PERFORMANCE INCENTIVES

PERFORMANCE INCENTIVES

Their Growing Impact on American K-12 Education

MATTHEW G. SPRINGER

editor

BROOKINGS INSTITUTION PRESS
Washington, D.C.

Copyright © 2009
THE BROOKINGS INSTITUTION
1775 Massachusetts Avenue, N.W., Washington, D.C. 20036
www.brookings.edu

Library of Congress Cataloging-in-Publication data

Performance incentives : their growing impact on American K-12 education / Matthew G. Springer, editor.
    p.   cm.
  Includes bibliographical references and index.
  Summary: "Offers an analysis of the promise and controversy around teacher pay for performance. Identifies potential strengths and weaknesses of performance-driven compensation policies and addresses key conceptual and implementation issues that have dominated the debate surrounding teacher compensation as an avenue for school reform"—Provided by publisher.
  ISBN 978-0-8157-8080-9 (hardcover : alk. paper) —
  ISBN 978-0-8157-8079-3 (pbk. : alk. paper)
  1. Teachers—Salaries, etc.—United States. 2. Merit pay—United States. 3. Teachers—Rating of—United States. I. Springer, Matthew G. II. Title.
  LB2842.22.P47 2010
  331.2'81371100973—dc22   2009021473

9 8 7 6 5 4 3 2 1
The paper used in this publication meets minimum requirements of the
American National Standard for Information Sciences—Permanence of Paper
for Printed Library Materials: ANSI Z39.48-1992.

Typeset in Adobe Garamond

Composition by Circle Graphics Inc.

Printed by R. R. Donnelley
Harrisonburg, Virginia

Contents

Acknowledgments

I owe my sincere gratitude to numerous people who contributed to this project. To begin, I would like to thank the many experts who contributed papers presented at the 2008 national research-to-policy forum hosted by the National Center on Performance Incentives, which was the impetus behind the collection of essays appearing in this volume. These individuals included Dale Ballou, Kevin Booker, Matthew Chingos, Michael Christian, Mark Ehlert, Steven Glazerman, Paul Glewwe, Dan Goldhaber, Jay Greene, Jane Hannaway, Nauman Ilias, Brian Jacob, Julia Koppich, Michael Kremer, Warren Langevin, Jessica Lewis, J.R. Lockwood, Ryan Marsh, Daniel McCaffrey, Robert Meyer, Karthik Muralidharan, Derek Neal, Steve Nelson, Michael Podgursky, Art (Xiao) Peng, Gary Ritter, Andrew Rotherham, Richard Rothstein, James Ryan, William Sanders, Timothy Silman, Venkatesh Sundararaman, Lori Taylor, Jacob Vigdor, Martin West, Marcus Winters, and S. Paul Wright.

I would also like to acknowledge those individuals who chaired conference panels and responded to papers presented at the research-to-policy forum. Thanks to Mark Berends, Linda Cavalluzzo, Bonnie Ghosh-Dastidar, R. Graham Greeson, Janet Hansen, Eric Hanushek, Carolyn Heinrich, J.R. Lockwood, Patrick McEwan, F. Howard Nelson, Paul Peterson, Michael Petrilli, Cynthia Prince,

Roger Sampson, Susan Sclafani, Brian Stecher, Paul Teske, Herbert Walberg, and Kate Walsh.

My thanks also to Grover (Russ) Whitehurst for preparing opening remarks on the proliferation of research on incentives in education and practical consider-ations for research-informed policy and to Randi Weingarten for delivering a thought-provoking keynote address on the role of teacher compensation reform in American K-12 public education.

The project was financed through the generous support of the United States Department of Education's Institute of Education Sciences, the Office of the Chancellor at Vanderbilt University, the Learning Sciences Institute at Vanderbilt University, the Peabody Center for Education Policy, the Peabody Professional Institutes, and an anonymous foundation. I also owe a special debt of gratitude to Timothy Caboni, Stephen Elliott, James Guthrie, and Mark Steinmeyer for their collaboration. The project further benefited from the leadership and support of the chancellor of Vanderbilt University, Nicholas S. Zeppos, and the dean of Peabody College of Vanderbilt University, Camilla P. Benbow.

In the course of editing this volume, it has been my pleasure to work with Christopher Kelaher at the Brookings Institution Press whose guidance and insight has proven invaluable and also to Janet Walker, Katherine Kimball, and other staff for their conscientious work, attention to detail, and substantial effort in preparing this volume for publication. Janet Hansen, Warren Langevin, and Herb Walberg also provided valued feedback on early versions of the manuscript.

Finally, I want to express my sincere thanks to the many staff at the National Center on Performance Incentives and Peabody College of Vanderbilt University, who spent innumerable hours in support of this project. Cate Gardner coordi-nated virtually all aspects of the conference and, in partnership with Rebekah Hutton, oversaw preparation and revision of the manuscripts. Susan Burns, Katherine Canon, Carolyn Fatheree, Kelly Fork, Helen Gleason, Alicen Hatter, Joyce Hilley, Martha Hutchinson, Susie Jackson, Jessica Lewis, Renee Morgan, and Palmer Payne were also critical to the success of the research-to-policy forum on numerous dimensions.

As editor, I appreciate reader interest in this volume and welcome any and all comments. It should also be noted that the views expressed here are those of the authors and should not necessarily be ascribed to the entities whose assistance is acknowledged above, to the National Center on Performance Incentives, or to any organizations with which the authors are affiliated.

1

Rethinking Teacher Compensation Policies: Why Now, Why Again?

Matthew G. Springer

In recent years, teacher compensation reform has resurfaced as a strategy to enhance academic outcomes in the U.S. public elementary and secondary school system. A number of school districts, state education agencies, and national and federal initiatives presently fund the development and implementation of programs that remunerate teachers based on their performance or differentiate teacher pay in response to market conditions. These programs are predicated on the argument that prevailing compensation practices provide weak incentives for teachers to act in the best interest of their students and that inefficiencies arise from rigidities in current compensation policies.

Financial incentives also have been advocated as a viable tool for motivating teachers to higher levels of performance, enticing more effective teachers to join or remain in the teaching profession, and aligning teacher behaviors and interests with institutional goals. Nonetheless, a sturdy and influential base of individuals and organizations remains fundamentally opposed to modifying the single salary schedule.[1] Opponents cite little evidence that pay-for-performance programs make schools better and further note that these programs render schools less effective by crowding out intrinsic rewards; they also say that the education system lacks appropriate measures for evaluating teacher performance.

Efforts to reconceptualize teacher compensation practices have garnered steady, if not increased, attention since the early- to mid-1980s, as illustrated in figure 1-1.[2] The notable spike in 1983 coincides with release of the influential *A Nation at Risk* report and then-president Ronald Reagan's proclamation that "teachers should be paid and promoted on the basis of their merit and competence. Hard-earned tax dollars should encourage the best. They have no business rewarding incompetence and mediocrity."[3] Also in 1983 a twenty-one-member congressional task force on merit pay established by Rep. Carl Perkins (D-Ky.) publicly supported and encouraged experimentation with performance-related pay reform. In fact, the U.S. Department of Education responded by allocating more than $2.5 million to fund seventy-one compensation reform efforts in thirty-seven states that year.[4]

Perhaps surprisingly, research on pay-for-performance programs in the United States has tended to focus on short-run motivational effects, and this research is highly diverse in terms of methodology, target populations, and evaluated programs.[5] In contrast to the applied natural and human sciences' practice of drawing causal inferences before policy decisionmaking, the education sector has tended not to rigorously evaluate policy innovations, particularly with respect to teacher pay. As such, the sector would benefit from deliberative assessment of past

Figure 1-1. *Number of References to Teacher Compensation Reform in Popular Media, 1950–2007*

Number

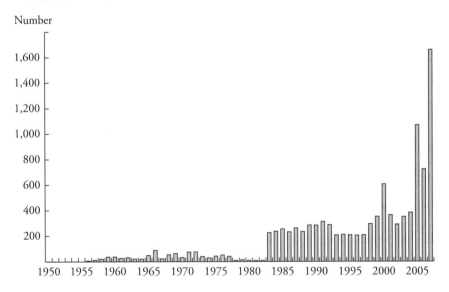

and present reform efforts as a means to differentiate fact from fiction. Now is a salient time to take stock of the teacher compensation reform movement.

The chapters in this volume focus primarily on two of the more prominent (and controversial) types of teacher compensation reform: awards based on pre-determined tasks or outcomes related to teacher and student behaviors (that is, pay for performance), or both; and recruitment and retention incentives or incentives for teaching in a hard-to-staff school or subject (that is, market-based compensation reforms). This introductory chapter presents a brief history of teacher compensation policy reforms and then discusses theoretical and empirical arguments for and against these reforms. The following section summarizes relevant evaluations of pay-for-performance and market-based compensation reforms, paying particular attention to evidence from experimental and quasi-experimental study designs. This chapter concludes with a short summary of the chapters in this volume.

A Brief History of Teacher Compensation Policies and Reforms

As the U.S. economy shifted from an agricultural to industrial foundation in the late nineteenth and early twentieth centuries, so too did the role of elementary and secondary public education. The public education system was recast as a way to produce effective citizens, unite society, and prevent crime and poverty. This new purpose and focus, combined with increased professionalism within teaching, enabled reconceptualization of teacher compensation practices, first through the grade-based compensation model and then through the single salary schedule.[6]

The grade-based compensation model paid teachers according to the level of schooling taught, and many of these models rewarded teachers based on annual performance reviews completed by school administration. This "merit pay" approach, however, typically violated procedural and distributive fairness as white males were more frequently awarded merit bonuses than nonwhite male teachers, and female teachers were paid considerably less than white male teachers.[7] The grade-based compensation model also paid secondary school teachers more than predominantly female elementary teachers.[8] About one-half of school districts in 1918 included similar merit pay provisions in their grade-based compensation programs.[9]

With the women's rights movement push for "equal pay for equal work," school systems began developing and adopting more egalitarian teacher compensation practices.[10] In 1921 Denver and Des Moines introduced the single salary schedule, which since has underpinned teacher pay practices. The single salary schedule determined pay according to two criteria thought to be most central to teacher productivity—years of service and degree held. It leveled the playing field relative to the grade-based compensation model by paying teachers on the same metric regardless of race, gender, or grade level taught and eliminating merit pay. Highly predictable, the single salary schedule also eased annual salary negotiations between school boards and teachers unions, a particularly attractive outcome considering the strained labor-management relations of this period.

There were individuals who opposed any compensation scheme that did not reward the performance of individual teachers or groups of teachers. Influenced largely by Frederick Taylor's principles of scientific management,[11] these individuals advocated for teacher pay systems that provided "as scientifically as possible for the best returns to society for the increasing public investment" by approaching salaries from their "economic and social aspects and not in terms of sentimentality."[12] As noted decades earlier by an Adams County, Pennsylvania, superintendent, Aaron Sheeley, opponents insisted that treating teachers as equals and not accounting for differences in teacher performance offered "a premium to mediocrity, if not to positive ignorance and incompetency."[13] Nonetheless, by 1950 the single salary schedule was adopted by 97 percent of all U.S. public elementary and secondary school districts and since has remained the dominant method for remunerating public school teachers.[14]

Efforts to reform teacher compensation policies have emerged in virtually every decade since the 1950s. Types of reforms can be classified into a handful of categories, including pay for performance, knowledge- and skills-based pay, career ladder programs, and market-based pay (for example, hard-to-staff subjects or schools or recruitment and retention stipends). While not an exhaustive summary, table 1-1 offers definitions and activities of the more prominent reforms proposed in the education sector.

What might not be entirely evident is the fact that pay-for-performance programs can vary markedly. There are a large number of complexities inherent in the design of compensation systems, including: Whose performance should determine bonus award eligibility? What performance indicators will monitor and appraise employee performance? Will the program reward school personnel on a relative or absolute standard? Who is part of the pay-for-performance system? How will bonus awards be distributed to school personnel? Consequently, building a solid research base is necessary for making firm judgments about programs generally as well as for deciding whether specific types of design features have more or less promise.

During the 1980s and 1990s, the focus of compensation reforms typically took the form of either career ladder programs or knowledge- and skills-based pay

Table 1-1. *Types of Teacher Compensation Reforms*

Type of program	Definition and activities
Pay-for-performance	Rewards based on predetermined tasks or outcomes, or both, related to teacher and student behaviors. *Input examples:* Teacher collaboration, professional development, and lesson preparation. *Output examples:* Student test scores, graduation rates, dropout rates, student and teacher attendance.
Knowledge- and skills-based pay	Rewards based on completion of teacher activities that are related to the development of knowledge and skills linked to improved student outcomes, as well as demonstration of classroom mastery. *Input examples:* Portfolio completion, dual certification, graduate degree in subject taught, standards-based teacher evaluation, National Board for Professional Teaching Standards (NBPTS) certification.
Career ladders	Provides new roles for teachers with additional pay and responsibilities as they increase their knowledge and skills. Plans typically involve vertical steps with multiple objectives within each step. *Input example:* Additional training and professional development, earning advanced degrees, assuming higher levels of instructional responsibility, and mentoring new teachers.
Hard-to-staff subjects	Incentives are targeted to teachers in subject areas where there are shortages, which are based on need at the school, district, or state level. Math, science, and special education are common examples. *Input examples:* Teachers trained in a high-need subject area teach in a school experiencing that shortage; teachers are compensated for pursuing subject area endorsements in high-needs areas.
Hard-to-staff schools	Incentives are offered for teaching in high-needs schools or districts, typically either high-poverty, low-performing, or geographically remote schools. Like hard-to-staff subject incentives, these incentives are designed specifically to address market factors influences. *Input example:* Teachers are awarded bonuses for working in high-needs, hard-to-staff schools.
Recruitment and retention awards	Rewards are offered to attract educators to a school and to encourage continued years of service. *Input example:* Awards are offered for signing a contract to work in a specific school or district. Annual bonuses are offered for each year of continued service in the school or district.

plans. Career ladder programs provided teachers new roles with additional pay and responsibilities, career advancement opportunities believed to encourage retention, and variation in responsibilities and activities designed to "counteract stagnation."[15] Knowledge- and skills-based pay programs rewarded teachers for successfully completing activities that represent higher levels of expertise and demonstrated understanding of exemplary teaching practices. Among these activities are portfolio completion, dual certification, earning a graduate degree in subjects taught, or high marks on standards-based teacher evaluations.[16]

A large number of states and school districts are exploring recruitment and retention incentives, including rewarding teachers who work in hard-to-staff schools or subjects. Market-based reforms are designed to address the inequitable distribution of highly effective teachers among schools as well as teacher shortages in such subjects as mathematics, science, and special education.[17] Even though the vast majority of states have funded incentive plans around teacher recruitment and retention, as observed by Susanna Loeb and Luke Miller, most of these programs are not well aligned with teacher labor market realities, nor is the receipt of an incentive award usually contingent on teacher effectiveness.[18] Hard-to-staff school and subject bonuses remain at the top of the policy agenda.

The present wave of compensation reform is best characterized by an increased focus on rewarding educational outputs, which is a departure from reform models proposed during the 1980s and 1990s that focused heavily on educational inputs and processes.[19] Pay-for-performance programs may use multiple measures to evaluate teacher performance and incorporate elements found in career ladder or knowledge- and skills-based pay plans; however, student outcomes on standardized assessments remain the most heavily weighted factor in determining bonus award eligibility.

Critiques of Teacher Pay-for-Performance Programs

Critics of pay-for-performance programs in education note that there is a great deal of collaboration among teachers. Introducing individual performance rewards, they argue, might reduce incentives for teachers to cooperate and collaborate with one another, thereby reducing rather than increasing school performance.[20] The team dynamic also may be disrupted between teachers as well as between teachers and administrators if a teachers' peers are put in a position of evaluating and rewarding their performance. The same may also hold true if the compensation system is designed as a rank-ordered tournament whereby teachers or teams of teachers are competing for a fixed amount of bonus money.

Critics argue further that pay-for-performance plans are destined for failure because teacher performance is more difficult to monitor than performance in other professions. Unlike, for instance, sales or the billable hours of a doctor or lawyer, a teacher's output is not measured readily in a reliable, valid, and fair manner. Teachers also may disagree about the optimal set of performance goals, or the evaluation system could lack transparency and teachers have no real idea how they are being evaluated. Given these problems, it is argued, the services provided by an individual teacher or group of teachers should not be linked to schooling outcomes, particularly if measures of teacher performance cannot account for the many factors beyond the teacher's control that influence student achievement.

A third criticism concerns the issue of multitasking.[21] The multitasking problem arises when the performance of a worker comprises multiple dimensions, only some of which are measured and incentivized. If there is a disconnect between an organization's mission and the activity to which incentives are attached, employees may shift work toward the metered, rewarded activity, and away from other important activities. As documented in several studies on minimum competency accountability programs, poorly designed incentive schemes create greater opportunity in the long run for cheating or related opportunistic behavior.[22]

In a similar vein, poorly designed reward systems may create perverse incentives whereby teachers may move away from low-performing schools in order to maximize their chances of earning additional pay. For example, North Carolina's school accountability system was found to make the recruitment and retention of high-quality teachers even harder on low-performing schools.[23] Potential unintended consequences related to the teacher labor market are critically important for policymakers and others to consider because proponents of pay-for-performance programs contend a positive compositional effect on the teacher workforce.

Another frequently cited argument against teacher pay for performance concerns individuals potentially losing interest in an activity as they are rewarded increasingly for that activity. Many individuals claim that sufficient incentives already reside in teaching and that the "primary attraction of teaching . . . continues to be the prospect of achieving success with children."[24] Introducing external rewards, this literature posits, will discourage risk taking, damage the cooperative nature of teaching, and negatively affect teachers' perception of their own ability.[25] Consequently, even if a pay-for-performance program elicits a positive behavioral response in the short run, the crowding out of intrinsic motivation over time may reduce effort, self-esteem, and originality to the point of negatively affecting teacher and school productivity.

Finally, recent compensation reforms have been faulted for focusing excessively on standardized assessments to determine if a teacher earns a bonus award.

In addition to test scores being noisy and volatile performance measures,[26] commentators argue that placing an inordinate amount of weight on student test scores is problematic because approximately two-thirds of teachers do not instruct in a single tested grade or subject. The typical student also engages in a large number of activities and classes beyond those subjects tested by a state's NCLB accountability program.[27] Thus a pay-for-performance program focused solely on monitoring and rewarding student test scores captures only part of a school's overall mission.

A Conceptualization of Problems with the Single Salary Schedule

Edward Lazear, a major contributor to the "new personnel economics" literature, provides a useful conceptualization of inefficiencies arising from the single salary schedule, and assesses the economics of alternative teacher compensation regimes, which he terms "payment for input" and "payment for output." He argues that payment for output always trumps payment for input in terms of raising overall productivity for two primary reasons: hiring practices and labor market selection.[28]

In terms of hiring practices, principals and building administrators must use noisy signals of "true" teacher effectiveness, such as years of experience, highest degree held, or past-employer recommendations. The hiring process's informational deficiencies are ameliorated in most professions by employee performance assessments and the close coupling of pay increases to actual productivity. However, the single salary schedule, along with teacher tenure, impedes principals' efforts to align pay and performance after hiring. For example, Brian Jacob reports that approximately 1 percent of all teachers working in urban school districts either are dismissed or do not have their contract renewed each year.[29] Once teachers earn tenure, contract nonrenewal can be triggered only by severe malfeasance on the part of the employee and, even then, termination is an arduous, controversial, and costly process.[30]

Lazear and others have also discerned a more subtle factor regarding the benefits of a pay-for-performance system. A pay-for-performance program will tend to attract and retain individuals who are particularly good at the activity to which incentives are attached and repel those who are not. That is, while incentives can raise the productivity of the typical worker employed, an incentive system also can raise the overall quality of the workforce simply through differential recruitment and retention of more effective workers. A case study of Safelite Glass Corporation, for example, reported that transitioning the company's compensation system from hourly wages to piece rates was associated with a 44 percent increase in worker productivity, half of which resulted from workers' gravitating to areas where they were most productive.[31]

Similarly, there is a growing concern that the single salary schedule creates a disincentive for the most capable job candidates from entering the teaching profession. A number of studies document that higher-ability college graduates are less likely to enter teaching,[32] and that the most academically talented female students are much less likely to enter teaching than forty years ago.[33] A recent provocative study of teacher turnover found evidence that the migration of high-ability women out of teaching between 1960 and the present primarily resulted from the "push" of teacher pay compression, which took away relatively higher earnings opportunities for teachers, as opposed to the "pull" of more lucrative nonteaching opportunities.[34] Although remunerative opportunities for teachers of high and low ability grew outside of teaching over this period, Caroline Hoxby and Andrew Leigh argue it was pay compression that accelerated the exit of higher-ability teachers.

Empirical Arguments for Moving Away from the Single Salary Schedule

A growing number of empirical studies estimating the influence of student, teacher, and school characteristics on student outcomes have concluded that teachers are the single most important determinant of student outcomes. Eric Hanushek was among the first scholars to undertake value added analysis of teacher effectiveness.[35] Using data collected as part of the Gary Income Maintenance Experiment, a welfare reform experiment in the early 1970s in Gary, Indiana, he assembled a unique longitudinal data file on approximately 1,800 students and their families. The results indicated that the city's most-effective teachers produced 1.5 grade-level equivalents of annual achievement growth in their students, while the least-effective teachers produced only 0.5 grade levels' worth of growth.

Subsequent studies have detected relationships between teacher effectiveness and student outcomes similar to those reported in the Gary study. William Sanders and June Rivers found a difference of 50 percentile points in student achievement between students that encountered three consecutive years of teachers at or above the 80th percentile of performance and those students that encountered three consecutive years of teachers in the bottom 20th percentile of performance.[36] Moreover, using student test score data from Texas, Hanushek and Steven Rivkin reported that a student who encountered five consecutive years of an above-average teacher could overcome the achievement gap in grade 7 mathematics typically found between students on the free or reduced-price lunch program and those from higher-income backgrounds.[37]

Advances in value added modeling have also elevated researchers' interest and ability to isolate an individual teacher's contribution to student learning and to determine the extent to which teacher, classroom, and school-level characteristics explain variation in student performance. These studies tend to find that teacher effectiveness is largely unrelated to measured teacher characteristics, such as the type of teaching certificate held, level of education, licensing exam scores, and experience beyond the first couple of years of teaching. Dan Goldhaber and colleagues, for example, found that these observable teacher characteristics only explain about 3 percent of the differences in student achievement that are attributable to the teacher.[38]

The fact that the vast majority of variation in teacher effectiveness cannot be explained by observable teacher characteristics (that is, the type of teaching certificate held, level of education, licensing exam scores, and years of teaching experience) has played a significant role in teacher compensation reform dialogues. Compensation payments for instructional personnel account for approximately 55 percent of current expenditures and 90 percent of instructional expenditures in public K-12 systems. Yet, these dollars are allocated to teachers in ways that are loosely related to student outcomes. Consequently, many critics of the single salary schedule contend there must be a more efficient and productive way to remunerate teachers.

Evaluations of Pay-for-Performance and Market-Based Incentive Programs

This section reviews previous evaluation studies assessing the impact of teacher pay-for-performance and market-based incentive programs, paying particular attention to evaluations relying on rigorous, experimental or quasi-experimental designs. When implemented properly, such designs are ideal for assessing whether a specific intervention truly produces changes in outcomes under study or whether observed changes in outcomes are simply artifacts of pretreatment differences between two or more groups participating in the study.[39] The evaluation literature is surprisingly thin considering the number of schools, districts, and states that have adopted teacher compensation reforms.

Table 1-2 summarizes key characteristics of these studies, including name of the program being evaluated, study period, sample size, the unit of accountability, the measures of teacher performance, and findings. The most rigorous evaluations conducted to date all come from abroad and tend to report a generally positive impact on student achievement. At the same time, it is less clear whether programs actually promoted long-run learning: some studies find that the effects do not persist from one year to the next or that opportunistic behavior on the part of teachers may actually explain alleged improvements. It is also worth noting that the incentive structure facing teachers and schools in some of the locations under study (for example, Andhra Pradesh, India, or rural Kenya) are much different from the operational context found within U.S. public elementary and secondary schools.

The information displayed in table 1-2 further indicates that several large-scale demonstration projects that employ a random assignment study design have been implemented in the United States. The programs vary widely in terms of program design: the Project on Incentives in Teaching experiment focuses on individual teacher-level incentive pay whereby teachers are eligible for bonus awards up to $15,000 based on their students' achievement gains, while according to New York City's School-Wide Performance Bonus Program, a school must meet predetermined performance targets and then a school-based compensation committee determines how award money will be allocated to school personnel. These projects are still being implemented and no results are available at this time.

There also is very little empirical information about market-based incentive programs, including teacher recruitment and retention stipends and additional pay for working in a hard-to-staff school or subject. Charles Clotfelter and colleagues found that an annual $1,800 bonus for being certified in mathematics, sciences, or special education and teaching in a high-poverty school reduced mean turnover rates among targeted teachers by 17 percent in North Carolina.[40] The Massachusetts Signing Bonus Program for New Teachers offered $20,000 to attract highly qualified individuals into teaching that might not otherwise have chosen to work in the profession (an initial payment of $5,000, with a remaining $15,000 to be paid over a four-year period), but the program was found to be less effective at recruiting and retaining new teachers than alternative certification programs.[41] Other policy interventions aimed at recruiting and retaining teachers include offering mentoring and induction programs, improving working conditions, and hiring and transfer programs.[42]

Table 1-2. *Summary of Experimental and Quasi-Experimental Evaluations of Teacher Pay-for-Performance Programs*

Program	Study design[a]	Study period	Sample
United States			
Project on Incentives in Teaching (Nashville, Tennessee)	RCT	2007–09	147 treatment and 152 control teachers (grades 5–8)
Project on Team-Level Incentives in Teaching (Round Rock, Texas)	RCT	2009	41 treatment and 41 control group teams (grades 6–8)
Recognizing Excellence in Academic Leadership Program (Chicago)	RCT	2008–11	32 Teacher Advancement Program (TAP) schools
Schoolwide Performance Bonus Program (New York City)	RCT	2008–09	191 treatment and 131 control group schools (elementary, middle, and k–8); more than 100,000 in grades 3–8
International			
Kenya's International Christelijk Steuenfonds Incentive Program	RCT	1998–99	100 primary schools; 1,000+ teachers; 50,842 students
Andhra Pradesh, India's Randomized Evaluation Project	RCT	2006–08	300 schools and 68,000+ student observations
Israel's Ministry of Education's School Performance Program	RD	1994–97	62 schools (37 nonreligious, 18 religious, and 7 Arab schools)
Israeli Teacher Incentive Experiment	RD	2001	4,109 students and 27 schools
Mexico's Carrera Magisterial	RD	1998–03	850,000+ classroom-year observations; 810 primary school teachers; 209 secondary school teachers
	RD	2000–02	76,567 teachers and 27,123 schools

a. RCT denotes randomized controlled trial design. RD denotes regression discontinuity design.

Unit of accountability	Performance measures	
	Measures of teacher performance	Results
Individual	Student test scores in mathematics, reading, social studies, and science	In progress
Group (grade-level teams)	Student test scores in mathematics, reading, social studies, and science	In progress
Hybrid (individual and school)	Mentor review, self-review, master teacher review, administrator review, classroom observations, teacher-developed portfolio, interviews, student test score gains, and overall school performance	In progress
Hybrid (individual and school)	Student test score levels and gains, student, teacher, and principal perceptions of school environment, and external enurmerators' rating of school's instructional climate	In progress
Group (school)	Student test score gains and student achievement levels	Modest, positive effect for high-stakes assessment; no effect on low-stakes assessment
Individual and group (school)	Student test score gains	Modest, positive effect on high-stakes assessment (approx. 0.12 to 0.19 standard deviations after year one and 0.16 to 0.19 standard deviations after year two)
Group (school)	Number of credit units per student, students receiving a matriculation certification, and school dropout rate	Modest, positive effect for average credit hours earned, average science credits earned, average test score, and proportion of students taking Israel's matriculation exam
Individual	Student achievement levels	Modest, positive effect for number of exit exam credits earned in mathematics (increased 18 percent) and in reading (increased 17 percent)
Individual	Educational degrees, years of experience, professional development, principal ratings, content knowledge mastery, student performance on standardized tests	No effect for primary school teachers; modest, positive effect for secondary school teachers (approx. 3 to 15 percent of standard deviation)
Individual	Educational degrees, years of experience, professional development, principal ratings, content knowledge mastery, student performance on standardized tests	Small, positive effects (< 10 percent of standard deviation)

Overview of the Book

The chapters in this volume are presented in three parts: perspectives on teacher compensation reform; incentive system design and measurement; and case studies and reviews of teacher incentive policies. The first part examines teacher compensation reform from multiple perspectives, including economic, legal, political, psychological, and sociological ones. The second part addresses issues related to the development and design of pay-for-performance programs and policies. The third section contains descriptive analyses of teacher mobility in Florida, case studies of incentive programs in North Carolina and the Little Rock School District in Arkansas, and a comprehensive review of educational policies in developing countries that change teacher incentives in an effort to improve the quality of schooling. Collectively, the chapters that make up this volume provide the foundation for understanding many of the historical and current issues associated with teacher pay reform.

Perspectives on Teacher Compensation Reform

In chapter 2, Dan Goldhaber examines the political positions of the National Education Association (NEA) and the American Federation of Teachers (AFT), how both organizations' views align with teachers' attitudes toward pay reform, and how these organizations influence the design and implementation of teacher compensation reform. He reports that the NEA and AFT "are generally opposed to teacher pay reforms, but diverge in terms of their specific positions on reform." For example, the NEA has opposed pay for performance and additional compensation to attract or retain individuals for hard-to-recruit positions, while the AFT has shown greater willingness to consider deviations from the single salary schedule.

In chapter 3, James Ryan assesses legal obstacles associated with creating differential pay programs for teachers. Although the legal landscape is fairly open to the creation of differential pay programs, according to Ryan, the key message regarding differential pay is compliance with federal guidelines for programs that are federally funded and consent of teachers unions where required by state law. Legal requirements also pertain to the individual rights of due process and protection against discrimination. The clearer and more objective the differential pay criteria, the less likely a program is to be subjected to legal challenges.

In chapter 4, Michael Podgursky offers a market-based perspective on teacher pay. Podgursky focuses on the interplay between the supply of and the demand for teachers and assesses the effects of policies that influence the teacher labor market. This market is characterized by rigidities that impede its efficient operation, resulting in chronic shortages by teaching field, disproportionate assignment of novice teachers to poor children, and failure to reward more effective teachers. Tenure and district size interact with the single salary schedule to exacerbate the schedule's contribution to inefficiency. These concerns are reflected in the growing attention paid by school districts to market-based and output-based pay reforms. Podgursky notes, however, that the use of alternatives to the rigid steps and lanes of the single salary schedule remains fragmentary and uneven.

In chapter 5, Richard Rothstein contends that education policymakers are not sufficiently aware of the costs and benefits of performance incentive systems. He reports that while supporters of test-based accountability for school personnel cite the private sector as a model, compensation systems in the private sector, though commonly including incentive pay, generally do not rely heavily on quantitative output measures to reward professionals. Because performance rewards are based too heavily on quantitative measures in the education sector, educators often engage in what Rothstein characterizes as three common distortions: mismeasurement of outputs; mismeasurement of inputs; and reliance on untrustworthy statistics.

Incentive System Design and Measurement

In chapter 6, Daniel McCaffrey, Bing Han, and J. R. Lockwood discuss the complex process of designing a system to award teacher bonuses on the basis of student achievement results. As evident in the step-by-step decisions that accompany designing performance-pay systems, including creating a student achievement database and choosing measures of teacher performance, the process of system design is more challenging than most districts and states may anticipate. McCaffrey and colleagues emphasize, "Most value added research to date has focused on the statistical properties of the measures from the perspective of methodological research rather than from the perspective of an algorithm that translates raw administrative data on students and teachers into dollars provided to individual people. The latter perspective forces consideration of many complex issues that are often taken for granted in pure methodological research and thus have not yet been given sufficient consideration."

In chapter 7, Derek Neal presents three challenges for public schools related to the design of incentive pay systems: the limits of performance statistics; the challenge of constructing performance rankings; and the decision to reward teacher or school-level performance. He considers which incentive pay designs may be more or less successful in the public education system, concluding incentive systems that measure and reward schoolwide performance based on rank order tournaments of comparable schools are likely the optimal strategy. The great myth about incentive pay, according to Neal, is that it brings "business practices" or "competitive pressures" to bear on the public education system. Consequently, he argues that in the absence of truly competitive market conditions, incentive pay is often rendered inefficient and ineffective, at least in its modern-day design and implementation.

In chapter 8, William Sanders, Paul Wright, and Warren Langevin examine whether estimates of teacher effectiveness are consistent when teachers transition between schools servicing different student populations. Although the number of teachers who moved from lower poverty to higher poverty schools was small, the authors report prior effectiveness still predicted effectiveness in the new school for these teachers, as it did for teachers who moved to schools with similar percentages of poor students. Situating their findings in the context of recent education dialogues, Sanders and colleagues conclude that "value added measures of teacher effectiveness should be included as a major component in determining which teachers are to be offered incentives to move to high-needs schools. Teachers selected on the basis of a policy that heavily weights prior value added estimates are more likely to be effective in facilitating academic growth for students, after moving to a new school, than teachers who are selected based on traditional credentials."

In chapter 9, Lori Taylor, Matthew Springer, and Mark Ehlert describe the teacher pay-for-performance programs implemented as part of the Governor's Educator Excellence Grant (GEEG) program in Texas. Most schools implemented an egalitarian award distribution structure. Actual bonus awards distributed to teachers ranged from $75 to $15,000, with nearly 80 percent of teachers who earned a bonus award receiving less than $3,000. Taylor and colleagues also examined a number of teacher and school characteristics that could be associated with the type of educator incentive program developed and adopted at a particular school. Given variation in plan designs, and the leading role that teachers played in designing and approving the incentive pay plans, their analysis offers important insights into the nature of compensation reforms that educators perceive to be acceptable.

Informing Teacher Incentive Policies

In chapter 10, Jacob Vigdor offers findings from a case study of North Carolina's ABCs of Public Education, a program that awards teachers with bonuses of up to $1,500 for schoolwide student test score gains, and examines whether the ABC program has improved student performance or lowered socioeconomic and racial achievement gaps or achieved both. He finds that even though the program appears to have an effect on test scores in high-stakes subjects, the effect does not appear on low-stakes assessments, while it also appears that socioeconomic and racial achievement gaps have increased over time. When offering lessons learned from North Carolina's experience with the performance incentive program, Vigdor reports, "Above all else, the results . . . suggest that incentive programs, when adopted in an effort to raise the performance of disadvantaged students, can be a two-edged sword. If teachers perceive bonus programs as yet another factor making jobs in advantaged schools more attractive, increased turnover rates in low-performing schools are a predictable consequence. This unintended side effect could be avoided so long as teachers perceive the bonus program as a fair reward for their effort, rather than a reward for student background or other inputs over which they have no direct control."

In chapter 11, Martin West and Matthew Chingos study the relationship among teacher effectiveness, mobility, and attrition in Florida. The authors find that the least effective teachers are somewhat more likely to leave in the first years of their careers and that schools with traditionally high-performing students do a far better job than most schools of retaining their most effective elementary school teachers and encouraging what appears to be voluntary departures or dismissals of the least effective teachers. In light of the fact that incentive policies in education often treat financial incentives for performance and retention as separate issues, West and Chingos propose exploring combining the two by offering larger performance incentives in hard-to-staff schools as a potentially promising approach to improve both overall teacher productivity and allocation of the most effective teachers across schools.

In chapter 12, Marcus Winters and colleagues report findings from an evaluation of the Achievement Challenge Pilot Project (ACPP) in Little Rock, Arkansas. ACPP ties performance bonuses to individual student fall-to-spring gains on a standardized student achievement test, ranging from $50 per student (0–4 percent gain) up to $400 per student (15 percent gain). In practice, ACPP's mechanism for awarding teacher bonuses yielded payouts ranging from $1,200 up to $9,200 per teacher per year. The authors report that ACPP appears to have improved student achievement and to have done so more for students of teachers who were previously less effective at producing learning gains. In addition, while teacher attitudes toward the program were generally supportive of ACPP, political activity by the union led to a change in the membership of the school board, and the new majority voted to cancel Little Rock's pay-for-performance system.

In chapter 13, Paul Glewwe, Alaka Holla, and Michael Kremer review a number of educational policies in developing countries that change teacher incentives in an effort to improve the quality of schooling. The review focuses on policies that attempt to improve the quality of schooling by improving working conditions to encourage teachers to come to work; providing direct payment to teachers based on their attendance or their students' performance; and altering teacher incentives by changing how schools are managed. Although the evidence tends to suggest incentives can result in desired changes, Glewwe and colleagues point out that more research is needed before making generalizations. They also address many aspects related to the design of incentive policies that can greatly affect teacher and system responses such as empowering local communities to hire teachers versus providing communities with information on student and teacher performance.

Notes

1. On July 5, 2008, for example, when then-Senator Barack Obama accepted the National Education Association endorsement for the Democratic presidential nomination, a crowd of more than 9,000 union leaders and members in attendance booed when he acknowledge support of performance-related pay incentives. For a more complete review of teachers unions, collective bargaining agreements, and compensation reform, see Randall W. Eberts, "Teacher Unions and Student Performance: Help or Hindrance?" *Future of Children* 17, no. 1 (2007): 175–200; Richard J. Murnane and Jennifer L. Steele, "What Is the Problem? The Challenge of Providing Effective Teachers for All Children," *Future of Children* 17, no. 1 (2007): 15–43; Jane Hannaway and Andrew J. Rotherham, "Collective Bargaining in Education and Pay for Performance," Working Paper 2008-11 (Nashville, Tenn.: National Center on Performance Incentives, 2008).
2. Data were obtained from a beta technology developed by Google that searches archived news information and generates data on the incidence of a particular topic being covered in the media. The search engine examines content from the more than 4,500 paid and unpaid subscription sources counting only one "hit" per story when a story was covered in several media outlets. For more information, visit http://news.google.com/archivesearch/about.html.
3. Speech at Seton Hall University, South Orange, N.J., May 1983, as cited in Susan Moore Johnson, "Merit Pay for Teachers: Poor Prescription for Reform," *Harvard Educational Review* 54, no. 2 (1984): 175–85; National Commission on Excellence in Education, *A Nation at Risk: The Imperative for Education Reform* (Washington: U.S. Department of Education, 1983).
4. Richard M. Brandt, *Incentive Pay and Career Ladders for Today's Teachers: A Study of Current Programs and Practices* (SUNY Press, 1990).
5. Michael Podgursky and Matthew Springer, "Teacher Performance Pay: A Review," *Journal of Policy Analysis and Management* 26, no. 4 (August 2007): 909–50.
6. Jean Protsik, *History of Teacher Pay and Incentive Reform* (Washington: Educational Resources Information Center, 1995); Richard J. Murnane and David Cohen, "Merit Pay

and the Evaluation Problem: Why Most Merit Pay Plans Fail and Few Survive," *Harvard Education Review* 56, no. 1 (1986): 1–17.

7. Gary A. Adkins, "Pros and Cons and Current Status of Merit Pay in the Public Schools," Virginia Association of Teacher Educators, Radford, Va. (Eric Resources Information Center No. ED238-162), 1983; Jerome Cramer, "Yes. Merit Pay Can Be a Horror, but Few School Systems Have Done It Right," *American School Board Journal* 170, no. 28 (1983): 33–34.

8. Fenwick English, "History and Critical Issues of Educational Compensation System," in *Teacher Compensation and Motivation,* edited by Larry Frase, pp. 3–26 (Lancaster, Pa.: Technomic Publishing, 1992).

9. Ibid.

10. Hazel Davis, "Teachers' Salaries," *Review of Educational Research* 13, no. 3 (1943): 276–84.

11. D. J. B. Mitchell, D. Lewin, and E. E. Lawler, "Alternative Pay Systems, Firm Performance, and Productivity," in *Paying for Productivity: A Look at the Evidence,* edited by Alan S. Blinder (Brookings, 1990).

12. Arthur B. Moehlman, *Public School Finance* (New York: Rand-McNally, 1927).

13. Allan Odden and Carolyn Kelly, *Paying Teachers for What They Know and Do: New and Smarter Compensation Strategies to Improve Schools* (Thousand Oaks, Calif.: Corwin Press, 1992).

14. Protsik, *History of Teacher Pay and Incentive Reform;* Murnane and Cohen, "Merit Pay and the Evaluation Problem"; English, "History and Critical Issues of Educational Compensation System."

15. Cresap, McCormick, and Paget, Inc., *Teacher Incentives: A Tool for Effective Management* (Washington: National Association of Secondary School Principals, 1984).

16. Michael Beer and Mark D. Cannon, "Promise and Peril in Implementing Pay-for-Performance," *Human Resource Management* 43 (2004): 3–48; Robert L. Heneman and Gerald E. Ledford Jr., "Competency Pay for Professionals and Managers in Business: A Review and Implications for Teachers," *Journal of Personnel Evaluation in Education* 12, no. 2: 103–21.

17. Cynthia D. Prince, *The Challenge of Attracting Good Teachers and Principals to Struggling Schools* (Arlington, Va.: American Association of School Administrators, 2002); Cynthia D. Prince, *Higher Pay in Hard-to-Staff Schools: The Case for Financial Incentives* (Arlington, Va.: American Association of School Administrators, 2002).

18. Susanna Loeb and Luke C. Miller, *A Review of State Teacher Policies: What Are They, What Are Their Effects, and What Are Their Implications for School Finance* (Palo Alto, Calif.: Institute for Research on Education Policy and Practice, Stanford University, 2007).

19. Dale Ballou and Michael Podgursky, *Teacher Pay and Teacher Quality* (Kalamazoo, Mich.: W. E. Upjohn Institute for Employment Research, 1997); Dale Ballou and Michael Podgursky, "Let the Market Decide," *Education Next* 1 (spring): 1–7; Eric A. Hanushek, "The Failure of Input-Based Schooling Policies," *Economic Journal* 113 (February 2003): F64-F98.

20. Murnane and Cohen, "Merit Pay and the Evaluation Problem."

21. Bengt Holmstrom and Paul Milgrom, "Multitask Principal Agent Analyses: Incentive Contracts, Asset Ownership, and Job Design," *Journal of Law, Economics, and Organizations* 7 (1991): 24–52.; Jane Hannaway, "Higher Order Skills, Job Design, and Incentives: An Analysis and Proposal," *American Educational Research Journal* 29 (1992):

3–21.; Avinash Dixit, "Incentives and Organizations in the Public Sector," *Journal of Human Resources* 37 (2002): 696–727.

22. Studies of high-stakes accountability systems have documented teachers focusing excessively on a single test and educators altering test scores, or assisting students with test questions, or doing both [Daniel Koretz, Sheila Barron, Karen Mitchell, and Brian M. Stecher, Perceived Effects of the Kentucky Instructional Results Information System (KIRIS) (Santa Monica, Calif.: RAND, 1996); Brian Jacob and Steven Levitt, "Rotten Apples: An Investigation of the Prevalence and Predictors of Teacher Cheating," *Quarterly Journal of Economics* 118, no. 3 (2003): 843–77]. Related analyses have found evidence of schools' strategic classification of students as special education and limited English proficiency [Donald Deere and Wayne Strayer, "Putting Schools to the Test: School Accountability, Incentives, and Behavior," Texas A&M University, unpublished, 2001; David Figlio and Lawrence Getzler, "Accountability, Ability, and Disability: Gaming the System?" Working Paper 9307 (Cambridge, Mass.: National Bureau of Economic Research, 2002); Julie B. Cullen and Randall Reback, "Tinkering toward Accolades: School Gaming under a Performance Accountability System," Working Paper 12286 (Cambridge, Mass.: National Bureau of Economic Research, 2006)]; use of discipline procedures to ensure that low-performing students will be absent on test day [David Figlio, "Testing, Crime, and Punishment," University of Florida, unpublished, 2003]; manipulation of grade retention policies [Brian Jacob, "Testing, Accountability, and Incentives: The Impact of High-Stakes Testing in Chicago Public Schools," *Journal of Public Economics* 89, nos. 5–6 (2005)]; and planning of nutrition-enriched lunch menus before test day [David Figlio and Joshua Winicki, "Food for Thought? The Effects of School Accountability Plans on School Nutrition," *Journal of Public Economics* 89, nos. 2–3 (2005): 381–94].

23. Charles Clotfelter, Helen Ladd, Jacob Vigdor, and Roger Aliaga Diaz, "Do School Accountability Systems Make It More Difficult for Low-Performing Schools to Attract and Retain High-Quality Teachers?" *Journal of Policy Analysis and Management* 23, no. 2 (2004): 251–71.

24. Susan Moore Johnson, "Incentives for Teachers: What Motivates, What Matters?" *Educational Administration Quarterly* 22, no. 23 (spring 1986): 54–79.

25. Alfie Kohn, "Why Incentive Plans Can't Work," *Harvard Business Review* (September–October 1993): 54–63; Roland Benabou and Jean Tirole, "Intrinsic and Extrinsic Motivation," *Review of Economic Studies* 70 (2003): 489–520; Edward L. Deci and Richard M. Ryan. *Intrinsic Motivation and Self-Determination in Human Behavior* (New York: Plenum, 1985).

26. Thomas Kane, Douglas Staiger, and Jeffrey Gepert, "Randomly Accountable," *Education Next* 2, no.1 (2002): 57–61; Dale Ballou, "Sizing Up Test Scores," *Education Next* 2, no.1 (2002): 10–15; Dennis Jansen, Timothy Gronberg, and Kevin Booker, "Volatility of School Output Measures and Implications for Use in School Funding Formulas and in Rankings of School and Teacher Performance," Working Paper (College Station: Texas A&M University, 2004).

27. The Center for Educator Compensation Reform, which provides technical assistance around the design and implementation of Teacher Incentive Fund grants, funded by the U.S. Department of Education, offers guidance on ways to address this challenge [Cynthia D. Prince and others, "The Other 69 Percent: Fairly Rewarding the Performance of Teachers of Non-Tested Grades and Non-Test Subjects" (Washington: Office of Elementary and Secondary Education, U.S. Department of Education, 2009)].

28. Edward Lazear, "Performance Pay and Productivity," *American Economic Review* 90, no. 5 (2000): 1346–61; Edward Lazear, "Paying Teachers for Performance: Incentives and Selection," Working Paper (Palo Alto, Calif.: Stanford University, 2001); Edward Lazear, "Teacher Incentives," *Swedish Economic Policy Review* 10 (2003): 197–213.

29. Brian A. Jacob, "The Challenges of Staffing Urban Schools with Effective Teachers," *Future of Children* 17, no. 1 (2007): 129–53.

30. See, for example, stories related to New York City's Teacher Reassignment Centers, which are estimated to cost in excess of $35 million per year and have become the focus of a forthcoming documentary film, "The Rubber Room."

31. Lazear, "Performance Pay and Productivity."

32. Michael Podgursky, Ryan Monroe, and Donald Watson, "Teacher Pay, Mobility, and Academic Quality," *Economics of Education Review* 23 (2004): 507–18; Dan Goldhaber and Albert Liu, "Occupational Choices and the Academic Proficiency of the Teacher Workforce," in *Developments in School Finance 2001–02*, edited by William Fowler (Washington: NCES, 2002), pp. 53–75; Eric A. Hanushek and Richard R. Pace. "Who Chooses to Teach (and Why)?" *Economics of Education Review* 14, no. 2 (1995): 101–17; Dale Ballou, "Do Public Schools Hire the Best Applicants? *Quarterly Journal of Economics* 111, no. 1 (1996): 97–133.

33. Sean Corcoran, William Evans, and Robert Schwab, "Women, the Labor Market, and the Declining Relative Quality of Teachers," *Journal of Policy Analysis and Management* 23, no. 3 (2004): 449–70.

34. Caroline M. Hoxby and Andrew Leigh, "Pulled Away or Pushed Out? Explaining the Decline of Teacher Aptitude in the United States," *American Economic Review* 93 (2004): 236–40.

35. Eric A. Hanushek, "The Trade-off between Child Quantity and Quality," *Journal of Political Economy* 100, no. 1 (1992): 84–117.

36. William L. Sanders and June C. Rivers, *Cumulative and Residual Effects of Teachers on Future Student Academic Achievement* (Knoxville: Value-Added Research and Assessment Center, University of Tennessee, 1996).

37. Eric A. Hanushek and Steven G. Rivkin, "How to Improve the Supply of High-Quality Teachers," *Brookings Papers on Education Policy* 2004: 7–25.

38. Dan Goldhaber, "The Mystery of Good Teaching," *Education Next* (Spring 2002): 1–7.

39. Regression discontinuity studies generate highly localized estimates of a treatment effect, and estimates tend to be of low power in many applications because they are reliant on a subset of observations immediately above and below a cutoff point.

40. Charles Clotfelter, Elizabeth Glennie, Helen Ladd, and Jacob Vigdor, "Would Higher Salaries Keep Teachers in High-Poverty Schools? Evidence from a Policy Intervention in North Carolina," *Journal of Public Economics,* 92 (2008): 1352–70;

41. Edward Liu, Susan Moore Johnson, and Heather G. Peske, "New Teachers and the Massachusetts Signing Bonus: The Limits of Inducements," *Educational Evaluation and Policy Analysis* 26, no. 3 (2004): 217–36.

42. Jennifer Imazeki, *Attracting and Retaining Teachers in High-Need Schools: Do Financial Incentives Make Sense?* (San Diego State University, 2008); Cassandra M. Guarino, Lucrecia Santibanez, and Glenn A Daley, "Teacher Recruitment and Retention: A Review of the Recent Empirical Literature," *Review of Educational Research* 76, no. 2 (2006): 173-208; Jacob, "The Challenge of Staffing Urban Schools with Effective Teachers."

PART ONE

Perspectives on Teacher Compensation Reform

2

The Politics of Teacher Pay Reform

Dan Goldhaber

Teacher pay reform is much in the news of late, as states, localities, and the federal government start not only considering but actually implementing various pay reform programs.[1] Florida, Minnesota, and Texas, for example, have all embarked on high-profile compensation reform efforts that include performance pay, arguably the most controversial type of pay reform, as a central component. These states are joined by urban school systems in Denver, Houston, and New York City, among others, that have launched reform initiatives. The federal government is providing additional encouragement with its Teacher Incentive Fund, which provides grants to states or localities for development of alternatives to the "single salary schedule," the pay system used by the overwhelming majority of school districts and which bases teacher pay solely on experience level and degree.

While interest in teacher pay reform may be on the rise, calls for reform are certainly not new.[2] Pay for performance (also called "merit pay") was, for example, one of the recommendations of the 1983 *A Nation at Risk Report*.[3] But the politics of pay reform may well have shifted, as calls for reform now appear to come from across the ideological spectrum. While it has traditionally been Republicans who have called for market-based teacher pay reforms, in the 2008 election cycle they were joined by the three front-runners for the Democratic nomination (Hillary

Clinton, John Edwards, and Barack Obama), each of whom has advocated teacher pay reforms that include pay-for-performance strategies of one form or another. Such reforms have recently been adopted with the agreement of local union affiliates in Denver and New York City, and drafts of the reauthorization of the No Child Left Behind Act have also included provisions for pay incentives for improved teacher performance and for teaching in high-needs areas. Given all this, the calls for teacher pay reform are unlikely to disappear anytime soon.

There are good reasons to focus on teacher compensation as an avenue for school reform. The structure of compensation in education, which is dictated by the single salary schedule, is clearly out of step with the way the broader labor market functions.[4] Private sector compensation generally reflects not only individual attributes such as cognitive or technical skills but also performance on the job.[5] There is some evidence that the dichotomy between the way teachers and private sector employees are paid may account in part for the decline in the quality of teaching staff (as measured by standardized test scores or the selectivity of colleges attended—or both) over time. These findings, combined with the weak estimated link between teacher credentials (for example, a master's degree) and student outputs, have led researchers as well as various commissions and task forces to call for reform.[6]

Teachers Unions, Teacher Preferences, and Pay Reform

The two major teachers unions—the National Education Association (NEA) and the American Federation of Teachers (AFT)—are generally opposed to teacher pay reforms, but they diverge in their specific positions on reform.[7] Unions in general work to increase the compensation and improve the working conditions of their members by using, among other things, the threat, implicit or express, of labor stoppages.[8] And the unions take explicit positions on matters of pay.[9] Of the two, the NEA tends to express the stronger position, opposing changes to the current teacher pay system (see table 2-1 for some comparisons of the two teachers unions). It supports the use of salary schedules that assign pay based on academic degrees, preparation, professional growth, and length of service and opposes performance pay or additional compensation to attract or retain teachers for hard-to-recruit positions. The AFT also tends to oppose the pay-for-performance strategy, particularly when bonuses reward individual teachers (as opposed to whole schools), but it is more likely than the NEA to endorse other deviations from the single salary schedule.[10] In one of its policy statements, for example, the AFT notes that the single salary schedule has "severe drawbacks" and "does not allow

Table 2-1. *Union Positions on the Structure of Teacher Pay*

Item	National Education Association	American Federation of Teachers
Issue Salary schedule	*Supports* "The single salary schedule is the fairest, best understood, and most widely used approach to teacher compensation—in large part because it rewards the things that make a difference in teacher quality: knowledge and experience."[a]	*Open to nonsalary schedule options* "In the absence of more proximate measures of teacher quality, it [the single salary schedule] had a commonsense validity—the more you know about the task and the longer you do it. . . . Recognizing the limitations of the single salary system, the AFT is encouraging its locals to explore various teacher compensation systems based on local conditions."[b]
Difficult-to-staff position	*Strongly or moderately opposes* Adamantly opposes extra pay for recruiting or retaining teachers in difficult-to-fill subject areas but does support carefully designed financial incentives to encourage experienced teachers to teach in low-performing schools.[c]	*Supports* Recognizes the need to place new teachers in shortage fields (for example, math and science) further up on the salary schedule.[d]
Additional knowledge or skill	*Supports* Comprehensive pay systems must encourage the factors that make a difference in teaching and learning—such as skills, knowledge, and experience—and National Board for Professional Teaching Standards certification.[e]	*Supports* Endorses additional compensation to teachers who earn advanced certification by passing the National Board for Professional Teaching Standards exam.[d]
Pay for performance	*Opposes* Forces teachers to compete rather than cooperate.[a]	*Strongly or moderately opposes* Might consider compensation systems with school-wide rewards based on multiple measures of student outcomes as well as other indicators, such as attendance rates, dropout rates, and others.[d]

a. See www.nea.org/pay/teachermyths.html.
b. See www.aft.org/topics/teacher-quality/comp.htm.
c. See www.nea.org/teachershortage/images/rrg-full.pdf.
d. See www.aft.org/about/resolutions/2002/compensation.htm.
e. See www.nea.org/lac/funding/041608testi.html.

teachers to be compensated like other professionals in our society." It does not endorse specific reforms but urges its local affiliates to explore alternative teacher evaluation and compensation systems and explicitly states that alternatives could include "financial incentives to teachers who acquire additional knowledge and skills, . . . [increased pay for those] who agree to teach in low-performing and hard-to-staff schools, . . . [or] increased pay for school-wide improvement, mentoring new and veteran teachers, and teaching in shortage areas."[11]

Union Influence

The policy positions the teachers unions take appear to be quite influential in determining the direction of education policy. Their influence may be direct, through negotiations at the collective bargaining table, strikes, or lawsuits designed to block reforms they see as at odds with union positions.[12] But it is likely that unions exercise greater influence indirectly, through their influence over legislation, policy, and determining who sits at decisionmaking tables. The teachers unions have significant financial and organizational roles in influencing state and national elections and are particularly important to Democrats: the NEA donated $2.4 million and the AFT $2.6 million in the 2006 election cycle, and an overwhelming majority of this money (88 and 99 percent, respectively) went to Democrats.[13]

Given its importance on elective office, union influence over legislation is not surprising. Representative George Miller (D-Calif.), a key Democratic point person on education issues, initially pushed to have performance pay be a component of the reauthorization of the federal No Child Left Behind Act. His position was abandoned, however, most likely in response to strong union opposition.[14] In New York State, the general assembly (with the backing of the teachers union) preemptively barred local policymakers from considering student achievement as a factor in making teacher tenure decisions.[15]

Teachers unions are likely to have even greater influence at the local level. As the political science professor Terry Moe points out, teachers (and their unions) play an outsized role in determining the political makeup of school boards and hence the policies of their localities.[16] School boards are often elected in off-year, low-turnout races in which small shifts in the number of voters opting for particular candidates can swing board elections.[17] That much of the voting public may know little about school board candidates (for instance, when the race is concurrent with city council elections) magnifies the influence of teachers in this type of race. Having teachers, or their designates, at polling places identifying board candidates as "the teachers' candidate" or "on the teachers' side" may be enough to tip the balance in some situations. Superintendents, while usually not directly elected, well understand the political dynamics of local races, and dealing with an unhappy teacher workforce is certainly part of their calculation in pushing for or implementing particular policies. When it comes to controversial policies that are sure to upset the apple cart, often the safest thing to do is implement a delay strategy, as a change in direction often accompanies the election of a new school board.

It should come as little surprise that school districts in which unions have less influence (for example, because they are in right-to-work states or do not have the right to collective bargaining to negotiate contracts) are far more likely to use pay-for-performance plans than are school districts in which unions have greater influence.[18] Not surprisingly, pay for performance is more prevalent in private and charter schools, where unions are generally less influential. As Michael Podgursky and Matthew Springer point out in a recent review, less than 10 percent of public schools (in the 1999–2000 school year) reported using a salary incentive to reward teaching excellence, compared with over 35 percent of charter schools and over 20 percent of private schools (more than 40 percent of nonreligious private schools report rewarding teaching excellence).[19]

While the union position (particularly that of the NEA) tends to oppose pay reforms, local school districts do sometimes negotiate reform contracts with union approval: Denver's ProComp plan, adopted with the cooperation of the local NEA affiliate, is one notable example. The successful implementation in Denver (and elsewhere, as other districts have used alternatives to the single salary schedule over the years, such as career ladders) is attributed largely to the willingness to engage the union and teachers from the beginning in thinking through the design and implementation of the proposed system and the push for reforms over a long period of time on the part of supporters, with significant support of foundations.[20] While ProComp is widely touted as a pay-for-performance plan, in fact it is but one component of a more comprehensive pay reform. In addition to pay that is linked to student learning growth, teachers are rewarded based on their knowledge and skills, a professional evaluation, and market incentives.[21] That ProComp encompasses a number of elements other than pay for performance, and that teachers under this system can be rewarded for credentials like certification from the National Board for Professional Teaching Standards, may help explain union buy-in.

Attitudes of Teachers

How well do the views of the teachers unions reflect the wider views of teachers? This question is important, as the politics of implementing reform is likely to be quite contentious if, for instance, teachers' views toward reforms are as hard-line as the position taken by the NEA. Unfortunately, opinion surveys do not provide a definitive answer to this question. Different polls of teacher attitudes toward pay reform suggest different levels of support for pay for performance, ranging from over 60 percent in favor to over 60 percent opposed.[22]

It is fairly clear that support for reform depends on how questions about it are framed. For example, a 2003 survey of public school teachers conducted by Public Agenda has found only about 50 percent support for school districts' moving away from the single salary schedule. But in that same survey, teachers appeared far more supportive of a deviation in the schedule when asked about some specific compensation reforms. Around 70 percent of teachers supported providing incentives to teachers "who work in tough neighborhoods with low-performing schools," and a similar percentage favored additional compensation for teachers "who consistently work harder, putting in more time and effort than other teachers." By contrast, far fewer (around 40 percent) were favorably inclined to support pay for performance or incentives for "hard-to-fill" subjects.

This general pattern of support for various types of reform is reflected in a 2006 survey of teachers in Washington state, conducted at the University of Washington.[23] As figure 2-1 demonstrates, this work suggests that teachers strongly sup-

Figure 2-1. *Teachers' Attitudes toward Various Pay Structures*
Percent

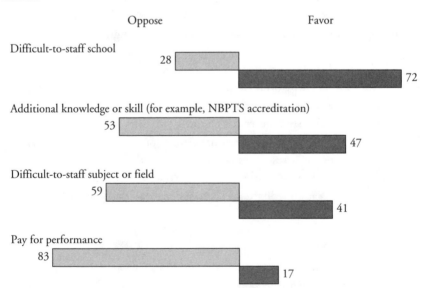

Source: Dan Goldhaber, Michael DeArmond, and Scott DeBurgomaster, "Teacher Attitudes about Compensation Reform: Implications for Reform Implementation," Working Paper 20 (Seattle, Wash.: School Finance Redesign Project, August 2007).

port extra pay for "work in tough neighborhoods with low-performing schools" and very strongly oppose rewarding "teachers whose students make greater gains on standardized tests than similar students taught by other teachers." Support for rewarding "teachers who specialize in hard-to-fill subjects such as science or mathematics" or those "who receive accreditation from the National Board for Professional Teaching Standards [NBPTS]" was more modest.[24]

Although these data are interesting and useful to those considering the likely teacher reaction to the idea of various pay reforms, there are limits to what one should infer based on broad-based teacher responses to survey questions. Some reforms might be more appropriate to specific educational contexts, and policymakers might also be interested in how teacher attitudes evolve after experiencing first-hand changes in the structure of their pay. Indeed, analysis of teacher attitudes toward pay reform suggests that context is in fact quite important in shaping teacher views.

Dale Ballou and Michael Podgursky find that support for performance pay varies not only on individual teacher attributes such as race and experience but also based on the characteristics of the students taught. For example, there appears to be a generational divide when it comes to pay for performance (which is also reflected in some of the above survey findings), with younger teachers far more favorably inclined toward this type of pay structure. But the authors also find that teachers working with disadvantaged and low-achieving students, or who have direct experience teaching in a system that has used it, are more likely to be favorably inclined toward pay for performance.[25]

More recent work by Dan Goldhaber, Michael DeArmond and Scott DeBurgomaster, and by Brian Jacob and Matthew Springer—which, like that of Ballou and Podgursky, analyzes the factors influencing teacher attitudes toward pay reforms—also finds that attitudes depend on individual teacher attributes, such as experience.[26] It is interesting that some evidence of divergence exists between the views of individual teachers and the unions. Consistent with the hardline union position, teachers who are members of a union are less likely to support merit pay; but Goldhaber, DeArmond, and DeBurgomaster, who investigate teacher attitudes toward other types of pay reforms, find union membership to have no statistically significant impact on whether teachers report supporting additional compensation for hard-to-staff schools or subjects. The survey results also indicate that teaching context matters, elementary-level teachers being less supportive of pay for performance than secondary-level teachers and, not surprisingly, teachers who have a positive view of their principals (or, in the case of Jacob and Springer, those who report greater self-efficacy) being more supportive of incentive pay.

Table 2-2. *Predicted Probabilities for Female Teachers' Support for Merit Pay*[a]

Item	Strongly favor	Somewhat favor	Somewhat oppose	Strongly oppose
Veteran high school teacher	0.03	0.14	0.24	0.59
Low teacher trust/high principal trust	0.09	0.25	0.29	0.37
High teacher trust/low principal trust	0.01	0.07	0.18	0.74
Novice high school teacher	0.04	0.18	0.27	0.51
Low teacher trust/high principal trust	0.13	0.3	0.28	0.29
High teacher trust/low principal trust	0.02	0.1	0.21	0.67

Source: Dan Goldhaber, Michael DeArmond, and Scott DeBurgomaster, "Teacher Attitudes about Compensation Reform: Implications for Reform Implementation," Working Paper 20 (Seattle, Wash.: School Finance Redesign Project, August 2007).

a. Teachers whose students make greater gains on standardized tests than similar students taught by other teachers.

The extent to which these factors influence teachers is not trivial. Table 2-2 shows the results from an analysis of the survey of teachers from Washington state, which was used to predict attitudes about pay reform for female teachers.[27] This analysis shows that teachers who have a high degree of trust in their principal and a low degree of trust of their colleagues are substantially more likely to at least somewhat favor pay for performance.

This review of union positions and teacher attitudes suggests that the successful engagement of teachers in reform efforts depends a great deal on local context and the process through which reforms are initiated. This in turn begs the question: what role do local decisionmakers play in teacher pay reform?

Local Decisionmakers, Political Coalitions, and Pay Reform

Although the attitudes of teachers and the policy positions of teachers unions are certain to play a role in influencing reform, these are not the only factors involved in acceptance of teacher pay reform. Union power is weak in many states and localities, and while use of alternatives to the single salary schedule is somewhat more prevalent in these districts, it is still only a tiny minority of such districts—for instance, in localities without collective bargaining—that employs alternative compensation models.[28]

Furthermore, surveys have suggested that of various types of pay reforms, teachers appear to be most favorably inclined toward pay incentives for hard-to-staff schools, and the AFT, unlike the NEA, actually supports this type of reform. Overwhelming evidence shows that effective teachers are inequitably distributed across student bodies, with the most disadvantaged students being far more likely to be taught by the least credentialed, least experienced teachers, and that incentives designed to rectify this issue can be successful.[29] Because much of this inequity is a result of within-district teacher distributions, such disparities could be addressed through district-level policies. Given these facts, it is surprising that pay reform designed specifically to address this inequity (hard-to-staff school incentives) is precisely the type of reform that is least likely to be used by school districts according to the 2003–04 wave of the *Schools and Staffing Survey,* administered by the U.S. Department of Education Institute of Education Science's National Center for Education Statistics.[30] Jacob and Springer, for example, report that in 2003–04, less than 5 percent of districts nationally used incentive pay to encourage teachers to take positions in less desirable locations as compared with more than 10 percent that reward teachers in a shortage field and nearly 20 percent that reward teachers for being certified by the National Board for Professional Teaching Standards.

If it is not teachers who oppose financial incentives for hard-to-staff schools, what explains the failure to use pay incentives to address within-district inequities? One speculative, but not unreasonable, suggestion is that responsibility lies with the political interests of elected officials—not in union opposition. Turnout in school board elections is unlikely to be uniform throughout a school district; affluent neighborhoods tend to have more-active parent populations, and thus these schools are likely to garner more attention from elected officials. As a result, it can be difficult to move a district's best teachers (through pay incentives or other policies) from the advantaged schools where they tend to be teaching to the disadvantaged schools where they are most needed.[31]

The anticipated political consequences of pay reforms certainly hinder their adoption, but other important details also probably play key roles in determining the likelihood of implementation and success of any attempted reforms. Reform is likely to depend on both coalition building and capacity. Moving reform from idea into practice requires a reasonably high level of consensus, which entails convincing parents, educators, and the business community that an investment of time and effort in such an endeavor is worthwhile for student achievement. This requires linking the importance of teacher quality to the use of pay as a managerial tool to influence it.

Perhaps more important, reform should be seen as reasonably safe—both in the sense that it has enough public support and that implementation is not likely to lead to disasters (such as a budget crisis or strike).

There are of course myriad different ways to build coalitions that make policy innovation safer, but one key approach would be to get teachers involved at the ground level in the reform effort, since it is often the teachers, through their union voice, who are seen as opposing reforms. This has begun to happen at the national level through the Teacher Leaders Network, which brings teachers together to discuss and design pay reform initiatives.[32] Piloting a reform before full-scale adoption also helps to lower the stakes and can help to buttress the notion that pay reform ideas, in and of themselves, are neither good nor bad; rather, their effects depend on the specifics of a policy's design, the capacity to administer a changed system, and the political reactions of key stakeholders to a reform.

Finally, there is nothing more likely to help make pay reform a safe political endeavor than its proven success. I argue, that success ought to be judged based on the impact of a reform on student outcomes, but a shorter-run metric for success that policymakers might point to is that a particular reform has been implemented and successfully administered in one or more localities. It is for this reason that readily adopted models like the Teacher Advancement Program, which is being used in multiple states and localities, and high-profile efforts like that of Denver are influential.

The Devil in the Details and Where We Go from Here

The broad discussion around reforming teacher pay tends to belie some of the complicated issues that arise when one attempts to figure out the practical details of how a given reform would actually work. It is easy, for instance, for policymakers to suggest that we ought to move away from a single salary schedule toward a pay-for-performance system, and in the abstract this concept may make perfect sense. But do we know precisely how to structure rewards? Should they be individual or group based? Should they cover teachers who are not working in tested areas? In the case of individual-based plans, do we know how to judge the value added of specific teachers? Do we know the appropriate size of incentives needed to induce the changes in teacher behavior that we wish to see? Do school systems have the support infrastructure—adequate data, sufficient capacity in human resource and accounting departments, and so on—to implement and administer a new pay system? Were pay reform to be adopted, how would we know whether it was effective? For the vast majority of school systems, the answer to most of these questions, I would argue, is no.

Group-based rewards, such as rewarding all teachers within a school, solve some of the sticky political issues that come up around pay reform in that they provide incentives for collaboration and can easily include teachers who are not in tested areas. Such rewards have a downside, however, in that they also encourage free riding and ignore within-school variation in performance. To my knowledge, there is no research that assesses the efficacy of group versus individual teacher performance-pay plans.

In the case of individual-based pay for performance, researchers are just beginning to explore the extent to which one can accurately evaluate individual teacher effectiveness based on student test scores, and they have already encountered significant limitations in using value added methodologies for this purpose (these issues are discussed in chapter 6 of this volume).[33]

Of course, linking teacher pay to student learning gains on standardized tests is not the only way of using pay for performance; one could, for instance, reward teachers based on assessments from their peers or supervisors. As the Denver Pro-Comp plan illustrates, deviations from the single salary schedule can certainly be more nuanced.

Although a number of districts have at times used alternatives to the single salary schedule, many probably as a reaction to the *Nation at Risk* report (which called for pay reform), little is known about how to structure other plans to make them effective.[34] This is because there are few credible quantitative studies on their effects.[35] The lack of quantitative evidence can be blamed mainly on the fact that only a handful of states currently have the data structure necessary to properly evaluate the effects of pay reforms (individual teacher-student links that can be tracked over time). This is slowly changing, as the No Child Left Behind Act of 2001 has led to significant upgrades in the amount of teacher and student data that are collected, and some recent pay reform legislation (the Teacher Incentive Fund, for example) requires that reforms be studied. Nevertheless, the available evidence base from which to draw inferences about different pay reform designs remains thin.

Moreover, as discussed above, the lack of evidence on how pay reform affects students surely plays into the willingness of policymakers to engage in reform. There are few, if any, localities that one can point to and say with credibility, "Look, it worked there," where *working* is defined as having an impact on students. Probably the best empirical evidence of the impact of pay for performance—the most contentious type of pay reform—comes from outside of the United States. Rightly or wrongly, this evidence is likely to be played down in policy debates, if it is known at all.

Contrast this situation with what is known about reduction in class size and the influence of the Student-Teacher Achievement Ratio experiment (popularly known as the STAR experiment) on the collective knowledge about efficacy of class size reduction. While various constituency groups (parents, teachers, business people) may not get the specifics right, many of them can point to the experiment as evidence that reducing class size is a proven way to increase student achievement. Furthermore, because the broad public understands the notion of an experiment, these findings carry a great deal of weight when it comes to evaluating the evidence for or against class size reduction policies.

Equally important, the Student-Teacher Achievement Ratio experiment helped policymakers move beyond the question of whether class size reduction does or does not work to infer more about the context (such as grade level or student characteristics) in which reducing class size is most likely to have an impact. It is no great leap to imagine that if policymakers had this level of information about how to structure pay incentives (see the questions posed at the beginning of this section), they would be more likely to implement them. Answering questions about the nuances of reforms helps to move the policy dialogue away from silly debates about whether pay reform is good or bad and toward more productive conversations about the design details that are likely to govern the impacts of a particular policy. The irony is that for technical details to be learned, pay reforms need to be implemented in an environment conducive to evaluation, yet it is the knowledge about the technical details that would enhance the likelihood that pay reforms will be adopted.

Ultimately, I do not believe that the lack of knowledge about what teacher pay ought to look like should be seen as a decisive argument against trying out alternative ways to structure teacher compensation. What is known about the single salary schedule suggests that it is not a system well suited to ensuring a high-quality teacher workforce that fairly allocates teachers across students. Teachers are paid according to characteristics that are, at best, only weakly related to their productivity, and they are rewarded in the labor market not through salary but through classroom assignment. When it comes to thinking about changing teacher pay to address this situation, people seek evidence that pay alternatives work. Thus even though the existing pay system does not appear to work well, the politics of pay reform generally make the standard of evidence for change higher than that applied to the status quo.

The increasing availability of data, and the consequent research showing the variation in teacher effectiveness, has no doubt tipped the scales of political debate over teacher pay toward experimentation. This is probably for the good, as what does or does not work can only be learned through program evaluations and, especially, well-designed experiments. But there are reasons to be cautious and to be realistic about the financial costs associated with reform. In particular, evidence to date suggests that lasting, effective pay reforms cannot be achieved on the cheap:

building the support, capacity, information, and evaluation system infrastructure is crucial.

Confronting the issue of institutional inertia is central to managing the politics of pay reform. Furthermore, figuring out how to nudge systems away from the entrenched single salary schedule is no small task. If school districts and teachers are pushed too hard, they are likely to push back. Recent experiences with pay reform initiatives in Florida, for example, suggest that many school districts will balk at implementing what they see as top-down reforms, as a result of which most state efforts, despite repeated attempts to boost teacher incentives in recent years, have been rejected.

More politically promising are reform initiatives (like those in Minnesota and the national Teacher Incentive Fund) that put additional monies on the table for school districts' use in pursuing reforms. The same logic would suggest an opt-in system for teachers in the existing workforce, with the understanding that opting in would most likely require some sweetening of the pay pot. Under the single salary schedule, teachers have little doubt about their future earnings. Convincing them to accept changes (or hiring teachers of equal or better quality) is likely to require increased salaries to compensate for any increased risk associated with a reformed pay structure.

The implementation of and support for pay reform programs may be at least as important in determining the success of a reform as the specifics of a program design. Perhaps one of the most important findings from surveys of teachers in states or districts that have undertaken pay reforms is that teachers often do not understand key features of how the reforms work or even that there is a reform in place.[36] This is likely to both lessen the effectiveness of a reform and open the door for misinformation (accidental or purposeful) that leads to political opposition. Consequently, investing in clear and direct lines of communication with teachers about the specifics of any reform program will be crucial to its success.

The single salary schedule, for all its shortcomings, has a number of appealing features. It is objective and easy to administer. It does not require any year-to-year adjustments or statistical analyses. This means it less costly to administer and less likely to create suspicion among teachers about the basis of their pay. Moreover, it is not certain that public school systems, whose central offices are populated with former teachers used to the single salary schedule, will generally have the capacity to support changes. Building capacity for pay reform is also likely to be costly in the short run.

There is some indication that voters and policymakers are willing to ante up additional funding for teacher salaries if the funding flows into a reform system.

Denver's ProComp is a good illustration of this. Implementation of the system first required voter approval of a ballot initiative to raise an additional $25 million in taxes annually to fund it. Similarly, the federal grants from the Teacher Incentive Fund result in an infusion of new monies into systems that are willing to implement pay reforms. These anecdotal examples suggest the outline of a grand bargain between teachers and their unions and pay reformers, whereby teachers accept some reforms if they come with a pay increase.

Unfortunately, individual political actors who successfully push reforms have strong incentives to declare victory and go home, regardless of the reform's efficacy. However, for those who are truly committed to pay reform this would be a mistake, since the next governor, legislature, superintendent, or school board is likely to reverse course. A history of failed attempts at pay reforms that were tried and abandoned for one reason or another illustrates the fact that over the long run, reformers will most likely bear the burden of proof in showing that a particular reform was in fact beneficial. In the absence of such evidence, it is hard to make a strong case for sustaining a more complex pay structure, one that tends to cause trouble with employees.

Sustaining any new education policy is always a risky enterprise, and advocates of pay reforms have only a thin evidentiary base on which to make their case. Given this, it makes sense when advocating reforms to also push for (and invest in) credible research that can help determine both the impacts of reform and ways in which it might be improved. The complicated political dynamics surrounding pay reform imply that rushing forward with ill-conceived or unsupported reforms that do not include an evaluation component could be costly in the long run. High-profile reform failures—whether real or perceived—are likely to undermine the notion that reforms can work. In some ways the stars appear to be aligned for reform in teacher pay systems: there is broad recognition of the importance of teacher quality and the likelihood that pay structure influences this, and there are national, state, and local reforms currently in place. It is unclear, however, how long this alignment will last, so it makes sense to take advantage of the current environment to learn as much as we can about the efficacy of particular reforms.

Notes

1. Note that I say teacher "pay" as opposed to teacher "compensation," which, in addition to pay, would also include benefits. While total compensation is very much an issue (see, for instance, Robert M. Costrell and Michael Podgursky, "Peaks, Cliffs, and Valleys: The

Peculiar Incentives of Teacher Pensions," *Education Next* 8, no. 1 [2008]: 22–28), there currently appears to be little policy debate over the value of changing the nonpay portions (including retirement benefits) of teacher compensation.

2. See Michael J. Podgursky and Matthew G. Springer, "Teacher Performance Pay: A Review," *Journal of Policy Analysis and Management* 26, no. 4 (2007): 909–49.

3. National Commission on Excellence in Education, *A Nation at Risk: The Imperative for Educational Reform* (U.S. Department of Education: National Commission on Excellence in Education, 1983).

4. See Eric Eide, Dan Goldhaber, and Dominic Brewer, "The Teacher Labour Market and Teacher Quality," *Oxford Review of Economic Policy* 20, no. 2 (2004): 230–44.

5. For more on individual attributes, see Dominic Brewer, Eric R. Eide, and Ronald G. Ehrenberg, "Does It Pay to Attend an Elite Private College? Cross-Cohort Evidence on the Effects of College Type on Earnings," *Journal of Human Resources* 34, no. 1 (1999): 104–23; Jeff Grogger and Eric Eide, "Changes in College Skills and the Rise in the College Wage Premium," *Journal of Human Resources* 30, no. 2 (1995): 280–310; and Richard J. Murnane, John B. Willett, and Frank Levy, "The Growing Importance of Cognitive Skills in Wage Determination," *Review of Economics and Statistics* 77, no. 2 (1995): 251–66. For more on performance on the job, see Robert D. Bretz and George T. Milkovich, "Performance Appraisal in Large Organizations: Practice and Research Implications," Cornell University, Center for Advanced Human Resource Studies, 1989.

6. See, for example, Eric A. Hanushek, "The Failure of Input-Based Schooling Policies," *Economic Journal* 113, no. 485 (2003): 64–98; Center for Teaching Quality, "Performance-Pay for Teachers: Designing Systems That Students Deserve" (2007); Committee for Economic Development, "Investing in Learning: School Funding Policies to Foster High Performance; A Statement on National Policy," Committee for Economic Development, 2004; and Business Roundtable, "Pay-for-Performance in Education: An Issue Brief for Business Leaders," 2000.

7. For more detail and a history of the two unions, as well as research on their effects on K–12 schooling, see Dan Goldhaber, "Are Teachers Unions Good for Students?" in *Collective Bargaining in Education: Negotiating Change in Today's Schools,* edited by Jane Hannaway and Andrew Rotherham (Harvard Education Press, 2006). The NEA refers to itself as a professional organization rather than a union, but the two organizations play similar functional roles. Both are large labor unions—the NEA with its roughly 3 million members is nearly twice the size of the AFT—and have built their influence around collective bargaining muscle, legislative brokering, and the sheer scale of their memberships.

8. Some good examples from this body of research are O. C. Ashenfelter, G. E. Johnson, and J. H. Pencavel, "Trade Unions and the Rate of Change of Money Wages in the United States Manufacturing Industry," *Review of Economic Studies* 39, no. 1 (1972): 27–54; Brian Bemmels, "How Unions Affect Productivity in Manufacturing Plants," *Industrial and Labor Relations Review* 40, no. 2 (1987): 241–53; Charles Brown and James Medoff, "Trade Unions in the Production Process," *Journal of Political Economy* 86, no. 3 (1978): 355–78; Henry S. Farber, "Nonunion Wage Rates and the Threat of Unionization" (Cambridge, Mass.: National Bureau of Economic Research, 2003); Robert N. Mefford, "The Effect of Unions on Productivity in a Multinational Manufacturing Firm," *Industrial and Labor Relations Review* 40, no. 1 (1986): 105–14; and Sherwin Rosen, "Trade Union Power, Threat Effects, and the Extent of Organization,"

Review of Economic Studies 36, no. 2 (1969): 185–96. The impacts of union actions on firms are not as clear as one might think. On the one hand, unions are thought to raise the cost of operation (Randall W. Eberts and Joe A. Stone, "Teacher Unions and the Cost of Public Education," *Economic Inquiry* 24, no. 4 [1986]: 631–43), but they also may serve the interest of employers by efficiently providing information to them about the preferences of employees, which in turn leads to greater productivity (Steven G. Allen, "Trade Unions, Absenteeism, and Exit-Voice," *Industrial and Labor Relations Review* 37, no. 3 [1984]: 331–45; Richard B. Freeman, "Individual Mobility and Union Voice in the Labor Market," *American Economic Review* 66, no. 2 [1976]: 361–68; and Richard B. Freeman and James L. Medoff, *What Do Unions Do?* [New York: Basic Books, 1984]).

9. For more detail, see the AFT website (www.aft.org/about/index.htm) and the NEA website (www.nea.org/home/19583.htm).

10. For specifics on the NEA and AFT positions, see National Education Association, *The 2007 NEA Handbook* (Washington, 2007) and American Federation of Teachers, "Professional Compensation" (www.aft.org/topics/teacher-quality/compensation/index.htm [November 2007]). Interestingly, Sandra Feldman, a former president of the AFT, has openly suggested that pay reforms could include both salary increases and rewards for "different roles, responsibilities, skills, and yes, results." "Rethinking Teacher Compensation: Equitable Pay for Teachers Is Part and Parcel of Improving Student Performance," in *American Teacher* 88, no. 6 (March 2004): 5 (www.aft.org/pubs-reports/american_teacher/mar04/AT_wws.html [February 2009]).

11. The AFT national policy includes additional compensation for knowledge and skills that advance or address high-priority educational goals; schoolwide improvement; National Board certification; mentoring new and veteran teachers, providing peer assistance and review, serving as lead teachers, and so forth; teaching in shortage areas; agreeing to teach in hard-to-staff or low-performing schools; assuming additional responsibilities; and instructional practice that meets mutually agreed upon high-quality professional standards. See "Professional Compensation for Teachers" (2002) (www.aft.org/about/resolutions/2002/compensation.htm [February 2009]) for additional details.

12. See Cynthia Prince, "Higher Pay in Hard-to-Staff Schools: The Case for Financial Incentives," American Association of School Administrators, Washington, June 2002.

13. As reported by the Center for Responsive Politics. See "National Education Association," Center for Responsive Politics (www.opensecrets.org/orgs/summary.php?id=D000000064 [February 2009]); and "American Federation of Teachers," Center for Responsive Politics (www.opensecrets.org/orgs/summary.php?id=D000000083 [February 2009]).

14. See testimony by the National Education Association before the House Committee on Education and Labor, *Hearings on the Reauthorization of the Elementary and Secondary Education Act,* September 10, 2007 (http://edlabor.house.gov/testimony/091007 RegWeaverTestimony.pdf); and testimony by the National Association of Elementary School Principals before the House Committee on Education and Labor, *Hearings on the Reauthorization of the Elementary and Secondary Education Act,* September 10, 2007 (http://edlabor.house.gov/testimony/091007MaryKaySommersTestimony.pdf), opposing the performance-pay component of the reauthorization of NCLB.

15. See "Albany Fails Again," *New York Times,* editorial, April 9, 2008.

16. Terry M. Moe, "Teacher Unions and School Board Elections," in *Besieged: School Boards and the Future of Education Politics,* edited by William G. Howell (Brookings, 2005),

pp. 255–87; Terry M. Moe, "The Union Label on the Ballot Box," *Education Next* 6, no. 3 (2006): 58–67. Moe tests the notion that teachers wish to influence school policies by examining whether they are more likely to vote in school board elections if they work and live in the same district. As he hypothesizes, teachers are significantly more likely to vote in such cases.

17. For example, see the summer 2006 issue of *Education Next,* which includes several articles on the relations between unions and school boards (www.hoover.org/publications/ednext/ 3211896.html [November 2007]).

18. See Dan Goldhaber and others, "Why Do So Few Public School Districts Use Merit Pay?" *Journal of Education Finance* 33, no. 3 (2008): 262–89.

19. Podgursky and Springer, "Teacher Performance Pay."

20. See Phil Gonring, Paul Teske, and Brad Jupp, *Pay-for-Performance Teacher Compensation: An Inside View of Denver's ProComp Plan* (Harvard Education Press, 2007).

21. For more information on ProComp, see its website (http://denverprocomp.org/ [February 2009]). For information on other pay-for-performance programs, see Podgursky and Springer, "Teacher Performance Pay."

22. See Brian Jacob and Matthew G. Springer, "Teacher Attitudes on Pay for Performance: A Pilot Study," National Center on Performance Incentives, 2007. A nuanced interpretation of the findings (at least this reader's interpretation) for teacher support for pay for performance suggests that support drops as measures of performance are more specifically stated.

23. See Dan Goldhaber, Michael DeArmond, and Scott DeBurgomaster, "Teacher Attitudes about Compensation Reform: Implications for Reform Implementation," Working Paper 20 (Seattle, Wash.: School Finance Redesign Project, August 2007) (www.crpe.org/cs/ crpe/view/csr_pubs/160).

24. Washington State Teacher Compensation Survey (University of Washington, 2006). For details on this survey and its findings, see Goldhaber, DeArmond, and DeBurgomaster, "Teacher Attitudes about Compensation Reform."

25. Dale Ballou and Michael Podgursky, "Teacher Attitudes toward Merit Pay: Examining Conventional Wisdom," *Industrial and Labor Relations Review* 47, no. 1 (1993): 50–61. Interestingly, Ballou and Podgursky find that teachers in pay-for-performance districts were more supportive of the practice, regardless of whether they themselves had received a performance bonus.

26. Goldhaber, DeArmond, and DeBurgomaster, "Teacher Attitudes about Compensation Reform"; Jacob and Springer, "Teacher Attitudes on Pay for Performance."

27. For simplicity, the reported simulation focuses on female teachers, who make up the overwhelming majority of the teacher workforce in the United States. However, it is worth noting that in the Goldhaber, DeArmond, and DeBurgomaster study, female teachers tended to be slightly less likely than male teachers to support pay reforms.

28. See Goldhaber and others, "Why Do So Few Public School Districts Use Merit Pay?"

29. See Charles T. Clotfelter and others, "Would Higher Salaries Keep Teachers in High-Poverty Schools? Evidence from a Policy Intervention in North Carolina" (Cambridge, Mass.: National Bureau of Economic Research, 2006); Charles T. Clotfelter, Helen F. Ladd, and Jacob L. Vigdor, "Teacher-Student Matching and the Assessment of Teacher Effectiveness," *Journal of Human Resources* 41, no. 4 (2006): 778–820; and Hamilton Lankford, Susanna Loeb, and James Wyckoff, "Teacher Sorting and the Plight of Urban Schools: A Descriptive Analysis," *Educational Evaluation and Policy Analysis* 24, no. 1 (2002): 37–62.

30. For details, see the National Center for Education Statistics website (http://nces.ed.gov/ surveys/sass/ [February 2009]).

31. As described in Goldhaber, "Teacher Pay Reforms: The Political Implications of Recent Research" (Washington: Center for American Progress, 2006), this may imply that some types of pay reforms are more likely to take hold at higher levels of government—for example, to be adopted by mayors or governors, who have a greater political stake in the quality of all schools in a region and who rely on broader constituencies than just public school parents.

32. See Center for Teacher Quality, "Performance-Pay for Teachers: Designing a System That Students Deserve," April 2007 (www.teachingquality.org/pdfs/TSreport.pdf [June 2008]).

33. For more on these issues, see Dale Ballou, "Value-Added Assessment: Controlling for Context with Misspecified Models," paper prepared for the Urban Institute Longitudinal Data Conference, Washington, March 2005; Dale Ballou, William Sanders, and Paul Wright, "Controlling for Student Background in Value-Added Assessment of Teachers," *Journal of Educational and Behavioral Statistics* 29, no. 1 (2004): 37–65; Daniel F. McCaffrey and others, "Models for Value-Added Modeling of Teacher Effects," *Journal of Educational and Behavioral Statistics* 29, no. 1 (2004): 67–101; Petra E. Todd and Kenneth I. Wolpin, "On the Specification and Estimation of the Production Function for Cognitive Achievement," *Economic Journal* 113, no. 485 (2003): F3–F33; and Dan Goldhaber and Michael Hansen, "Is It Just a Bad Class? Assessing the Stability of Measured Teacher Performance," Working Paper 2008-5 (Seattle, Wash.: Center on Reinventing Public Education, November 2008).

34. See Michael DeArmond and Dan Goldhaber, "A Leap of Faith: Redesigning Teacher Compensation," University of Washington at Seattle, Center on Reinventing Public Education, 2007; Harry P. Hatry, John M. Greiner, and Brenda G. Ashford, *Issues and Case Studies in Teacher Incentive Plans,* 2nd ed. (Washington: Urban Institute Press, 1994); and Richard J. Murnane and David K. Cohen, "Merit Pay and the Evaluation Problem: Why Most Merit Pay Plans Fail and a Few Survive," *Harvard Educational Review* 56, no. 1 (1986): 1–17. For example, should incentives be targeted to individual teachers or groups? How large should different types of incentives be?

35. Some evidence suggests that group-based pay-for-performance awards affect school-level performance (Charles T. Clotfelter and Helen F. Ladd, "Recognizing and Rewarding Success in Public Schools," in *Holding Schools Accountable: Performance-Based Reform in Education,* edited by Helen F. Ladd [Brookings, 1996], pp. 23–64), and some international evidence suggests that individual teacher-based pay-for-performance systems enhance teacher productivity (Victor Lavy, "Evaluating the Effect of Teachers' Group Performance Incentives on Pupil Achievement," *Journal of Political Economy* 110, no. 6 [2002]: 1286–1317; Victor Lavy, "Performance Pay and Teacher's Effort, Productivity, and Grading Ethics" [Cambridge, Mass.: National Bureau of Economic Research, 2004]), but only one major quantitative study has been done on the impact of individual teacher-based pay-for-performance in the United States (David N. Figlio and Lawrence W. Kenny, "Individual Teacher Incentives and Student Performance," *Journal of Public Economics* 91, nos. 5–6 [2007]: 901–14).

36. See Clotfelter, Ladd, and Vigdor, "Teacher-Student Matching and the Assessment of Teacher Effectiveness"; and Jacob and Springer, "Teacher Attitudes on Pay for Performance."

3

A Legal Perspective on Teacher Compensation Reform

James E. Ryan

Although the single salary schedule remains a ubiquitous feature in teacher compensation, differential pay has become more popular over the past decade. Differential pay takes a number of forms, but two general types are most prominent: performance-based pay, sometimes called merit pay, which rewards teachers based on the performance improvements of their students; and recruitment and retention incentives, given to teachers who teach in difficult-to-staff subjects or in hard-to-staff schools. Although they remain the exception, school districts across the country are already using one or both forms of differential pay.

Hundreds of school districts are experimenting with some type of performance-based pay system. At least six states have statewide or pilot programs, and the federal government has spent close to $100 million on the Teacher Incentive Fund, designed to encourage the use of performance-based pay systems in high-needs districts and schools.[1] An even larger number of school districts and states currently offer recruitment and retention incentives for teachers in hard-to-staff subjects like math or science or for those who agree to teach in hard-to-staff schools, which are typically urban, high poverty, and high minority.[2]

Teachers unions remain largely opposed to performance-based pay. The union position is not monolithic, however, and there have been some important break-throughs, including a recent agreement on a performance-pay plan between the

Bloomberg administration and the New York City teachers union.[3] The unions also remain largely opposed to bonuses based on subject area, generally believing it inappropriate to distinguish among teachers based on the subjects they teach. But they are supportive of bonuses given to teachers who agree to teach in difficult-to-staff schools.[4]

Differential pay raises a host of important empirical and political questions. Which programs are most likely to attract and retain capable teachers? Which are most likely to boost student achievement and why? How important is teacher support for merit pay? Which level of government—local, state, or federal—is best suited to develop and implement differential pay schemes? Social scientists are paying increasing attention to these and other questions, as is demonstrated in the other chapters in this volume.

This chapter focuses on a different but equally important question: are there legal obstacles to the creation and implementation of some or all differential pay programs? As the chapter describes in some detail, the legal landscape is fairly open to the creation of such programs. The most serious unresolved legal question is whether differential pay is the subject of mandatory bargaining requirements imposed by state law. Even if—or where—differential pay is found to be the subject of mandatory bargaining requirements, this does not necessarily preclude such programs. It simply means that unions must first be consulted and agree to include differential pay in teacher contracts. Such a requirement may prove to be more of an obstacle with some forms of differential pay than with others, depending on the unions' support of or opposition to the plan. Any such legal requirement may also push in the same direction as policy insofar as securing the consent of teachers to a new pay system may be critical to a successful transition.

The various legal issues raised by differential pay programs can usefully be divided into two categories: governmental authority and individual rights. Under the first category, the basic question is whether the government—federal, state, or local—has the authority to develop a differential pay system. Under the second category, that the government has such authority is assumed; the key question is whether individual teachers possess any rights that must be protected in the implementation of those programs.

With respect to these legal issues, the analysis usually does not vary depending on the particular type of differential pay program at issue. For this reason, in the discussion that follows the various types of differential pay programs— performance-based pay or recruitment and retention bonuses—are separated out only where legal requirements would instead vary by type of program.

Governmental Authority

All three levels of government—federal, state, and local—play a role in shaping education law and policy. Each level of government is subject to different rules about the reach of its power. The federal government is, famously, a government of enumerated powers. For the federal government to enact any kind of program, it must point to a provision in the federal constitution that grants the government the authority to act in that particular area.

State governments, by contrast, are not so limited, at least not by the federal constitution. They need not point to a specific enumerated power in the federal constitution to justify legislation but rather may legislate in any area provided that the legislation furthers the general welfare of their citizens. Under every state constitution, moreover, states have the duty, not simply the authority, to provide for public education.[5] It is for this reason, as well as tradition, that states are generally considered primarily responsible for education in this country.

States share this power with local school districts. As a matter of state law throughout the country, however, localities possess only those powers granted to them by state governments. Local control over education is a fairly long tradition, but the degree of control has ebbed and flowed over time, and states remain largely free to add to or subtract from local authority over schools.

Federal Government

As noted above, the federal government has already instituted a program—the Teacher Incentive Fund—to encourage performance-based pay of teachers. Members of Congress have also introduced other proposals—each one controversial—to expand the federal government's role in this area, including a draft bill to incorporate performance-based pay into a revised version of the No Child Left Behind Act.[6] At first blush, one might think that the federal government has no authority in the area of teacher pay. After all, the U.S. Constitution says nothing about teachers or education, and the Tenth Amendment to the Constitution provides that "powers not delegated to the United States by the Constitution, nor prohibited by it to the states, are reserved to the states respectively, or to the people."[7] Given the silence of the Constitution and the command of the Tenth Amendment, one might conclude that states, and only states, can govern regarding the issue of performance-based pay or any other form of differential pay.

The federal government, however, has indirect as well as direct authority to regulate. The key feature of existing and proposed federal programs regarding teacher pay, as in the field of education generally, is that they involve federal spending.

The federal government does not command states to enact certain education policies, whether related to teacher pay or special education; instead, it conditions receipt of federal funding on states' agreement to enact those policies. Although the Constitution does not give the federal government authority to regulate education directly, it does give the federal government the power to spend money and fairly broad discretion as to how that money should be spent. The so-called spending clause explicitly gives Congress the power to tax and spend "to provide for the common defense and general welfare of the United States."[8]

Congress's authority pursuant to the spending clause is vast, at least as interpreted by the Supreme Court. Through the spending clause, Congress can attach all sorts of conditions to spending bills and thereby accomplish indirectly what it might not be able to require directly. Thus even if Congress cannot command states to institute differential pay, the spending clause gives Congress another route to the same end: it can offer states money in exchange for their agreement to institute differential pay systems. To appreciate the importance of this power, a review of the relatively sparse law on the subject is in order.

Since the spending clause grants Congress the authority to tax and spend for the "general welfare," the scope of authority granted by this clause turns on the definition of *general welfare.* Unfortunately, this term is not defined in the Constitution. Two different ways to interpret its scope, and therefore the scope of the spending power, were apparent almost immediately after the Constitution was ratified. They were urged by two of the most influential founding fathers, James Madison and Alexander Hamilton.

First, as Madison argued, one could interpret the clause to require that spending for the general welfare be restricted to spending that carries out one of Congress's enumerated powers. On this view, Congress could not spend money on education if it did not have the enumerated power to regulate education directly. This position, Madison argued, would bar Congress from using the spending clause to accomplish indirectly what it could not accomplish directly. Hamilton, by contrast, argued that Congress could use its spending authority to pursue goals outside of those encompassed by its other enumerated powers, provided that the spending advanced the "general welfare" of the United States, an obviously capacious concept and thus a weak to nonexistent limitation.[9]

Hamilton's view eventually prevailed. In 1936, in *United States* v. *Butler,* the Court held that the "power of Congress to authorize expenditure of public moneys for public purposes is not limited by the direct grants of legislative power found in the Constitution."[10] As a consequence, Congress could attach conditions to federal funds that require recipients to perform acts or administer regulations Congress could not directly command.

The intuitive notion underlying this approach is that federal spending programs operate like contracts. In return for federal funds, states or localities agree to comply with federally imposed conditions. As the court recently explained, "The residents of the state retain the ultimate decision as to whether or not the state will comply. If a state's citizens view federal policy as sufficiently contrary to local interests, they may elect to decline a federal grant."[11] Thus just as an employee can quit rather than accept payment and conditions from an employer, a state can always turn down the federal government's offer of money.

The problem with this view is that states, as a practical matter, may not always be in a position to decline federal funds. The Supreme Court has recognized this problem and has acknowledged that Congress's power under the spending clause must be somewhat limited, given the vast financial resources of the federal government. Otherwise, Congress could "render academic the Constitution's other grants and limits of federal authority."[12] The Court has therefore established five limitations on the exercise of the federal spending power.[13] These limitations, however, are fairly anemic, both singly and in combination.

The most basic requirement is that the spending power must be in pursuit of the general welfare. This requirement stems directly from the language of the spending clause, but it does not offer much in the way of a restriction. As the Court instructed in 1987 in *South Dakota* v. *Dole,* which remains its most thorough pronouncement on the scope of the spending clause, "Courts should defer substantially to the judgment of Congress" when considering whether a particular expenditure is designed to advance the general welfare. Indeed, the Court suggested that the level of deference is such that the general welfare requirement may not be "a judicially enforceable restriction at all."[14]

The second requirement is also largely meaningless, though for different reasons. Congress cannot induce states, through conditional funding, to engage in otherwise unconstitutional behavior.[15] Congress could not, for example, offer states funding on the condition that they outlaw the Catholic Church. The Court would presumably enforce this requirement if necessary, but because Congress is not typically in the business of using its conditional spending power to induce states to violate the Constitution, this is not a particularly meaningful limitation.

The third requirement is that any condition placed on federal funds must be stated unambiguously so that in considering whether to accept funds, states are fully aware of the consequences.[16] This clear-notice requirement has a bit more bite than the first two and has been used by the Supreme Court and lower courts to invalidate attempts to enforce ambiguous conditions by withdrawing federal funds.[17] Such cases remain rare, however, and the clear-notice rule in general does not impose a substantive limit on Congress's authority. It simply requires Congress to speak clearly when attaching conditions to funding, and it indirectly prevents federal agencies—in this case, the Department of Education—from adding conditions to the funding after the legislation is passed and the money distributed.

It is possible, of course, that federal legislation regarding differential pay might leave some details unclear and that the Department of Education might attempt to dictate those details over a state's objection. However, as long as Congress specifies what states must do in exchange for the funding, and as long as the Department of Education does not overreach, this requirement should be easy to satisfy.

The final two requirements could potentially impose serious restrictions on Congress's authority to attach funding conditions, but they have not been enforced with much zeal. One demands that conditions on federal funding be germane; in the Court's words, the conditions must not be "unrelated to the federal interest in particular national projects or programs."[18] At first blush, this seems to be a serious requirement, one that would enable courts to strike down conditions on funds that are only tangentially related to the purpose of the federal program. The Court, however, has indicated that the federal interest can be stated at a high level of generality and that the relationship between the conditions and the spending can be fairly tenuous and still survive constitutional review.

In *South Dakota* v. *Dole,* for example, the Court upheld a federal program that conditioned money for highways on an agreement by recipient states to raise their minimum drinking age to twenty-one. The Court held that this condition was related to the federal interest in "safe interstate travel," which, it concluded, was one of the "main purposes for which highway funds are expended."[19] The Court described the federal interest in highway spending at a fairly abstract and general level, as one of safety rather than, say, construction and maintenance of roads. This in turn made it much easier for the condition on that spending to be relevant to the interest, for the simple reason that the more broadly and abstractly the federal interest is described, the more conditions will relate to that interest.

In addition, the relationship between raising a drinking age and safe interstate travel is plausible but not precise. Indeed, Justice Sandra Day O'Connor dissented in *Dole* because she thought the relationship should have to be tighter to uphold a condition on federal funds.[20] The majority of the Court has yet to agree with O'Connor's dissent in *Dole,* however, as it reiterated in a more recent opinion (written, ironically, by O'Connor) that there need only be "*some* relationship" between the conditions and the purposes of the federal spending.[21]

Finally, the Court has stated that the financial inducement offered by Congress must not be "so coercive as to pass the point at which pressure turns into compulsion."[22] Like the germaneness requirement, the coercion limitation seems at first glance to place a serious obstacle to Congress's use of the spending power. After all, while states remain free in theory to refuse federal funds, there will always be a great deal of pressure on them to accept the funding, since the alternatives will be either to use state funds (and perhaps increase state taxes) or to forgo the program.

At the same time, however, divining the line between pressure, which is permitted, and compulsion, which is forbidden, will never be an easy task. As the Court observed in 1937 and repeated again in its 1987 *Dole* decision, temptation should not be confused with coercion. "To hold that motive or temptation is equivalent to coercion is to plunge the law in endless difficulties. The outcome of such a doctrine is the acceptance of a philosophical determinism by which choice becomes impossible."[23]

Perhaps because of these difficulties, the Supreme Court has never found a conditional spending program to be unconstitutionally coercive, and lower courts have rarely done so. A number of lower courts have acknowledged the difficulty of discerning the difference between an offer that states "cannot refuse" and one that is "merely a hard choice," and some have questioned whether any "sovereign state which is always free to increase its tax revenues [could] ever be coerced by the withholding of federal funds."[24]

No court, moreover, has given much guidance as to how the point of coercion should be identified. The Supreme Court in *Dole* concluded that the condition was not coercive because states that did not raise the minimum drinking age to twenty-one would lose only 5 percent of their federal highway funds. This "relatively mild encouragement" meant that enactment of the minimum drinking age remained "the prerogative of the state not merely in theory but [also] in fact."[25]

The Court's statements in *Dole,* however, raise more questions than they answer. Why is the percentage of federal funds used as the benchmark? Even assuming this is the correct benchmark, what percentage must be at stake before coercion is found? If a state stands to lose, say, 80 percent of federal funding for education, but federal funding makes up only a small percentage of overall funding for schools, should coercion be found? Suppose federal funding instead constituted 95 percent of all education funding, and 10 percent of those funds were at stake. Should that count as coercion? No court has given a good answer to questions like these, perhaps because a good answer does not exist. There is simply no principled way to select the correct benchmark and no obvious point at which temptation becomes coercion.

For practical purposes, the important point is that courts are quite reluctant to find unconstitutional coercion in conditional spending programs, which means that the federal government has wide latitude to affect education policy by attaching conditions to federal funds. As long as the conditions are stated clearly, it seems beyond doubt that the federal government has the authority to require states to institute differential pay programs in exchange for receiving education funding.

State Governments

State governments possess general authority, under the federal constitution, to pass legislation that promotes the welfare of their citizens. States may nonetheless restrict their own power, either by statute or by constitutional provision. The only restrictions on state power that are relevant in this context are state labor laws, which require state and local governments to bargain over certain subjects with public employee unions. In all but two states, collective bargaining requirements are imposed by state statute; in Florida and Hawaii, by contrast, state and local governments are required by state constitutional provisions to engage in collective bargaining.[26]

It follows that in all states but Florida or Hawaii, legislatures that wish to develop a statewide program of differential pay for school teachers can simply enact a statute commanding such. To avoid mandatory bargaining requirements, that statute might have to make clear that it creates an exception to existing state labor laws, but the crucial point to recognize is that states possess the authority to modify statutes that restrict their power or the power of local governments.[27] If a state passed a labor law in 1980, for example, that required differential pay programs to be subject to mandatory bargaining, it could simply pass another law in 2008 that authorized such programs to be implemented unilaterally. In Florida and Hawaii, by contrast, a statewide program requiring differential pay would be permissible only if found consistent with state constitutional provisions regarding collective bargaining or if the state constitution were amended.

Local Governments and Mandatory Bargaining Requirements

The central and unresolved legal question regarding differential pay arises when local school boards decide, in the absence of explicit state authority, to institute such a program. Local governments, as discussed, possess only the authority granted to them by their state governments, either by statute or state constitutional provision. Even when granted general authority over a subject, such as teacher compensation, local governments must comply with specific restrictions on this authority. In this context, the relevant restrictions are contained in state labor laws that require mandatory bargaining with teachers unions over certain issues related to their employment.

Collective bargaining laws are intended to reduce the inequality of bargaining power between employees and employers by forcing employers to negotiate in good faith with the representatives of the employees.[28] Although there are extensive federal laws governing labor relations, states and state political subdivisions such as cities and school districts are exempt from the federal requirements.[29] Many states have filled this gap and passed their own labor relation laws, which do cover local and state employees.

Not all states, however, have collective bargaining laws, which leads to a crucial point: the relevant law on this topic is quite diverse. State collective bargaining legislation covering public employees did not even exist until the 1950s, when a few states, most notably Wisconsin, granted public employees the right to bargain with municipal governments. Since that time, many more states have enacted collective bargaining laws, but these vary quite a bit. Some states, including North Carolina and Virginia, actually prohibit collective bargaining among public employees and their government employers.[30]

Other states, totaling about forty, authorize collective bargaining for public employees. These laws vary quite a bit on such subjects as which groups of employees are covered; the extent of any duty to bargain and the subjects covered by mandatory bargaining requirements; limitations regarding the ability of public employees to strike; and whether local governments—in addition to state governments—have the authority to bargain with their employees. In addition, some states have one collective bargaining law for all government employees, while others leave it to local governments to come up with their own laws. Still others have a series of collective bargaining laws that cover different types of government employees such as firefighters or teachers. Given this diversity, it is not surprising that the legal framework surrounding public sector collective bargaining has been described as a "crazy patchwork quilt with some glaring holes."[31]

That said, and notwithstanding the differences among state laws, there are some points of convergence. Two are most important. First, in the forty or so states in which collective bargaining is authorized by law, teachers tend to be among the employees covered, and school districts have some duty to bargain with the teachers unions.[32] Second, the basic legal question regarding differential pay tends to be the same in every state, and that question is fairly straightforward: is differential pay an issue over which state or local governments *must* bargain with teachers unions? This question is important because if differential pay is the subject of mandatory bargaining, local governments effectively cannot institute such programs without the consent of teachers unions. Given the traditional opposition of teachers unions to some types of differential pay, especially merit pay, a requirement that the consent of teachers unions be obtained before going forward might be enough to doom the program.

To determine whether differential pay is the subject of mandatory bargaining, state law must be consulted. Here, again, there is a good deal of convergence among the states, as most state laws require that employers and employees bargain over wages, terms, and "other conditions" of employment.[33] The obvious question, therefore, is whether the differential pay at issue—be it merit pay, a recruitment bonus, or an incentive to teach math or science—should be considered a wage or some other term or condition of employment. Unfortunately, the law is somewhat unclear, in large part because there have been relatively few cases on the subject.

At first glance, the question might seem simple: any payment to a teacher by a school district must be considered a wage, as it is a form of compensation from an employer to an employee. Indeed, there is some support for this proposition, both indirect and direct. As for the indirect support, some court decisions have interpreted a similar provision in the National Labor Relations Act and concluded that merit pay is indeed a part of an employee's wages. Although there have not been many cases on this point, the general trend is that "where a union has been recognized as a bargaining agent of the employees[,] the employer cannot grant merit increases in wages to individual employees independent of the consent or act of the union."[34]

Interpretations of federal labor laws do not control interpretations of state labor laws, even when the language in the two laws is identical. That said, some state courts look to and rely upon federal court interpretations of similarly worded federal laws, whether statutes or constitutions. One could expect state courts to do the same here. In addition, looking to federal court interpretations of the National Labor Relations Act simply helps one to predict how state courts might interpret similar language, even if they are not bound or even influenced by federal court decisions.

More direct support for the notion that at least performance-based pay is a wage is found in some administrative court decisions. In most states that have collective bargaining laws, administrative hearings precede any court action. The collective bargaining laws create an administrative process through which disputes must first pass before courts become involved. So, for example, if a teachers' union believes that a school district has violated either the relevant labor law or the collective bargaining agreement itself, the union will typically first have to exhaust any available administrative remedies before going to court. If unhappy with the results of the administrative process, the union can then—but only then—press its case in court.

As a result of this administrative apparatus, there is a body of decisions from administrative officials regarding their respective state collective bargaining laws. Some of these decisions have to do with merit or performance-based pay, and some support the notion that performance-based pay is indeed a wage. The hearing examiner in a 1994 New Jersey dispute, for example, determined that Camden County had violated its bargaining obligation by unilaterally instituting a merit pay program for Department of Health and Human Services employees.[35] Citing a string of similar decisions in New Jersey, the hearing examiner wrote that "compensation, specifically the implementation of a merit pay program, is mandatorily negotiable."[36] A similar conclusion was reached by the Florida Public Employees Relations Commission in a 1992 decision. The commission interpreted a Florida statute that required a public employee to bargain collectively with regard to "wages, hours, terms and conditions of employment."[37] The commission concluded that "step or merit pay salary increases are considered 'wages'" and are therefore subject to mandatory bargaining.[38]

These administrative decisions, though telling, have little precedential value. Courts are not required to follow them, even within the same state. However, taken together with the federal cases involving the National Labor Relations Act, these administrative decisions lend credence to the notion that, properly understood, differential pay programs involve wages. In other words, these decisions suggest that, if and when faced with this question, at least some state courts would find that differential pay programs are a subject of mandatory bargaining. Indeed, one commentator, writing in 1999, thought the issue obvious, saying in a footnote to an article regarding merit pay that "it is clear that such plans are mandatorily negotiable."[39]

There seems little reason to predict that courts would make distinctions among the various types of differential pay and treat, for example, merit pay one way and a recruitment bonus another. For example, in *Crete Education Association* v. *Saline County School District,* decided in 2002, the Nebraska Supreme Court concluded that a signing bonus offered to a single employee was indeed part of the employee's wages and therefore subject to mandatory bargaining. The court reasoned that gifts not tied to work or services do not count as wages, but "gifts or bonuses [that] are so tied to the remuneration which employees received for their work . . . are in reality wages and within the statute."[40] It would be surprising were this same court to conclude, using this test, that signing bonuses count as wages but merit pay does not.

Not all courts agree on the issue of whether differential pay counts as a wage. In fact, some cases have reached precisely the opposite conclusion, though they rely on a legal test similar to that used by the Nebraska Supreme Court. The best known is *United Teachers of Dade* v. *Dade County Sch. Bd.,* a 1986 decision by the Supreme Court of Florida. In *Dade County,* the court held that a monetary award given to some teachers pursuant to the Florida Master Teacher Program was not a wage and was thus not subject to mandatory collective bargaining.[41]

The Florida Master Teacher Program granted monetary awards to successful public school teachers. Participation in the program was completely voluntary. The plaintiffs in the case argued that the monetary award was a "merit wage" and was thus a direct payment to teachers, in violation of the teachers' state constitutional right to bargain over wages.[42]

To reach its conclusion, the court looked to an analogous case from Iowa. In *Fort Dodge Community School District* v. *Public Employment Relations Board,* the question facing the Supreme Court of Iowa was whether a cash incentive for early retirement was a wage and therefore subject to mandatory collective bargaining. The Supreme Court of Iowa reasoned that the incentive payment was not a wage, as the term *wage* was not commonly understood to "include payment for services not rendered or labor not performed."[43]

The Florida Supreme Court appeared to use the same legal test, with one important modification. It concluded that the Florida Master Teacher Program award was not a "wage" because "no *additional* teaching services are required to be performed by the teachers who voluntarily choose to compete for the payment."[44] Why the court thought it relevant to focus on "additional" teaching services is a bit of a mystery, as presumably a pay raise from one year to the next would be considered a wage even if it did not require additional teaching services.

That the merit payment did not replace any of the provisions of the existing teachers' contracts with the school board and that the award would not be used as a basis for determining future salary increases or promotions were also persuasive. Based on these facts, the Florida Supreme Court determined that the Master Teacher Program award did not count as a wage and thus the implementation of the program did not violate the plaintiffs' rights to bargain collectively.[45]

The varying conclusions reached by courts that have wrestled with differential pay may be a function of the personal inclinations of the particular judges. There is a large literature regarding the influence of politics and ideology on judicial decisions, and it seems beyond question that some judges interpret vague laws in ways consistent with their political or ideological preferences.[46] There is little reason to believe that questions of teacher compensation, about which opinions tend to run strong, would be exempt from this pattern.

These decisions also expose the fault line in laws regarding collective bargaining with public employees. Public employees are entitled to the protection offered by collective bargaining rules and they should not be permitted to ignore those rules whenever they find it convenient to do so. However, some employment-related matters involving public employees also raise broader issues of public interest. Where these sorts of public policy issues are raised, the notion that they must be decided by collective bargaining, rather than by duly elected officials, seems incongruous with basic principles of democratic decisionmaking.

Differential pay programs straddle this line dividing the private and public. Wage increases and bonuses are obviously important to teachers and their careers. They are equally important to the public, however, insofar as they are a tool that might well enhance the efficiency and equity of public education. Depending on one's perspective, the issue of differential pay might seem perfectly suited for collective bargaining or an issue that is too important to the public to be left to contract negotiations. Perhaps for precisely this reason, the question of whether differential pay programs must be subject to collective bargaining remains open and will probably continue to be the source of disagreement among state courts.

One interesting possibility is that private foundations might provide merit pay or bonuses and thereby circumvent collective bargaining agreements. Some private foundations, most notably the Milken Family Foundation, provide annual monetary awards to outstanding teachers.[47] Such programs have received relatively little attention, most likely because they are small and offer one-time awards to only a few teachers. They do not represent any real threat to existing salary structures.

Whether such programs, assuming they were expanded, would face legal hurdles remains an unexplored and interesting question. Antibribery statutes or myriad state laws limiting the outside income of public employees, although they might seem relevant at first blush, should rarely if ever come into play. Offering or accepting an award for good teaching hardly seems to constitute corruption or undue influence, the actions targeted by bribery statutes. Statutes that limit the receipt of outside income, in turn, either do not apply to teachers or specifically exempt monetary awards or income from philanthropic organizations.[48]

On the other hand, it is possible that such programs could violate collective bargaining laws if school districts cooperated with private foundations in an effort to avoid mandatory bargaining rules. It is easy to see how this might become a problem if private awards were to grow more widespread. Without the participation of school officials, identifying successful teachers might be quite difficult. (The Milken Family Foundation, for example, relies on recommendations from state departments of education.) With the participation of school officials, however, school boards might be guilty of unfair labor practices if the program is sufficiently widespread to constitute a de facto merit pay system. All of this remains purely hypothetical, however, which means that any predictions regarding legality must be made with some caution.

A final point to consider is the intersection of law and policy. The law may allow for the implementation of differential pay programs without recourse to collective bargaining. Given the legal uncertainty, however, the safer bet at the moment is to obtain the consent of teachers unions when possible. Evidence also suggests that this might be a wise choice from a policy perspective. Teacher cooperation, for example, is cited by a number of researchers as crucial to the success of performance-based pay programs.[49] Teacher "buy-in" does not always equate with union consent, of course, and one could imagine that teachers at a particular school might favor performance-based pay even though their union opposed it. But union consent is often likely to be at least an imperfect proxy for teacher consent. Where this is the case, law and policy point in the same direction: the wisest course is to bargain over the terms of differential pay programs rather than implement them unilaterally.

Individual Rights

Individual rights generally act as cross-cutting checks on government authority. Even where the federal, state, or local government has authority to act, this is only the first question with regard to whether the act itself is legal. The second question is whether the act violates a protected individual right. To use a simple example, the federal government has the authority to regulate interstate commerce, and thus it has the authority to ban certain items from being shipped across state lines. If it decided, however, to ban the shipment of the *New York Times* across state lines, it would violate the First Amendment right to a free press.

In the context of differential pay, the rights to due process and to freedom from governmental discrimination are the two most relevant. With respect to differential pay for teachers, these rights would only come into play once the system had been adopted; they would form the basis of challenges to the operation of the pay system, not its creation. One set of potential challenges would focus on whether the procedural safeguards were sufficient and the decisionmaking free from arbitrariness and caprice. The other would focus on whether the system is being used to discriminate on forbidden grounds such as race, sex, religion, or age. Neither due process nor antidiscrimination protections should be difficult or onerous for school districts to provide. Whether there will be complaints and litigation regardless of the protections provided is another matter.

Due Process

Both the Fifth and Fourteenth Amendments to the U.S. Constitution protect against the deprivation of "life, liberty, or property, without due process of law."[50] The Fifth Amendment applies to the federal government, the fourteenth to state governments. They both provide identical protection; the only difference is the entity from whom the individual is protected. State constitutions generally contain similar provisions securing due process of law. Most state courts interpret these state provisions as providing the same protections as the federal constitution, though some state courts apply their respective due process clauses with more vigor.[51]

Before the protections of the federal due process clause can be invoked, it must be shown that a life, liberty, or property interest is at stake. This is often not an issue in cases involving incarceration or those involving the destruction of real property, where liberty or property interests are clearly at stake. In cases involving government benefits, however, it is not clear whether the requisite interest exists. The basic and important question is whether the person seeking to invoke the due process clause has a property interest in receipt of the governmental benefit. In this context, the more precise question is whether teachers have a property interest in whatever form of differential pay—merit pay or a recruitment bonus, for example—is at issue.

The law, unfortunately, is easier to state than to understand. The Constitution does not define what counts as a property interest, and the Supreme Court has instructed that such interests must be established by an independent source, such as state law. To establish that a property interest is at stake, a plaintiff must show that state law created a legal entitlement to the benefit at issue, which, in turn, requires that the plaintiff show that he or she had a legitimate expectation of receiving the benefit.[52] A unilateral expectation or subjective hope is not sufficient to demonstrate a property interest.

The problem with this approach is not hard to detect. The procedures used to determine under what circumstances the benefit should be provided or withheld might constitute the best proof regarding the legitimate expectations of recipients. Yet taken to its logical conclusion, this approach leads to the perverse outcome that the due process clause does not apply when the procedures for granting a benefit are completely lacking or utterly arbitrary. Imagine that the government offers welfare recipients little in the way of procedural protections, retains wide discretion to withhold benefits, and never explains why it makes a decision one way or the other. If a court were to look just to these procedures, it would be hard to conclude that anyone had a legitimate expectation of continuing to receive welfare payments. The lack of reasonable procedures would in effect constitute the justification for not providing any procedural protections whatsoever, which seems more than a little odd. It seems backward to say that the more arbitrary the procedures, the less opportunity there is to challenge them.

A lower court decision from 1982, involving a merit pay program, provides a good example of the problem. In *Kanter* v. *Community Consolidated School District 65,* a tenured teacher argued that her rights to due process were violated when she did not receive a merit pay increase.[53] The school failed to establish written criteria for awarding merit pay, and it also failed to give her written reasons for denying her an award. The district court used the absence of procedural protections to conclude that Maxine R. Kanter, the teacher, was not entitled to any protections because she did not have a property interest in merit pay. In the case at bar, the court reasoned, merit pay was "based on subjective factors of teacher merit as judged by the teacher's peers and the superintendent of the school district." It followed that Kanter could not have a property interest because awards of merit pay were largely discretionary—if not downright mysterious. "Therefore," the court concluded, "Kanter has no constitutional right guaranteeing any particular procedural due process."[54]

The Supreme Court, in a case decided after *Kanter,* tried to resolve some of the confusion by clarifying that it was inappropriate to look solely to existing procedures to determine the existence of a property interest. In *Cleveland Board of Education* v. *Loudermill,* a 1985 decision, the Court addressed what had become known as the "bitter with the sweet" doctrine, which essentially allowed governments to decide for themselves whether to protect benefits from deprivation without due process.[55] According to this doctrine, because a legislature did not have to provide benefits at all, it could also provide little in the way of procedural protections for those denied the benefit.

In *Loudermill,* the Court explicitly rejected this doctrine. In the Court's words,

The point is straightforward: the Due Process Clause provides that certain substantive rights—life, liberty, and property—cannot be deprived except pursuant to constitutionally adequate procedures. The categories of substance and procedure are distinct. Were the rule otherwise, the Clause would be reduced to a mere tautology. "Property" cannot be defined by the procedures provided for its deprivation any more than can life or liberty. The right to due process is conferred, not by legislative grace, but by constitutional guarantee. While the legislature may elect not to confer a property interest in [public] employment, it may not constitutionally authorize the deprivation of such an interest, once conferred, without appropriate procedural safeguards.[56]

Having entombed the bitter-with-the-sweet doctrine, however, the Court still left open the question of how exactly to decide whether state law creates a property interest.

In the context of differential pay programs, the question is somewhat difficult to answer. There is little doubt that teachers, especially teachers with tenure, have a property interest in continued employment. They have a legitimate expectation, in other words, that their employment will continue absent a good justification for their dismissal. The same may well be true for teachers before tenure, provided they have some protection against dismissal provided by a shorter-term contract.

The harder question, however, is whether a property interest in continued employment is sufficient to establish a property interest regarding *conditions* of that employment. Presumably, at some point, it must; otherwise, schools would be free to make conditions of employment so deplorable as to effectively push teachers out of their jobs without facing due process scrutiny. On the other hand, it does not seem reasonable to expect that every decision regarding a condition of employment, no matter how minor, constitutes a potential deprivation of a property interest.

Unfortunately, differential pay falls somewhere in the middle: the denial of such pay to a particular teacher can hardly be seen as an effective ouster from employment, but neither is it a trivial condition of employment. Thus the question will most likely boil down to whether teachers can ever claim to have a legitimate entitlement to receive the payment at issue. Here, it remains difficult, despite abandonment of the bitter-with-the-sweet doctrine, to avoid considering the criteria used to award differential pay. The more those criteria are objective and require payment if certain conditions are met, the easier it is to conclude that teachers who meet those criteria are entitled to the pay. The more the criteria are subjective and awards are unpredictable, the harder it is to conclude that teachers will ever have a legitimate claim of entitlement. The circularity problem thus seems difficult to escape.

The trend with regard to performance-based pay seems to be in the direction of establishing relatively objective standards to guide the award of such pay.[57] To the extent this trend continues, and there seem to be sound policy reasons to support it, one could safely conclude that most courts will find a property interest at stake. Similarly, school districts that provide bonuses for teachers of certain subjects or in certain schools tend to rely on fairly objective criteria. They provide, for example, signing bonuses to all those who will teach math or science or to all those who teach in low-performing schools. Here, too, one can safely bet that courts would find a property interest at stake. The question is hardly free from uncertainty, however, and it remains entirely possible that some due process challenges will falter at the starting line, in which case the question of whether the procedures are sufficient would never be addressed.

Assuming, however, that teachers possess the requisite property interest, the next question is what sorts of procedures satisfy the due process clause. Here the law, or at least federal law, is fairly clear. The teacher must receive notice of any decision regarding merit pay, an explanation for the basis of that decision, and an opportunity to be heard, meaning an opportunity to contest a negative decision.[58] The ultimate decision, moreover, must not be arbitrary or capricious, which essentially means that it cannot be wildly inconsistent with the evidence surrounding the decision.[59] None of these requirements is especially difficult to meet, and courts are generally quite deferential to government decisionmakers. If teachers receive notice, an explanation, and an opportunity to be heard, and the decision does not seem impossible to understand based on the established facts, school districts with differential pay programs should rarely lose a due process challenge brought by disappointed teachers.

At least school districts should not lose in federal court. As mentioned, state courts, applying due process protections grounded in state constitutions, tend to be as deferential as federal courts applying federal due process protections. Some state courts, however, apply their state due process protections with more vigor and thus take a closer look at the basis for governmental decisions.[60] In these courts, school districts may well need to supply stronger proof that the payment at issue is awarded on a truly rational basis. Disappointed teachers, in turn, may have a greater opportunity to challenge the basis for the award. Of all the various forms of differential pay, the most vulnerable may be merit pay programs that link bonuses to student test performance. Recruitment and retention bonuses to fill staffing gaps seem sufficiently rational to withstand even heightened scrutiny, but merit pay programs rest on the sometimes tenuous relationship between student and teacher performance. Given the complexity of fairly linking teachers and student performance, teachers may well succeed in showing that merit pay programs are irrational, at least if they appear before courts willing to second-guess the actual operation and reasoning behind legislative programs.

Whether schools will be subject to challenges, regardless of whether they ultimately prevail, is another question. Here, common sense is as good a guide as any. The more that differential pay programs are based on objective and rational criteria, clearly spelled out and understood, the more likely it is that teachers will accept the programs, and the less likely that the programs will invite challenge and litigation. If teachers subject to the program accede to the criteria—if they "buy in" to the program, in other words—the likelihood of a due process challenge will diminish even further, assuming that the criteria are followed.

Antidiscrimination Laws

Federal and state laws contain a wide array of protections against discrimination based on certain characteristics, including race, sex, religion, disability, and age. These protections are found in the equal protection clause of the U.S. Constitution, in similar provisions in state constitutions, in federal statutes, and in state statutes. The laws differ in their details and the degree of protection offered. Policies or decisions based on race, for example, are more vulnerable to constitutional challenge than those based on sex or disability. Policies or decisions that intentionally discriminate on the basis of race or sex, moreover, are typically more vulnerable than those that simply have a disparate impact.[61]

To add to the complications, some statutes provide for individual enforcement, such as Title VII of the 1964 Civil Rights Act, which prohibits discrimination on the basis of sex. Others generally allow only for administrative enforcement, such as the disparate impact regulations of Title VI of the 1964 Civil Rights Act. In addition, the availability of damages for violations of the statutes varies from statute to statute.

For purposes of this chapter, a general outline of the key legal principles, as opposed to a recitation of the bewildering details, should suffice. At the outset, it is worth noting that some single salary schedules were first adopted in response to lawsuits brought by Thurgood Marshall of the National Association for the Advancement of Colored People (NAACP) in the 1940s, which challenged unequal pay given to white and black teachers. To avoid legal challenges alleging that differential pay plans discriminated on the basis of race, some states simply adopted single salary schedules and moved away from considerations of merit-based pay.[62]

From the legal cases initiated by Thurgood Marshall emerged the most important antidiscrimination principle, which remains pertinent today: differential pay programs should not be used as a basis for discriminating among teachers except on the basis of relevant criteria, relating either to performance or staffing needs. If the programs are used instead to discriminate on personal characteristics such as race, sex, religion, or disability, that use will most likely—and should—be found illegal. This is especially true where there is clear evidence of intentional discrimination.

In most instances, such proof will not exist. The smoking gun is a rare find. There may instead be evidence suggestive of discrimination. If a disproportionate number of men have been given performance-based pay, for example, that at least suggests the possibility that sex discrimination is at play. In these instances, speaking generally, where there is evidence of a disproportionate impact in the implementation of performance-based pay programs, the burden will shift to the school to justify its decisions. The school would then have to explain why, for example, more men had received salary increases than women, an explanation that would obviously have to pertain to performance rather than gender.

The law is slightly more complicated than this, in large part because not all groups receive the same amount of protection, given variations in federal and state law. Some groups realistically are protected only against intentional discrimination, meaning that proof of a disparate impact would not be enough to place the burden upon the school to justify its decisions. Other groups are protected by statute from policies that have a clear, disparate impact that is not sufficiently justified. Schools and districts that institute performance-based pay programs need only be aware that they might be vulnerable to charges of discrimination if a pattern of decisions favors one identifiable group—for example, men—over another. Provided that they have a rational explanation for that pattern, however, they should have little trouble succeeding in any challenge to their programs.

One final source for challenges comes from teacher tenure laws, which in some states provide that all teachers must be paid according to a single salary schedule.[63] Generally speaking, school districts remain free to establish different salary grades for teachers, but they must treat all those within a particular grade equally.[64] Although at least one state court has ruled that merit pay is inherently inconsistent with laws requiring a single salary schedule, most courts give districts plenty of discretion to create the criteria that define the various salary grades.[65] Those criteria could include consideration of student performance or the teaching of difficult-to-staff subjects; the only limitation, again, is that similarly situated teachers be treated equally.

Antidiscrimination challenges can be avoided or reduced in the first place in the same way that due process challenges can be avoided or reduced. Schools or school districts that create programs that rely on objective, easily understood criteria will necessarily generate less suspicion that some other, insidious factor guided the decision. Moreover, to the extent teachers buy into the program, the level of suspicion will drop accordingly.

Conclusion

The crucial legal issue regarding differential pay is whether the consent of teachers unions is needed before schools implement such programs. That question remains unanswered, and it will likely continue to be the subject of controversy and disagreement among state courts. Until this legal uncertainty is settled, which will have to happen state by state and therefore will take some time, clearly the safer legal course is to obtain union consent to differential pay programs.

Given the traditional hostility expressed by unions toward some forms of differential pay, especially merit-based pay, requiring consent could derail some experiments with differential pay programs. In these circumstances, school districts might well decide to force the legal issue by pressing ahead with the program and defending against the inevitable lawsuit. On the other hand, obtaining agreement for a change to the pay system, at least from individual teachers if not their unions, seems to be a wise policy in any event, so districts might have independent reasons to do their best to obtain consent.

The remaining legal requirements, whether pertaining to the authority of the federal government or the rights to due process and against discrimination, should not present obstacles to differential pay programs at the federal, state, or local level. The only exception might be in states whose courts apply state due process protections with vigor; in those states, merit pay programs may well be vulnerable to due process challenges if there is not a demonstrably reliable way to link student and teacher performance. That exception notwithstanding, a clearly articulated and fairly implemented differential pay program should be immune from due process and discrimination claims. Again, law and policy push in the same direction. The clearer and fairer the standards used to award differential pay, the less likely it is that the program will be the subject of litigation and the more likely that the policy will be accepted by teachers. The law does not always march in time with wise policy, but in this instance, the two at least seem headed in the same direction.

Notes

1. Lynn Olson, "Teacher Pay Experiments Mounting amid Debate," *Education Week,* October 3, 2007, pp. 1, 14.
2. Cynthia D. Price, "Higher Pay in Hard-to-Staff Schools: The Case for Financial Incentives," American Association of School Administrators, June 2000, pp. 2–3. See also Michael J. Podgursky and Matthew G. Springer, "Teacher Performance Pay: A Review," *Journal of Policy Analysis and Management* 26, no. 4 (2007): 909–50.
3. Elissa Gootman, "Bloomberg Unveils Performance Pay for Teachers," *New York Times,* October 17, 2007, p. A1.
4. Price, "Higher Pay in Hard-to-Staff Schools," pp. 13–17.
5. James E. Ryan and Thomas Saunders, foreword to "Symposium on School Finance Litigation: Emerging Trends or New Dead Ends?" *Yale Law and Policy Review* 22 (2004): 463–80, 466.
6. Olson, "Teacher Pay Experiments Mounting," p. 1.
7. U.S. Constitution, amend. 10.
8. U.S. Constitution, art. 1, sec. 8, cl. 1.
9. For a discussion of Madison's and Hamilton's views of the proper scope of the spending clause, see, for example, Celestine McConville, "Federal Funding Conditions: Bursting through the *Dole* Loopholes," *Chapman Law Review* 4 (Spring 2001): 163–94, 168.
10. 297 U.S. 1, 65 (1936). Ironically, after stating this view of the spending clause, the Court nonetheless struck down the act, under the Tenth Amendment, because it regulated agriculture, which the court held was beyond Congress's power to control (ibid., 68). The Court thus endorsed Hamilton's view but seemed to apply Madison's, making this "one of the few truly ridiculous opinions delivered in two centuries of Supreme Court jurisprudence." David E. Engdahl, "The Spending Power," *Duke Law Journal* 44 (October 1994): 1–99, 36. The endorsement of Hamilton's view has been repeated in later opinions; the application of Madison's view has not.
11. *New York* v. *United States,* 505 U.S. 144, 168 (1992).
12. Ibid., 167.
13. The Court discusses all five of these limitations in *South Dakota* v. *Dole,* 483 U.S. 203, 207–08, and n. 2 (1987).
14. Ibid., 207–08 and n. 2.
15. Ibid., 210–11.
16. Ibid., 207.
17. See, for example, *Pennhurst State School and Hospital* v. *Halderman,* 451 U.S. 1 (1981); *Virginia Department of Education* v. *Riley,* 106 F.3d 559 (1997); *Arlington Central School District Board of Education* v. *Murphy,* 548 U.S. 291 (2006).
18. *Dole,* 207 (internal quotation marks omitted).
19. Ibid., 208.
20. See *Dole,* 212–18 (O'Connor, J., dissenting).
21. *New York,* 167 (emphasis added).
22. *Dole,* 211.
23. Ibid. (quoting *Steward Machine Co.* v. *Davis,* 301 U.S. 548, 589–90 [1937]).
24. See McConville, "Federal Funding Conditions," pp. 180–81 and n. 4 (discussing and quoting decisions). See also *Riley,* 569–72.

25. *Dole,* 211–12.
26. Joseph R. Grodin and others, *Public Sector Employment* (St. Paul, Minn.: Thomson/West, 2004), p. 82.
27. Courts generally apply a fairly strong presumption against implied repeals and try to interpret the more recent statute in a way that reconciles it with the first. See, for example, *Morton* v. *Mancari,* 417 U.S. 535 (1974). If a state legislature does not make clear that a differential pay statute creates an exception to an older law requiring mandatory bargaining over wages, courts might read the more recent statute to provide for differential pay only with the consent of unions.
28. See, for example, 29 U.S.C., sec. 151 (2007).
29. 29 U.S.C. 152(2) (2007).
30. Grodin and others, *Public Sector Employment,* pp. 81–83.
31. Ibid., p. 82 (internal quotation marks omitted).
32. Ibid., pp. 89–91.
33. Deborah Tussey, "Bargainable or Negotiable Issues in State Public Employment Labor Relations," in *American Law Reports,* 3rd ed. (Thomson Reuters/West, 2008), 84:242. There are exceptions, however. New Jersey, for example, has one law that requires bargaining over terms and conditions of employment and another law that expressly grants school boards authority to withhold salary increases for "inefficiency or other good cause." A state court held that school boards could, as a consequence, withhold salary increases without the consent of teachers unions. See *Clifton Teachers Association* v. *Board of Education of Clifton,* 346 A.2d 107 (N.J. App. Div. 1975). This decision, however, simply addressed the withholding of an individual teacher's salary increase; it did not address whether such increases themselves can be tied to teacher performance absent collective bargaining.
34. L. S. Tellier, "Merit Increase in Wages as Subject of Collective Bargaining or Unfair Labor Practice," in *American Law Reports,* 2nd ed. (Thomson Reuters/West, 2007), 33:997.
35. *In the Matter of County of Camden,* 20 New Jersey Public Employee Reporter, par. 25177 (New Jersey Public Employee Relations Committee Hearing Examiner's Decision, July 22, 1994).
36. Ibid. Whether this conclusion would apply to schoolteachers, in light of the statute granting school boards authority to withhold salary increases for inefficiency, discussed above in note 33, remains an open question.
37. *Tarpon Springs Fire Fighters Association* v. *City of Tarpon Springs,* 19 Florida Public Employee Reporter, par. 4013 (Florida Public Employees Relations Commission, December 8, 1992).
38. Ibid. Note, however, that in 1986, the Florida Supreme Court ruled that a monetary award to successful public school teachers did not constitute a wage. See *United Teachers of Dade* v. *Dade County School Board,* 500 So.2d 508 (Fla. 1986). It follows that not all "merit" awards will necessarily be considered wages, in Florida or elsewhere.
39. David A. Farmelo, "Bargaining and Labor Relations Issues of School Reform: Higher Standards for Certification/Recertification of Teachers and Merit Pay Based on Student Performance," in *School Law in Review 1999* (National School Boards Association, 1999), pp. 6–8, n. 21.
40. 654 N.W.2d 166, 179 (Neb. 2002) (internal quotation marks omitted).
41. 500 So.2d 508, 514 (Fla. 1986).

42. Ibid., 509.
43. 319 N.W.2d 181, 184 (Iowa 1982).
44. *United Teachers of Dade,* 514.
45. Ibid.
46. A leading work in the field is Jeffrey A. Segal and Harold A. Spaeth, *The Supreme Court and the Attitudinal Model Revisited* (Cambridge University Press, 2002).
47. For a description of the Milken Foundation and its teaching awards, see the foundation's website (www.mff.org/mea/ [June 2008]).
48. See, for example, 20 U.S.C., sec. 209 (exempting awards); *Code of Alabama,* sec. 36-6-4 (2008) (allowing public officers and employees to receive supplemental income from "any philanthropic source").
49. See, for example, Allen Odden and Carolyn Kelley, *Paying Teachers for What They Know and Do: New and Smarter Compensation Strategies to Improve Schools,* 2nd ed. (Thousand Oaks, Calif.: Corwin Press, 2002), pp. 180–81 ("In many ways, teachers play the most critical role in compensation reform. Without the cooperation, professionalism, and commitment of teachers to make compensation reform work for them, the likelihood of success is very low").
50. U.S. Constitution, amends. 5 and 14.
51. See, for example, Anthony B. Sanders, "The 'New Judicial Federalism' before Its Time: A Comprehensive Review of Economic Substantive Due Process under State Constitutional Law since 1940 and the Reasons for Its Recent Decline," *American University Law Review* 55 (December 2005): 457–540.
52. See, for example, *Board of Regents of State College* v. *Roth,* 408 U.S. 564, 277 (1972).
53. 558 F. Supp. 890, 892 (D.C. Ill. 1983).
54. Ibid.
55. 470 U.S. 532.
56. Ibid., 542.
57. See Podgursky and Springer, "Teacher Performance Pay," pp. 913–22 (reviewing existing performance-based pay programs).
58. For example, *Daniels* v. *Williams,* 447 U.S. 327, 331 (1986).
59. Ibid., 331.
60. For example, *Twigg* v. *County of Will,* 255 Ill. App. 3d 490 (Ill. Ct. App. 1994)
61. See generally Charles F. Abernathy, *Civil Rights and Constitutional Litigation: Cases and Materials,* 4th ed. (St. Paul, Minn.: Thomson/West, 2006).
62. Bruce Beezer, "Black Teachers' Salaries and Federal Courts before *Brown* v. *Board of Education:* One Beginning for Equity," *Journal of Negro Education* 55, no. 2 (1986): 200–13, quotation 212.
63. For example, *Sherwood National Education Association* v. *Sherwood-Cass-R-VII School District,* 168 S.W.3d 456 (Mo. Ct. App. 2005).
64. P. H. Vartanian, "Compensation of Tenure Teacher," in *American Law Reports,* vol. 145, 2nd ed. (Thomson Reuters/West, 2008), p. 408.
65. *Sherwood National Education Association,* 168 S.W.3d at 462 ("It simply is difficult to square the concept of merit pay with the Teacher Tenure Act, which had as one of its purposes the minimization of the part that 'malice, political or partisan trends, or caprice' might play in the employment of teachers"); Vartanian, "Compensation of Tenure Teacher," p. 148.

4

A Market-Based Perspective on Teacher Compensation Reform

Michael Podgursky

During the 2004–05 school year, the most current year for which national data are available, U.S. public schools spent $179 billion on salaries and $50 billion on benefits for instructional personnel. These compensation payments account for 55 percent of K–12 current expenditures and 90 percent of current instructional expenditures. As large as these expenditures are, they do not fully capture the resources committed to K–12 compensation, since they do not include billions of dollars of unfunded liabilities in the form of pension funds and retiree health insurance for teachers and administrators.[1] If productivity doubled for an input accounting for 1 percent of total cost, there would be only a modest overall social gain. However, given the large share of K–12 costs that arise from educators' compensation, even small gains in efficiency would yield large social dividends. It is the central thesis of this chapter that large inefficiencies arise from the teacher compensation system in U.S. public schools.

A burgeoning research literature outside of K–12 education highlights the importance of human resource policies within organizations. To quote a leading textbook in the field (written by two economists), *Human resources [HR] are key to organizational success or failure. It is perhaps going too far to say that excellent HR policies are sufficient for success. But success with poor HR policies* is probably impossible, and the effects of improved HR success are potentially enormous."[2] Compensation is a central part of a strategic human resources policy.

Unfortunately, in public K–12 education, the compensation system is neither strategic nor integrated. Rather, it is best seen as an amalgam of different components, reflecting pressures from different constituencies, legislative tinkering, and legacies from earlier vintages of collective bargaining agreements but with little attention to overall human resources efficiency. For example, base pay for teachers is set by salary schedules that have evolved through generations of collective bargaining agreements or, in many nonbargaining states, legislative fiat. Base pay is augmented by various types of districtwide or statewide salary supplements (for example, coaching, career ladder).

Finally, deferred compensation in the form of retirement pay inhabits another silo altogether, with policy set by statewide pension boards dominated by senior educators and administrators. Teacher compensation is the sum of all of these parts (plus fringe benefits, such as health insurance).

Single Salary Schedules

Salary schedules for teachers are a nearly universal feature of public school districts, and pay for public school teachers is largely determined by these schedules. In large school districts the pay of thousands of teachers in hundreds of schools—from kindergarten teachers to secondary teachers in math and science—is set by a single district schedule. The nearly universal use of salary schedules in public school districts is seen in data from the 1999–2000 National Center for Education Statistics' Schools and Staffing Surveys. Ninety-six percent of public school districts accounting for nearly 100 percent of teachers report use of a salary schedule.[3]

Table 4-1 illustrates the salary schedule for public school teachers in Columbus, Ohio, by level of teacher education and experience. The pay levels associated with higher levels of education may not be tied to a teacher's field. For example, it is commonplace for a teacher to earn graduate credits and degrees in education administration while being employed full time as a classroom teacher.

Such schedules are sometimes referred to as *single salary schedules,* a term that reflects their historical development. Joseph Kershaw and Roland McKean describe three phases in the historical development of teacher pay regimes. During the first phase, which lasted roughly until the beginning of the twentieth cen-

Table 4-1. *Salary Schedule for Public School Teachers, Columbus, Ohio, 2007–08*

Years of experience	Prelicense bachelor's degree	Bachelor's degree	Bachelor's degree and 150 hours	Master's degree	Master's degree and 30 semester hours
0	29,313	36,779	37,844	40,788	44,220
1	30,490	38,251	39,353	42,406	43,252
2	31,703	39,795	40,935	44,098	44,981
3	32,991	41,376	42,553	45,863	46,746
4	34,278	43,031	44,282	47,702	48,622
5	35,676	44,760	46,047	49,615	50,571
6	n.a.	46,525	47,886	51,601	52,594
7	n.a.	48,401	49,799	53,661	54,727
8	n.a.	50,350	51,785	55,794	56,897
9	n.a.	52,337	53,844	58,037	59,177
10	n.a.	54,433	56,014	60,354	61,531
11	n.a.	56,640	58,258	62,782	63,995
12	n.a.	58,883	60,575	65,283	66,570
13	n.a.	61,237	63,002	67,894	69,218
14	n.a.	63,701	65,540	70,616	72,013

Source: Data from the Columbus Education Association website (www.nctq.org/salary_schedule/55-07.pdf).

tury, teacher pay was negotiated between an individual teacher and a local school board. As school districts consolidated and grew in size, this type of salary determination became increasingly unpopular with teachers. With consolidation and growth, the monopoly power of school districts in the labor market increased, and charges of favoritism were common. In response to these problems, there was gradual movement toward the second phase, the use of salary schedules that differed by grade level and position. "Typically the salaries differed from grade to grade, and high school salaries would inevitably be higher than those at the elementary level."[4]

The third and current phase began in the 1920s and accelerated during World War II and the immediate postwar period. This is characterized by the single salary schedule—the current norm. An education commentator writing in the 1950s noted that "the distinguishing characteristic of the single salary schedule is that the salary class to which the classroom teacher is assigned depends on the professional qualifications of the teacher rather than the school level or assignment." According to Kershaw and McKean, "The single salary schedule was regarded as bringing a feeling of contentment and *professionalism.* A teacher would no longer be an *elementary* teacher, but a *teacher,* a member on equal footing of the profession that included all teachers." By 1951 the single salary schedule was used by 98 percent of urban school districts.[5]

Since elementary school teachers were nearly all women and high school teachers were predominantly male, early struggles for a single salary schedule were seen by some commentators as an important part of feminist struggles for pay equity.[6] Eventually, the unification of pay schedules for elementary and secondary school teachers was embraced by the National Education Association as well as the American Federation of Teachers and embedded in collective bargaining agreements and, in some cases, state legislation.

These salary schedules for teachers contrast with the situation in most other professions. In medicine, pay to doctors and nurses varies by specialty. Even within the same hospital or health maintenance organization, pay will differ by specialty field. In higher education there are large differences in pay between faculty by teaching fields. Faculty pay structures in most higher education institutions are flexible. Starting pay is usually market driven, and institutions will often match counteroffers for more-senior faculty whom they wish to retain. Merit or performance-based pay is commonplace. Dale Ballou and Michael Podgursky report generally similar findings for private K–12 education. Even when private schools report that they use a salary schedule for teacher pay, payments "off schedule" seem commonplace.[7]

Rigid salary schedules would not be as costly if the factors rewarded, teacher experience and graduate education, were strong predictors of teacher productivity. Value added studies of the effect of teachers on student achievement find little support for a positive effect of teacher master's degrees, and teacher experience has little effect beyond the first few years.[8]

There is a saying in economics (the origin of which I do not know): "You can't repeal the law of supply and demand." By this economists mean that if prices are not allowed to clear a market then some other mechanism will. For example, if city governments use rent controls to set rates below the market clearing level, then shortages will develop. In such a case the market will "clear" in the sense that individuals will have to invest more of their time in searching for an apartment. Some will give up and quit. Others will pay bribes. And the overall quality of the apartment stock may decline. All of these nonprice mechanisms will act to clear the market instead of price. It is important to keep this idea of nonprice clearing in mind in considering the effects of teacher salary schedules on the level and distribution of teacher quality.

Shortages by Teaching Field

The single salary schedule suppresses pay differentials by field. All teachers in a district with the same experience or education level earn the same base pay. Thus a second-grade teacher will earn the same pay as a high school chemistry teacher. However, many districts have little difficulty in hiring elementary school teachers but face chronic shortages of applicants in special education, math, and science. Given the wide variation in human capital investments by teaching field (for example, elementary education versus secondary physical science) it is almost certainly the case that nonteaching opportunity earnings differ greatly as well. Limited data on the ratios of qualified applicants to vacancies show sharp differences by field.

National data on teacher recruiting, presented in table 4-2, bear this out. These data are from the 1999–2000 and 2003–04 Schools and Staffing Surveys, national surveys of schools and teachers undertaken at regular intervals by the U.S. Department of Education. These are assessments of market conditions by

Table 4-2. *Ease of Filling Vacancy, by Teaching Field, 1999–2000 and 2003–2004*

Percent

Teaching field	Easy	Somewhat difficult	Very difficult	Could not fill
1999–2000				
Elementary	67.6	26.2	5.5	0.7
Social studies	70.0	24.7	4.7	0.6
English as a second language	56.5	33.2	9.5	0.8
Math	29.0	34.8	33.3	2.8
Biological science	34.0	38.5	26.2	1.3
Physical science	31.7	35.7	30.2	2.4
Special education	25.5	35.8	32.8	5.8
2003–04				
Elementary	75.1	21.1	3.3	0.5
Social studies	71.5	24.4	3.6	0.4
English as a second language	59.0	32.9	7.1	1.1
Math	33.3	37.8	25.5	3.4
Biological science	34.9	44.2	19.0	1.9
Physical science	34.6	37.7	25.3	2.4
Special education	29.1	41.8	25.7	3.5

Source: National Center for Education Statistics, Schools and Staffing Surveys, 1999–2000, 2003–04; author's calculations from School District Survey using microdata file.

Table 4-3. *Ease of Filling Vacancy, High- and Low-Poverty Schools,*
by Teaching Field, 2003–2004[a]
Percent

Teaching field	Easy	Somewhat difficult	Very difficult	Could not fill
Elementary				
Low poverty[a]	85.4	13.0	1.4	0.2
High poverty[b]	62.7	29.0	6.9	1.4
Math				
Low poverty	37.4	40.1	21.6	1.4
High poverty	31.1	29.4	32.5	7.1

Source: See table 4-2.

a. Low poverty is defined as the bottom 25 percent of the income distribution; high poverty is defined as the top 25 percent of the income distribution.

administrators who have recently recruited at least one teacher in various fields. Respondents are asked to rate how difficult or easy it was to fill a vacancy in a particular field. Seventy-five percent of school administrators reported in 2003–04 that it had been easy to fill vacancies in elementary education, and fewer than 4 percent reported that it was "very difficult" or that they had not been able to fill the position. The situation changes dramatically with math, science, and special education, where a large share of districts reported it was "very difficult" or that they were unable to fill a vacancy. Data in table 4-3 show that this pattern also prevails in high-poverty schools. Although filling any vacancy is easier for low-poverty schools than for high-poverty schools, finding elementary teachers is still relatively easy even for high-poverty schools, 63 percent of which reported it easy to fill vacancies in elementary education.

In a market with flexible wages, our prediction would be straightforward. Relative earnings of elementary teachers would fall relative to those of science, math, and special education teachers. However, districts' salary schedules do not permit this relative wage adjustment to occur. Thus the market "clears" in terms of quality rather than price. Numerous reports have documented the extent of "teaching out of field" or teachers' practicing with substandard licenses in the fields of science, math, and special education, whereas more than 95 percent of elementary school teachers are fully licensed in elementary education.[9]

In this regard, it is interesting to contrast the K–12 system with higher education. Average pay of faculty varies greatly by field. Largely because of the high salaries they can command outside of teaching, finance professors earn much more than history or English professors. Higher-education costs would increase massively if it were necessary to pay all faculty in a university at the same rate as finance professors. Short of that, attempts by higher-education institutions to suppress pay gaps between finance and other disciplines by leveling down would simply cause the market to "clear" in terms of quality rather than price—the quality of finance faculty would fall relative to that in other disciplines. "Teaching out of field" in finance would become the norm rather than the exception.

It is also interesting to note that in other professional fields such as medicine, law, nursing, or dentistry, while there is considerable differentiation in remuneration between various specialties, there is a good deal of common core training among practitioners. Family practitioners and orthopedic surgeons have a good deal of training and coursework in common. By contrast, how much do first-grade teachers and high school chemistry teachers have in common in terms of professional preparation? Very little. Yet one artifact of the compensation system (and "bargaining units" under collective bargaining law) is to lump these very different types of professionals (chemistry and first-grade teachers) under the same job title, contract, and salary schedule.

Novice Teachers and Poor Children

The single salary schedule suppresses differentials by schools within districts. In larger urban districts dozens or even hundreds of schools are covered by the same salary schedule. The working environments for teachers vary greatly between these schools. Some may even be dangerous places to work, whereas other schools will be more pleasant places to work. Often teachers in the less desirable schools will be able to use their seniority to transfer to a more pleasant school, or they may simply quit at a higher rate. Because the salary schedule assigns lower pay to teachers with less experience within a school district, an unintended consequence of a district-wide salary schedule is lower spending per student in high-poverty schools.[10] High-poverty schools will also have relatively newer or inexperienced teachers. One fairly consistent finding in the literature on teacher effects is that students taught by novice or inexperienced teachers have lower achievement gains than students with more experienced teachers.[11]

Since they are based on a sample rather than the universe of schools and teachers, the national Schools and Staffing Surveys cannot be used to examine this intradistrict allocation of novice teachers. Instead I rely on school-level administrative data on students and teachers collected by the Missouri education department to explore this phenomenon. The empirical literature cited above finds that novice teachers are less effective than more experienced teachers but provides no precise guidance as to where this damage threshold abates. All would agree, however,

Table 4-4. *Relationship between Percent of Teachers Inexperienced and Student Poverty, Missouri Public Elementary Schools, 2005–06*[a]
Percent

	First-year teachers		Teachers with less than three years' experience	
Dependent variable	OLS[b]	FE–district[c]	OLS[b]	FE–district[c]
Percent in school eligible for free and reduced-price lunch	0.051 (5.81)	0.066 (4.15)	0.077 (5.62)	0.115 (4.42)
Number of schools	1,250	1,250	1,250	1,250
Number of districts	n.a.	522	n.a.	522

Source: Missouri Department of Elementary and Secondary Education, author's calculations from administrative data from a restricted use file.
a. *t*-statistics in parentheses.
b. Ordinary least squares.
c. School district fixed effects.

that the newest teachers (for example, first-year teachers) are less effective. Thus in this analysis I use two definitions of *novice teacher:* in the narrow definition, as a teacher with no prior experience (that is, in his or her first year of teaching) and, more broadly, as one with less than three years' experience. I then compare the exposure rate of students to novice teachers in high- and low-poverty elementary schools by regressing the percentage of novice teachers in a school (narrowly and broadly defined) on the student poverty rate in the school. These results are shown in the columns labeled OLS (ordinary least squares) in table 4-4. For both measures, there is a significant positive association indicating that, on average, poor children are more likely to be exposed to a novice teacher.

This association between novice teachers and school poverty can arise from two sources. First, it may be that high-poverty school districts have relatively more novice teachers on staff. Second, it may be that within a district, schools with above-average levels of student poverty have relatively more novice teachers. These explanations are not mutually exclusive. Which is the dominant factor is an empirical point. The estimates labeled FE–district (fixed effects at the district level) neutralize the former effect and estimate the strength of the relationship owing to intradistrict variation alone in student poverty and novice teaching. In both cases, the size of the coefficient increases significantly. This indicates that the intradistrict association is the dominant factor producing the association. Since pay is rigid, intradistrict markets clear on teacher experience and quality.

Figure 4-1. *Relationship between Student Poverty and Teachers' Inexperience, Elementary Schools in Nine Largest Missouri School Districts, 2005-2006*[a]

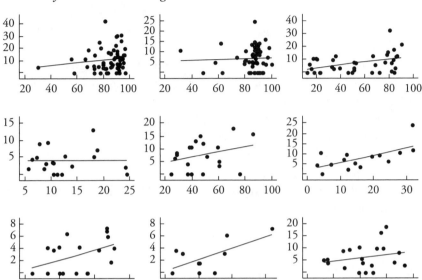

Source: See table 4-4.

a. *x*-axis = percentage of students eligible for free or reduced-price lunch; *y*-axis = percentage of teachers in their first year of teaching; • = 1 percent full-time equivalent; —— = fitted values.

This same relationship is illustrated in figure 4-1, which plots the relationship between student poverty and the percentage of first-year teachers in elementary schools for the nine largest public school districts in Missouri. In most cases there is a positive relationship within the district. However, it is also worth noting that in nearly all cases the outlier schools with the highest share of novice teachers usually have a student poverty rate that is above the district average.

To return to the market-clearing thesis, if the attractiveness of working conditions varies among schools within a district, then evenly distributing teacher pay will cause an uneven distribution in teacher quality. To equalize teacher quality, teacher pay needs to be disequalized.

Insufficient Rewards for Effective Teachers

One consistent finding in the teacher value added literature is that there is a large variation in teacher effectiveness.[12] Even within the same school building, some fourth-grade teachers are much more effective at raising student achievement than others. Some teachers work harder and elicit greater effort from students than others. Some teachers are burnt out and simply putting in time until retirement (more on pension system incentives below). The single salary schedule suppresses differences between more- and less-effective teachers (however defined). The best way to understand what the effect of the single salary schedule is would be to imagine what the effect of a performance-pay regime might be. Rewarding more-effective teachers on the basis of performance would have two important consequences. The first is a motivation effect. Incumbent teachers would have an incentive to work harder to raise whatever performance measure is rewarded. In addition, over the longer term, a performance-pay system would have a selection effect. It would draw into the workforce teachers who are relatively more effective at meeting the performance targets and would help retain such teachers as well. Equalizing teacher pay among teachers at different levels of effectiveness lowers the overall quality and performance of the teaching workforce. Once again, the market clears in terms of quality rather than price.

Tenure and the Size of Districts

The costs associated with teacher salary schedules are aggravated by two other features of K–12 human resources policy: tenure and the size of wage-setting units (that is, districts). In statistics and medicine it is commonplace to refer to "interaction effects." Pharmacists now rely on computer-based data systems to flag potentially harmful interaction effects of drugs. The basic idea is that the overall effect of two drugs is not equal to the sum of their separate effects. In fact, the combination may enhance or dampen their separate effects or may produce harmful side effects. The same is true for the components of a compensation system. The effect of policy A may be larger or smaller, depending on the presence of policy B.

Consider the effect of teacher tenure. Even if experience by itself does not raise a teacher's effectiveness, a seniority-based wage structure might, in principle, be efficient if less-effective teachers are weeded out over time. However, personnel policies in traditional public schools are not likely to produce such an effect. Teachers in traditional public school districts receive automatic contract renewal (tenure) after two to five years on the job. It is difficult to dismiss a teacher for poor job performance after he or she has received tenure, a finding that has been widely documented.[13] Thus the presence of teacher tenure laws, and collective bargaining language, which further hampers dismissal of low-

Figure 4-2. *Distribution of Teachers in Public and Private Schools, by Size of District*

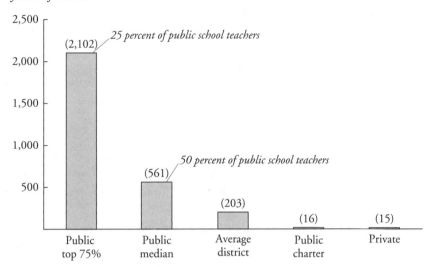

Source: Michael Podgursky, "Teams versus Bureaucracies," in *Charter School Outcomes*, edited by Mark Berends, Matthew Springer, and Herbert Walberg (New York: Lawrence Erlbaum, 2007).

performing teachers, makes the economic costs associated with single salary schedules even greater.

Another factor that increases the cost of rigid district salary schedules is the size of the district as the wage-setting unit. Other things equal, the larger the size of the unit, the greater the economic damage. The wage-setting unit in private and charter schools is typically the school, whereas in traditional public schools wages are set at the district level. In fact, most personnel policy concerning teachers—the level and structure of teacher pay, benefits, recruiting—is centralized at the district level in traditional public schools. This has two effects. First, it makes the market for teachers less flexible and competitive. In general it would be better to have five "districts," each of which determines the pay scale for twenty schools, than one district that sets pay for one hundred schools. At least the five could compete with one another and adjust their schedules to meet their own internal circumstances. A second consequence is that large wage-setting units make the process more bureaucratic and less amenable to merit or market adjustments.[14]

Figure 4-2 illustrates the dramatic differences in the size of the wage and personnel units of traditional public and private schools. There are approximately fifteen thousand public school districts in the United States, but the size distribution of these districts in terms of teacher employment is highly skewed. As a consequence, most teachers are employed in large school districts. One-quarter of teachers in traditional public schools are employed in districts with 2,100 full-time equivalent teachers, and half of traditional public school teachers are in districts with at least 561 full-time equivalent teachers. Thus the typical teacher works in a large organization with standardized, bureaucratic wage setting. By contrast, the average charter school—an independent employer—employs just 16 full-time equivalent teachers, barely larger than the average private school (15 full-time equivalent teachers).

In business, the size of the employing unit is an important factor in understanding a firm's choice of personnel policies. In small teams, it is much easier for supervisors or fellow workers to monitor job performance. This makes merit or performance-based pay less controversial. Large school districts, on the other hand, have a great deal of trouble implementing merit pay systems for teachers.[15] In part, this is because they must come up with evaluation systems that guarantee horizontal "equity" across the many schools in the district bargaining unit—essentially a hopeless endeavor. Private and charter schools are under no requirement that their performance assessments be identical to those of other schools. They need only assure their teachers that they are treated fairly within the school. Teachers unhappy with the pay system at the school can always "vote with their feet" and go to another school with a more desirable pay regime.

In principle, public school districts need not be so bureaucratic. They could adopt more decentralized systems of personnel policy, give school principals more control over teacher recruitment and pay, and adopt a more a team-oriented model. In fact, school districts are taxing districts. I am aware of no economic arguments for centralization of wage setting. That wage setting is observed in private schools—including Catholic diocesan schools—following a more decentralized model suggests that there are no efficiency gains to be had from centralization. However, this highlights an important difference between traditional public schools and charter or private schools. In terms of the percentage of teachers covered, collective bargaining agreements are far less common in charter schools than in traditional public schools, and in private schools they are virtually nonexistent. Tabulations from the 1999–2000 Schools and Staffing Surveys find that 70 percent of public school districts, which employ 73 percent of the districts' teachers, have collective bargaining agreements covering their teachers. This contrasts with the 14 percent of charter schools (employing 18 percent of charter school teachers) who bargain collectively.[16] The absence of a binding collective bargaining agreement is an important source of personnel flexibility in charter schools. Teachers unions in general have been opposed to more flexible market- or performance-based pay systems, although there are exceptions, such as the widely publicized Denver performance-pay plan. However, even in Denver, the plan is districtwide rather than school based. Collective bargaining laws, by defining the district as the "appropriate bargaining unit," have tended to push personnel policy and wage setting to the district level and lock them into place there.

Trends in Market-Based Pay

Given the efficiency costs of rigid salary schedules and growing pressure on schools to raise performance, it is not surprising that interest in market- and performance-based pay is growing. Several states and districts have implemented incentives to encourage experienced educators to teach in low-performing schools.[17] Florida, Minnesota, and Texas have implemented state programs to encourage schools and districts to use performance-based pay systems for teachers. Congress has also provided an impetus through its Teacher Incentive Fund, a five-year, $500 million program to encourage states to set up pilot programs of teacher performance incentives.[18] The website of the National Center for Performance Incentives at Vanderbilt University now does a good job of tracking programs by state. Unfortunately, there are not many "microeconomic" data on the actual implementation of these programs in schools. State data systems generally do not capture these program details. Even states that have good data on teacher salaries and their components generally cannot break out teacher performance or incentive bonuses.

The best data currently available on national levels and trends are to be found in various waves of the Schools and Staffing Surveys, conducted by the National Center for Education Statistics. The Schools and Staffing Surveys follow a large nationally representative sample of roughly 8,000 public schools and 43,000 public school teachers.[19] There have been five waves of surveys, associated with five school years: 1987–88, 1990–91, 1994–95, 1999–2000, and 2003–04. A sixth administration (2007–08) is currently "in the field," but results of that survey will not be available for some time. While the surveys cover two decades of public school experience and have included various questions about performance- and market-based pay, unfortunately, many of these have not been compatible over time. Thus I focus attention on data in the most recent waves of the survey, which contain consistent items.

District administrators were asked whether they provided pay bonuses or other rewards for certain teacher characteristics or behaviors.[20] These are listed in the

Table 4-5. *Incidence of Performance-Based Teacher Compensation*
Percent

	Teacher weighted		
Item	1999–2000	2003–04	Percent change[a]
District rewards			
National Board for Professional Teaching Standards certification	22.9	39.8	17.0
Excellence in teaching	13.6	14.0	0.3
In-service professional development	38.8	35.9	–3.0
Teaching in less desirable location	11.2	13.1	1.9
Teaching in fields of shortage	23.6	25.3	1.7
Number of incentives			
None	39.2	31.1	–8.0
One	33.1	35.5	2.5
Two	16.0	21.0	5.0
Three	5.9	10.2	4.2
Four	2.0	4.5	2.5
Five	3.9	0.7	–3.2
Schools awarded bonuses for student achievement[a]			
Cash bonus or additional resources for schoolwide use	n.a.	19.6	n.a.
Cash bonus or additional resources for teachers	n.a.	15.4	n.a.
Nonmonetary forms of recognition to schools	n.a.	30.4	n.a.
Teacher salary schedule in district	n.a.	n.a.	n.a.

Source: 1999–2000 and 2003–04 Schools and Staffing Surveys, School District Survey.
a. From 1999–2000 to 2003–04.

top rows of table 4-5. The most common bonus—offered to 40 percent of teachers in 2003–04, is for certification from the National Board for Professional Teaching Standards. The next most common bonus among districts is for professional development. Smaller numbers of districts reported the type of market-based bonuses discussed above: in the 2003-04 survey, 25 percent of teachers were employed in districts that reported some sort of bonus for shortage fields, and 13 percent of districts reported rewards for teaching in a less desirable location.[21] According to my tabulations of the 2003–04 data, 31 percent of districts reported that they provided no incentive rewards. This share dropped between the 1999–2000 and 2003–04 surveys. Almost three-quarters of teachers were employed in districts that provided one or more such incentives, and 15 percent of teachers were in districts providing three or more such incentives.

The first block in table 4-5 focuses on individual teacher bonuses. The next, at the bottom of the table, concerns schoolwide bonuses. Some states and districts have begun to provide schoolwide incentives for staff. Unfortunately, these questions were only asked in the 2003–04 survey. Of most interest for our purposes is the question concerning cash payments to teachers. Fifteen percent of teachers are employed in districts reporting schoolwide cash bonuses or additional resources based on student achievement.

Although all of the Schools and Staffing Surveys had questions on market- and performance-based pay, few of the questions were consistently asked from one administration of the survey to the next. One block of questions that was nearly identical over the years concerned recruitment bonuses by field. This question asked district administrators whether they offered additional rewards in shortage fields, and in which teaching fields these incentives are used. The results are presented in table 4-6.

Table 4-6. *Recruitment Incentives in Fields of Shortage, by Teaching Field, Various Years, 1987–2004*[a]
Percent

Item	1987–88	1990–91	1993–94	1999–2000	2003–04	Percent change[b]
Percent districts that provide incentives (teacher-weighted)	11.3	16.6	18.7	23.6	25.3	14.0
Elementary	n.a.	n.a.	n.a.	2.4	2.6	n.a.
Special education	6.7	11.8	13.4	14.3	20.6	13.9
English and language arts	n.a.	n.a.	n.a.	5.3	4.2	n.a.
Social studies	n.a.	n.a.	n.a.	1.6	2.4	n.a.
Computer science	1.4	2.9	1.3	3.4	3.4	2.0
Mathematics	5.2	5.8	3.9	8.9	15.7	10.5
Physical sciences	3.6	5.0	3.9	8.4	13.4	9.8
Biological sciences	3.8	4.3	3.7	8.4	12.8	8.9
English as a second language	3.3	7.6	8.1	11.1	15.5	12.2
Foreign language	2.4	3.1	2.4	5.3	9.4	7.0
Music or art	n.a.	n.a.	n.a.	4.9	6.4	n.a.
Vocational or technical education	n.a.	4.7	3.2	8.0	7.3	n.a.
Other fields	4.2	4.2	1.6	n.a.	n.a.	n.a.

Source: Schools and Staffing Surveys, various years; School District Surveys.

a. Based on responses to the survey question, "Does this district currently use any pay incentives to recruit or retain teachers to teach in fields of shortage?"

b. From 1987–88 to 2003–04.

First, the sharp increase over the sixteen-year interval in the incidence of field-based incentives is noteworthy. In the first administration of the Schools and Staffing Surveys during the 1987–88 school year, only 11 percent of teachers were eligible for such incentives.[22] That share climbed to 25 percent of teachers by the 2003–04 school year. Consistent with the recruitment difficulty responses seen in table 4-2, these incentives are most commonly used in the areas of special education, math, science, and English as a second language.

Teacher Pension Incentives

Retirement benefits are an important part of a strategic compensation package. Recognizing the need for a flexible benefit system to attract mobile young professionals, private sector employers have moved dramatically away from traditional pension systems toward individual retirement accounts or similar defined contribution plans.[23] Moreover, many employers maintaining defined benefit plans have changed the plans to incorporate defined contribution features that do not punish mobile young workers.[24] Defined benefit pensions have long been an important part of compensation for teachers in public schools. Traditionally, salaries for public employees have been relatively low, but benefits, particularly retiree benefits, have been relatively high. This mix of current versus deferred income was rationalized by the contention that the public good was best served by the longevity of service that would be induced by these pension plans.[25] In recent decades, however, evidence is growing that many of these plans, by encouraging early retirement, may shorten rather than lengthen professional careers. For example, a study by Leora Friedburg and Anthony Webb has found that a switch by employers to a defined contribution retirement benefit system has been associated with later retirement.[26]

Robert Costrell and Michael Podgursky have shown that defined benefit systems create strong incentives for teachers to retire at relatively early ages and that this tendency has been accentuated by legislative changes over the years in a number of states.[27] What are the incentive effects of such defined benefit systems? First of all, they punish mobility. Teachers who leave before conventional retirement age suffer severe losses in pension wealth. Second, they encourage early teacher retirement. Many teachers retire in their mid-fifties. The median age for retirement and withdrawal from the teaching workforce is fifty-eight.[28]

It is difficult to come up with an efficiency rationale for these spikes in pension wealth accrual. The fairly massive backloading of benefits might be justified if there were strong evidence of large returns to experience and important job-specific human capital investments. However, most value added econometric studies of teacher effectiveness find that novice teachers (that is, teachers with less than three years of experience) on average are less effective than more senior teachers, but the returns to experience level off quickly. There is little evidence that a teacher with twenty years' experience is any more effective in the classroom than a teacher with ten years' experience. Ironically, in a steady state, the current pension system, by pushing many teachers into retirement at a relatively young age, actually raises the share of novice teachers in the workforce and thereby lowers overall teacher effectiveness.[29]

Conclusion

The management of human resources—the recruitment, retention, and motivation of employees—is increasingly recognized as a critical variable in the success of an organization. An integrated and coherent compensation policy is a central core of an efficient human resources policy. In private and many public organizations, the compensation package is considered as a strategic whole, carefully designed to get the most return from each dollar of compensation. In public K–12 education, by contrast, the compensation system is much more fragmented and uncoordinated, with each different piece responding to pressures from different groups or inherited from an earlier collective bargaining agreement but with little or no systematic consideration of the logic or incentive effects of the whole.

Accountability pressures are forcing school districts to address the inefficiencies built into this compensation system and rethink how they are spending roughly $250 billion annually on compensation of instruction personnel. Federal programs such as the Teacher Incentive Fund are encouraging states to experiment with performance- and market-based pay. Minnesota, Florida, and Texas, among others, have developed programs to encourage their districts to develop performance-based pay programs. A number of large urban districts, most notably Denver, have taken important steps in this direction. Performance- and market-based incentives are much more common in charter schools and are growing with the charter school base.[30] Our examination of various waves of the Schools and Staffing Surveys finds increasing evidence of performance- and market-based pay even among traditional public schools. Much less movement has occurred in the area of teacher retirement benefits. However, large unfunded liabilities for pensions and retiree health insurance are likely to force reforms in this area as well.

Experience from the private sector and other government employment suggests that trial and error, combined, one hopes, with evaluation, will be necessary to arrive at highly effective systems. Nonetheless, given the massive public spending on compensation of K–12 professionals, even modest gains in efficiency can produce large social dividends.

Notes

1. The Pew Center on the States, "Promises with a Price: Public Sector Retirement Benefits," September 12, 2008 (www.pewcenteronthestates.org/uploadedfiles/Promises%20with%20a%20Price.pdf [March 8, 2009]).

2. James Barron and David Kreps, *Strategic Human Resource Management* (New York: John Wiley, 1999); emphasis in original.

3. Michael Podgursky, "Teams versus Bureaucracies," in *Charter School Outcomes,* edited by Mark Berends, Matthew Springer, and Herbert Walberg (New York: Lawrence Erlbaum, 2007), pp. 61–84.

4. Joseph A. Kershaw and Roland N. McKean, *Teacher Shortages and Salary Schedules,* RAND research memorandum (Santa Monica, Calif.: RAND, 1962).

5. Ibid., pp. 23, 25. See also Myron H. Lieberman, *Education as a Profession* (New York: John Wiley, 1956), pp. 391–93.

6. Marjorie Murphy, *Blackboard Unions: The AFT and NEA, 1900–1980* (Cornell University Press, 1990).

7. Dale Ballou and Michael Podgursky, *Teacher Pay and Teacher Quality* (Kalamazoo, Mich.: W. E. Upjohn Institute for Employment Research, 1997); Dale Ballou, "Pay for Performance in Public and Private Schools," *Economics of Education Review* 20, n. 1 (2001): 51–61.

8. Steven G. Rivkin, Eric A. Hanushek, and John F. Kain, "Teachers, Schools, and Academic Achievement," *Econometrica* 73, no. 2 (2005): 417–58.

9. U.S. Department of Education, National Center for Education Statistics, *Qualifications of the Public School Teaching Force: The Prevalence of Out-of-Field Teaching, 1987–88 to 1999–2000,* NCES 2002603 (National Center for Education Statistics, August 2004).

10. Marguerite Roza and others, "Do Districts Fund Schools Fairly?" *Education Next* 7 (Fall 2007): 68–74; Patrice Iaterola and Leanna Steifel, "Intradistrict Equity and Public Education Resources and Reform," *Economics of Education Review* 22, no. 1 (2003): 60–78.

11. See Rivkin, Hanushek, and Kain, "Teachers, Schools, and Academic Achievement"; Daniel Aaronson, Lisa Barrow, and William Sander, "Teachers and Student Achievement in Chicago High Schools," *Journal of Labor Economics* 25, no 1 (2007): 95–136; Donald Boyd and others, "How Changes in Entry Requirements Alter the Teacher Workforce and Affect Student Achievement," *American Education Finance Association* 1, no. 2 (2006): 176–216.

12. See Rivkin, Hanushek, and Kain, "Teachers, Schools, and Academic Achievement"; Aaronson, Barrow, and Sanders, "Teachers and Student Achievement in Chicago High Schools."

13. Edwin Bridges, *The Incompetent Teacher: The Challenge and Response* (New York: Routledge, 1992); Frederick Hess and Martin West, *A Better Bargain: Overhauling Teacher Collective Bargaining for the 21st Century* (Harvard University, Kennedy School of Government, Program in Educational Policy and Governance, 2006) (www.hks.harvard.edu/pepg/PDF/Papers/BetterBargain.pdf). A proposed teacher performance-pay plan in

Idaho takes explicit recognition of this interaction of performance pay with tenure. Under the plan (ISTARS), teachers would earn individual bonuses (based on duties and additional certification and endorsement areas) in lieu of tenure. A flat dollar bonus would be paid to all teachers who entered the plan This plan was discussed during the 2008 Idaho legislative session but did not become law (www.sde.state.id.us/istars/details.asp#leadership [March 8, 2009]).

14. Podgursky, "Teams versus Bureaucracies."

15. Harry P. Hatry, John M. Greiner, and Brenda G. Ashford, *Issues and Case Studies in Teacher Incentive Plans,* 2nd ed. (Washington: Urban Institute Press, 1994).

16. The Schools and Staffing Surveys do not ask a collective bargaining question of private schools. However, we are aware of no private school organized by the major teachers unions. Some Catholic dioceses negotiate agreements with Catholic teacher associations. However, these agreements are far less restrictive than anything negotiated in public schools, and Catholic school teachers do not have tenure.

17. Cynthia Prince, "Higher Pay in Hard-to-Staff Schools: The Case for Financial Incentives" (Arlington, Va.: American Association of School Administrators, June 2002) (www.aasa.org/files/PDFs/Publications/higher_pay.pdf [March 8, 2009]).

18. Michael Podgursky and Matthew Springer, "Teacher Performance Pay: A Review," *Journal of Policy Analysis and Management* 26, no. 4 (2007): 909–50.

19. The Schools and Staffing Surveys include private schools and teachers, as well; however, the focus of the present study is trends in public schools.

20. "Does the district currently use any pay incentives such as a cash bonus, salary increase, or different steps on a salary schedule to reward . . . ?"

21. Interestingly, the rank order of district implementation of these incentives is nearly opposite that of teacher preferences, as reported in a recent study of Washington teachers by Dan Goldhaber, Michael DeArmond, Scott DeBurgomaster, "Teacher Attitudes about Compensation Reform: Implications for Reform Implementation," Working Paper 20 (University of Washington, Center on Reinventing Public Education, School Finance Redesign Project, August 2007). Teaching in a less desirable location was the most favored incentive (63 percent), followed by National Board for Professional Teaching Standards certification (20 percent), teaching in shortage fields (12 percent), and performance pay (6 percent). See Roza and others, "Do Districts Fund Schools Fairly?"

22. These recruitment incentives can take the form of cash bonuses or higher pay or higher initial placement on the salary schedule. The latter is more subtle, and thus less controversial, than explicit bonuses or differentiated pay structures.

23. Under a traditional or defined benefit plan, the employer guarantees an annuity payment of a certain amount to the worker on retirement. With an individual retirement account or similar defined contribution plan, the employer merely agrees to contribute a certain amount to a retirement account for the worker but does not guarantee any particular annuity payment upon retirement. Defined contribution plans now account for the vast majority of private sector plans. See Janet Hansen, "Teacher Pensions: A Background Paper," Committee for Economic Development, Washington, 2008 (www.ced.org/images/library/reports/education/report_educ200806pensions.pdf [March 8, 2009]).

24. In particular, roughly 25 percent of private defined benefit plans have been converted to "cash balance" plans (Hansen, "Teacher Pensions"). In cash balance systems, employees maintain a nominal private account that earns a guaranteed rate of return. If the employee

separates before retirement, the balance in the account stays with the employer but continues to earn the guaranteed rate of return. At retirement the employee has the option to convert the cash balance into an annuity.

25. National Education Association, *Understanding Defined Benefit and Defined Contribution Pension Plans* (Washington, 1995). As the report points out, however, this purpose has "been lost for many in the mists of time," and "many pension administrators would be hard-pressed to give an account of why their systems are structured as is except to say that 'the Legislature did it' or 'It is a result of bargaining'" (p. 3).

26. Leora Freidberg and Anthony Webb, "Retirement and the Evolution of Pension Structure," *Journal of Human Resources* 40, no. 2 (2005): 281–308.

27. Robert Costrell and Michael Podgursky, *Golden Peaks and Perilous Cliffs: Rethinking Ohio's Teacher Pension System* (Washington: Fordham Institute, 2007) (www.edexcellence.net/doc/060707_Pensions_Report.pdf [March 8, 2009]).

28. Michael Podgursky and Mark Ehlert, *Teacher Pensions and Retirement Behavior: How Teacher Pension Rules Affect Behavior, Mobility, and Retirement,* CALDER Working Paper 5 (Washington: Urban Institute, 2007) (www.caldercenter.org/PDF/1001071_Teacher_Pensions.pdf [March 8 2009]).

29. The problem of retiree health insurance is only beginning to appear on the radar screens of state legislatures. New public sector accounting rules from the Governmental Accounting Standards Board (GASB 43 and 45) require state and local governments to estimate and report the magnitude of unfunded retiree health insurance benefits. A few states pay for retiree health insurance through a state fund. However, for the most part this is a benefit provided by school districts. Available evidence suggests that many, perhaps most, districts that provide these benefits finance them on a pay-as-you-go basis. Not surprisingly, then, on first glimpse the unfunded liabilities are very large. For example, the Los Angeles Unified School District provides complete coverage for the teacher and her or his spouse for employed and retired teachers with more than five years' seniority. The estimated unfunded accrued liabilities to date are $10 billion. State of California, Public Employee Post-Employment Benefits Commission, *Funding Pensions and Retiree Health Care for Public Employees,* 2007 (www.pebc.ca.gov/images/files/final/080107_PEBCReport2007.pdf [March 8, 2009]).

30. Podgursky, "Teams versus Bureaucracies."

5

The Influence of Scholarship and Experience in Other Fields on Teacher Compensation Reform

Richard Rothstein

In 1935 a nineteen-year-old political science major at the University of Chicago interviewed Milwaukee administrators for a term paper. He was puzzled that when money became available to invest in parks, there was no agreement between school board and public works officials on whether to spend it by hiring more playground supervisors or improving physical maintenance of the city's open spaces. The student concluded that rational decision-making in this case was impossible because "improving parks" included multiple goals: school board members thought mostly of recreational opportunities, while public works administrators thought mostly of green space to reduce density.

The next year, the director of the International City Managers Association hired the young graduate as his assistant. Together, they attempted to evaluate municipal services, including police, fire, public health, education, libraries, parks, and public works. Their 1938 book, *Measuring Municipal Activities,* concludes that quantitative performance measures are mostly inappropriate because public service goals cannot easily be defined in numerical terms.

The senior author, Clarence E. Ridley, directed the city managers association until his 1956 retirement. His assistant, Herbert A. Simon, later won the Nobel Prize in Economics for a lifetime of work demonstrating that organizational behavior is characterized by "bounded rationality": measurement of costs and benefits, he states, does "not even remotely describe the processes that human beings use for making decisions in complex situations."[1]

In *Measuring Municipal Activities,* Ridley and Simon observe that public services have multiple purposes; even if precise definitions for some purposes were possible, evaluating the services overall would require difficult judgments about which purposes were relatively more important. Moreover, it is never possible to quantify whether outcome differences between cities are attributable to differences in effort and competence of public employees or to differences in the conditions—difficult to measure in any event—under which agencies work.

The authors note that "the most serious single problem which still stands in the way of the development of satisfactory measurement techniques is the difficulty of defining the objectives of municipal services in measurable terms." Objectives like "improv[ing] health . . . or develop[ing] good citizens must be stated in much more tangible and objective terms before they adapt themselves to measurement."[2]

Ridley and Simon suggest that before attempting quantitative measurement, questions should be addressed, such as the following: For evaluating library services, should judgments be made about the quality of books being circulated? For a mortality index for public health, should all lives be considered equally valuable, those of the elderly, of very young children, and of productive workers?[3] Ridley and Simon had something to say about measuring school effectiveness as well:

> The chief fault of the testing movement has consisted in its emphasis upon content in highly academic material. . . . That a particular pupil shows a marked improvement in reading or spelling may give some indication that a teacher is improving her performance . . . but the use to which the pupil puts that knowledge is the only significant point in determining the significance of subject tests in measuring the educational system. . . .
>
> The final appraisal of the school system must be in terms of its impact upon the community through the individuals that it trains. How effective is the school system in raising the cultural level of the community? . . . What is the delinquency rate in the community? . . . Is the economic situation improving as a result of intelligent effort on the part of the people? . . . What is the proportion of registered voters to the eligible voting population? . . .
>
> From a practical standpoint, no one is so optimistic as to believe that all these results can be directly measured.[4]

Politicians and policymakers are showing growing enthusiasm for quantitative accountability to maximize public service efficiency, but they have rushed to develop measurement systems without giving great thought to whether these systems truly measure ultimate outcomes of the kind that Ridley and Simon had in mind. In Great Britain, Margaret Thatcher attempted to rationalize public enterprises: where they could not be privatized, her government hoped to regulate them, using rewards and sanctions for numerically specified outcomes. Tony Blair accelerated these efforts, while in the United States, the Clinton administration's Government Performance Results Act of 1993 proposed to "reinvent government" by requiring measurable outcomes for all agencies.

Enthusiasm for holding schools accountable for student test scores is but part of this trend, which proceeded oblivious to the warnings not only of Herbert Simon but of other social scientists as well. In 1979 Donald T. Campbell formulated a law of performance measurement: "The more any quantitative social indicator is used for social decision-making, the more subject it will be to corruption pressures and the more apt it will be to distort and corrupt the social processes it is intended to monitor."[5]

A decade later, in his study titled *Bureaucracy,* James Q. Wilson wondered why public agencies did not employ "carefully designed compensation plans" that would permit public employees to benefit financially from good performance. "Part of the answer," he states, "is obvious. Often we do not know whether a manager or an agency has achieved the goals we want because either the goals are vague or inconsistent, or their attainment cannot be observed, or both."[6]

Before the Soviet Union collapsed in 1989, Western publications often reported on the goal distortion and corruption endemic to Soviet attempts to manage the economy by mandating quantitative results. Industrial planners established targets for enterprise production and punished managers who failed to meet them. There were targets, for example, for the number of shoes to be produced. Certainly, increasing output was an important goal of the Soviet shoe industry, but it was not the only goal. Factories responded to the incentives by using the limited supply of leather to produce a glut of small sizes that consumers could not use. Planners specified the number of kilometers that freight transport enterprises should cover each month. Certainly, transporters who cover more distance can deliver more goods. But when distance itself was incentivized, the haulers fulfilled their quotas by making unnecessary journeys or driving circuitous routes.[7]

Some Soviet incentives retarded technological progress. Electrifying the vast country was an important economic objective, but creating incentives to increase output gave electricity managers no reason to reduce inefficiency from the loss of current in transmission. Quotas for other industries set in tons created incentives to avoid developing lighter materials.[8]

In the United States today, attempts to hold schools accountable for students' math and reading test scores have similarly corrupted education by reducing the attention paid to other important curricular goals. Such corruption has parallels in other fields, often studied and reported by social scientists and management theorists. Education policymakers have paid little attention to this expertise. Instead, they duplicated the worst features of flawed accountability in other public and private services when they designed No Child Left Behind and similar state systems.

Some advocates of test-based accountability in education, confronted with evidence of goal distortion, have concluded that these problems stem only from the inadequacy of teachers. As one critic argues, good teachers "can and should" integrate subject matter so that raising math and reading scores need not result in diminished attention to other curricular areas.[9] But this expectation denies the intent and power of incentives, which, if successful, should redirect attention and resources to those outputs that are rewarded. The consistency with which professionals and their institutions respond in this fashion in all fields should demonstrate that this outcome is not a problem with the ethos of teachers but is rather an inevitable consequence of any quantitative incentive system.

A Few Familiar Examples

As Campbell observed, perhaps the most tragic example of goal distortion from quantifiable accountability stems from the work of a former Harvard Business School professor, financial analyst, business executive, and, later, public official. During the Vietnam War, Secretary of Defense Robert McNamara believed in quantitative measures of success and demanded reports from generals of relative "body counts" of Americans and North Vietnamese. True, just as high reading test scores are usually a reliable indicator of reading proficiency, relative casualties are usually a reliable indicator of a nation's military fortunes; a strong inverse correlation between a nation's casualties and its success in the broader political and economic objectives of warfare should normally be expected. But an army can be corrupted if imposing casualties becomes an end in itself and if local commanders' performance is judged by this relatively easily measured indicator. Generals or their civilian leaders may then lose sight of political and economic objectives. In Vietnam, as body counts became the objective itself, generals attempted to please their superiors by recording fewer deaths of American soldiers than of the enemy.

As it was impossible to hide American deaths from the political leadership, generals found ways to inflate the numbers of enemy deaths. In some cases, death became an end in itself, in other cases the categorization of deaths was corrupted (for example, by counting civilian as enemy deaths) or the numbers simply exaggerated. High enemy body count numbers led American leaders to believe the war was being won. These leaders confused U.S. superiority in body counts with the achievement of political and economic objectives. The war was then lost.[10]

There are other commonplace examples of the dangers of quantitative accountability, familiar even to those who have not studied the social science and management literature. Motorists stopped by police for trivial traffic violations may experience an accountability system in which police departments evaluate officers by whether they meet ticket quotas. Certainly, citing traffic violations is one act of good policing, but judging officers by this easily quantifiable outcome creates incentives for them to focus on trivial offenses that meet a quota rather than investigate more serious crimes for which the payoff may be less certain. The numerical accountability system generates false arrests and creates incentives for police officers to boost their measured productivity by disregarding suspects' rights.

Management theorists and criminologists have long decried the quota practice, but police departments continue to be seduced by this apparently easy way to ensure that officers are not wasting time at doughnut shops.[11] In 1966 the criminologist Jerome Skolnick wrote, "The goals of police and the standards by which the policeman's work is to be evaluated are ambiguous. . . . Even within the ranks of police specialists there is no clear understanding of goals"; consequently, judgment about effectiveness based on a simple quantitative indicator is bound to distort police priorities.[12]

The Federal Bureau of Investigation tracks local police clearance rates, which become the basis for evaluating detectives' effectiveness. The clearance rate is the percentage of reported crimes that result in convictions. Just as high math scores characterize effective schools, high clearance rates characterize effective police departments. But as with math scores, once clearance rates become ends in themselves, Campbell's law of performance measurement takes over, and the indicator distorts and corrupts the social processes it is intended to monitor. Police can increase the clearance rate by offering reduced charges to suspects who confess to other crimes, even crimes they may not have committed. Such plea bargains give detectives big boosts in their clearance rates. Meanwhile, those who plead guilty only to the crime for which they were arrested typically get harsher penalties than those who make false confessions to multiple crimes. Incentives to raise clearance rates are still commonplace, although this use of a numerical measure of police performance undermines just law enforcement—the difficult-to-quantify but true objective of police forces.[13]

As a 1968 presidential candidate, Richard M. Nixon promised a war on crime. After his election, the Federal Bureau of Investigation publicly reported crime statistics by city. The statistic it used to judge whether police departments were effective was the sum of crimes in seven categories considered most important: murder, forcible rape, robbery, aggravated assault, burglary, auto theft, and serious larceny. Serious larceny was defined as theft resulting in a loss in value of at least $50. Many cities subsequently posted significant reductions in crime.

The crime reductions were apparently realized by manipulating crime classifications. The biggest reductions were in larcenies of $50 or more. When police take crime reports, valuing larceny is a matter of judgment, so police placed lower values on losses after accountability was implemented than before. Although the number of alleged $50 larcenies (which counted as serious larceny) declined, the number of alleged $49 larcenies (which did not) increased.[14]

Policemen nationwide acknowledged being ordered to downgrade crime classifications to show progress in their cities' crime index numbers.[15] Donald Campbell concludes: "It seems to be well-documented that a well-publicized, deliberate effort at social change—Nixon's crackdown on crime—had as its main effect the corruption of crime-rate indicators . . . , achieved through underrecording and by downgrading the crimes to less serious classifications."[16]

U.S. News and World Report publishes an annual ranking of colleges. The rankings are truly an accountability system; college boards of trustees may consider the rankings when determining compensation for their presidents.[17] The *U.S. News* rankings are based on several factors, including the judgments of college presidents and other administrators about their peer institutions' quality and how selective a college is, determined partly by the percentage of applicants who are admitted (a more selective college admits a smaller share of applicants). The rankings illustrate Campbell's law because these factors would be quite reasonable if there were no stakes attached to measuring them. College presidents and other administrators are in the best position to know the strengths and weaknesses of institutions similar to their own, and asking for their judgment should be a good way to find out about college quality. But once an accountability rating is based on these answers, presidents have incentives to dissemble, giving competitive institutions poorer ratings to make their own appear superior in comparison.

Similarly, higher-quality colleges are likely to accept relatively fewer applicants because demand for admission is comparatively strong. But once this indicator became an accountability measure, colleges had incentives to boost the number of applicants who would be rejected, for example by sending promotional mailings to unqualified applicants or dropping application fees. The indicator persists in *U.S. News* ratings, although it has now lost considerable validity.[18]

Health Care Report Cards

Health care is an area in which corruption stemming from quantitative accountability has been extensively documented in Great Britain and the United States. Beginning in the late 1980s, both governments (and several American states) hoped to persuade patients to choose more effective care, especially because public funds (Medicare and Medicaid in the United States) might otherwise be wasted. So the governments created "report cards" to compare the extent to which patients of different doctors and hospitals survived open-heart surgery. Goal distortion was one result.

Health care, like education, has multiple goals that providers must balance. For heart patients, one goal is certainly to prolong life and thereby reduce mortality. But a second goal is to respect the wishes of terminally ill patients who choose to avoid artificial life-prolonging technology, hoping for a more dignified experience when death is inevitable. To this end, federal legislation requires hospitals to provide patients with information about living wills. The two goals are always difficult to balance and can be reconciled only by on-site judgment of physicians and families, who weigh subtle factors. Heart surgery report cards undermined this balancing process. By rewarding hospitals for reducing their easily measured mortality rates, the government created incentives to ignore the other goal of respecting the dignity of patients (and avoiding excessive costs incurred when extending an unacceptable quality of life).[19]

Britain's National Health Service also ran up against Campbell's law when it attempted to compare the performance of maternity services, to encourage mothers to use those of higher quality. To this end, the National Health Service published comparative data on providers' perinatal mortality rates—the rate of infant deaths in the period immediately before and after birth. This is certainly the most easily quantifiable outcome of obstetrics. But there are other objectives as well, including reducing the severity of handicaps with which high-risk infants survive and providing a more comfortable and competent experience for pregnant mothers.

These more difficult-to-quantify objectives require maternity services to devote resources to prenatal care. The incentive system, publishing only the quantifiable perinatal mortality rate, affected the way maternity services balanced their efforts between community-based prenatal care and hospital deliveries. With limited resources, maternity services invested less in prenatal care so they could invest more in hospital services. The perinatal mortality rate declined, just as the incentive system intended. But another result was an increase in poor developmental outcomes for live births—more low-birthweight deliveries and more learning difficulties and behavioral problems for children because less attention was paid to prenatal care.[20]

The National Health Service also established a standard that no patient should have to wait more than two years for elective surgery. This created incentives for surgeons to spend more time on surgery and less on postoperative care, which is unmeasured in the accountability system. Such a shift may have reduced overall patient welfare. Because surgical urgency is on a continuum, not neatly divided between elective and urgent procedures, the target for elective surgery caused practitioners to make relatively minor procedures (some cataract surgeries, for example) a greater priority and more serious, but not quite urgent, procedures a lesser priority; in that way, all surgeries could be performed within the target time frame. A consequence was that average waiting times for surgery increased, to achieve the target that all surgeries be performed within two years.[21]

A serious problem facing test-based accountability systems in education is how to adjust for differences in student characteristics. A school with many low-income children, who tend to have serious health problems, high rates of residential mobility, great family stress, and little literacy support at home, may be a better school, even if its test scores are lower, than another whose pupils have fewer such problems. Educators try to get around this by comparing what are considered similar schools—those, for example, with similar proportions of minority students or similar proportions of students who are low income (eligible for the federal free and reduced-price lunch program).

But such adjustments are insufficient. Stable working-class families, with incomes nearly double the poverty line, are eligible for subsidized lunches; schools with such students can easily get higher scores than schools with poorer students, yet the latter may be more effective schools. Charters can enroll minority students whose parents are more highly motivated than neighborhood school parents, leading charters falsely to claim superiority when their test scores are higher.[22]

The difficulty of adjusting for differences in unmeasured background characteristics is not unique to education; it was an important problem identified by Clarence Ridley and Herbert Simon in their 1938 study of municipal functions. In comparing the effectiveness of fire departments in different cities or years, they found, it is impossible to use simple quantitative measures, such as the value of fire losses in a year or the number of fires per capita. From one year or place to another, there might be a change in the amount of burnable property or in the proportion of industrial property, and a more severe winter; "a multitude of other factors beyond the control of the administrator would have an important effect upon the loss rate."[23]

Ridley and Simon consider fire the easiest of municipal activities to measure. Comparisons of police effectiveness, they argue, have to account not only for racial and ethnic differences in populations but also for housing quality, economic conditions, availability of "wholesome recreational facilities," the way courts are administered, and "other intangible factors of civic morale." Evaluation of public health workers' performance has to be adjusted for similar factors, as well as for climate, epidemics, and other chance fluctuations in population health. Construction of a mortality index for measuring the adequacy of public health departments must distinguish "only those diseases which are partly or wholly preventable through public health measures."[24]

Medical care faces similar problems; some patients are sicker and thus harder to cure than others with the same disease. Patients' ages, other diseases, prior treatment, health habits (for example, smoking), diet, and home environment must all be considered. So before outcomes are compared, health care report cards must be "risk-adjusted" for patients' initial conditions. Yet although risk adjustment in medicine is more sophisticated than education's available controls for minority status or free-lunch eligibility, health policy experts still consider their inability to adjust performance comparisons adequately for patient characteristics as a flaw in medical accountability systems.

The U.S. Health Care Financing Administration initiated its accountability system for cardiac surgery in 1986, reporting on death rates of Medicare patients in fifty-five hundred U.S. hospitals. The agency used a complex statistical model to identify hospitals whose death rates after surgery were greater than expected, after accounting for patient characteristics. Yet the institution labeled as having the worst death rate, even after sophisticated risk adjustment, turned out to be a hospice caring for terminally ill patients.[25]

The following year, the Health Care Financing Administration added more patient characteristics to its model. Although the agency now insisted that it adequately adjusted for all critical variables, the ratings invariably resulted in higher adjusted mortality rates for low-income patients in urban hospitals than for affluent patients in suburban hospitals. Campbell's law swung into action: when surveyed, physicians and hospitals admitted that they were refusing to treat sicker patients.[26]

In 1989 New York's St. Vincent's Hospital was put on probation after it placed low in state hospital rankings for cardiac surgery. The next year, it ranked first in the state. St. Vincent's accomplished this feat by refusing to operate on tougher cases.[27] Surgeons' performance numbers were not adversely affected by the deaths of patients who had been denied surgery.

Just as schools are sometimes judged satisfactory according to state ratings but inadequate by No Child Left Behind standards (or vice versa), whether hospitals have high or low mortality rates depends on the particular risk-adjustment formula employed in the ratings. An analysis of gastrointestinal hemorrhage cases in Great Britain has found successive revisions of hospital rankings as additional adjustments for patient characteristics were applied.[28]

In 1991 a team of U.S. health policy researchers reanalyzed federal Medicare data. The researchers obtained additional information on patient characteristics, enabling them to control for even more background factors than did the Medicare system itself. Nearly half of the 187 hospitals that Medicare had identified as having high mortality rates for cardiac surgery, purportedly because of poor quality of care, no longer were in the high mortality group when patient characteristics were more adequately controlled.[29]

Risk adjustment in medical incentive systems has also invited data corruption. Many background characteristics used for risk adjustment must be coded by and collected from the physicians who are themselves being held accountable for risk-adjusted outcomes. Physicians have always used great discretion in their coding. After New York State began reporting death rates from cardiac surgery, the share of cardiac patients reported by physicians to have serious risk factors before surgery rose dramatically: for example, those reported also to suffer from chronic obstructive pulmonary disease more than doubled, and those reported to be suffering from renal failure jumped sevenfold. Since the definitions of many comorbid conditions are not precise, it is unclear to what extent physicians consciously manipulated the data. Nonetheless, 41 percent of New York's reduction in risk-adjusted mortality from cardiac bypass was attributable to the apparently artificial increase ("upcoding") in the reported severity of patients' conditions.[30]

The Medicare performance indicator system was abandoned in 1993. Bruce Vladeck, administrator of the Health Care Financing Administration at the time, conceded that the methodology was flawed. "I think it's overly simplistic," he told an interviewer. "It doesn't adequately adjust for some of the problems faced by inner-city hospitals." Added Jerome Kassirer, then editor-in-chief of the *New England Journal of Medicine,* "The public has a right to know about the quality of its doctors, yet . . . it is irresponsible to release information that is of questionable validity, subject to alternative interpretations, or too technical for a layperson to understand." Kassirer concludes that "no practice profile [that is, physician report card] in use today is adequate to [the] task."[31]

In 1994 the U.S. General Accounting Office published an analysis of health care report cards. Although the federal Medicare report card had been abandoned, several state incentive systems were still in place, as were others that had been devised by private insurers. The office found that no public or private report card had been able to develop a method to adjust for patient characteristics that was "valid and reliable." Kaiser Permanente in Northern California, for example, published a report card that included more than a hundred measures of performance. Yet the General Accounting Office observed that "each performance indicator may need its own separate adjustment because patient characteristics have a unique affect on every condition and disease."[32] Similar problems arise when we attempt to adjust for risk factors in education—for example, family characteristics apparently have a more powerful impact on reading scores than on math scores, the latter being more sensitive to school quality and the former to family intellectual environment.

In 2002, following publicity surrounding mistreatment in nursing homes, the Centers for Medicaid and Medicare Services established a report, the Nursing Home Quality Initiative, requiring nursing homes to report whether they adhered to fifteen recognized quality standards—such as the percentage of residents who have pressure sores (from being turned in bed infrequently). These public reports were intended to give consumers information about relative quality.

However, nursing home administrators and nurses caring for the elderly must balance many more than these fifteen aspects of quality. For example, because nurses' time is limited, spending more time turning patients in bed (a Nursing Home Quality Initiative standard) may leave them less time to maintain hygienic standards by washing their hands regularly (not a Nursing Home Quality Initiative standard). Although the initiative, intended to be easily understood by consumers, is limited to fifteen standards, the Centers for Medicaid and Medicare Services monitors some 190 measures (such as hand washing) on a checklist when it inspects nursing homes for purposes of certifying eligibility for Medicaid or Medicare reimbursement. Following the introduction of the Nursing Home Quality Initiative, performance on the fifteen selected indicators improved, but adherence to the 190 standards overall declined, resulting in more citations for violations issued by the Centers for Medicaid and Medicare Services.[33] As the General Accounting Office had observed in its 1994 review of health care report cards, "Administrators will place all their organizations' resources in areas that are being measured. Areas that are not highlighted in report cards will be ignored."[34]

In 2003 a team of American economists published an analysis of health care report cards. Their paper concludes that report cards on health care providers "may give doctors and hospitals incentives to decline to treat more difficult, severely ill patients." The accountability system has "led to higher levels of resource use [because delaying surgery for sicker patients necessitates more expensive treatment later] and to worse outcomes, particularly for sicker patients. . . . At least in the short run, these report cards decreased patient and social welfare."[35]

One of the paper's authors was Mark McClellan, a member of President George W. Bush's Council of Economic Advisers when No Child Left Behind was designed and implemented. The paper concludes that although report cards advertise that some hospitals had dramatically better outcomes, "on net, these changes were particularly harmful. . . . Report cards on the performance of schools raise the same issues and therefore also need empirical evaluation."[36]

Dr. McClellan subsequently served as administrator of the Centers for Medicare and Medicaid Services from 2004 to 2006. Apparently ignoring McClellan's earlier conclusions, the federal government reinstituted Medicare accountability report cards in 2007, publishing the names of forty-one hospitals with higher-than-expected death rates for heart attack patients. The government plans next to add a report card for pneumonia. Michael Leavitt, then secretary of health and human services, acknowledged that the list of failing hospitals is still imperfectly adjusted for patient characteristics but promised that "it will get nothing but better as time goes on." Also ignoring McClellan's and his colleagues' conclusions, as of late 2006 six states continued to publish their own report cards on cardiac surgery mortality rates in their hospitals, and three published performance reports for individual surgeons.[37]

Accountability in Job Training and Welfare

In a 1955 study, the organizational sociologist Peter M. Blau described a state employment agency that registered jobless workers for benefits and for assistance in finding new jobs. He described how the state initially attempted to hold caseworkers accountable by rating them according to the number of interviews they conducted. But this resulted in goal displacement, giving caseworkers incentives to sacrifice quality for speed. So the state added seven new quantitative indicators, including the number of job referrals and actual placements and the ratio of placements to interviews. Even these quantitative indicators were still deemed insufficient to balance all aspects of effective performance, so the agency prohibited supervisors from basing more than 40 percent of an employee's evaluation on quantitative indicators.[38]

The government has frequently attempted to impose accountability systems on job training and welfare agencies that use federal funds. As in health care, Campbell's law usually wins out: the reliance on quantitative indicators distorts and corrupts the agency functions that these indicators hope to monitor.

Under the Job Training Partnership Act of 1982, the government offered financial rewards to agencies that had better records of placing workers in jobs. The Department of Labor defined successful placements as those that lasted at least ninety days. This created incentives for agencies to place workers in low-skilled and short-term jobs that might last not much longer than ninety days. Training for long-term stable employment required more resources, and success rates were somewhat lower, although placement in long-term stable employment was an important though unmeasured goal of the act.

In some cases, job training agencies provided special services to support employment, such as child care, transportation, or clothing allowances. Such services were terminated after the ninetieth day of employment. Similarly, case managers followed up with employers, urging them to keep recent trainees on the payroll. Such follow-up often also ended on the ninetieth day. Before the Job Training Partnership Act established a ninety-day standard for measuring performance, these practices were rare.[39]

The federal program could have reduced goal distortion by extending the monitoring program beyond ninety days, but the Department of Labor could not afford the additional expense. James Heckman, a Nobel laureate in economics, concluded that the Job Training Partnership Act's "performance standards based on short-term outcome levels likely do little to encourage the provision of services to those who benefit most from them."[40]

Gaming the System

In education, high-stakes testing has led to gaming by administrators and teachers. Teaching narrow curricular areas expected to be tested rather than teaching to the full domain, classifying students in subgroups where they do the least harm to proficiency percentages, and suspending low-scoring students during testing periods are among the corruptions of education that scholars have observed. In job training, the ninety-day employment standard also created opportunities for gaming of the accountability system. Outcomes in the reward system were counted only for job seekers actually enrolled in a training program. This gave agencies an incentive to train clients informally, waiting to formally enroll trainees until they were certain to find employment. In other cases, since outcomes were measured ninety days after the end of formal training, agencies failed to graduate and continued "training" some clients who had little hope of finding employment, long after any hope for success had evaporated. Such gaming behavior continued under the Workforce Investment Act of 1998, the successor to the Job Training Partnership Act. As the General Accounting Office observed, "The lack of a uniform understanding of when registration occurs and thus who should be counted toward the measures raises questions about both the accuracy and comparability of states' performance data."[41]

The accountability plans of both the Workforce Investment Act and its predecessor required local agencies to demonstrate continuous performance improvement each year. As with education's No Child Left Behind, the law recognized that conditions differed from state to state, so states were permitted to establish their own target levels. As a result, many states established deliberately low initial targets for their training agencies, to ensure more room for subsequent improvement.[42] This too anticipated states' behavior in education: many states attempted to meet No Child Left Behind proficiency standards by defining proficiency at a level far below "challenging." Public administration theory refers to this behavior as the *ratchet effect,* a term taken from analyses of similar behavior in the Soviet economy when factory managers deliberately slowed production so that planners would not increase the following year's quota to more difficult levels.

Adjusting for Background Differences

As in health care, an inability to adequately adjust performance expectations for background differences has also frustrated accountability designs in job training programs. In any accountability system, no matter how carefully subgroups are defined, professionals who have direct contact with clients will always know more detail than policymakers about client characteristics and will be able to game the system. This is certainly true in schools, where teachers know more about their students' potential than administrators or policymakers can infer from prior test scores and a few demographic markers. In health care, Mark McClellan and his colleagues observe, "Doctors and hospitals likely have more detailed information about patients' health than the developer of a report card can, allowing them to choose to treat unobservably (to the analyst) healthier patients."[43]

Accountability in the Private Sector

Calls for test-based accountability systems in education are frequently accompanied by claims that this is the way it is done in the private sector. Such demands for accountability are usually accompanied by proposals for incentive pay, whereby teachers and principals of students with high test scores earn higher salaries. When New York City mayor Michael Bloomberg announced in 2007 a teachers union agreement to pay cash bonuses to teachers at schools whose test scores rose, he said, "In the private sector, cash incentives are proven motivators for producing results. The most successful employees work harder, and everyone else tries to figure out how they can improve as well." Eli Broad, whose foundation promotes incentive pay plans for teachers, added, "Virtually every other industry compensates employees based on how well they perform. . . . We know from experience across other industries and sectors that linking performance and pay is a powerful incentive."[44]

Such claims misrepresent how private sector firms motivate employees. Although incentive pay systems are commonplace, they are almost never based exclusively, or even primarily, on quantitative output measurement for professionals. Indeed, though the share of private sector workers who get performance pay has been increasing, the share who get such pay based on numerical output measures has been decreasing. There has been a decline in commissions and piece rates for sales and production workers, along with a growth in performance pay for employees who get bonuses based largely on subjective supervisory evaluations.[45] The business management literature nowadays is filled with warnings about incentives that rely heavily on quantitative rather than qualitative measures.[46]

In general, business organizations use quantitative performance measures warily and almost never exclusively. Like teaching or other employment in the public sector, most private sector jobs include a composite of more and less easily measured responsibilities. Adding multiple measures of accountability is, by itself, insufficient to minimize goal distortion.

For example, one of the nation's largest banks determined to reward branch managers not only for short-term branch financials but also for other measures that contributed to long-term profitability, such as customer satisfaction as determined by an independent survey of customers who visited bank branches. One manager boosted his ratings, and thus his bonuses, by serving free food and drinks, but this did nothing to boost the bank's long-term financial prospects.[47]

Multiple measures are also no panacea because if the weighting (the relative importance) of each measure in the accountability system is not explicit and well justified, there will likely be a tendency over time to increase the weights of quantitative measures, relative to qualitative ones, because the former seem superficially to be more objective and take much less time and effort to collect. Thus over time the bank's measurement system came increasingly to rely on short-term branch financial results that the multiple measures had been intended to dilute.[48]

Because of the ease with which most employees game purely quantitative incentives, most private sector accountability systems blend quantitative and qualitative measures, with most emphasis on the latter. McDonald's, for example, does not evaluate its store managers by sales volume or profitability alone. Instead, a manager and his or her supervisor establish targets for easily quantifiable measures such as sales volume and costs but also the less easily quantifiable product quality, service, cleanliness, and personnel training, because these factors may affect long-term profitability as well as the reputation (and thus profitability) of other outlets. Store managers are judged by the negotiated balance of these various factors. Wal-Mart uses a similar system. A practice of negotiating quantitative and qualitative performance goals is also common for professionals in the private sector.[49]

Certainly, supervisory evaluations of employees are less reliable than objective, quantitative indicators. Supervisory evaluations may be tainted by favoritism, bias, inflation and compression (that is, narrowing the range of evaluations to avoid penalizing or rewarding too many employees), and even kickbacks or other forms of corruption. The apparent correlation between labor market success and employees' physical attractiveness confirms that supervisory evaluations are flawed tools for objective evaluations of performance. Yet the fact that subjective evaluations are so widely used, despite these flaws, suggests that, as one personnel management review concludes, "it is better to imperfectly measure relevant dimensions than to perfectly measure irrelevant ones." Or, in the words of the Harvard Business School professor George Baker, "The prevalence of subjectivity in the performance measurement systems of virtually all [business] organizations suggests that exclusive reliance on distorted and risky objective measures is not an efficient alternative."[50]

Management of accountability systems in the private sector is labor intensive. Bain and Company, the management consulting firm, advises clients that judgment of results should always focus on long-term, not short-term (and more easily quantifiable), goals. A company director estimated that at Bain itself, each manager devotes about a hundred hours a year to evaluating five employees for purposes of its incentive pay system. "When I try to imagine a school principal doing 30 reviews, I have trouble," he has observed.[51]

Most private (as well as public) sector jobs have outcomes that are partially attributable to individual effort and partially attributable to group effort. For this reason, contrary to Eli Broad's claim, individual merit pay plans are relatively rare in the private sector; the greater the relative proportion attributable to group effort, the rarer are individual incentives. Even in manufacturing, piece rate systems are not the rule because they create incentives for workers "to shift their attention from the team activity where their individual contributions are poorly measured to the better measured and well-compensated individual activity."[52]

A widespread business reform in recent decades, known as total quality management and promoted by W. Edwards Deming, warns that businesses seeking to improve quality and thus long-term performance should do away with work standards (quotas), eliminate management by numbers and numerical goals, and abolish merit ratings and the practice of management by objective, because all of these encourage employees to focus on short-term results. "Management by numerical goal is an attempt to manage without knowledge of what to do, and in fact is usually management by fear," Deming insists. Only good (subjective) leadership, not restricted to mechanical and quantitative judgment, can maximize long-term results.[53]

Also first proposed in the early 1990s, a now-popular corporate accountability tool is the balanced scorecard conceived by management theorists who conclude that quantifiable short-term financial results are not accurate guides to future profitability. Firms' goals were too complex to be reduced to a few quantifiable measures, which generally refer only to past performance, while future performance relies not only on a track record of financial success but also on "intangible and intellectual assets, such as high quality products and services, motivated and skilled employees, responsive and predictable internal processes, and satisfied and loyal customers." Each of these should be incorporated, and measured if possible, in an organizational accountability system. In the balanced scorecard approach to business accountability, corporate leaders supplement quantifiable measures with judgments about the quality of organizational process, staff quality and morale, and customer satisfaction. Evaluation of a firm's performance should be "balanced between objective, easily quantifiable outcome measures and subjective, somewhat judgmental, performance drivers of the outcome measures."[54]

For "best-practice firms" employing the balanced scorecard approach, the use of subjective judgments reflects a belief that results-based compensation may not always be the ideal scheme for rewarding managers [because] many factors not under the control or influence of managers also affect reported performance [and] many managerial actions create (or destroy) economic value but may not be measured.[55]

Curiously, the federal government uses a balanced scorecard approach, simultaneously with its quantitative outcome-focused Government Performance Results Act and its exclusively quantitatively based No Child Left Behind Act. Each year since 1988, the U.S. Department of Commerce has given Malcolm Baldrige National Quality Awards to exemplary institutions in manufacturing and other business sectors. Numerical output indicators play only a small role in the department's award decisions: for the private sector, 450 out of 1,000 points are for results, although even here, some results, such as ethical behavior, social responsibility, trust in senior leadership, workforce capability and capacity, and customer satisfaction and loyalty, are based on points awarded for qualitative judgments. Other criteria, which also rely on qualitative evaluation, make up the other 550 points, such as "how . . . senior leaders set organizational vision and values" and "protection of stakeholder and stockholder interests, as appropriate."[56] The Department of Commerce concluded that Baldrige principles of private sector quality could be applied as well to health and education institutions, so these were added to the reward system in 1999. In assessing educational institutions, only 100 of 1,000 points are awarded for student learning outcomes, with other points awarded for subjectively evaluated measures, such as "how senior leaders' personal actions reflect a commitment to the organization's values."[57]

The most recent Baldrige award in elementary and secondary education went in 2005 to the Jenks, Oklahoma, school district. In making this award, the Department of Commerce cited the district's test scores as well as low teacher turnover and innovative programs such as an exchange relationship with schools in China and the enlistment of residents of a local long-term care facility to mentor kindergartners and prekindergartners. Yet in 2006 the Jenks district was deemed by the federal Department of Education to be substandard under the provisions of No Child Left Behind, because Jenks's economically disadvantaged and special education students failed for two consecutive years to make "adequate yearly progress" in reading as determined by test scores.[58] Policies of the federal Departments of Commerce and Education are incoherent, at best.

That exclusively quantitative accountability systems result in goal distortion, gaming, and corruption in a wide variety of fields is not inconsistent with a conclusion that such systems nonetheless improve average performance. How much gain in reading and math scores is necessary to offset the goal distortion—less art, music, physical education, science, history, character building—that inevitably results from rewarding teachers or schools for score gains only in math and reading? How much misidentification of high- or low-performing teachers or schools is tolerable in order to improve their average performance? How much curricular corruption are we willing to endure when we engage in, as one frequently cited work in the business management literature puts it, "the folly of rewarding A while hoping for B"?[59]

Several of the analyses by economists, management experts, and sociologists cited in this chapter conclude that narrowly quantitative incentive schemes have, at times, somewhat improved the average performance of medical care, job training, welfare, and private sector agents. The documentation of perverse consequences does not indicate that, in any particular case, the harm outweighs the benefits of such narrow quantitative accountability. The Soviet Union did, after all, industrialize from a feudal society in record time.

The General Accounting Office, while condemning the perverse incentives resulting from report cards in health care, nonetheless concludes, "We support the report card concept and encourage continued development in the field." Performance incentive plans in medicine, both in the United States and Great Britain, did improve average outcomes in many respects, including cardiac surgery survival rates, the most frequently analyzed procedure. Accountability for waiting times for elective surgery in Great Britain did reduce average waiting times, notwithstanding some other perverse consequences. One careful analysis of emergency room waiting times in Great Britain was unable to find evidence of perverse consequences expected from a narrow quantitative incentive. It could be, the authors conclude, that "it is better to manage an organization using imperfect measures than using none at all."[60]

However, these are not the only alternatives. It is possible, indeed practical, to design an accountability system in education to ensure that educators meet their responsibilities to deliver the broad range of outcomes that the American people demand without relying exclusively on measures as imperfect as test scores. Such a system would be more expensive than our current regime of low-quality standardized tests, and it would not give policymakers the comfortable, though false, precision that they expect quantitative measures like test scores to provide.

Notes

1. Herbert A. Simon, "Rational Decision-Making in Business Organizations" (Nobel Memorial Lecture, December 8, 1978), pp. 352, 366.
2. Clarence E. Ridley and Herbert A. Simon, *Measuring Municipal Activities: A Survey of Suggested Criteria for Appraising Administration* (Chicago: International City Managers Association, 1943), pp. vii, 2. Citations are to the 1943 edition.
3. Ibid., pp. 47–48, 26.
4. Ibid., pp. 43, 45.
5. Donald T. Campbell, "Assessing the Impact of Planned Social Change," *Evaluation and Program Planning* 2 (1979): 67–90, p. 85.
6. James Q. Wilson, *Bureaucracy: What Government Agencies Do and Why They Do It* (New York: Basic Books, 1989), p. 117.
7. Alexander Nove, "Economic Irrationality and Irrational Statistics," in *Economic Rationality and Soviet Politics; or, Was Stalin Really Necessary?* edited by Alexander Nove (London, 1964), pp. 286–99, specifically pp. 294 and 289; P. M. Mullen, "Performance Indicators: Is Anything New?" *Hospital and Health Services Review* (July 1985): 165–67; see p. 165.
8. Mullen, "Performance Indicators: Is Anything New?" p. 165.
9. Martin West, "Testing, Learning, and Teaching: The Effects of Test-Based Accountability on Student Achievement and Instructional Time in Core Academic Subjects," in *Beyond the Basics: Achieving a Liberal Education for All Children,* edited by Chester E. Finn Jr. and Diane Ravitch (Washington: Thomas B. Fordham Institute, 2007), pp. 45–61; see p. 57.
10. Campbell, "Assessing the Impact of Planned Social Change," p. 86.
11. W. Edwards Deming, *Out of the Crisis* (Cambridge, Mass.: MIT, Center for Advanced Engineering Study, 1986), p. 104; Mark A. Uhlig, "Transit Police Remove Officer for Quota Plan," *New York Times,* December 21, 1987; Tom Jackman, "Falls Church Police Must Meet Quota for Tickets," *Washington Post,* August 8, 2004, p. C1; Solomon Moore, "In California, Deputies Held Competition on Arrests," *New York Times,* October 5, 2007, p. A16.
12. Jerome H. Skolnick, *Justice without Trial: Law Enforcement in Democratic Society* (New York: Wiley, 1966), p. 164.
13. Ibid., pp. 176, 181.
14. David Seidman and Michael Couzens, "Getting the Crime Rate Down: Political Pressure and Crime Reporting," *Law and Society Review* 8, no. 3 (1974):457–94, p. 462.
15. W. R. Morrissey, "Nixon Anti-Crime Plan Undermines Crime Statistics," *Justice Magazine* 5–6 (June–July 1972): 8–14; Roger Twigg, "Downgrading of Crimes Verified in Baltimore," *Justice Magazine* 5–6 (June–July 1972): 15–19.
16. Campbell, "Assessing the Impact of Planned Social Change," p. 85 (citations in text omitted).
17. Scott Jaschik, "Should U.S. News Make Presidents Rich?" *U.S. News and World Report,* March 19, 2007 (www.insidehighered.com/news/2007/03/19/usnews).
18. Alan Finder, "College Ratings Race Roars on Despite Concerns," *New York Times,* August 17, 2007.
19. Jesse Green, Leigh J. Passman, and Neil Wintfeld, "Analyzing Hospital Mortality: The Consequences of Diversity in Patient Mix," *Journal of the American Medical Association* 265 (1991): 1849–53, p. 1853.
20. Peter Smith, "Outcome-Related Performance Indicators and Organizational Control in the Public Sector," *British Journal of Management* 4 (September 1993): 135–51, p. 141–42.

21. Ibid., pp. 146–47; Maria Goddard, Russell Mannion, and Peter C. Smith, "The Performance Framework: Taking Account of Economic Behaviour," in *Reforming Markets in Health Care*, edited by P. C. Smith (Buckingham, U.K.: Open University Press, 2000), pp. 139–61, 141–42, 149; Peter Smith, "On the Unintended Consequences of Publishing Performance Data in the Public Sector," *International Journal of Public Administration* 18, nos. 2–3 (1995): 277–310, p. 291.

22. Martin Carnoy and others, *The Charter School Dust-Up: Examining the Evidence on Enrollment and Achievement* (Teachers College Press, 2005).

23. Ridley and Simon, *Measuring Municipal Activities*, p. 3.

24. Ibid., pp. 10, 17, 28.

25. Lisa I. Iezzoni, "Risk and Outcomes," in *Risk Adjustment for Measuring Health Care Outcomes*, edited by Lisa I. Iezzoni (Ann Arbor, Mich.: Health Administration Press, 1994), pp. 1–28, 4.

26. Allen Schick, "Getting Performance Measures to Measure Up," in *Quicker, Better, Cheaper: Managing Performance in American Government*, edited by Dall W. Forsythe (Albany, N.Y.: Rockefeller Institute Press, 2001), pp. 39–60, 41; Lawrence P. Casalino and others, "General Internists' Views on Pay-for-Performance and Public Reporting of Quality Scores: A National Survey," *Health Affairs* 26, no. 2 (2007): 492–99, p. 495.

27. Marc Santora, "Cardiologists Say Rankings Sway Choices on Surgery," *New York Times*, January 11, 2005; Casalino and others, "General Internists' Views on Pay-for-Performance," p. 496; Lawrence K. Altman, "Heart-Surgery Death Rates Decline in New York," *New York Times*, December 5, 1990.

28. Martin McKee, "Discussion," in "League Tables and Their Limitations: Statistical Issues in Comparisons of Institutional Performance (with Discussion)," edited by Harvey Goldstein and David J. Spiegelhalter, *Journal of the Royal Statistical Society, Series A (Statistics in Society)* 3, no. 159 (1996): 385–443, p. 430; Lisa I. Iezzoni and others, "Using Severity-Adjusted Stroke Mortality Rates to Judge Hospitals," *International Journal for Quality in Health Care* 7, no. 2 (1995): 81–94.

29. Green, Passman, and Wintfeld, "Analyzing Hospital Mortality," p. 1852; Henry Krakauer and others, "Evaluation of the HCFA Model for the Analysis of Mortality Following Hospitalization," *Health Services Research* 27, no. 3 (1992): 317–35, p. 330.

30. U.S. General Accounting Office (GAO), *Health Care Reform: "Report Cards" Are Useful but Significant Issues Need to Be Addressed*, GAO/HEHS 94-219 (September 1994), p. 38; Martin McKee and Duncan Hunter, "What Can Comparisons of Hospital Death Rates Tell Us about the Quality of Care?" in *Outcomes into Clinical Practice*, edited by Tony Delamothe (London: British Medical Journal Press, 1994), pp. 108–15, 112; Smith, "Outcome-Related Performance Indicators," p. 148; Jesse Green and Neil Wintfeld, "Report Cards on Cardiac Surgeons: Assessing New York State's Approach," *New England Journal of Medicine* 332, no. 18 (1995): 1129–33, table 1; Arnold Epstein, "Performance Reports on Quality: Prototypes, Problems, and Prospects," *New England Journal of Medicine* 333, no. 1 (1995): pp. 57–61.

31. Associated Press, "Rating of Hospitals Is Delayed on Ground of Flaws in Data," *New York Times*, June 23, 1993; Jerome P. Kassirer, "The Use and Abuse of Practice Profiles," *New England Journal of Medicine* 330, vol. 9 (1994): 634–36.

32. GAO, *Health Care Reform: "Report Cards,"* pp. 5–6, 26, 42.

33. Susan Feng Lu, "Multitasking, Information Disclosure, and Product Quality: Evidence from Nursing Homes," Kellogg Institute, November 15, 2007 (www.kellogg.northwestern.edu/faculty/lu/multitasking.pdf).

34. GAO, *Health Care Reform: "Report Cards,"* p. 55.

35. David Dranove and others, "Is More Information Better? The Effects of 'Report Cards' on Health Care Providers," *Journal of Political Economy* 111, no. 3 (2003):555–88, pp. 555–56, 577.

36. Ibid., p. 583–85.

37. Gardiner Harris, "Report Rates Hospitals on Their Heart Treatment," *New York Times,* June 22, 2007; Robert Steinbrook, "Public Report Cards: Cardiac Surgery and Beyond," *New England Journal of Medicine* 355, no. 18 (2006): 1847–49.

38. Peter Michael Blau, *The Dynamics of Bureaucracy: A Study of Interpersonal Relations in Two Government Agencies,* rev. ed. (University of Chicago Press, 1963), pp. 38–42, 45–46.

39. Burt S. Barnow and Jeffrey A. Smith, "Performance Management of U.S. Job Training Programs: Lessons from the Job Training Partnership Act," *Public Finance and Management* 4, no. 3 (2004): 247–87, pp. 271–72.

40. Pascal Courty, Carolyn Heinrich, and Gerald Marschke, "Setting the Standard in Performance Measurement Systems," *International Public Management Journal* 8, no. 3 (2005): 321–47, p. 338; Brian Stecher and Sheila Nataraj Kirby, eds., *Organizational Improvement and Accountability. Lessons for Education from Other Sectors,* report prepared for the William and Flora Hewlett Foundation (Santa Monica, Calif.: RAND) (www.rand.org/pubs/monographs/2004/RAND_MG136.pdf [2004]), p. 384; James J. Heckman, Carolyn Heinrich, and Jeffrey Smith, "The Performance of Performance Standards," *Journal of Human Resources* 37, no. 4 (2002): 778–811, p. 808; Ann Blalock and Burt Barnow, "Is the New Obsession with 'Performance Management' Masking the Truth about Social Programs?" in *Quicker, Better, Cheaper: Managing Performance in American Government,* edited by Forsythe, pp. 485–518, 505.

41. Barnow and Smith, "Performance Management of U.S. Job Training Programs," pp. 269–70; GAO, *Workforce Investment Act: Improvements Needed in Performance Measures to Provide a More Accurate Picture of WIA's Effectiveness,* GAO-02-275 (February 2002), p. 17.

42. Courty, Heinrich, and Marschke, "Setting the Standard in Performance Measurement Systems," p. 331, 341–42.

43. Dranove and others, "Is More Information Better?" p. 581.

44. Quoted in Elissa Gootman, "Teachers Agree to Bonus Pay Tied to Scores," *New York Times,* October 18, 2007 (www.nytimes.com/2007/10/18/education/18schools.html?scp=1& sq=Teachers%20Agree%20to%20Bonus%20Pay&st=cse); Michael Bloomberg, Mayor's Press Release 375, October 17, 2007 (www.nyc.gov/html/om/html/2007b/pr375-07.html [January 2008]).

45. Scott J. Adams, John S. Heywood, and Richard Rothstein, *Teachers, Performance Pay, and Accountability* (Economic Policy Institute, 2009), tables 2 and 7.

46. When this chapter distinguishes quantitative from qualitative measures, it describes as quantitative only those, such as test scores or production, in which data are typically presented in numerical form in the first instance. This chapter does not suggest that qualitative evaluations cannot also be expressed in quantitative form. Thus a supervisor's evaluation, although based on judgment rather than an employee's measurable output, can be expressed as a numerical rating. Accountability systems that combine quantitative and qualitative measures can still rank employees or institutions in numerical order, and many do so.

47. Christopher D. Ittner and David F. Larcker, "Coming Up Short on Nonfinancial Performance Measurement," *Harvard Business Review* 81, no. 11 (2003): 88–95, p. 89.

48. Christopher D. Ittner, David F. Larcker, and Marshall W. Meyer, "Performance, Compensation, and the Balanced Scorecard," University of Pennsylvania, Wharton School, November 1, 1997 (knowledge.wharton.upenn.edu/papers/405.pdf), pp. 23–24.

49. Robert S. Kaplan and Anthony A. Atkinson, *Advanced Management Accounting,* 3rd ed. (Englewood Cliffs, N.J.: Prentice-Hall, 1998), p. 692–93; Richard Rothstein, "Making a Case against Performance Pay," *New York Times,* April 26, 2000.

50. Ittner, Larcker, and Meyer, "Performance, Compensation, and the Balanced Scorecard," p. 9; Daniel S. Hamermesh and Jeff E. Biddle, "Beauty and the Labor Market," *American Economic Review* 84, no. 5 (1994): 1174–94; William H. Bommer and others, "On the Interchangeability of Objective and Subjective Measures of Employee Performance: A Meta-Analysis," *Personnel Psychology* 48, no. 3 (1995): 587–605, p. 602; George Baker, "Distortion and Risk in Optimal Performance Contracts," *Journal of Human Resources* 37, no. 4 (2002): 728–51, p. 750.

51. Rothstein, "Making a Case against Performance Pay."

52. Bengt Holmstrom and Paul Milgrom, "Multitask Principal-Agent Analyses: Incentive Contracts, Asset Ownership, and Job Design," special issue, *Journal of Law, Economics, and Organization* 7 (1991): 24–52, p. 35.

53. Deming, *Out of the Crisis,* pp. 76, 101–02; see also Jeffrey Pfeffer, "Six Dangerous Myths about Pay," *Harvard Business Review* 76, no. 3 (1998): 108–119; and W. Edwards Deming Institute, "Teachings," 2007 (www.deming.org/theman/teachings02.html).

54. Kaplan and Atkinson, *Advanced Management Accounting,* p. 368; Schick, "Getting Performance Measures to Measure Up," p. 50.

55. Robert S. Kaplan and David P. Norton, *The Balanced Scorecard: Translating Strategy into Action* (Harvard Business School Press, 1996), p. 220.

56. For a discussion, see Stecher and Kirby, *Organizational Improvement and Accountability;* and Baldrige National Quality Program, "Criteria for Performance Excellence" (U.S. Department of Commerce, National Institute of Standards and Technology, 2007) (www.quality.nist.gov/PDF_files/2007_Business_Nonprofit_Criteria.pdf).

57. Baldrige National Quality Program, "Education Criteria for Performance Excellence" (U.S. Department of Commerce, National Institute of Standards and Technology, 2007) (www.quality.nist.gov/PDF_files/2007_Education_Criteria.pdf).

58. Baldrige National Quality Program, "2005 Award Winner" (U.S. Department of Commerce, National Institute of Standards and Technology, 2007) (www.quality.nist.gov/PDF_files/Jenks_Public_Schools_Profile.pdf); Shaun Epperson, "Jenks School Misses NCLB Standard," *Tulsa World,* November 14, 2007.

59. Steven Kerr, "On the Folly of Rewarding A While Hoping for B," *Academy of Management Journal* 18, no. 4 (1975): 769–83.

60. GAO, *Health Care Reform: "Report Cards,"* p. 56; Goddard, Mannion, and Smith, "The Performance Framework," p. 141; Gwyn Bevan and Christopher Hood, "What's Measured Is What Matters: Targets and Gaming in the English Public Health Care System," *Public Administration* 84, no. 3 (2006): 517–38 , pp. 526–27; Steven Kelman and John N. Friedman, "Performance Improvement and Performance Dysfunction: An Empirical Examination of Impacts of the Emergency Room Wait-Time Target in the English National Health Service," Working Paper RWP07-034 (Cambridge, Mass.: Kennedy School of Government Faculty Research, August 2007).

PART TWO

Incentive System Design and Measurement

6

Turning Student Test Scores into Teacher Compensation Systems

Daniel F. McCaffrey, Bing Han, and J. R. Lockwood

A key component to the new wave of performance-based pay initiatives that is sweeping across the country is the use of student achievement data to evaluate teacher performance. The requirements of the No Child Left Behind Act have resulted in the testing of greater numbers of students than ever before. Annual testing in grades 3 to 8 and in one high school grade has yielded longitudinal data on students. While greater amounts of data are being collected, researchers have been developing and applying innovative statistical and econometric models to the longitudinal data to develop measures of individual teachers' contributions to their students' learning.[1] Generally referred to as value added models, this class of models has found significant variation among teachers in their performance and has demonstrated that this variation is a significant source of variation in student outcomes.[2]

The reputation of value added models for providing fair comparisons of teachers has fostered a belief that such models can validly support pay-for-performance systems. However, most value added research to date has focused on the statistical prop-

This chapter is based on work supported by the U.S. Department of Education Institute of Education Sciences under R305A060034. All opinions, findings, conclusions, and recommendations expressed here are those of the authors and do not necessarily reflect the views of any sponsoring organization.

erties of the measures from the perspective of methodological research rather than from the perspective of an algorithm that translates raw administrative data on students and teachers into dollars provided to individual people. The latter perspective forces consideration of many complex issues that are often taken for granted in pure methodological research and thus have not yet been given sufficient deliberation.

The Logic of Performance-Based Pay and Implications for Developing the System

Performance-based compensation systems are proposed as a means of motivating teachers to higher levels of performance and enticing the most capable to join and remain in the profession.[3] The logic of a performance pay or bonus system implicit in its operation is that by rewarding teachers who are performing well, the system demonstrates high and low performance standards to teachers and identifies high-performing teachers. On the basis of that information, low-performing teachers may work to improve their performance, motivated by financial incentives and the knowledge that their performance is low, or they may decide to leave teaching should they find the cost of improving is too great. The logic of performance-based pay assumes that increased compensation will encourage high-performing teachers to continue their effective practices and entice them to remain in the profession. Thus the basic logic of performance pay is that the results of the system (that is, the dollar awards teachers receive) provide implicit signals to teachers about their performance and that they will respond to this information on the basis of personal and financial incentives. These implicit signals are not directly communicated to participants but may be implied in the workings of the system.

A performance compensation system also has explicit signals. Explicit signals are specific and detailed standards that are clearly expressed to participants. These are the rules used to measure performance and to determine how those measures translate into financial compensation. When teachers evaluate the signal of their financial reward and consider changing their behaviors, they will look to these explicit signals to understand what they need to do to maintain or improve their performance. Thus both the rules and the outcomes of the system give signals to teachers about what they need to do to be successful and receive financial rewards.

Teachers' evaluations of the entire system are also critical for its success. Teachers will respond to the system only when they believe the system provides fair, reliable, and accurate measures of their performance and compensation commensurate with their perceptions of their own and their colleagues' performance; they believe the measures used by the system will be responsive to their actions; and they value the student outcomes measured by the system. Teachers will evaluate the rules and outcomes of the system to determine whether they meet these requirements. Such considerations pertain to current teachers as well as the prospective teachers that proponents of performance-based compensation argue such systems will attract to the profession.

Creating the Student Achievement Database

The process of compensating teachers on the basis of their students' achievement begins with the task of creating a database linking the achievement of students with their teachers. The importance and inherent challenges of this first step are often overlooked, and it is taken for granted that clean data appropriate for analysis already exist and will be used for the estimation of effects and the final bonus decisions. In our experience, administrative data, even from good systems, require extensive processing before they can be used to generate performance measures. The processing can affect both the explicit and implicit signals provided by the system in possibly contradictory ways and will require making decisions that balance the competing objectives of these two types of signals.

Selecting Teachers for a Performance-Pay Program

One of the first tasks is to determine which teachers are eligible for bonuses and what courses are to be included when a teacher's performance is measured. Policymakers would like every teacher to be eligible for a bonus, regardless of teaching responsibilities. This ideal is unlikely to be feasible for systems designed to award performance measured by student achievement tests, however, because for many subjects and for some grade levels such testing does not exist. Hence the use of the standard accountability test data as the basis for compensation decisions requires that the program be restricted to teachers instructing tested subjects and grades. Moreover, if prior test scores are to be used in measuring performance, then bonuses will need to be restricted to teachers in grades after the first grade of testing.

Tested grades and subjects, however, are not sufficient to determine which teachers to evaluate according to the student achievement database. Teaching involves a complex array of tasks that vary by the numbers of students taught, the grade levels of the students, the courses being taught, and the relationship of those courses to the tests. This complexity results in indeterminacies about which teachers to include in the sample, and resolving these indeterminacies requires choices that can affect the explicit and implicit signals of the system.

Clearly the signals provide information about each individual teacher's tasks; but perhaps less obvious is that they also provide information about the peer group used in normative evaluation of teacher performance and compensation decisions.[4] Educators, policymakers, and researchers do not generally have an objective standard for evaluating teacher performance. Rather, performance measures typically implicitly define a teacher's contribution to student learning by comparing student outcomes when taught by the teacher to counterfactual outcomes that would have occurred under alternative conditions.[5]

The counterfactual used to define teacher contributions to learning is often tacitly chosen by the analytic procedures used to create a performance measure. Common reference points are the average performance for students across teachers in a district or state.[6] Many statistical models include parameters for district mean by grade level so that the comparison is with the performance of the average teacher in the district at the same grade level. Methods that use data from the entire state to estimate expected performance use the average performance across teachers from the entire state as the point of reference.[7]

Compensation decisions also typically involve comparing performance among teachers combined into a peer group (for example, all middle school mathematics teachers). The Florida Special Teachers Are Rewarded system proposed creating awards for teachers in the top quintile of their peer group in the state.[8] In other programs, awards are based on comparisons of teachers with statistical populations—for example, awarding bonuses to all teachers whose students score above the 80th percentile of an appropriately scaled normal distribution.

In any of these methods for measuring performance or awarding compensation, the choice of the peer groups can be significant. Changing the teachers included in a peer group can change a teacher's performance measure and how that measure is valued. Different groups can be used in estimation and compensation decisions, but the decision of which teachers to evaluate on a specific subject and include in the population needs to be carefully considered relative to the goals of the system and the performance measure to be used.

EXPLICIT SIGNALS

The choice of teachers to evaluate and compensate on the basis of any test provides explicit signals about the expectations for the teacher's performance and his or her peer group. The database links teachers by course to students and their test scores. This indicates to teachers which tasks they are accountable for and what test will be used to measure performance. For every teacher, the determination must be made about which subjects and grade levels constitute a sufficiently substantial portion of the teacher's job responsibility and are sufficiently related to the standard achievement assessments that his or her students' performance on the tests in this grade level are appropriate for evaluating the teacher's job performance. These decisions can have important effects on teaching practice since theory suggests teachers will focus on evaluated tasks and use the signals from the performance measures and compensation to guide their work on those tasks.[9]

Teachers will also scrutinize these explicit signals to determine whether they align with their expectations about their primary teaching assignments and the validity of the test for measuring this performance. The extent to which the signals do not conform to teachers' expectations can weaken their support for the compensation system and its ability to influence their teaching. Furthermore, the system must be sufficiently rigorous to elicit a response; otherwise those eligible for a performance award do not need to change behavior to meet the performance benchmark. In essence, they may receive a performance bonus for doing what they already were doing.

The choice of teachers to be evaluated and compensated on the basis of standardized assessments can be quite challenging. Some teachers, such as resource and special education teachers, teach only a few students in a particular subject or grade level, and the class sizes might be even smaller when student samples are restricted to those who complete testing.[10] Individuals interested in designing and implementing a performance-pay plan must decide whether a teacher with few students in a given subject meets the criteria for being a teacher of that subject for evaluation purposes. Should a teacher with few mathematics students be accountable for this instruction when the teacher primarily teaches other subjects? Will teachers agree this is a sufficiently important component of their teaching responsibility to warrant its being used in the evaluation?

The range of courses being taught is another factor that complicates the choices of which teachers should be evaluated using student test scores. Many secondary schools offer students a complex array of courses even in the basic subject areas of mathematics and English language arts. Mathematics courses in middle schools, for example, can include special education courses, sheltered mathematics courses for English language learners, traditional grade-level courses, prealgebra, algebra I, and advanced courses, including geometry and algebra II. Most policymakers and researchers want to consider teachers of all these courses as mathematics teachers and to hold them accountable for student mathematics performance. It is debatable, however, whether the standardized statewide assessments adequately measure the learning that the teacher is responsible for supporting. This is particularly true for special education and advanced courses.

English language arts courses are even more complex. There are many English language–related classes that might not be considered the primary coursework of students. Some middle school students take courses in drama and speech in addition to standard English courses, and there may be legitimate debate over whether drama and speech teachers should be grouped with other language arts teachers for assessment and compensation purposes. It is not directly clear whether school administrators should evaluate reading teachers and English language arts teachers on the basis of a reading test, a language arts test, or both types of assessments.

Choices of courses to include might have particularly important implications for explicit signals about the normative groups. The teachers will assess the courses included in the evaluation and determine whether comparison with all teachers of these courses provides a valid measure of their own performance. Will language arts teachers accept comparison to reading teachers, or social studies teachers, who also teach reading, writing, and vocabulary skills? Conversely, will social studies and reading teachers feel comparison to language arts teachers provides a fair measure of their contributions to students' reading and writing achievement? Similarly, decisions about the inclusion of special education teachers, different grade levels, and teachers with different class sizes could all affect teachers' perceptions of the system.

Implicit Signals

The choices of which teachers to include in a performance assessment system will also affect the implicit signals of the compensation system. Clearly, a teacher's performance measure will be determined by the tests and courses used in the evaluation. The statistical errors in the performance measures will depend on class size: smaller classes will yield estimates of performance that have more uncertainty and less stability, so that measures for teachers with small classes might contain large errors and give confusing signals about those teachers' performance. The normative group will also determine how teachers rank among other teachers in their peer group and the size of the bonuses they receive. These outcomes will affect not only the information teachers receive about their own performance but also how they perceive and react to the system.

The variability of estimates across years could influence teachers' evaluation of the reliability of this system. Several studies have examined the intertemporal stability of value added estimates, most of which find that these measures of teacher productivity are only moderately stable over time and that the stability of these estimates varies by grade level. Recent work by Daniel McCaffrey, T. R. Sass, and J. R. Lockwood finds that only about 34 percent of teachers ranked in the bottom quintile of the distribution of teachers in one year would be ranked in the same quintile the following year.[11] In designing and implementing a teacher pay-for-performance plan, it is important to remember that if performance measures appear unreliable teachers may not support their use or may become skeptical that their efforts will actually influence how the measure quantifies their performance.

The choices about which teachers to include in the sample in order to produce the most desirable implicit signals might conflict with those that provide the most desirable explicit signals. Implicit signals can be improved by excluding teachers of small classes, for example, but excluding such classes might give undesirable explicit signals about the worth of special education teachers or imply that teachers of multiple subjects can limit their efforts on some classes.

Selecting Students for Evaluation of Teachers

After identifying which teachers will be evaluated on the basis of a given test, the students to be used in the evaluation of a teacher must be selected. There are two primary issues that contribute to determining whether a student should be linked to a particular teacher: days enrolled in the teacher's classroom and the possible influence of multiple teachers when the administrative data include links to multiple teachers in the same subject for a student. Again, the choice will have ramifications for explicit signals, implicit signals, and teachers' perceptions of and reactions to the pay-for-performance program.

In terms of days enrolled, a student must have been under the teacher's tutelage for a sufficient number of days for the teacher's teaching to have affected the student's learning. Most people believe a teacher probably had minimal effect on a student who was enrolled in his or her class for only a few days. Most teachers would also probably feel that it would be inappropriate to hold them accountable for such a student's progress. The exact number of days providing a reasonable cutoff has not been researched but will require careful consideration. The cutoff must meet general expectations about which students' outcomes might reasonably be attributable to actions of the teacher.

On the other hand, choosing to exclude some students from teacher evaluations has the potential negative consequence of encouraging teachers to focus on other students who are to be included. More restrictive rules for inclusion will create greater potential for negative consequences because more students will be at risk for exclusion and at risk for reduced attention for a larger portion of the school year. But making the rules too lax by including students for whom the teacher might have had only minimal input could weaken teacher confidence in the evaluation system and potentially add error to the performance measures. The cutoff must find a balance that avoids negative consequences for the pay program from being either too few or too many days.

An important consideration in determining the length of time a student is enrolled is the quality of the administrative data on student enrollment in schools and courses. Many local school districts are likely to have reasonably accurate data for school enrollment records because of legal and financial responsibilities dictated by state education agencies, but course enrollment data for individual classes may be less accurate. Course enrollment data early in the school year often contain many errors because students more frequently change courses at the beginning of the school year and because teaching vacancies may yet need to be filled, causing students and courses to be reshuffled among teachers. In our experiences working with such data, input from teachers, building administrators, and district personnel was helpful in correcting these errors.

Our work with administrative data systems also found a sizable proportion of middle school students linked to multiple teachers for the same subject in a single school year. Some of these links result from the errors described above, but many are legitimate, as students can, for example, take an English language arts elective throughout the school year, have separate reading and language arts teachers, or take both regular and special education classes in mathematics. Students sometimes switch courses midyear because of school transfers and teaching assignment changes within a school. It must be determined which teachers have sufficient responsibility for teaching the material covered by the test and which might affect student learning. If multiple teachers truly are responsible, then it must be determined how to distinguish among the different teachers' contributions in light of the impact on the explicit and implicit signals and teachers' evaluations of them. These determinations must also consider the feasibility of accounting for multiple teachers' contributions with the chosen statistical procedures used for estimating performance as well as the accuracy of the data.

One potential approach to disentangling the problems associated with multiple teachers and part-year enrollment is to include all students in the evaluation but to weight students' contributions to a teacher's performance-pay evaluation in proportion to each teacher's contribution to their learning. This approach is appealing because all student data contribute, eliminating the potential for signaling that some students "do not count," but it requires that each teacher's share of every student's learning be assessed. However, it is not clear that time in the classroom is proportional to the share of learning. Teachers of a year-long drama course and a year-long English language arts course might not make equal contributions to the students' learning as measured by a language arts assessment.

Another potential challenge to this approach is convincing teachers that their contributions are fairly measured. This is currently a controversy in New York City schools because state testing occurs in January and there is concern about how teachers from two adjacent years contribute to the learning and the measures.[12] Entities interested in designing and implementing a performance-pay program need to explore alternative approaches to understand the sensitivity of performance measures to this problem and teachers' evaluations of the validity of such alternatives.

EXPLICIT SIGNALS

The choice of students to include tells teachers which students contribute to their measure of performance and indirectly which students are valued by the system. Of particular concern is that economic theory suggests that teachers are likely to focus their efforts on students who are included in the evaluations, potentially at the expense of students who are excluded from the calculations. Decisions to exclude students must acknowledge the potential risk for negative consequences for these students. At the same time, decisions about which students to include must also consider whether these are the students teachers should be focusing on and on whose performance teachers should be evaluated. Another factor that must be considered is whether the included students will match teachers' perceptions of the students they should be held accountable for and whose learning they can influence. If the selected students do not match teachers' expectations, this could weaken teachers' support for the performance-pay system and their belief in their ability to affect the likelihood of being awarded a performance bonus.

IMPLICIT SIGNALS

The choice of students can affect class size, which, in turn, can affect the precision of estimated performance measures. Including students whose learning is unrelated or only weakly related to a teacher's activities because they were not in the teacher's classes for much of the school year, or were taught by multiple teachers, could further contribute to errors in teacher performance measures and bonus decisions. Conversely, excluding students could also systematically distort estimated teacher effects if excluded students have different outcomes or respond differently to the teachers' efforts than those students continuously enrolled in a teacher's class. All of these factors not only contribute to how teachers evaluate their own performance but also affect how teachers evaluate the compensation system.

Other Factors in Creating the Database

Administrative data are often messy and challenging, in part because these systems are typically designed for administrative purposes, not complex statistical analysis. For example, we encountered three issues when transposing administrative data systems to a form that permits calculating teacher effect estimates:

—Information on select students from one administrative data system may contradict data contained in a different data system. For example, the grade level in the test-score file for a particular student might differ from the grade level in the enrollment file for a given school year. This may occur for a variety of reasons: students' being tested out of grade, students' not advancing grade levels from one school year to the next, or a coding error in the administrative data file.

—Some students may be present in one data system and not in another. We routinely find students present in an enrollment file for a given school year but not in the course listing and test-score files. The reverse may also be true, that is, a student has a valid record in the test-score file but does not appear in the enrollment file.

—Students may have multiple records for a given school year in one or more files. For example, a student may have two different sets of test scores for the same school year.

Although these types of problems are familiar to most analysts who have worked with administrative data and who typically develop ad hoc rules for editing such errors, such common data errors are more problematic when the data are used for high-stakes compensation decisions. Decisions made in data processing for compensations, unlike those in research studies, can give signals to teachers about what is expected of their performance. For example, dropping student records that contain inconsistencies can signal to teachers that certain students do not count and could have negative consequences for these students. Hence the potential implications of any editing decision must be carefully considered, and practices that avoid unintended signals must be used. For instance, practices to retain all the available data are likely to be important. Furthermore, because of the high stakes involved, the data used for determining compensation might be highly scrutinized by teachers or their representatives. In particular, teachers who are dissatisfied with the compensation decisions might question their performance measures. Any data of questionable accuracy might support their challenges and could undermine other teachers' confidence in the system, possibly eroding any motivating effects of a performance-pay system. Careful review of the data with knowledgeable district staff and teacher verification of data before assigning awards are likely to be necessary components of any performance-pay system.

Measuring Teacher Performance

Assembling the appropriate data sources is only the first step in translating raw data to award decisions. The keystone of a performance-pay system is the next step: choosing a performance measure. There are many possible analytic methods for measuring teacher performance using student achievement data, and the method chosen to evaluate teacher performance will have implications for the explicit and implicit signals and for teachers' perception of the performance-pay system.

There are two general classes of performance measures that are or might be used in practice: standardized and ad hoc methods. We use the term *standardized* to refer to methods based on general statistical or econometric models and estimators that can be applied to any locale with minor modifications to account for local data availability. These include the value added approaches that exist in the statistical and econometric literature. Standard measures range from simple approaches, such as average gain scores (current-year score minus prior-year score) to complex approaches, such as the multivariate mixed-model approach introduced by William L. Sanders, Arnold M. Saxton, and Sandra P. Horn and expanded by our 2004 work with colleagues.[13]

Ad hoc methods, the other class of measures, are developed by individual schools, school districts, or states for their particular needs. These measures might derive from standard approaches but may include nonstandard statistical procedures or combine standard measures with other empirical evaluations. For example, one school district we are aware of is using average percentage gains in achievement to evaluate school performance for the purpose of compensating principals because the measure places greater value on lower-performing students. Another district is measuring school performance by combining value added measures with the percentage of students who graduate from high school.

The use of ad hoc measures appears to be motivated by the desire to provide strong explicit signals to teachers about expected performance. Teachers may also accept these ad hoc measures because they are comprehensible and believed to be trustworthy based on face validity (that is, it looks like it measures what it is supposed to measure). The statistical properties of these measures are rarely considered and may be difficult to assess. As a consequence, the implicit signals for individual teachers are not considered, and implications of these properties for the teacher evaluations of the system are generally ignored.

There is a growing literature on the statistical properties of standard methods for calculating a teacher's productivity. These methods are easiest to evaluate on the basis of their likely implicit signals and effects on the resulting performance-pay system. It is much more difficult to evaluate these methods on their explicit signals, especially the complex methods, because of the difficulty in determining how individual student data contribute to teachers' performance measures. Even developers of the methods struggle to identify these contributions.[14] Clearly, if even the developers are unsure exactly what and how students contribute to the effectiveness estimate of a teacher, these measures will not have strong explicit signals.

The lack of transparency of some value added methods has implications for teachers' evaluation of the performance-pay system. If the teachers cannot understand how their students' test-score data contribute to their own individual performance measures, they are likely to lack trust in the performance-pay system or to attempt to change their behavior in response to its rewards—regardless of the implicit information in those rewards. Although our conjecture has not been tested empirically in the education system, it does create a tension in choosing among performance measures because according to statistical theory and the case study described below, complex methods yield performance measures with better statistical properties than simpler methods, though some transparency is lost.

Case Study of Performance Measures

In preparing this chapter, we designed a case study to better understand the potential implications of the value added measure chosen to evaluate teacher performance. The case study used data on 37,887 middle school students and their mathematics teachers from a large urban school district. The student sample is roughly 50 percent African American, 36 percent white, 11 percent Hispanic, and about 3 percent Asian or other ethnic group and includes all students who attended any of the district's thirty-eight middle schools (excluding special education and alternative schools but including magnet schools) in grades 5 to 8 for at least part of one or more of the 2004–05 through 2006–07 school years. The teacher sample includes all teachers who taught mathematics to students during the 2005–06 or 2006–07 school years. In total, our sample is made up of 615 teachers, 339 who taught in both the 2005–06 and 2006–07 school years and 267 more who taught only in the one of the two years (139 in the 2005–06 school year, 137 in the 2006–07 school year).

In the 2003–04 through 2006–07 school years, students in grades 3 to 8 were tested in mathematics, reading, English language arts, social studies, and science.

In the 2002–03 school year students in grades 3, 5, and 8 were tested in mathematics and reading. The test scores in mathematics and English language arts are presented on a developmental scale with scores linked across grades and years from the 2003–04 school year forward. The social studies and science tests are not vertically linked or linked across school years but are scaled to have roughly the same mean and variance at each grade level and year. The analyses used both the raw scale scores and rank-based z scores—raw scores nonlinearly transformed to improve bivariate relationships among scores from adjacent grades of testing.[15]

When estimating teacher effects, we grouped all mathematics teachers in a single sample, and a single effect is estimated for each teacher in each year, combining data across grades for teachers of multiple grades. However, the models included grade-level specific intercepts, so that each teacher's performance is evaluated relative to the performance of other teachers teaching at the same grade level. Because compensation is an annual decision, our case study calculates annual measures of teacher performance using only current and prior data.[16] The case study considers seven different value added performance measures ranging from simple to complex.

AVERAGE GAIN SCORES

Gain scores equal a student's current-year score less his or her prior-year score, and they are a direct measure of growth.[17] A simple value added method uses the average gain score for each teacher's students as the performance measure. Average gain scores are appealing performance measures because they are transparent, easy for educators to understand, and depend on student growth in an obvious manner. However, they require that achievement test scores be scaled so that differences in scores from adjacent grade levels have meaning. Average gain scores are also sometimes treated as objective rather than normative measures of teacher performance.

LOOKUP TABLES

Notionally, a teacher's effect on student learning can be thought of as the difference between students' achievement after being in a teacher's classroom compared with their likely achievement had they been taught by a different teacher. In the lookup table approach, a student's likely achievement had he or she had alternative teachers is estimated by the statewide average score for all students who had the same score in the prior year. The expected achievement comes from a large lookup table of prior-year scores and average current-year scores for students with this score. The classroom average of the differences between students' expected scores from the lookup table and their true scores equals the value added performance measure.

LINEAR REGRESSION MODELS

A statistical technique known as linear regression provides another method to estimate expected achievement of a student and then use this information to calculate a teacher's value added effect estimate. Unlike the lookup tables approach, only students in the school district are used to estimate the expected scores, which are assumed to be a linear function of a single prior-year mathematics score. For example, the average grade 5 mathematics score for a student with a grade 4 mathematics score of y_4 is assumed to be equal to $a + by_4$, where a and b are estimated by selecting the best line to fit to the data from the district. In this model, students who differ by one point in their grade 4 scores are assumed to differ by b points on average in their grade 5 mathematics scores. Students whose true scores are greater than the predicted values achieved better-than-average learning, and if the average of such deviations for a teacher's students is positive, then this teacher is assumed to be performing better than average.

A common modification to the basic linear regression approach is to augment the simple model with indicator variables for individual teachers to improve the estimation by not attributing a portion of teacher effects to differences in prior scores. This augmented model is the model for classical analysis of covariance methods, and so we refer to this as the ANCOVA method. Again, the value added measure is the average of the deviations between true and predicted scores.[18]

Linear models like ANCOVA can yield seriously biased predictions when the prior scores have measurement error, which can undermine the usefulness of this approach in estimating teacher performance. Another potential problem with this method is that students whose prior-year test scores are missing cannot be used in the calculation of teacher effects.

MULTIVARIATE ANCOVA

The multivariate ANCOVA approach extends the simple ANCOVA method by including all the available prior scores, in both mathematics and other subject areas, as covariates in the linear model for predicting expected scores. Using multiple prior test scores can greatly improve the accuracy of the predictions and reduce the bias from measurement error that results from working with a single predictor. However, including all the prior test scores can be problematic because data are often incomplete and lack scores from prior years for some students. Without special attention all students with missing data would be excluded from the estimation of the teacher performance measures. This loss of data can be avoided by parameterizing the model so that it uses only the available data for each student, which allows students with at least one prior score to contribute to the estimation of teacher effects. The multivariate ANCOVA in this case study uses this special parameterization for estimating the performance measures.

FIXED EFFECTS ON LEVEL SCORES

This complex approach uses a model for the entire vector of mathematics scores for each student rather than a model just for the current-year score. It assumes a student component, or "student fixed effect," that is common across all scores from a particular student. Controlling for this component controls for differences in students across classes, and the statistical model also includes indicator variables for individual teachers. The value added performance measure is roughly the classroom average of the differences between each student's score in the current year and his or her average scores across all years. This approach can be implemented in standard statistical software for moderate problems but requires specialized software when the number of teachers gets large. Scores from students with at least one test score from any of the prior years contribute to the estimation of the teacher effect.

Care must be taken with this model to make sure the teacher indicator variables are coded to support the model parameterization that contrasts each teacher to the mean of all teachers. Effects are differences between the teacher of interest and some other teacher or teachers. The most interpretable comparison is the difference between a given teacher and the average for all teachers. This comparison is necessary for ensuring stability in the effects across years and pooling information across grades. By default most statistical software packages estimate effects that equal the difference between a given teacher and an arbitrary "holdout" teacher. Recoding of the indicator variables can provide the desired estimates with standard software, but recoding does require expertise with regression models and statistical software packages.[19]

FIXED EFFECTS ON GAIN SCORES

This approach replicates the fixed-effect approach using gain scores rather than students' achievement scores as the outcome variable. The value added estimated teacher effect is roughly the average of the differences between each student's gain score in the current year and his or her average gain score. This approach can be seen as generalization of the simple average gain-score approach because multiple years of gain scores are modeled simultaneously and the student fixed effects are used to control for any persistent difference among students in their growth across multiple school years.

This method requires that students have a current-year gain score and at least one gain score from a prior year for their data to contribute to the estimation of the teacher effect. The gain scores do not need to be from an adjacent year, but because of this additional requirement fewer student scores contribute to the estimated effects than with the fixed effects on levels method.

MULTIVARIATE MIXED-EFFECT MODELS

The multivariate mixed-effect approach again uses a statistical model for each student's vector of scores. However, rather than explicitly using a fixed effect for each student, it captures commonality among scores from the same student by allowing for unspecified correlation. The correlation of scores among students implicitly serves to control for differences in the prior achievement of students from different teachers. The model also assumes teacher effects are random variables and allows for the estimation of how these effects persist from one year to the next. We implemented two multivariate mixed-effect models in the Bayesian framework: the complete persistence, or layered, model and the variable persistence model.[20]

This method can use data from all students, even those without any prior scores, to estimate the teacher effect. However, the estimation method downweights the contributions to the estimated teacher effects of students with incomplete data, as scores from students with more prior scores get greater weight. Some analysts place restrictions on the model so that students with few prior scores do not contribute to the estimated teacher effects. We did not use such a restriction in our estimates.

The estimation methods cannot be implemented using common statistical software and can require extensive computing resources for large samples. The method has also been criticized for being overly complex and difficult for some teachers to understand and accept as accurate. Table 6-1 gives a summation of the details of each measure.

Each approach was applied to both the raw scores and the z score transformations, except the lookup table, which uses only raw scores because z scores were not available from the state, and the multivariate mixed models, which use only z scores, because of the computation time required to fit these models. We also calculated both raw estimates and empirical Bayes or shrunken estimates for approach. Empirical Bayes estimates multiply the raw estimates by a "shrinkage" factor that is less than 1, which, under certain statistical assumptions, minimizes

Table 6-1. *Value Added Performance Measures*

Method	Complexity	Adjustment for prior achievement	Implementation issues
Average gain scores	Simple	Subtracts prior scores.	Requires scores to be scaled so that differences in scores from different grades can be interpreted. Uses only students with an adjacent prior-year score in estimating teacher effects.
Lookup tables	Simple	Uses deviations from the students' predicted score estimated by the mean of all students in the state who had the same score in the prior-year.	Uses only students with an adjacent prior-year score in estimating teacher effects. Measurement error in the prior-year test score can result in predictions for expected scores that do not fully capture differences among students and do not properly adjust for differences among classes.
Linear regression models	Simple	Uses deviations from the students' predicted score estimated by a linear regression on the prior-year score.	Uses only students with an adjacent prior-year score in estimating teacher effects. Measurement error in the prior test score can result in predictions for expected scores that do not fully capture differences among students and do not properly adjust for differences among classes.
Multivariate ANCOVA	Moderate	Uses deviations from the students' predicted score estimated by a linear regression on all the scores from all the prior scores.	Will use only students with complete data across all years unless parameterized to use incomplete student record. Can be implemented in standard software, but care is needed to code the data so that incomplete records contribute to estimation.

(continued)

Table 6-1. *Value Added Performance Measures (continued)*

Method	*Complexity*	*Adjustment for prior achievement*	*Implementation issues*
Fixed effects on level scores	Complex	Uses the difference between the student's current-year score and his or her average score by including indicator variables for students and teachers in a linear regression model in which test scores from all years are modeled simultaneously as outcome variables.	Uses data from all students with two or more test scores in estimating teacher effects. Can be implemented in standard software for moderate sample sizes but requires extra coding to ensure that effects contrast the teacher with the average teacher rather than an arbitrary holdout. Can be computer intensive for large samples.
Fixed effects on gain scores	Complex	Uses gain scores and the difference between the student's current gain score and his or her average gain score by including indicator variables for students and teachers in a linear regression model in which gain scores from all years are modeled simultaneously as outcome variables.	Uses data from all students with two or more gain scores. Again, requires special coding to be estimate treatment effect relative to the average teacher.
Mutlivariate mixed-effect models	Complex	Implicitly adjusts scores by modeling the correlation among the multiple score from a student. Treats the vector of student scores as a multivariate outcome variable.	Uses data from all students for estimating teacher effects. Requires specialized software and can be computer intensive. Criticized for being very complex.

the expected value of the square of the prediction errors for the estimates, where prediction error equals the difference between the estimated performance and the teacher's true performance. Shrinkage is implicit in Bayesian models, so we include shrunken estimates only for the multivariate mixed models.

Quality Indexes for Performance Measures

The errors in the value added measures will influence the implicit signals provided by the performance-based compensation system. We decompose estimated teacher effects into three components: accumulated individual errors, aggregate errors, and true effect.[21] This can be expressed as

Estimated effect = true effect + aggregate errors + accumulated individual errors,

where

true effect is the true effect of the teacher,

aggregate errors are errors in estimated effect that result from commonalities among scores from students in the same class that remain after statistical adjustment but are unrelated to the teacher, and

accumulated individual level errors are errors in estimated effects that result from aggregating the data on the individual students in the teacher's class. We refer to these errors as *noise.*[22]

Aggregate errors can be systematic and related to student or school characteristics or due to a spurious event such as malfunctioning climate control on test day. Another potential source of aggregate error is nonrandom assignment of students to classes that results in classes that differ on factors related to student achievement and which are not properly controlled by the value added modeling used for estimating the performance measures. Noise results from errors that would arise even if the students were randomly assigned to classes or if the statistical procedures had fully succeeded in leveling the playing field and effectively accounted for all differences among classrooms. The variability of the noise decreases with class size, and all commonly used estimates of the prediction errors of teacher performance measures only account for noise and incorrectly ignore other sources of error.

Two features of the errors are likely to be particularly important: the size of the errors and the extent to which the errors are correlated with the attributes of the teachers' classes so that teachers with certain types of students (or schools) are systematically more likely to have positive or negative errors in their estimated performance; for example, effects for teachers in schools serving high-income students are likely to be too high.

The traditional statistical measure of noise is the mean of the squared prediction error (MSE). Other traditional measures of noise are the reliability coefficient, which equals the ratio of an estimate of variability in true teacher effects to the variability in estimated teacher effects, and the cross-year correlation of estimated effects for the same teacher.

The MSE provides an absolute measure of the variability owing to noise and is relevant when one considers the effect of noise on comparisons of teacher performance to an objective standard such as exceeding zero; it is not necessarily monotonically related to errors in other quantities of interest such as ranks or percentiles of the distribution of effects. Two performance measures with equal MSEs might not provide equally good information on ranks, because ranking depends on both the spread of the teacher effects and the errors around an individual teacher effect, but the MSE estimates only the likely size of errors around individual effects. The reliability accounts for both the spread of effects and likely variability of each estimator around each individual effect; consequently, reliability is the relevant metric for comparing value added methods on the basis of the precision of ranks and percentiles.[23] Cross-year correlation measures the intertemporal stability of the estimated effects: since errors vary from year to year, performance measures with relatively greater error will have smaller cross-year correlation. However, because cross-year correlation depends not only on the size of the errors but also on the year-to-year variability of true performance across time, it serves only as a means of ordering value added methods.

Both cross-year correlation and reliability are useful measures of the size of error, but they alone might not be the best metrics for comparing value added methods. Both these values can be distorted by aggregate error. Aggregate error can inflate the spread of teacher effects relative to prediction error, which will inflate reliability. Furthermore, if the student or school factors that contribute to aggregate errors are stable across years, then aggregate errors can create intertemporal stability in estimated teacher effects, yielding higher correlation. Reliability and correlation are meaningful quantities, but if value added methods have different levels of aggregate errors then these metrics might not order value added methods by desirability for use.

We created two alternative metrics of the size of error to overcome the limitations of the MSE, reliability, and cross-year correlations for comparing value added methods. The first is the scaled MSE.[24] The notion behind this metric is that for two value added measures with an equal spread of teachers, a greater MSE implies a lower reliability. However, the average shrinkage factor for shrunken estimates can make estimates with more shrinkage have smaller MSEs but not necessarily greater reliability. Consequently, we divided the MSE by the average shrinkage to obtain our metric.

As an alternative to cross-year correlations as a measure of intertemporal instability, we would like to measure the year-to-year variability in aggregate errors. Although we cannot observe this quantity, we can observe the year-to-year variability in the sum of aggregate errors plus true teacher effects. Given that the variability in true teacher effects does not depend on the value added method, ranking methods by the variability in the sum of the true effects and aggregate errors is equal to ranking them by aggregate errors.[25] Hence we used an estimate of this variability as a metric of the error in the value added methods. Again, overall levels of shrinkage can distort this value, so we divided by the average shrinkage.

We also used two measures of systematic error. We decomposed the variability in estimated teacher effects from two years into three sources: the noise within year; the time-varying aggregate errors plus time-varying teacher performance; and stable aggregate errors and stable teacher performance. We then determined the proportion of each of the last two components explained by students' prior achievement from two years earlier and their race (African American or Hispanic versus white or Asian). Two-year lagged scores were used to avoid spurious correlations with gain scores.

Comparison of Performance Measures

Figures 6-1, 6-2, and 6-3 display the scores of the various alternative value added measures on the seven metrics: MSE, reliability, and cross-year correlation in figure 6-1; scaled MSE and the scaled within-teacher between-year aggregate variance component in figure 6-2; and systematic error measures in figure 6-3. We use two sets of error metrics because the first three metrics need to be considered in light of other information, whereas the last two are meant to allow for comparison of value added measures without consideration of other errors.

The figures indicate that the errors in gain score–based methods are generally not related to the student characteristics we explored, but the errors are large relative to other methods. Alternatively, the ANCOVA methods have smaller errors than gain-based methods, but aggregate errors are relatively highly related to student attributes. Gain-score methods are like a coin flip—fair but capricious; ANCOVA methods are like a misaligned rifle—consistent in where they hit but not necessarily on target. Among the simple methods the lookup tables generally have the most robust performance—never the best but never extremely poor,

Figure 6-1. *Evaluation of Alternative Performance Measures on Three Noise Metrics*[a]

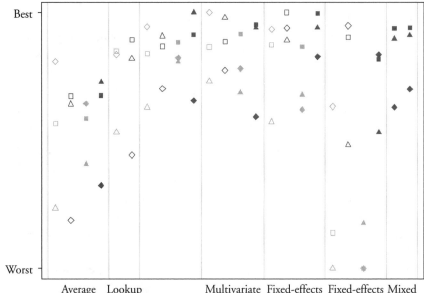

a. Metrics are: mean squared (prediction) error (squares), reliability coefficient (diamonds), and cross-year correlation coefficient (triangle). Open symbols are used for performance measures based on raw scale scores, and solid symbols are used for performance measures based on z-scores. Dark gray symbols are used for measures with shrinkage, and light gray symbols are used for measures without shrinkage. The left column in (multivariate) mixed models is the constant persistence (layered) model, and the right column is the variable persistence model.

either. Fixed effects on levels with *z* scores and multivariate ANCOVA generally perform well across all methods. The two multivariate mixed-models specifications also perform moderately well. Both perform about equally on all five noise measures, although the complete persistence (layered) models perform slightly less well on the MSE. Both also perform fairly well on the time-varying systematic error measure, but the variable persistence model performs moderately poorly on the measures of time-invariant systematic error. The two-year averages of the teacher effects from this measure are relatively strongly correlated with student attributes compared with the other value added estimates. Compared with the other measures, the estimates from the variable persistence model will be more likely to favor teachers of students at low risk for low achievement.

Figure 6-2. *Evaluation of Alternative Performance Measures on Two Alternative Noise Metrics*[a]

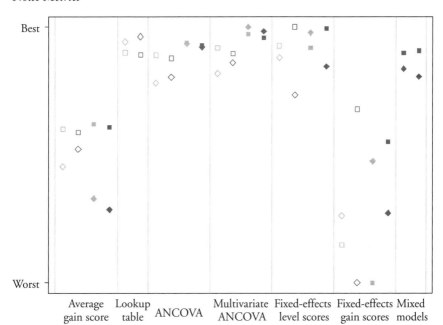

a. Metrics are scaled mean squared (prediction) error (squares) and scaled year-to-year aggregate error plus teacher-effect variability (diamonds). Open symbols are used for performance measures based on raw scale scores, and solid symbols are used for performance measures based on z-scores. Dark gray symbols are used for measures with shrinkage and light gray symbols are used for measures without shrinkage. The left column in (multivariate) mixed models is the constant persistence (layered) model, and the right column is the variable persistence model.

We explored the implications of these differences for evaluating teacher performance by comparing the teachers whose performance is significantly better than average (zero) according to each value added performance measure. A value added method finds a teacher significantly better than average if the lower limit of the prediction interval (the estimate plus or minus two times the standard error of prediction) exceeds zero. We discuss the findings for four of the measures: gain scores (without shrinkage and raw scores), ANCOVA (without shrinkage and raw scores), fixed effects on level scores (with shrinkage and z scores), and mixed models (the variable persistence model). We chose these estimates because they span the collection of measures in terms of complexity and scores on the metrics. Gain scores and ANCOVA are most likely to be considered by practitioners because

Figure 6-3. *Evaluation of Alternative Performance Measures on Two Systematic Error Metrics*[a]

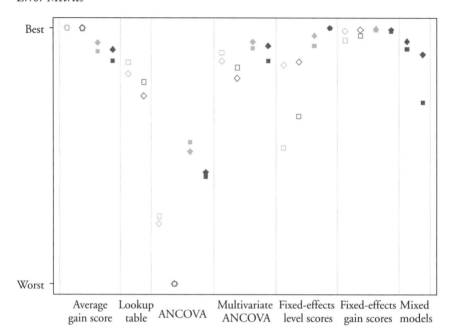

a. Metrics are proportion of time-invariant estimated-teacher-effect variability explained by student variables (race-ethnicity and two-year lag prior test scores) (squares) and proportion of time-varying aggregate estimated-teacher-effect variability explained by student variables (race-ethnicity and two-year lag prior test scores) (diamonds). Open symbols are used for performance measures based on raw scale scores and solid symbols are used for performance measures based on z-scores. Dark gray symbols are used for measures with shrinkage, and light gray symbols are used for measures without shrinkage. The left column in (multivariate) mixed models is the constant persistence (layered) model, and the right column is the variable persistence model.

they are transparent and easy to implement. Fixed-effects and multivariate mixed models receive greater attention from methodologists.

Table 6-2 provides a summary of the data on teachers whose performance is classified as significantly better than average by each of the four value added measures. The table presents the percentage of teachers in different groups who receive this classification and the Kappa statistic as a measure of agreement in the classification across the two school years.[26] The Kappa statistic equals the percentage of agreement in classification adjusted for chance agreement.

Some general patterns are clear from the table. The systematic errors identified in the ANCOVA methods result in classification of more teachers whose

Table 6-2. *Summary of Teachers Whose Performance is Classified as Significantly Average, by Four Selected Performance Measures*

Item	ANCOVA	Student gains	Mixed models	Fixed effects
All teachers	29	20	19	19
Teachers by class size				
Less than ten students	7	14	4	11
Ten to nineteen students	12	17	13	15
Twenty or more students	44	23	27	23
Teachers by average student prior achievement				
Less than one standard deviation below mean	6	18	7	15
Between one standard deviation below and the mean	23	21	18	20
Between the mean and one standard deviation above	42	19	24	21
More than one standard deviation above the mean	70	23	40	20
Teachers by course taught				
Only general education courses[a]	36	21	23	22
Only special education courses	5	17	5	12
Only advanced courses[b]	88	13	63	13
Cross-year agreement (Kappa statistic)	0.55	0.24	0.53	0.5

a. Excludes teachers who taught special education, algebra, or other advanced mathematics courses.
b. Includes teachers who taught only algebra or other advanced mathematics courses.

performance is classified as significantly above average than with any of the other methods, and the method strongly favors teachers of high-achieving students. With the ANCOVA method, only 6 percent of teachers teaching classes with the lowest prior achievement (in which the average prior achievement is less than one standard deviation below the mean of all classes) receive this designation, whereas 70 percent of teachers teaching classes with the highest average prior achievement (in which the average prior achievement is greater than one standard deviation above the mean for all classes) receives this designation. Substantially more teachers in the group teaching the highest-performing students are designated above average with the ANCOVA method than with any of the other performance measures. A related consequence of the systematic error in this measure is the high proportion of teachers who teach only advanced classes and are designated as above-average performers. This is a small group of teachers, but nearly all of them are designated as superior by the ANCOVA method, whereas other methods identify as few as 13 percent of these teachers as superior. Because a teacher's course assignments are stable across time, ANCOVA consistently favors teachers of advanced classes and higher-achieving students across years (Kappa is 0.55).

Performance measures based on gain scores behave in a manner opposite to those based on the ANCOVA measure. The relatively large noise results in a very low Kappa statistic (0.24) and the classification of large proportions of teachers with small classes as above-average performers. A tendency of gain scores to be negatively correlated with students' prior achievement results in roughly equal percentages of teachers being classified as above average regardless of their students' prior achievement. Also the proportion of special education teachers classified as superior performers is high (17 percent) compared with all the other measures.

Performance measures based on fixed effects for z scores with shrinkage and measures based on gain scores identify similar types of teachers as above-average performers. However, the fixed-effects measure is more stable across years, with a Kappa statistic of 0.50. Performance measures based on mixed models tend to favor teachers of students with high prior achievement but not to the extent that the ANCOVA method does. Moreover, this does not falsely identify the large number of teachers that ANCOVA does. For example, the performance of only 40 percent of teachers of students with the highest prior achievement is designated as significantly better than average compared with ANCOVA. However, 63 percent of teachers teaching only advanced classes are designated as superior performers under mixed models.

Direct comparisons of the methods reflect these overall trends. As shown in table 6-3, direct comparisons of ANCOVA with other methods reveal that ANCOVA identifies as above average many teachers who are not so classified by the other methods, and these differences persist across the two years of data. For instance, fixed-effects and ANCOVA methods disagree on 20 percent of teachers, and more than 40 percent of the teachers classified as above average by the ANCOVA measures but not the fixed-effects measures have the same difference in classifications in both school years. Hence using ANCOVA-based measures would tend to systematically favor individual teachers of low-risk students compared with teachers of high-risk students as well as create a system that favored such teachers.

Table 6-3. *Pairwise Comparison of Four Performance Measures on the Basis of Teachers Classified as Significantly Better than Average*

Method A = fixed effects; method B = multivariate mixed models;
Pearson correlation coefficient = 0.86

Classified as significantly above average by both methods

Method B	Method A		
	Above average	*Other*	*Total*
Above average	135 (14 percent)	45 (5 percent)	180 (19 percent)
Other	45 (5 percent)	729 (76 percent)	774 (81 percent)
Total	180 (19 percent)	774 (81 percent)	. . .

Classified as significantly above average by one method but not the other

Item	By method A but not method B	By method B but not method A
Average percentage minority students	0.70	0.46
Average prior achievement	−0.77	0.72
Percent special education teachers	0.40	0.02
Average LMT[a] score	−0.44	0.43

Method A = fixed effects; method B = gain scores;
Pearson correlation coefficient = 0.59

Classified as significantly above average by both methods

Method B	Method A		
	Above average	*Other*	*Total*
Above average	122 (13 percent)	58 (6 percent)	170 (18 percent)
Other	58 (6 percent)	721 (76 percent)	779 (82 percent)
Total	180 (19 percent)	769 (81 percent)	. . .

Classified as significantly above average by one method but not the other

Item	By method A but not method B	By method B but not method A
Average percentage minority students	0.67	0.65
Average prior achievement	−0.12	−0.27
Percent special education teachers	0.12	0.33
Average LMT[a] score	0.17	0.16

(continued)

Table 6-3. *Pairwise Comparison of Four Performance Measures on the Basis of Teachers Classified as Significantly Better than Average (continued)*

Method A = fixed effects; method B = ANCOVA;
Pearson correlation coefficient = 0.51

Classified as significantly above average by both methods

Method B	Method A		
	Above average	*Other*	*Total*
Above average	132 (13 percent)	129 (14 percent)	261 (27 percent)
Other	48 (5 percent)	640 (67 percent)	688 (73 percent)
Total	180 (19 percent)	769 (81 percent)	. . .

Classified as significantly above average by one method but not the other

Item	By method A but not method B	By method B but not method A
Average percentage minority students	0.72	0.50
Average prior achievement	−0.74	0.56
Percent special education teachers	0.33	0.02
Average LMT[a] score	−0.30	0.34

Method A = multivariate mixed models; method B = gain scores;
Pearson correlation coefficient = 0.66

Classified as significantly above average by both methods

Method B	Method A		
	Above average	*Other*	*Total*
Above average	120 (13 percent)	50 (5 percent)	170 (18 percent)
Other	59 (6 percent)	722 (76 percent)	781 (82 percent)
Total	179 (19 percent)	772 (81 percent)	. . .

Classified as significantly above average by one method but not the other

Item	By method A but not method B	By method B but not method A
Average percentage minority students	0.53	0.69
Average prior achievement	0.52	−0.81
Percent special education teachers	0	0.52
Average LMT[a] score	0.42	−0.41

Table 6-3. *Pairwise Comparison of Four Performance Measures on the Basis of Teachers Classified as Significantly Better than Average (continued)*

Method A = multivariate mixed models; method B = ANCOVA;
Pearson correlation coefficient = 0.74

Classified as significantly above average by both methods

	Method A		
Method B	Above average	Other	Total
Above average	165 (17 percent)	96 (10 percent)	261 (27 percent)
Other	14 (1 percent)	676 (71 percent)	690 (73 percent)
Total	180 (19 percent)	769 (81 percent)	. . .

Classified as significantly above average by one method but not the other

Item	By method A but not method B	By method B but not method A
Average percentage minority students	0.71	0.53
Average prior achievement	−0.49	0.36
Percent special education teachers	0.21	0.06
Average LMT[a] score	0.31	0.20

Method A = ANCOVA; method B = gain scores;
Pearson correlation coefficient = 0.87

Classified as significantly above average by both methods

	Method A		
Method B	Above average	Other	Total
Above average	129 (14 percent)	41 (4 percent)	170 (18 percent)
Other	132 (14 percent)	649 (68 percent)	781 (82 percent)
Total	261 (27 percent)	690 (73 percent)	. . .

Classified as significantly above average by one method but not the other

Item	By method A but not method B	By method B but not method A
Average percentage minority students	0.52	0.75
Average prior achievement	0.55	−0.98
Percent special education teachers	0	0.56
Average LMT[a] score	0.35	−0.49

a. Learning Mathematics for Teaching Project's Multiple Choice Measures of Mathematical Knowledge for Teaching.

No such differences exist with gain scores and fixed-effects or multivariate mixed models. Fixed-effect and mixed-model methods are highly correlated and disagree on just 10 percent of teachers when the data from the two school years are combined. Moreover, the differences between these two methods are not persistent. Few of the teachers for which the methods disagree in 2005–06 have the same disagreement in 2006–07. At the margins the two methods favor slightly different teachers, but because of noise and true year-to-year variability in performance the individual teachers at the margins are not the same every year.

Table 6-3 also compares results from the Learning Mathematics for Teaching Project's Multiple Choice Measures of Mathematical Knowledge for Teaching (LMT).[27] The test, administered to 126 of the district's mathematics teachers (all teachers were invited to complete the tests), assesses the mathematics knowledge needed for teaching and serves as an external measure of teacher quality. Teachers classified as above average by mixed models but not fixed effects have, on average, higher LMT scores than teachers classified as above average by fixed effects but not by mixed models. This could indicate that those teaching higher-performing students are better teachers and that the difference is being identified only by the mixed models. Further research would be needed to fully understand how these two measures differ.

Conclusions

The key tenet of performance-based pay systems is that financial rewards provide incentives for teachers to change their behaviors, and the signals given by the system inform teachers about the way to change behavior that is consistent with the policymakers' desires and likely to yield rewards. We identified two types of signals: explicit and implicit.

Explicit signals come from the rules for measuring performance and determining compensation. The implications of the signals may be tacit. For example, the rule that only continuously enrolled students contribute to the performance measure tells teachers which students count and is not meant to specifically direct teacher behavior, but economic theory suggests that it can affect how teachers direct their efforts and could lead them to focus on continuously enrolled students.

Implicit signals come from the compensation rewards. The actual realized values of the compensation decisions tell teachers who is performing well and who is not. Implicit signals could also have a significant effect on teachers' evaluation of the compensation system or the system-wide signal. Teachers might be motivated to change only if they believe that the performance system is fair, reliable, and accurate. The distribution of compensation across teachers will determine in part their assessment of the system. Explicit signals also contribute to evaluation of the system: teachers will evaluate the rules on which students are used in measuring performance to determine whether the system is fair and accurate; they will also study the design of the performance measure to assess whether it is trustworthy and has face validity.

Given that the performance-based pay system is meant to provide signals and is likely to be somewhat controversial and highly publicized, every component of the system will be highly scrutinized by teachers and their representatives. The development of the database for estimating performance will yield explicit signals about the tasks and students that count for teacher performance. These explicit signals will also contribute to the evaluation of the quality of the entire system. However, equally important, the development of the database will provide implicit signals to teachers through its effect on the statistical properties of performance measures (for example, by determining comparison sets of teachers and class sizes) and the compensation decisions. These implicit signals will influence teachers' behaviors and their evaluation of the system. Similarly, the choice of performance measure clearly has implications for both explicit and implicit signals and will have an enormous impact on demonstrating to teachers what performance is valued and on determining teachers' evaluations of the system. Finally, the choice of rules for converting performance measures into compensation will affect the nature of errors, the uncertainty of the rewards, and the extent of systematic errors in teachers in certain types of schools or teaching certain types of students who receive greater or less compensation as equally effective teachers in other settings. The rules may also have explicit signals that teachers will use in determining their behaviors.

The existence of both explicit and implicit signals, which are affected by every aspect of the compensation system, creates a tension for developing the system. Choices leading to the most desirable explicit signals may conflict with the choices leading to the most desirable implicit signals. The most obvious example of such a tension is the choice of a performance measure, where theory suggests that simple and transparent measures with face validity and clear signals on what is valued are important for directing teachers and yielding confidence in the system, whereas the evaluation of the statistical properties of value added performance measures suggests that more complex measures are likely to provide better implicit signals and a system that over time may appear to be more fair, reliable, and accurate. The tension between explicit and implicit signals also exists in the data processing, where, for example, excluding teachers with small classes would be the desirable choice for yielding reliable and stable performance measures but would create a negative explicit signal about which teachers and students count, given that many small classes involve special education students.

Our review of anecdotes about the development of performance-based compensation systems suggests that developers working with education agencies tend to use explicit signals to guide their choices with relatively little consideration of implicit signals that will arise and that database construction might be occurring without careful consideration of its implications for the system at all. Alternatively, methodologists developing value added measures and debating their merits tend to focus on factors that will affect implicit signals with little consideration of the explicit signals and their contribution to system-wide evaluations of the system.

Developers must consider both types of signals. Theory suggests that a system that lacks face validity will not motivate teachers. Similarly, a system that fails to provide clear and consistent signals about what constitutes successful teaching cannot direct effective changes in behavior. Developing systems that make optimal compromises among signals is currently challenging because there is little research on how teachers interpret the rules governing the system to determine the explicit signals and equally limited research on how they read the signals of the compensation decisions to determine the implicit signals for their own behaviors.

Researchers need to work with teachers to study their interpretations of signals of compensation systems. But policymakers must also make it a priority to collect such information as they evaluate any compensation systems they enact. Teachers' true evaluations will be revealed only when they participate in such a system. Given the large number of choices to be made and their potential to have contradictory effects on explicit and implicit signals, no amount of planning based on external research is likely to yield a system in which all the choices are optimal, given teachers' actual interpretations. Hence evaluations have a critical formative role in ongoing development of the performance systems that are most effective. These evaluations also have a critical role in providing information about teachers' attitudes that cannot be gathered elsewhere but is essential to the design of databases, performance measures, and final compensation plans for future pay-for-performance systems.

Notes

1. See William L. Sanders, Arnold M. Saxton, and Sandra P. Horn, "The Tennessee Value-Added Assessment System: A Quantitative Outcomes–Based Approach to Educational Assessment," in *Grading Teachers, Grading Schools: Is Student Achievement a Valid Evaluational Measure?* edited by J. Millman (Thousand Oaks, Calif.: Corwin Press, 1997), pp.137–62; W. Webster and R. Mendro, "The Dallas Value-Added Accountability System," in *Grading Teachers, Grading Schools,* edited by Millman, pp. 81–99; Daniel McCaffrey and others, "Models for Value-Added Modeling of Teacher Effects," *Journal of Educational and Behavioral Statistics* 29 (2004): 67–101; and D. Harris and T. Sass, "Value-Added Models and the Measurement of Teacher Quality," Florida State University, April 2006.

2. See Steven Rivkin, Eric A. Hanushek, and John F. Kain, "Teachers, Schools, and Academic Achievement," *Econometrica* 73 (2005): 417–58; T. Kane, J. Rockoff, and D. Staiger, "What Does Certification Tell Us about Teacher Effectiveness? Evidence from New York City," *Economics of Education Review,* forthcoming; and R. Gordon, T. Kane, and D. Staiger, "Identifying Effective Teachers Using Performance on the Job," White Paper 2006-01 (Brookings, 2006).

3. See Michael Podgursky and Matthew Springer, "Credentials versus Performance: Review of the Teacher Performance Pay Research," *Peabody Journal of Education* 82 (2007): 551–73; and R. Buddin and others "Merit Pay for Florida Teachers: Design and Implementation Issues," Working Paper WR-508-FEA (Santa Monica, Calif.: RAND, 2007).

4. A normative evaluation of performance defines a teacher's performance relative to other teachers in the population. For example, performance might be evaluated by comparing the average score for students in a teacher's classroom to the average score for all students. The teacher's evaluation depends on the effectiveness of other teachers as well as his or her own inputs. In contrast, No Child Left Behind uses an objective standard. Performance is measured against an objective standard, proficiency, and the percentage of students who meet this standard. A school's measure under No Child Left Behind does not depend on other schools in the population. Normative compensation decisions determine compensation on the basis of how a teacher performs relative to other teachers. For example, teachers in the top quintile of the population receive bonuses.

5. For example, other teachers. See Daniel McCaffrey and others, "Evaluating Value Added Models for Teacher Accountability," MG-158-EDU (Santa Monica, Calif.: RAND, 2003).

6. Regression methods are all based on predicting students' performance under some alternative condition and comparing the students' performance to the expected value to determine the teacher's input. One method for estimating performance measures that does not require implicit comparisons to a standard in the estimation process is average gain score (that is, the student's current-year score minus his or her prior-year score). Gain scores estimate performance as the change in performance for a teacher's students without centering these gains against a standard. However, implicit in this estimation method is the assumption that in the absence of variation in teacher effectiveness, average gain scores would be equal across classrooms.

7. Two relevant examples are the lookup-table method described in this chapter and the Student Growth Percentiles measure used in Colorado. See D. W. Betebenner, *Estimation of Student Growth Percentiles for the Colorado Student Assessment Program* (Dover, N.H.: National Center for the Improvement of Educational Assessment, 2007).

8. See Buddin and others, "Merit Pay for Florida Teachers."

9. See B. Holmstrom and P. Milgrom, "Multitask Principal-Agent Analyses: Incentives, Contracts, Asset Ownership, and Job Design," *Journal of Law, Economics, and Organization* 7 (1991): 24–52; A. Dixit, "Incentives and Organizations in the Public Sector: An Interpretive Review," *Journal of Human Resources* 37 (2002): 696–727.

10. As discussed in T. J. Kane and D. O. Staiger, "Volatility in School Test Scores: Implications for Test-Based Accountability Systems," in *Brookings Papers on Education Policy,* edited by Diane Ravitch (Brookings, 2002), pp. 123–98, the students in a school in any year can be considered a sample draw of all possible cohorts that might have attended the school. As such, the estimate of a school effect depends on the luck of the draw in any year, and standard statistical theory suggests that measures will be more volatile for schools with small numbers of students. Kane and Staiger provide a detailed discussion of how this variability in the sample of students contributes to measures of the school's performance. The same theory holds for teachers. Every classroom of students is a sampling of the students the teacher might have taught, and the performance measure depends on the idiosyncratic characteristics of the sample. Estimates from classes with fewer students will be more sensitive to these idiosyncratic features of the sample than classes with many students.

11. Daniel F. McCaffrey, T. R. Sass, J. R. Lockwood, and K. Mihaly, "The Inter-Temporal Variability of Teacher Effect Estimates," *Education Finance and Policy,* forthcoming; Dale Ballou, "Value-Added Assessment: Lessons from Tennessee," in *Value-Added Models in Education: Theory and Applications,* edited by R. Lissetz (Maple Grove, Minn.: JAM Press, 2005); Daniel Aaronson, Lisa Barrow, and William Sander, "Teachers and Student Achievement in the Chicago Public High Schools," *Journal of Labor Economics* 25, no. 1: 95–135; Cory Koedel and Julian R. Betts, "Re-Examining the Role of Teacher Quality in the Educational Production Function," Working Paper 2007-03 (Nashville, Tenn.: National Center on Performance Initiatives, 2007).

12. See L. Casey, "Finding Real Value: Making Sound Policy out of the Value-Added Debate," paper prepared for conference, Value Added Measures: Implications for Policy and Practice, Washington, May 23, 2008.

13. Sanders, Saxton, and Horn, "The Tennessee Value-Added Assessment System; McCaffrey and others, "Models for Value-Added Modeling of Teacher Effects."

14. L. T. Mariano, Daniel F. McCaffrey, and J. R. Lockwood, "A Model for Teacher Effects from Longitudinal Data without Assuming Vertical Scaling," *Journal of Educational and Behavioral Statistics* (forthcoming) provides an example of a detailed evaluation of the contributions of individual student scores to estimated performance measures.

15. For each subject and grade level, the percentile ranking of each score was calculated, and these percentiles were converted to the corresponding quantiles of the standard normal distribution with an adjustment to allow for drift in the population mean and standard deviation across years. See Daniel McCaffrey, Bing Han, and J. R. Lockwood, "From Data to Bonuses: A Case Study of the Issues Related to Awarding Teachers Pay on the Basis of Their Students' Progress," Working Paper (Santa Monica, Calif.: RAND, 2008).

16. Our estimates of teacher productivity do not use data from future years. For example, data from the 2006–07 school year were not used in estimating the teacher effects from the 2005–06 school year. Although some estimation methods (for example, multivariate mixed models or fixed-effects methods; see details below) can make use of future data by jointly modeling all years of data and waiting until future data are available to produce estimates

for a given school year, we did not use such methods because we thought it unrealistic for compensation decisions to be delayed for more than an entire school year in order to include future data in the estimation process.

17. D. R. Rogosa, "Myths and Methods: Myths about Longitudinal Research," in *The Analysis of Change*, edited by J. M. Gottman (Hillsdale, N.J.: Lawrence Erlbaum Associates, 1995), pp. 3–66.

18. R. G. D. Steel and J. H. Torrie, *Principles and Procedures of Statistics: A Biometrical Approach*, 2nd ed. (New York: McGraw-Hill, 1980).

19. See McCaffrey, Sass, Lockwood, and Mihaly, "The Inter-Temporal Variability of Teacher Effect Estimates."

20. On the former, see W. L. Sanders, A. M. Saxton, and S. P. Horn, "The Tennessee Value-Added Assessment System (TVAAS): A Quantitative, Outcomes-Based Approach to Educational Assessment," in *Grading Teachers, Grading Schools*, edited by J. Millman (Thousand Oaks, Calif.: Corwin Press, 1997). On both models, see J. R Lockwood, D. F. McCaffrey, L. T. Mariano, and C. Setodji, "Bayesian Methods for Scalable Multivariate Value-Added Assessment," *Journal of Educational and Behavioral Statistics* 32, no. 2: 125–50.

21. McCaffrey, Sass, Lockwood, and Mihaly, "The Inter-Temporal Variability of Teacher Effect Estimates."

22. These errors are consistent with errors that would arise even if students were randomly assigned to classes or if statistical procedures had fully succeeded in leveling the playing field and effectively accounted for all differences among classrooms. The variability of these errors decreases with class size, and all common measures of prediction error account for only these errors.

23. J. R. Lockwood, T. A. Louis, and D. F. McCaffrey, "Uncertainty in Rank Estimation: Implications for Value Added Modeling Accountability Systems," *Journal of Educational and Behavioral Statistics* 27 (2002): 255–70.

24. Because we use both raw scores and *z* scores and both gains and level scores, we divided all estimates by the marginal variance of the student scores on the outcome used in the measure.

25. This assumes that values have been scaled by the overall scale of the outcome measures and that aggregate errors are uncorrelated with true teacher effects.

26. See Joseph L. Fleiss, *Statistical Methods for Rates and Proportions* (New York: John Wiley and Sons, 1981).

27. See Learning Mathematics for Teaching Project's Multiple Choice Measures of Mathematical Knowledge for Teaching; H. C. Hill, S. G. Schilling, and D. L. Ball, "Developing Measures of Teachers' Mathematics Knowledge for Teaching," *Elementary School Journal* 105 (2004): 11–30.

7

Designing Incentive Systems for Schools

Derek Neal

Much debate concerning the design of performance incentives in education centers on specific psychometric challenges. Advocates of the use of performance incentives in education often argue that student test scores provide objective measures of school output, but their opponents raise concerns about the breadth and reliability of assessments, the alignment of assessments with curriculum, and the potential for schools to manipulate assessment results through various forms of coaching or even outright cheating. In sum, many doubt that school systems can or will construct student assessments that truly form a basis for measuring and rewarding educational performance.[1] Although these psychometric concerns are first order, I argue that policymakers and researchers must pay more attention to challenges that would remain in a world with perfect assessments.

Assume for a moment that the only mission of schools is to foster the math skills associated with a particular curriculum. Furthermore, assume that policy-

I thank the participants at the National Center on Performance Incentives conference for useful comments. I thank Matthew Springer for detailed suggestions. I thank Margarita Kelrikh and Richard Olson for research assistance. I thank Gadi Barlevy, Edward Haertel, and Canice Prendergast for useful discussions. I thank the Seale Freedom Trust for research support. I also thank Lindy and Michael Keiser for their support through a gift to the University of Chicago's Committee on Education.

makers in this setting possess an ideal instrument for assessing math skill and are able to make assessments of every student at the beginning and end of each school year. Even these ideal assessments do not provide the information policymakers need to rank schools according to their performance.

If a factory produces five hundred widgets today, we know that the value of this output is five hundred times the price of a widget. If Johnny's math scale score rises from 140 to 145, we may conclude that Johnny's expected number of correct answers, in a setting that requires him to try all the items in a specific domain, has increased by 5. However, we do not know what this increase in expected correct answers is worth to Johnny or to society. In addition, we do not know whether a 5-point increase would have been worth more to society if Johnny had begun the school year with a baseline score of 130 or 150 instead of 140. Finally, because Johnny may receive tutoring and support from his parents as well as his teachers, we cannot straightforwardly determine what portion of Johnny's score increase should be credited to his school rather than his family.

Education is not the only field in which it is difficult to attach dollar values to the marginal contribution of a given worker or a group of workers who function as a production unit. Private firms that face these measurement issues often abandon the task of trying to produce cardinal measures of output for individual workers or teams. Instead, firms take on the more manageable task of forming performance rankings among workers or groups of workers and then deliver bonuses, raises, and promotions as a function of these rankings.[2]

However, the task of constructing performance rankings in public education differs from the task of constructing performance rankings in most private firms because there is no clear way, a priori, to collapse the multiple dimensions of school performance into a single index. Private sector firms may not be able to precisely measure the contribution of a worker or group of workers to overall profits, but firms know that this is the criterion by which they seek to rank performance. In public education, policymakers must begin the process of designing incentive systems by developing a clear definition of performance and then pay close attention to the mapping between this definition and the performance ranking procedures they adopt.

Some scholars suggest that because the potential benefits of cooperation among teachers are large relative to the costs of cooperation, incentive systems in education should provide rewards and punishments at the school level. Others have touted the benefits of allowing individual schools or organizations that manage groups of schools to compete not only in academic performance contests but also in the labor market for teachers. Systems that assign reward pay at the school level but allow each school to allocate resources among teachers according to its own personnel policies foster competition in the market for teachers that may speed the rate of social learning about the best ways to hire, mentor, and motivate teachers.

Most of the analyses offered here rest on the implicit assumption that there exists a benevolent education authority that faithfully represents the interests of taxpayers, but it may be the case that the public provision of education invites political corruption that contaminates the design of incentive systems. This observation raises the possibility that voucher systems serve as complements to rather than substitutes for incentive pay and accountability systems.

The Limits of Performance Statistics

Private firms have the ability to hand out bonuses, promotions, and other forms of reward pay based not only on objective information and procedures but also on the subjective evaluations of owners or the managers who work for them. This arrangement is possible because workers know that owners are losing their own money when firms fail to retain, motivate, and promote their best employees. However, there are no residual claimants in government agencies, and officials who run public organizations may suffer no harm if they hand out bonuses and reward pay to their friends and family instead of to those who are most deserving. This feature of public agencies generates demands by public employees that performance incentive systems in government tie rewards and punishments to objective performance measures, and these performance statistics are often reported to the public.

In 1976 Donald Campbell made the following observation concerning government statistics that is often referred to as Campbell's law: "The more any quantitative social indicator is used for social decision-making, the more subject it will be to corruption pressures and the more apt it will be to distort and corrupt the social processes it is intended to monitor."[3] Campbell's law in fact makes two assertions: First, when governments attach important stakes to specific government statistics, actors within governments often face incentives to engage in activities that improve these statistics without actually improving the conditions that the statistics are meant to monitor. Such activities corrupt the statistics in question because the statistical improvements induced by the activities do not coincide with real improvements in welfare. Second, the same activities that corrupt performance statistics may actually cause direct harm.

Campbell provides numerous examples of this phenomenon, and in chapter 5 in this volume, Richard Rothstein provides more detail concerning Campbell's observations and related observations from several different fields. Because Rothstein's summary of existing evidence suggests that Campbell's law may be an appropriate label, education policymakers should be wary of performance incentive or accountability systems that rely heavily on performance statistics. Workers change their behavior in response to the adoption of any particular performance measurement system, and these responses often compromise the value of the performance measures in question.

Modern economists typically use Bengt Holmstrom and Paul Milgrom's multitasking model to organize their analyses of the phenomena that Campbell describes. Holmstrom and Milgrom built their model to explain why private firms often choose not to attach incentives to performance statistics even when they have access to statistics that are highly correlated with actual performance. Their insights concerning the settings in which private firms are reluctant to attach high stakes to performance measures help us understand why Campbell drew such pessimistic conclusions about the use of performance statistics in government.[4]

In the multitasking model, agents may take many different actions at work, and by assumption, employers have two tools for directing the efforts of their workers. First, firms may pay the costs required to monitor their workers' actions directly. Second, firms may link worker pay to performance statistics. These statistics are noisy signals of worker outputs, and the key assumption is that the relationships between worker actions and measured output are not the same as the relationships between worker actions and actual output. Some actions have a greater impact on measured output than actual output, while the reverse is true for other actions.

Advocates of recent trends in education reform hope that high-stakes assessments will prompt teachers to allocate more effort toward activities like teaching math and less toward activities that amount to leisure for teachers and extra recess for students, and any fair assessment of test-based accountability programs would likely conclude that accountability systems do create these types of changes in effort allocation.[5] However, the logic of the multitasking model suggests that other reallocations should also be expected.

Everyone knows the saying, "You get what you pay for," but the multitasking model takes this line of reasoning a step further. Because effort is costly, if firms pay for performance as measured by a statistic, workers will not only allocate more effort to the actions that have the greatest impact on the statistic in question but also allocate less effort to actions that do not have large direct impacts on this statistic. Furthermore, this reallocation will occur even if it means that less effort will be devoted to actions that have large positive impacts on actual output. In education, these reallocations may involve teachers' spending less time on activities that foster creativity, problem-solving skills, the ability to work well in teams, or other important skills that are not directly assessed. Thus even if teachers put forth more total effort following the introduction of assessment-based incentive pay, these types of reallocations may leave students worse off.[6]

Campbell's empirical observations combined with the insights of the multi-tasking model are warning signs for those who wish to design incentive pay systems for public schools. However, considering the design challenges inherent in constructing incentive pay systems for educators, the corruption of assessments is only the tip of a large iceberg.

Necessary Ingredients

Here, I discuss the task of ranking educators in an environment with ideal assessments. Incentive pay systems for educators require two components. First, these systems require a method for ranking schools or teachers according to performance. Second, they require the assignment of specific rewards and penalties to the various performance ranks that schools or teachers may receive.

Assume the following are true:

—There are exactly K skills that schools are supposed to foster.
—Each school has N students.
—There exists an assessment for each of the K skills.
—Each of the K assessments has perfect reliability.
—Neither students nor teachers can corrupt the assessment results.
—Variation in achievement growth among students is determined entirely by school performance.

The assumption of no corruption implies that the only way schools can enhance their students' test scores is to engage in activities that create more skill among their students. The final assumption implies that policymakers can isolate the contribution of schools to student skill development.

This ideal setting brings to the forefront a fundamental issue that must be settled before the process of designing incentive systems for schools can begin. To design a system that rewards performance, performance must first be defined. Note that, at a point in time, all the assessment information for the students in a given school can be placed in an $N \times K$ matrix. Each row contains all the assessment results for a particular student, and each column contains the results of a particular assessment for all the students in that school. If we index schools by

$s = 1, 2, \ldots S$, we can define a set of S matrixes as $X = (X^1, X^2, \ldots X^S)$. Each matrix is $N \times K$, and together these matrixes contain all skill assessments for all students in all schools at a point in time. For simplicity, I assume that these measures are taken on the first day of school. Next, I define X' as the collection of measurements $X' = (X^{1'}, X^{2'}, \ldots X^{S'})$ taken among the same students on the last day of the same school year. Given that society began the school year at X, how does society evaluate the relative values of ending the year at any one of the billions of possible X' outcomes? Furthermore, if I take the matrixes of test scores from the beginning and end of the school year for any two schools, how do I use these four matrixes to decide which school performed better?

In a truly perfect world, an incredibly skilled team of econometricians possessing the largest research grant in the history of social science research would have already devised a method for estimating the social value (in dollars) of moving the students in school s from any X^S to any $X^{S'}$, and given this method, it would be easy to design incentives for educators. Education authorities could simply allow competing school districts or school management companies to bid for the opportunity to operate schools in given locations and then pay each of these entities a lump sum at the end of the year equal to the social value of the change in human capital among all of its students minus the total amount bid for the right to operate schools.

This simple approach is not possible in education, and this idealized setting shows that the central reason is orthogonal to common observations concerning the difficulty of accurately assessing all the skills produced in schools. Even if policymakers possessed measures of all skills produced in schools, and these measures were reliable and expressed on interval scales, policymakers would still have no idea how to value various improvements on these scales in monetary terms.

Even psychometrically perfect assessments provide no rational basis for constructing pay-for-performance systems that look like piece rate or commission systems; furthermore, they do not provide the information required to simply rank schools or teachers according to performance. Because school output is multidimensional, that is, there are $N \times K$ outcomes at each point in time in each school, it is not clear a priori how one collapses this information into a one-dimensional performance ranking for schools or teachers.

Many owners and managers in the private sector also operate in environments that do not permit them to assign a dollar value to the marginal contributions of each of their employees, but the task of constructing performance rankings is probably more complicated in education than in these private firms. If the partners in an accounting firm sit down to create a ranking of their associates, all partners know the criterion they are supposed to use. They are supposed to rank associates based on their best guesses concerning how much each associate could add to the total value of the partnership. However, if the superintendent of a large school district or even a state decides to rank schools or teachers according to their performance, she or he must first construct a definition of performance.

Any sensible method of constructing performance rankings in education must be guided by three principles that are all variations on the same theme: spell out priorities; clearly map priorities and procedures; and define sensible comparison sets. A coherent definition of performance must serve as an anchor for the procedures used to construct performance rankings.

Spelling Out Priorities

First, the documents describing any accountability or incentive pay system should spell out the priorities of policymakers. These documents should clearly delineate the types of achievement that the system is intended to foster and, to the extent possible, should explore how policymakers view the relative importance of achievement in various subjects or by various types of students. Thus, policymakers should begin by formulating clear answers to questions like the following:

—Is progress in reading more valuable than progress in math or civics, and if so, how much?

—Is it more socially valuable to bring a disadvantaged student closer to grade level than to bring a gifted student closer to her or his full potential, and if so, how much?

—What are the relative values of noncognitive traits, like persistence, and cognitive skills?

Schools are supposed to simultaneously foster many skills in hundreds of students at the same time. Without clear answers to these questions and many others, the task of objectively ranking the overall performance of any two schools is a hopeless endeavor.[7]

Mapping Priorities and Procedures

Second, the mapping between the policy priorities that define an incentive system for educators and the procedures used to create performance rankings for schools and teachers should be clear and precise. This step is challenging, but those who design and implement incentive systems risk failure if they do not devote enough attention to this essential task.

Consider the No Child Left Behind Act of 2001 (NCLB) as an example. The language of the act, beginning with its title, signals that addressing the educational needs of the most academically disadvantaged is a high priority. However, Derek Neal and Diane Schanzenbach argue that, in states that measure school performance by counting the number of students who score above a statewide proficiency standard, the levels of the proficiency standards on various assessments determine which students are most pivotal for a school's performance rating. Students who test below the proficiency standard but are able to achieve the standard given modest interventions are the students whose achievement gains matter most in determining their school's status under No Child Left Behind. Thus even though the rhetoric surrounding NCLB highlights the need to improve outcomes among our most disadvantaged students, NCLB implicitly places greater social value on the learning of students in the center of the achievement distribution than on that of students who are currently far below their state's proficiency standard.[8]

In states that use value added systems to measure school or teacher performance, choices of scales for the exams combined with choices concerning how to weight improvements that occur in different ranges of the test-score distribution determine the rewards that schools receive for directing attention to different students and different subjects, but policymakers often fail to offer a rigorous justification for these choices. A concrete example helps make this point clear. In the 2006–07 school year, Florida implemented the Special Teachers Are Rewarded (STAR) incentive system. An important component of the STAR program involved assigning performance points to teachers based on their students' gains on standardized tests using the value table method. Table 7-1 is an example of a value table. The Florida Department of Education offered this table as a model for how points should be assigned to teachers under STAR based on their students' reading outcomes.

Table 7-1. *Elementary Reading Value*

Year-1 level, 2005	Year-2 level, 2006					
	1a	1b	2	3	4	5
1a	0	100	455	550	675	725
1b	−50	50	145	265	340	500
2	−100	−50	125	205	245	350
3	−175	−100	−90	170	210	250
4	−200	−150	−140	−75	195	215
5	−250	−200	−160	−125	25	210

There are six levels of reading achievement for students in Florida elementary schools, and the table specifies points associated with each of the thirty-six possible student transitions. As the table indicates, if a student moves from level 2 to level 3 in one year, her or his teacher receives 205 points. However, the teacher of another student who moves from level 1b to level 2 receives only 145 points. The department of education intentionally awarded more points for improvements that are less common, but it is hard to see why these particular gradients are the right ones.

The additional reward for bringing a student past level 3 and up to level 5 in year 2 varies greatly depending on the baseline achievement level. The marginal reward is much greater if the student began at level 1b than at either levels 1a or 2. Why would this be the case? Shouldn't one expect that the value to society of bringing a child from level 3 to level 5 is roughly the same regardless of the child's identity? If Johnny began the year behind Sue but both Johnny and Sue are at the same reading level by January, is there any reason that society should value Johnny's learning during the spring more or less than Sue's?

Because the STAR proposal did not contain a detailed discussion of the relative social importance of different types of progress among different types of students, it would be easy to generate an equally plausible set of point allocations for the entries in table 7-1 that would imply notably different results in terms of which teachers are ranked among the top performers in their district. The STAR system and other systems that do not create clear ties between how performance is defined and how performance is measured inevitably yield performance rankings that lack credibility.

Defining Comparison Sets

Third, incentive systems should group schools according to the types of students and families they serve and then rank schools either relative to other schools that serve similar students or to a performance standard designed for such schools. Any attempt to create a single performance ranking over all schools in an entire state or large district necessarily encounters serious conceptual problems. When school A is ranked above school B, the implication is that school A performs better than school B. However, if the two schools are educating students from extremely different backgrounds, one must ask, "Better at what?"

In 2006 Hillsborough County, Florida, decided to participate in the STAR merit pay system. Although STAR's value table approach sought to place all teachers on a level playing field, the 2006–07 results in Hillsborough suggest that the STAR procedures generated performance rankings that overstated the true performance of teachers in affluent schools relative to the those in disadvantaged schools. County officials moved quickly to modify the plan, and the revised plan involves schools' being placed in leagues according to their Title I status.[9]

The Hillsborough experience is not surprising given that the original plan sought to make performance comparisons among teachers who, in important respects, were not performing the same job.[10] The tasks of defining and measuring job performance in education are necessarily complicated because educators perform complex jobs, but these tasks become meaningless when policymakers insist on making performance comparisons among persons who are not working with comparable students.

The gains that students make, in a given year, on any particular assessment scale reflect the interaction of their initial skill level and the quality of the instruction they receive. Thus data on students from two classrooms who began the year at widely different levels of achievement do not provide any information that allows one to directly compare the quality of instruction in the two classrooms. One can never rule out the possibility that students in one classroom simply began in a region of the scale where it is easier to make significant gains.

Auxiliary Benefits of Competition within Leagues

Some will worry that a system requiring schools to compete only against other schools that draw from similar student populations may do little to improve performance in disadvantaged communities because it may be possible for some schools to outperform most schools in disadvantaged communities without actually performing at an exceptionally high level. However, this line of reasoning does not take into account that teachers and principals might change where they choose to teach in response to such a system.

Imagine that there are ten different leagues in a state and that these leagues are defined by the early preparation and family backgrounds of entering students. If an "easy" league exists in which it is less costly to win reward pay or avoid sanctions, talented principals and teachers will face a strong incentive to move to a school in this league. More important, teachers and principals who are best suited to teaching in the schools that belong to that particular league face the strongest incentive to move.

Furthermore, in a system with league-specific tournaments, differences in reward pay across leagues can be used as an effective means of attracting the right teachers and principals to serve in disadvantaged communities. Those who respond to the extra reward pay are not only those who are willing to teach in disadvantaged communities but also those who are willing to bet that they know how to do it successfully.

Finally, by using schools with observationally similar students to define the performance standard for any given school, one minimizes an important performance measurement problem that has been assumed away in the analyses presented so far. If Johnny's math score rises by ten points this year, it is hard to know what part of this gain should be attributed to the efforts of Johnny's teacher and what part to inputs Johnny receives outside school from parents, grandparents, or other adults.

To the extent that teachers and principals have information about the backgrounds of their children that are not reflected in the measures of preschool preparation or family background available to policymakers, it will not be possible to form perfect comparison groups for any school. However, to the greatest extent possible, whenever school A receives a better ranking than school B, this outcome should imply that school A performed better than school B and not simply that school A worked with more-advantaged students.

The state of California actually produces a performance ranking of each school within a set of schools that are similar in resources and the background of their students. Nevertheless, policymakers in California treat similar schools' rank data as simply "additional contextual information."[11] Neither the state accountability system nor the state implementation of NCLB attaches important rewards or sanctions to the ranking system's outcomes.

The federal government, in its implementation of NCLB, and numerous states continue to make the mistake of asserting that rewards and punishments for educators must be determined by measures of schools' performance relative to either statewide standards or all other schools in the state. Defenders of this approach argue that it is the only way to implement high achievement standards for all children, but this argument confuses two distinct uses of statistics.

Statistics that accurately indicate whether an organization is reaching stated goals are not necessarily the statistics that organizations should employ in their incentive pay systems. If the object is to determine whether the children in a given state are reaching a minimum level of achievement as set by the state, then the performance of each student will need to be measured against a common standard that reflects this target. However, if assessment results are to be used as part of a set of personnel practices that rewards and punishes teachers and principals for their job performance, then comparisons must be made among persons who are working in comparable environments and thus doing comparable jobs.

Neither value added models nor growth models offer a way around this concern. The original Hillsborough approach sought to rank teachers using measures of achievement growth, and it still produced results that were not credible. If the baseline achievement distributions for two classrooms have little overlap, the data permit few direct comparisons between students who began the year at similar achievement levels but attended different classrooms. Although researchers or policymakers can always create models that produce estimates of how the teachers in these two classrooms are performing relative to one another, it is the modeling choices of analysts, not data on actual relative performance, that drive these estimates. Some will argue that Hillsborough simply chose the wrong growth model, but the county's real mistake was trying to make performance comparisons among teachers who were not working in comparable classrooms.

School versus Teacher Performance

Thus far this chapter has not drawn distinctions between incentive systems that operate at the school level and those at the teacher level and has often discussed incentive pay and accountability systems as if they operate at the school level. Nonetheless, the process of designing incentive systems in education requires that choices be made concerning the extent to which policymakers attach incentives to measures of overall school performance rather than of individual teacher performance.

Three different scenarios form interesting baselines. First, a districtwide or statewide system might link measured performance for individual teachers to teachers' pay and job security. Second, district or state policies might tie incentive pay for teachers to measures of how their schools or departments perform. Finally, a system might link all government performance incentives to school-level outcomes but allow those who run schools to adopt their own policies concerning how incentive payments at the school level are allocated among different teachers within schools. For a variety of reasons, the latter two approaches are likely preferable to the first.

Cooperation and Information Sharing

It seems reasonable to assume that the teachers in a school possess a great deal of information concerning how the performance of their peers could be improved. However, incentive systems that rely solely on rewards and punishments for individual teachers do not provide any motivation for teachers to share this valuable information with their peers. Thus even if an assessment-based system can accurately show that teacher A is not performing as well as her peers, the system will not foster efficient improvement in teacher A's performance if teacher A is the only person affected by her performance.

For at least two reasons, an efficient system will provide incentives for teacher A's principal and peers to help her improve. First, they are likely to have the best information concerning how she might improve. Second, the costs of sharing this information, relative to the benefits, are often low. When one teacher shares with another teacher lessons learned from experience and experimentation, the time costs required to convey information may often be quite low relative to the benefits, and it takes little imagination to come up with numerous examples. Information concerning pedagogy, organization, or even the personalities and needs of particular students in the school may often be shared at low cost but to great benefit.[12]

Incentive systems based on measures of individual teacher performance not only provide no incentive for teachers to engage in this type of information sharing but may also provide clear incentives to withhold such information. Any system that makes performance comparisons among teachers working in the same school actually creates incentives for teachers to sabotage the performance of their peers. Although some may view this conclusion as far-fetched, economists point to this possibility as one reason that incentive systems used in the private sector are often designed to avoid direct competition among workers who are supposed to cooperate with one another in joint production activities.[13]

Some may argue that these undesirable effects can be avoided by having individual teachers compete against a fixed performance standard rather than one another. However, competition against fixed performance standards creates other problems. To begin, competition against a performance standard is competition against some historical notion of what was possible in the past in a particular type of classroom. This form of competition cannot require educators to perform at efficient levels unless standards are constantly revised to reflect what is possible in different school environments given new methods of pedagogy, instructional technologies, and other resources.[14] Furthermore, this need for revision and updating creates opportunities for political forces to build low performance expectations into the system. Competitions that allow the possibility that everyone can be a winner invite mischief that lowers standards.

In contrast, when incentive systems involve direct competition among schools for reward pay, individual teachers have clear incentives to help their peers improve because they receive no reward pay unless their school performs better than other schools. Furthermore, if they have the freedom to hand out different shares of their school's total reward pay based on their own aggregation of test-score outcomes and their subjective evaluations of each teacher, principals can build reputations for rewarding not only individual performance but also cooperation among teachers. Principals have strong incentives to pursue this course of action if their pay and job security depend on their overall performance rankings in their schools, and principals who follow this course strengthen incentives for teachers to help one another improve.

None of the above arguments against attaching incentive pay to measures of individual teacher performance deny that variation in individual teacher performance is an important factor in determining variation in student outcomes. Everyone who has ever been a student knows that some teachers are much better than others, and recent work by Steve Rivkin, Eric Hanushek, and John Kain provides clear evidence that this is the case. Identifying, training, and retaining talented teachers is key to running an effective school, and these tasks are too difficult to accomplish within systems that do not encourage all agents in a given school to use their information in ways that improve not only their individual performance but also the performance of others.[15]

An Easier Measurement Problem

Incentive pay systems based on school performance are also easier to implement than systems built around measures of individual teacher performance because it is difficult to measure differences in performance among teachers. The existing empirical literature provides clear evidence that teachers differ in efficiency but less clear evidence that statisticians can build reliable measures of teacher performance that form a credible basis for incentive pay. Several issues complicate the task of creating performance measures for individual teachers, especially statistical noise and classroom teacher assignments.

NOISE

Estimates of individual teacher effects for a given year are quite noisy when one attempts to include reasonable controls for student and classroom characteristics. Although a number of researchers have argued that a particular type of value added model can produce more reliable estimates of individual teacher effects by using multiple years of data, I do not see how a method that delivers precise estimates of teacher performance over periods of three to five years is useful as a basis for making personnel decisions and handing out reward pay.[16]

Most professionals in the private sector work in environments that involve some form of reward pay on at least an annual basis that comes in the form of bonuses, raises, or profit sharing. Although decisions about promotions are made at less frequent intervals, promotion systems not only provide incentives for current effort but also affect the efficiency of the entire organization by allocating the most talented and productive people to positions in which success depends most heavily on talent and productivity. Performance measures for individual teachers derived from many years of data may be useful inputs for a tenure evaluation process, but they are not useful as a means of providing incentives for existing teachers, especially tenured ones, to provide efficient effort levels on a continuous basis.

Ignoring Classroom Assignments

Jesse Rothstein highlights a second challenge for those who wish to use statistical methods to rank teachers based on their contribution to student achievement. Using North Carolina data, Rothstein shows that the identity of a student's teacher in a future grade helps predict performance in the current school year. This pattern is consistent with the hypothesis that the allocation of students to teachers within a school is driven, at least in part, by how individual students are progressing through school. Rothstein presents evidence that this sorting of students to teachers is driven not solely by fixed student characteristics but also by how the student develops academically over time, and he argues that estimated teacher effects based on methods that seek to control for this type of student tracking over time are not highly correlated with estimates from more standard models.[17]

Standard methods that researchers use to measure the relative performance of individual teachers rely on the assumption that given standard student background variables, the assignment of children to teachers is a random process and can therefore be ignored. However, the assignment of teachers to students within schools reflects a set of choices made by principals based on information that researchers cannot see. Some teachers excel at working with children who are naturally hard workers, while other teachers have a comparative advantage in working with kids who are struggling in school or at home. Thus when researchers assume that the assignments of teachers to students can be ignored, they are, in effect, assuming that principals systematically fail to do their jobs.

Ignorable assignment is still a challenge at the school level. Parents' choice of schools for their children most likely reveal information about unmeasured family characteristics that influence academic outcomes for their children. However, there are scenarios that make ignorable assignment at the school level much more palatable.

California already has a set of procedures that are designed to identify a comparison set of similar schools for any given school in California. In large states, it may be possible to form comparison sets that are not only homogeneous with respect to student characteristics but also geographically separated. Imagine a set of fifty elementary schools that serve as the comparison set for elementary school A. Assume that all fifty schools are similar to A with respect to early preparation for school and the demographic characteristics of students, and also assume that no student in any of these fifty schools lives within a one-hour commute of school A. That students in school A did not attend one of the fifty schools in this comparison set provides no information about school A or the comparison schools. The comparison schools were not realistic options for the students in school A. Furthermore, that students in the comparison schools did not attend school A is not informative about either school A or the comparison schools because school A was not an option for these students.

If such a comparison set is used to create a performance measure for school A, unmeasured factors at the community level may still create problems. However, there is no set of decisions facing parents, teachers, or principals that can be expected to directly generate correlations between these unobserved factors and the assignment of students to either school A or the schools in its comparison set.

The Value of Labor Market Competition

Assume that a state or large district allows independent companies and nonprofit organizations to bid for opportunities to manage public schools. Furthermore, imagine an incentive system that provides reward funds at the school level based on an index of school performance and also provides for the termination of an organization's management contract if the same index falls below a specified level. This index might be based entirely on assessment results or a combination of assessment results and the results of school inspections, parent surveys, and other information. Regardless, the key assumption is that the index is a reliable indicator of how a particular school performs relative to similar schools that serve students from the same backgrounds.

In addition, assume that the organizations that manage schools are responsible for distributing reward money to teachers and for designing their own policies and procedures for evaluating teachers, screening new hires, terminating existing teachers, granting tenure, and determining career ladders for teachers within their schools. Thus school management organizations compete with one another not only in determining the educational practices used within their schools but also in developing and implementing the personnel policies and procedures that identify and retain the best teachers. Because the resources of these organizations are tied to their performance, they face clear incentives to select personnel policies that retain and reward the teachers who make the greatest contributions to overall school quality. Furthermore, as different organizations experiment with different management models, successful innovations will spread to other organizations and other schools.

This type of labor market competition among schools is almost never seen in the developed world. Although many European countries have education systems with voucher components that foster competition among schools for students, collective bargaining on a national or regional level sets most personnel policies for both private and public schools in these systems.[18]

The personnel economics literature describes many ways that private firms implement desirable performance incentive systems even in environments like education, in which it is impossible to precisely measure the marginal contributions of individual workers to the profits of firms. However, these papers usually describe incentive schemes that are possible only when firms know a great deal about both the preferences of their workers and the details of their production technologies.[19] Economists justify this approach to characterizing what firms actually do by noting that competition among firms for talented workers moves the actual personnel policies of firms toward the efficient ones.[20] Inefficient policies waste resources either by paying too much for the effort that workers provide or by encouraging workers to provide effort that does not generate returns in excess of the incentive payments made to workers. Because firms that do not discover efficient ways to provide incentives for their workers waste resources and cannot compete over the long term with firms that do, competition in the product market enhances efficiency in the labor market.

For this reason, systems that promote competition among schools while allowing schools to compete for teachers by experimenting with different personnel policies offer greater promise than systems that impose a single set of incentive pay policies on all schools. Imagine that a state or district superintendent must design a single incentive pay system for an entire state or district. Even if possessing an ideal system for creating teacher performance rankings based on peer evaluations, principal evaluations, student assessment results, and other relevant information, the superintendent would need a second crystal ball to help determine the rewards and penalties that should be attached to particular performance ranks. In competitive labor markets, efficient innovators thrive and prosper while those who pursue inefficient personnel policies either abandon them or go out of business, but few competitive forces discipline the personnel policies adopted by nations, states, or even large school districts.

This observation also raises concerns about the ability of large government agencies to determine the reward structures and ranking procedures that govern competition among schools. The benefits of competition among schools will be determined in part by the extent to which policymakers not only choose valid ranking procedures but also attach the correct reward structure to various ranks. Policymakers require enormous amounts of information to perform these tasks well.

Conclusion

The great myth about incentive pay or accountability systems is that they bring business practices or competitive pressures to public education, but such claims are not valid. In contrast to private firms, public school systems are not directly accountable to their customers, that is, the families they serve. In the traditional public school model, teachers and principals, as public employees, are accountable to the appointed agents of elected officials. In accountability or incentive pay systems, teachers and principals are accountable to formulas and procedures created by these same agents. These systems may foster competition to earn the rewards governments offer, but if governments design these competitions poorly, there is no guarantee that they will correct their mistakes in a timely manner.

Decades ago school boards began to adopt policies that guaranteed salary increases for all teachers who obtained master's degrees in education, and our university libraries are now filled with research papers that find no relationship between the acquisition of these degrees and the performance of teachers.[21] Yet there is no indication that districts intend to break the link between master's degrees and pay levels any time soon. If state education agencies or school districts adopt incentive pay systems that are as ill advised as the decision to grant automatic raises to a teacher who obtains a master's degree, what forces will correct such errors?

Hidden actions of agents can corrupt performance statistics. The multitasking model demonstrates that once government agencies attach important incentives to a particular statistic, government employees will take actions to improve the value of this statistic even if these actions contribute nothing or do harm to those that their organization is intended to serve. However, the political process may corrupt government performance statistics in a more direct manner if interest groups exert influence over the adoption of specific performance measures and reward schemes for use in incentive pay systems.

The analyses presented here implicitly assume the existence of a benevolent education authority and described the policies this authority might adopt given its access to information. However, it is easy to imagine ways that ranking procedures and reward structures might be corrupted by the political process. Is it inconceivable that an alliance of teachers unions and postsecondary schools of education could demand that state officials consider the number of master's degrees among faculty members or the total number of hours in professional development classes as a key factor in determining a school's overall performance ranking? It is easy to imagine the adoption of state- or districtwide incentive pay systems that specify a mapping between certain performance statistics and total pay according to rules that do not vary at all with grade, subject taught, or school environment, even though it is almost impossible to justify this approach on efficiency grounds.

These observations suggest that voucher systems and statewide performance measurement systems should be seen not as policy substitutes but rather as policies that could work well together. Consider a system that provides comprehensive performance rankings for schools but also allows parents to use this information as only one of many factors when deciding where their children should attend school. In this scenario, the choices of parents determine the overall budgets of each school, and those who run schools engage in competition for resources by choosing the education and personnel policies that deliver educational services that parents value.

This approach gives parents the opportunity to act on information they have that cannot be found in any database and also the opportunity to aggregate the information at their disposal based on their values and priorities. By granting parents control over the public funds that are allocated for their children's education, society gains an army of education performance monitors. Lacking this control, parents have less incentive to acquire information about the quality of their child's school and no means to credibly communicate the information they possess.[22]

Those who are convinced that parents cannot possibly be trusted to choose schools for their children may wish to amend this system by making total school resources dependent not only on student enrollment but also on some government assessment of school quality. But even with such an amendment, a system of real competition among schools may serve as an important catalyst for improving the practices that determine the hiring, retention, and payment of teachers.

It is also worth noting that high-powered incentives may not even be the optimal approach to personnel policy in education. The Holmstrom and Milgrom multitasking model points directly to this possibility. In addition, Timothy Besley and Maitreesh Ghatak note that many nonprofit organizations in education, health, or related services choose personnel policies that include relatively little incentive pay. In these types of organizations, they argue, it is often efficient to devote considerable resources to the screening of potential hires and to then hire only candidates with high levels of personal commitment to the mission of the organization. When it is possible to identify such individuals, incentive pay is no longer necessary.[23]

Current trends in education reform operate on the assumption that teachers should face high-powered performance incentives, but it is possible that this assumption is wrong. It is possible that, rather than incentive pay systems, schools need much better means for identifying and developing talented persons who enjoy helping children learn. Whether or not this is the case, real competition among schools and organizations that manage schools may be the best mechanism available for societal learning about desirable methods for identifying, training, and motivating teachers.

Notes

1. See chapter 5 in this volume.
2. Edward P. Lazear and Sherwin Rosen, "Rank-Order Tournaments as Optimum Labor Contracts," *Journal of Political Economy* 89, no. 5 (1981): 841–64, began the economics literature that describes these forms of incentive pay as prizes associated within rank-order performance tournaments.
3. See Donald T. Campbell, "Assessing the Impact of Planned Social Change," Occasional Working Paper 8 (Hanover, N.H.: Dartmouth College, Public Affairs Center, December 1976).
4. Bengt Holmstrom and Paul Milgrom, "Multitask Principal-Agent Analyses: Incentive Contracts, Asset Ownership, and Job Design," special issue, *Journal of Law, Economics, and Organization* 7 (January 1991): 24-52.
5. See Eric A. Hanushek and Margaret E. Raymond, "Does School Accountability Lead to Improved Student Performance?" Working Paper 10591 (Cambridge, Mass.: National Bureau of Economic Research, June 2004); and Eric A. Hanushek, "Impacts and Implications of State Accountability Systems," in *Within Our Reach,* edited by John E. Chubb (New York: Rowman and Littlefield, 2005).
6. This scenario may be avoided if teachers find that the process of preparing children for specific assessments actually lowers the cost of building other skills. If the process of preparing children for a high-stakes assessment makes it easier to teach critical thinking skills, social skills, and the like, it may be possible to design an accountability system that gener-

ates improved performance on a specific assessment without taking attention and effort away from the skills that are not directly assessed.

7. Avinash Dixit, "Incentives and Organizations in the Public Sector," *Journal of Human Resources* 37, no. 4 (2002): 696–727, correctly notes that many different advocacy groups act as performance monitors in public education, and these groups do not always have the same priorities. Seen in this light, the typical failure of existing incentive pay systems to take clear and coherent stands on how performance should be defined and measured is not completely surprising. However, my goal is not to explain why current government policies are what they are but rather to outline normative criteria that incentive policies should meet.

8. Derek Neal and Diane Whitmore Schanzenbach, "Left Behind by Design: Proficiency Counts and Test-Based Accountability," University of Chicago, February 2008; Neal and Schanzenbach draw their conclusions based on data from Chicago. Randall Reback, "Teaching to the Rating: School Accountability and the Distribution of Student Achievement," *Journal of Public Economics* 92, nos. 5–6 (2008): 1394–1415, draws similar conclusions based on earlier data from Texas. Matthew G. Springer, "The Influence of an NCLB Accountability Plan on the Distribution of Student Test Score Gains," *Economics of Education Review* 27, no. 5 (2008): 556–63, does not find similar patterns using data from Idaho, but he cannot replicate the Neal and Schanzenbach ("Left Behind by Design") methodology because he does not have access to assessments taken before the introduction of NCLB.

9. See Letitia Stein, "Hillsborough's Merit Pay Experiment Benefits Affluent Schools," *St. Petersburg Times,* February 24, 2008 (www.sptimes.com/2008/02/24/Hillsborough/ Hillsborough_s_merit_.shtml) for details. The new Hillsborough plan is part of the Merit Awards Program that replaced STAR statewide.

10. Chapter 6 in this volume, by Daniel McCaffrey, Bing Han, and J. R. Lockwood, explores in more detail how rankings of teacher performance vary depending on numerous choices that policymakers must make when building an empirical model to produce the rankings.

11. See State of California, Department of Education, Office of Policy and Evaluation, "Construction of California's 1999 School Characteristics Index and Similar Schools Ranks," PSAA Technical Report 00-1, April 2000.

12. Hideshi Itoh, "Incentives to Help in Multi-Agent Situations," *Econometrica* 59, no. 3 (1991): 611–36, shows that when the cooperation or helping costs among workers are low enough relative to benefits, it is optimal for firms to adopt incentives policies that operate only at the team level. In another paper presented to the 2008 conference of the National Center on Performance Incentives, Karthik Muralidharan and Venkatesh Sundararaman, "Teacher Incentives in Developing Countries: Experimental Evidence from India," Working Paper 2008-13 (Nashville, Tenn.: National Center for Performance Incentives, February 2008), using experimental data from India, find no difference in achievement gains associated with teacher incentives as against school incentives. However, the schools involved in their experiment contained only a handful of teachers, and the organization of these schools differs greatly from that of modern schools in developed countries. Gains from cooperation may be greatest in larger schools where a number of teachers are teaching similar material to different students. Victor Lavy, "Evaluating the Effect of Teachers' Group Performance Incentives on Pupil Achievement," *Journal of Political Economy* 110, no. 6 (2002): 1286–1317, documents noteworthy responses to a school-level incentive plan in Israel.

13. See Edward P. Lazear, "Pay Equality and Industrial Politics," *Journal of Political Economy* 97, no. 3 (1989): 561–80.

14. The tournament model of Jerry R. Green and Nancy L. Stokey, "A Comparison of Tournaments and Contracts," *Journal of Political Economy* 91, no. 3 (1983): 349–64, clarifies the potential drawbacks of the performance standard approach.

15. Steven G. Rivkin, Eric A. Hanushek, and John F. Kain, "Teachers, Schools, and Academic Achievement," *Econometrica* 73, no. 2 (2005): 417–58.

16. See Daniel F. McCaffrey and others, *Evaluating Value-Added Models for Teacher Accountability* (Santa Monica, Calif.: RAND, 2003). for a comprehensive review of value added methods. See chapter 6 in this volume for a detailed case study that explores how variation in methods used to measure teacher effects as well as policies that link reward pay to different performance ranks can, in practice, generate noteworthy variation in distributions of reward pay among teachers. See Daniel F. McCaffrey, Tim R. Sass, and J. R. Lockwood, "The Intertemporal Stability of Teacher Effect Estimates," June 2008, for a detailed treatment of the stability of estimated teacher productivity effects.

17. Jesse Rothstein, "Do Value-Added Models Add Value? Tracking, Fixed Effects, and Causal Inference," Princeton University, November 20, 2007.

18. Denmark, Netherlands, and Sweden are examples. See Neal (2009) forthcoming for details.

19. In Lazear and Rosen's seminal paper on tournaments, "Rank-Order Tournaments as Optimum Labor Contracts," firms know the exact willingness of workers to supply different levels of effort and the precise relationship between effort and true output, even though neither the worker's contribution to output nor the worker's effort are observed. Similar assumptions are common in many models of bonus pay and promotions. See Canice Prendergast, "The Provision of Incentives in Firms," *Journal of Economic Literature* 37, no. 1 (1999): 7–63.

20. Here, *efficient* does not necessarily mean the first-best outcome in a world with perfect information but rather the best firms can do subject to the information constraints they face.

21. See Kate Walsh and Christopher O. Tracy, "Increasing the Odds: How Good Policies Can Yield Better Teachers," National Council on Teacher Equality, December 2004.

22. Daron Acemoglu, Michael Kremer, and Atif Mian, in "Incentives in Markets, Firms, and Governments," *Journal of Law, Economics, and Organization* (forthcoming), argue that real competition among educators may cause harm. They reach this conclusion because parents in their model are not able to monitor schools directly and thus rely on public statistics like test scores. In this setting, Holmstrom and Milgrom's ("Multitask Principal-Agent Analyses") multitasking model suggests that intense competition among educators may waste resources and harm students.

23. Holmstrom and Milgrom, "Multitask Principal-Agent Analyses"; Timothy Besley and Maitreesh Ghatak, "Competition and Incentives with Motivated Agents," American Economic Review 95, no. 3 (June 2005): 616–36.

8

The Performance of Highly Effective Teachers in Different School Environments

William L. Sanders, S. Paul Wright, and Warren E. Langevin

Teacher quality is a major concern of policy leaders and practitioners interested in the condition of American public schooling. A considerable amount of policy debate and media coverage related to issues of teacher quality has focused on schools with large concentrations of economically disadvantaged and minority students. Over the course of their public school education, students in these schools are, on average, not likely to receive instruction of the same quality as students in other schools.[1] This general pattern in the distribution of teacher effectiveness and student outcomes is also being reported with greater frequency in academic journals. If public school students are assigned to classrooms with a disproportionate number of less effective teachers, then the cumulative effects of their lack of exposure to highly effective teachers will likely result in meaningful differences in school attainment and an individual's future earnings.[2]

In response to concerns over teacher quality, federal and state policymakers have demonstrated a heightened interest in designing practical solutions to motivate highly effective teachers to either move to or remain in high-needs schools.[3]

The working paper on which this chapter is based was supported, in part, by the National Center on Performance Incentives, which is funded by the U.S. Department of Education's Institute of Education Sciences (R305A06034). The views in this paper do not necessarily reflect those of sponsoring agencies or affiliated institutions.

Financial incentives are the most frequently discussed mechanism to enhance the quality of the teacher labor force.[4] These recruitment and retention incentives come in various forms, including signing bonuses, certification stipends, tuition reimbursement, loan forgiveness, tax credits, and housing subsidies.

The theory driving these programs assumes that offering financial incentives will help recruit and retain more teachers in the upper tail of the ability distribution in hard-to-staff subjects or schools while also encouraging less effective teachers either to improve or to exit the system for a nonteaching position. A common argument of proponents of financial incentives is that schools need to be able to respond to labor market conditions when hiring faculty members at less competitive campuses, typically located in rural or densely urban areas, or in more competitive subject areas. Since most public school teachers are compensated on the basis of a single salary schedule that does not permit any salary differentials across different fields, local administrators must invest greater resources to search for candidates qualified to teach in math and science at the elementary or secondary level. Financial incentives might also play a role as a market signal in a compensation system that rewards teachers on the basis of performance. If a local school district has the legal capacity and budgetary resources to offer monetary bonuses to its highest-performing employees, then school administrators may have a competitive advantage over peer employers in retaining highly effective teachers in the system.[5]

There is a general lack of consensus on the relative merits of different approaches to motivate teachers to accept job assignments in schools with economically disadvantaged students or those failing to meet state accountability standards.[6] Teachers appear to be highly sensitive to the demographic composition of the student population as well as the academic achievement level of the school.[7] Additionally, a large proportion of newly hired teachers with strong academic records are drawn from outside urban areas, and teachers who live farther from home are more likely to quit or transfer to a different job.[8] On the other hand, a large share of local school districts indicate it is difficult to fill teaching positions in mathematics, science, and special education, difficulties that are exacerbated by certain socioeconomic demographics of a school or school district.[9]

The policy implications of the social science literature on teacher recruitment and retention are not sufficiently precise to guide practitioners in local school districts around the country, and issues of teacher quality with relation to financial incentives and student achievement require further investigation. A key challenge for programs offering financial incentives to highly effective teachers is a lack of quantitative research on whether teachers produce comparable results when they move to a school with a different socioeconomic environment from that of their previous school. If highly effective teachers are recruited to move to high-needs schools through the successful implementation of an incentive program, can their previous measured effectiveness be sustained when they are teaching in a different school environment? Do estimates of teacher effectiveness obtained in one set of schooling environments yield a different set of estimates when teachers move to a different school serving a different set of students?

This chapter examines the relationship between measures of teaching effectiveness before and after teachers change schools that enroll student populations with a different set of demographic characteristics from those of the previous school. The data used in this empirical study include teacher effectiveness estimates for more than 5,300 mathematics teachers in the state of Tennessee responsible for the instruction of fourth through eighth grades between the 2002–03 and 2006–07 school years. Teacher effectiveness is measured using the methodology of the Tennessee Value-Added Assessment System, a statistical approach for estimating the impact of individual teachers on the academic progress of their students.

Our statistical analysis points to several findings of interest for policymakers involved in the design of recruitment and retention incentives. A positive and statistically significant estimate on teacher effectiveness was found when teachers moved from high-poverty to lower-poverty schools. The magnitude of this effectiveness estimate was not sufficiently large, however, to overcome the relationship between a teacher's effectiveness measures before and after moving to a lower-poverty school. That is, the strongest predictor of a teacher's future effectiveness was the teacher's past effectiveness. Another important observation is that the relationship between a teacher's effectiveness before changing schools was higher in the second year after the move than in the first year of the move. This pattern is viewed to be consistent with the experience of teachers adjusting to their new surroundings and the academic achievement levels of their students.

Although the total number of teacher movements observed in Tennessee was much smaller than expected based on practitioner accounts and media reports,[10] few teachers identified in the "least effective" category had an estimate of effectiveness greater than the sample average following their move to a different school. During the window of observation for this analysis, only fifty-four teachers moved to schools with a significantly higher proportion of students eligible for free and reduced-priced lunch. Yet this finding should not dissuade policymakers as they consider strategies for motivating highly effective teachers to move to or remain in high-needs schools. A limitation of this study is the use of teacher effectiveness estimates for each teacher based on a single year of student test-score results. If a policy is designed to identify candidates for recruitment who will be offered monetary incentives to move to schools with greater needs, the implementation of two- or three-year estimates for prospective candidates will increase the reliability of the estimates and minimize the risk of recruiting a classroom instructor who does not demonstrate the same level of effectiveness in a different environment. The scope of this study is also limited to the case of teachers who move to a different school in the same district and does not permit comparisons of teachers who move across district or state lines in response to salary differentials and financial incentives.

Tennessee Public Education System

Teachers and school administrators are working in concert with state officials to better meet the needs of high-poverty students throughout the state of Tennessee. During the 2006–07 school year, the public elementary and secondary education system of 1,709 schools employed 61,856 classroom teachers, who were responsible for the instruction of 1,000,630 pupils.[11] At $43,815 a year, the average salary of a classroom teacher in Tennessee is lower than national and regional averages, particularly in relation to the neighboring states of Georgia, North Carolina, and Virginia.[12] Recognizing the challenge of competing for successful teachers with states that offer higher salaries, greater resources, and incentive packages, state administrators have pledged to increase salaries and develop new incentives for the recruitment and retention of highly effective teachers in low-performing schools.[13]

The rise of teacher quality as a major concern for the state of Tennessee follows the enactment of the No Child Left Behind Act in 2002. A condition of the federal categorical grant is that state departments of education must regularly report the number of teachers who do not meet the state's highly qualified teacher definition and then, if highly qualified teachers are found to be disproportionately allocated to certain types of schools, to devise and implement a remedy.[14]

The Tennessee Department of Education's teacher equity plan reports that highly qualified teachers taught four out of every five core academic courses (80.9 percent) in the 2004–05 school year, but those teachers were not similarly represented across different grade spans and demographic levels.[15] The disaggregated data in the report indicate that a lower percentage of core academic courses at both the elementary and secondary levels were taught by highly qualified teachers in high-poverty schools than in low-poverty schools. The challenge of raising teacher quality is reflected in the reality that students in high-poverty schools were also more likely to have novice or inexperienced teachers and teachers who did not hold master's or higher degrees compared with more economically advantaged schools.[16]

A recent analysis released by the Tennessee Department of Education indicates that the distribution of highly effective teachers in the public school system, as determined by standardized test-score results, is working to the detriment of students in schools with large concentrations of economically disadvantaged and minority students.[17] The report defines teacher effectiveness on the basis of a teacher's contribution to the academic growth of his or her students. Highly effective teachers are identified as those teachers who produce statistically significant increases in student test scores on the Tennessee Comprehensive Assessment Program exams. Least effective teachers are identified as those teachers whose students do not progress as much as expected from one school year to the next.

Figure 8-1 displays the relationship between teacher effectiveness, years of teaching experience, and a school's demographic composition.[18] Schools with large concentrations of economically disadvantaged and minority students have a near-equal share of highly effective teachers with fewer than five years of teaching experience. However, the percentage of highly effective teachers with five or more

Figure 8-1. *Distribution of the Most Effective Teachers, by Years of Experience and School Demographics*

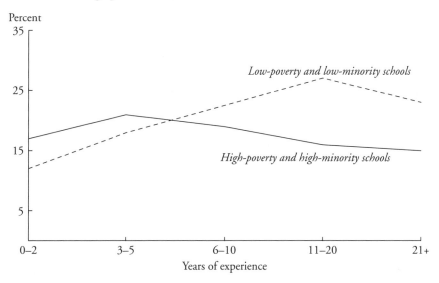

Source: Data from Tennessee Department of Education (see note 17).

years of experience declines in schools with a significant percentage of economically disadvantaged and minority students. The converse appears to be true for the relationship between teacher effectiveness and years of experience within more economically advantaged schools.

This chapter builds upon this descriptive analysis of teacher effectiveness by looking at recent data from Tennessee on mathematics teachers in the fourth through eighth grades. Specifically, we consider several questions with relevance to the policy debate about teacher mobility and effectiveness in schools with different levels of economically disadvantaged students. What are the characteristics of teachers who moved to different schools within a district? What are the demographic characteristics of the schools where they previously worked? What are the teacher effectiveness estimates for teachers who moved? How did teachers perform in the classroom at different schools?

Methodology

The relationship between teacher mobility and effectiveness may be empirically studied by looking at the progress of students on standardized tests monitored by local and state administrators. This research study measures teacher effectiveness using data from a vertically linked series of achievement tests administered to students and the statistical procedures developed for the Tennessee Value-Added Assessment System.[19]

The general structure of a value added assessment may be introduced using the hypothetical case of a third-grade student over two years of classroom instruction.[20] The graphical representation in figure 8-2 shows the student's progress in terms of standardized test scores for mathematics in the third and fourth grades. The district average score in mathematics is given by point D_3 for third-grade students and point D_4 for fourth-grade students. The hypothetical student produces a test score given by point H_3 in third grade and point H_4 in fourth grade. A solid line between D_3 and D_4 indicates the progress of the average student in the district advancing from third to fourth grade. The dashed line from H_3 to P_4 indicates the predicted growth of a student who scored at point H_3 in third grade and progressed at the expected rate of similarly situated students in the district to reach point P_4.

What was the contribution of the fourth-grade instructor to the progress of the hypothetical student? Since the hypothetical student demonstrated a test score at a higher level (H_4) than predicted by the district average gain (P_4), the additional gain in test scores from one year to the next may be attributed to the

Figure 8-2. *Value Added Modeling of Teacher Effectiveness for Hypothetical Student, by Test Scores, Grades 3 and 4*

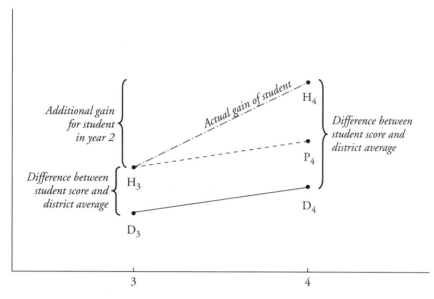

fourth-grade teacher. By taking into account the performance of all representative students in a teacher's class and a set of technical adjustments for predicting the average effectiveness of teachers in the state and variation in test-score gains from student to student, a researcher can generate a teacher effect estimate to serve as a dependent variable in an analysis of teacher effectiveness across multiple years in Tennessee.[21]

Analytic Strategy

A two-way repeated measures analysis of variance, with one between-subjects factor and one within-subjects factor, is used in this study to test hypotheses about teacher effectiveness and mobility. The dependent variable in the analysis was a *t* value calculated from Tennessee Value-Added Assessment System teacher effects in mathematics, grades 4 through 8, from the 2002–03 through 2006–07 school years. We converted teacher effect estimates to *t* values (that is, estimated teacher effect divided by its standard error) since the scale for measuring teacher effectiveness changed during this time period from using scale score units to using normal curve equivalent units. Subsequently, such a *t* value is referred to as a "teacher effectiveness indicator" (TEI). We do not include observations before the 2002–03 school year because school-level demographic data on percentage of students eligible for free and reduced-price lunch is unavailable. The statistical process of generating TEI values for secondary analyses is based on multivariate, longitudinal models that assess the contributions of individual teachers to the academic growth of students. This calculation uses all available student data over multiple grades and years in multiple subjects and allows the use of incomplete student data. This approach generates a random teacher effect estimate defined as the contribution of a teacher to a student's academic growth in a given subject-grade-year expressed as a deviation from the average growth for the school district as a whole.[22]

The between-subjects factor in the two-way repeated measures analysis of variance is the teacher mobility group. Teacher mobility was delineated into four groups: teachers who do not change schools (stayers); teachers who move to a new school with a similar percentage of students eligible for free and reduced-price lunch (move to same); teachers who move to a school with a greater percentage of free and reduced-price lunch students (move to poorer); and teachers who move to a school with a smaller percentage of free and reduced-price lunch students (move to richer). A move to a "richer" or "poorer" school is said to take place if the difference between the two schools in the percentage of students eligible for free and reduced-price lunch is greater than 10 percentage points. A move to a "same" school took place if the difference between the two schools in the percentage of students eligible for free and reduced-price lunch was no greater than 10 percentage points.

The within-subjects factor in the analysis of variance is relative year. In all cases, a move to a new school took place between the first and second years of a three-year time span. The first year of the three-year span is referred to as the pre-move year. The pre-move year was 2003, 2004, or 2005. The second year was the year of the move (2004, 2005, or 2006) and represents a teacher's first year in the new school. The third year (2005, 2006, or 2007) is referred to as the post-move year and represents the second year in the new school.

The analysis was restricted to those teachers who had single-year estimates in math for three consecutive years corresponding to one of the three-year spans listed above. To eliminate the potentially confounding influence of district effects on estimates of teacher effectiveness, all comparisons are made on a within-district basis, and all teacher moves were restricted to within-district movements. Teachers need not have taught the same grade in all three years.

Table 8-1. *Distribution of Math Teachers, by Mobility Group*

Mobility group	Whole state		Four largest districts	
	N	Percent	N	Percent
Move to poorer	54	1.02	24	1.62
Move to same	186	3.53	62	4.18
Move to richer	126	2.39	66	4.44
Stay	4,906	93.06	1,333	89.76

Characteristics of Teachers Who Moved to Different Schools

Table 8-1 displays the number of math teachers in each mobility group included in this study. These data reflect a sample of teachers for the entire state and the four largest urban school districts in Tennessee: Hamilton County Schools (Chattanooga), Knox County Schools (Knoxville), Memphis City Schools, and Metropolitan Nashville Public Schools. The percentage of teachers who had a three-year span of consecutive teacher estimates and who changed schools over these time spans was very small relative to the number of teachers in the sample. Only 6.94 percent over the whole state and 10.24 percent for the four largest urban districts met these criteria.

A second point to consider is that the four urban districts account for half of the teacher school changes in our sample classified as moving to poorer (24 of 54, 44.4 percent) and to richer (66 of 126, 52.4 percent). Teacher mobility in these urban districts accounted for a disproportionately smaller share of teachers who moved to a school with similar percentage of free and reduced-price lunch students (62 of 186, 33.3 percent) and stayers (1,333 of 4,906, 27.2 percent).

Table 8-2 reports simple descriptive statistics for teacher years of experience by mobility group. The mean years of experience of the teachers who moved ranged from 11.2 to 12.7 years and were not dramatically different across the three types of moves. Teachers who changed schools were not clustered at any one point on the teacher years of experience distribution but rather represented the entire range of the distribution.

Characteristics of Schools Where the Teachers Worked

Table 8-3 reports descriptive statistics on the percentage of students eligible for free and reduced-price lunch in the schools at which the teachers taught. These

Table 8-2. *Descriptive Statistics for Years of Experience of Teachers in Pre-Move Year*

Mobility group	N	Mean	SD	Min.	Max.
Move to poorer	54	11.2	7.9	2	33
Move to same	186	11.9	8.2	2	38
Move to richer	126	12.7	7.9	2	33
Stay	4,906	15.1	10.1	1	53

statistics illustrate the magnitude of the demographic change for those teachers who stayed or relocated to a new school within the district. For teachers who did not move, the school's percentage of students eligible for free and reduced-price lunch averaged around 49 percent, and for those who moved to a school of similar demographics the average was about 57 percent. For those teachers who moved to a school with different demographics, either to a poorer school or to a richer school, the percentage of students eligible for free and reduced-price lunch averaged near 56 percent in the poorer schools and around 33 percent in the richer schools.

Table 8-3. *Descriptive Statistics for Percent Free and Reduced-Price Lunch Students for Schools in Which the Teachers Taught*

Mobility group	Relative year	Mean	SD	Min.	Lower quartile	Median	Upper quartile	Max.
Move to poorer	Pre-move	34.6	20.6	0	20.8	34.3	48.4	82.2
(*n* = 54)	Move	58.7	21.4	18.0	42.7	56.0	73.8	96.7
	Post-move	55.2	21.0	7.8	38.0	53.9	71.2	97.2
Move to same	Pre-move	57.7	26.0	1.2	42.2	55.7	82.2	97.9
(*n* = 186)	Move	57.7	26.1	0.1	41.7	57.2	84.5	99.8
	Post-move	59.0	26.5	1.7	41.3	58.6	85.1	99.6
Move to richer	Pre-move	61.3	23.1	17.5	39.2	63.2	83.0	97.7
(*n* = 126)	Move	33.8	22.3	2.0	11.9	32.6	49.4	85.0
	Post-move	38.2	20.1	2.2	23.6	36.4	51.5	85.7
Stay (*n* = 4,906)	Pre-move	48.7	22.8	0	34.0	48.7	62.1	100
	Move	48.9	23.4	0	33.0	48.8	62.6	100
	Post-move	50.2	23.3	0	35.0	50.3	64.3	100

Table 8-4. *Descriptive Statistics for Teacher Effectiveness Indicator before and after the Move*

Mobility group	Relative year	Mean	SD	Min.	Max.
Move to poorer	Pre-move	−0.13	1.45	−4.25	2.87
(n = 54)	Move	−0.21	1.26	−3.58	3.01
	Post-move	−0.39	1.62	−3.36	4.48
Move to same	Pre-move	0.18	1.46	−5.19	5.26
(n = 186)	Move	0.06	1.69	−5.39	6.08
	Post-move	0.27	1.6	−3.61	6.15
Move to richer	Pre-move	−0.12	1.51	−3.72	6.75
(n = 126)	Move	0.53	1.72	−4.57	6.19
	Post-move	0.67	1.98	−3.63	7.21
Stay (n = 4,906)	Pre-move	0.19	1.55	−6.97	19.81
	Move	0.19	1.6	−6.77	11.77
	Post-move	0.11	1.63	−10.57	10.81

Teacher Effectiveness Estimates for Teachers Who Moved

Table 8-4 presents descriptive statistics on TEI values for each mobility group at each relative year. The mean effect estimate of teachers who moved to a school with a similar demographic composition has a positive and higher value (0.18) in the year before a move than that of a teacher who moved to a richer school (−0.12) or a poorer school (−0.13). Teachers who moved to a richer school demonstrated a higher mean effect in the second year after the move (0.67) than teachers who moved to a demographically similar school (0.27) and those who moved to a poorer school (−0.39).

A set of comparisons between the mean TEI values provided by the repeated measures analysis of variance is shown in table 8-5. Among teachers who changed schools, only those teachers who moved from a poorer school to a richer school had a statistically significant mean change in their TEI. This specific change in a positive direction is consistent with a higher level of teaching effectiveness after the move.

Teachers' Classroom Performance at a Different School

The question remains what percentage of teachers who changed buildings actually had a major shift in their respective teacher effects distributions. Table 8-6

Table 8-5. *Specific Comparisons among Teacher Mobility Groups*[a]

Contrast	Estimate	t value	Pr > |t|
Year 3 – year 1	−0.263 (0.237)	−1.11	0.2669
Year 2 – year 1	−0.083 (0.222)	−0.37	0.7084
Year 3 – year 2	−0.180 (0.219)	−0.82	0.4114
Year 3 – year 1	0.094 (0.128)	0.73	0.4632
Year 2 – year 1	−0.118 (0.120)	−0.98	0.3266
Year 3 – year 2	0.211 (0.118)	1.79	0.0734
Year 3 – year 1	0.791 (0.155)	5.1	<.0001
Year 2 – year 1	0.648 (0.146)	4.45	<.0001
Year 3 – year 2	0.143 (0.143)	1.0	0.3176
Year 3 – year 1	−0.076 (0.025)	−3.05	0.0023
Year 2 – year 1	0.007 (0.023)	0.29	0.7755
Year 3 – year 2	−0.082 (0.023)	−3.59	0.0003

a. Standard errors in parentheses.

places the TEI values in three categories: less than −1 (below average), between −1 and +1 (average), and greater than +1 (above average). Teachers were then classified by their TEI category in the first and third years of their three-year span (that is, before and after the move, for those who changed schools).

The fourth panel of table 8-6 shows frequencies and row percentages for the 4,096 teachers who did not change schools. The table indicates 2,556 teachers (52.1 percent) were in the same category in the first year (before the move) and the third year (after the move). The total number of teachers who remained in the same category is calculated as the sum of the 404 teachers of below average effectiveness, 1,591 teachers of average effectiveness, and 561 teachers of above-average effectiveness. If teacher effectiveness after the move were independent of teacher effectiveness before the move, only 1,948 (rather than 2,556), or 39.7 percent, would be expected to be in the same category in the first and third years. This indicates that the observed level of agreement is considerably higher than would be expected by chance.

On the other hand, only 247 teachers (5.0 percent) changed in effectiveness from one extreme to the other: 111 went from below average to above average (11.8 percent of the first row total), and 136 went from above average to below average (10.9 percent of the third row total). By chance, one would expect 517 (not 247), or 10.5 percent (not 5.0 percent) to move between the extreme categories: the observed number is considerably below the chance level.

Table 8-6. *Frequencies and Row Percentages in Teacher-Effect Categories for Teachers before and after the Move to a Different School*[a]

Status	Teacher effectiveness category in year before move	Teacher effectiveness category in year after move			
		< -1	-1 to 1	> 1	n
Move to poorer					
	< -1	7 (53.9)	6 (46.2)	0 (0.0)	13
	-1 to 1	9 (29.0)	17 (54.8)	5 (16.1)	31
	> 1	3 (30.0)	5 (50.0)	2 (20.0)	10
Move to same					
	< -1	13 (37.1)	14 (40.0)	8 (22.9)	35
	-1 to 1	18 (17.3)	64 (61.5)	22 (21.2)	104
	> 1	4 (8.5)	18 (38.3)	25 (53.2)	47
Move to richer					
	< -1	11 (34.4)	11 (34.4)	10 (31.3)	32
	-1 to 1	14 (19.4)	33 (45.8)	25 (34.7)	72
	> 1	2 (9.1)	9 (40.9)	11 (50.0)	22
Stay					
	< -1	404 (42.9)	426 (45.3)	111 (11.8)	941
	-1 to 1	557 (20.5)	1,591 (58.7)	564 (20.8)	2,712
	> 1	136 (10.9)	556 (44.4)	561 (44.8)	1,253

a. Percentages in parentheses.

The other three panels show similar frequencies and row percentages for each category of teacher who changed schools. For teachers who moved to a school with a similar percentage of students eligible for free and reduced-price lunch, results are similar to those for teachers who did not move: 102 (13 + 64 + 25) of the 186 teachers (54.8 percent) were in the same category before and after the move (versus the 39.9 percent expected by chance); 12 teachers (6.5 percent) changed from one extreme to the other (versus 10.3 percent expected by chance). For teachers who moved to a poorer school, 26 of the 54 teachers (48.1 percent) stayed in the same category (versus 40.6 percent expected by chance), and 3 teachers (5.6 percent) changed from one extreme to the other (versus 9.6 percent expected by chance). For teachers who moved to a richer school, 55 of the 126 teachers (43.7 percent) stayed in the same category (versus 35.9 percent expected by chance), and 12 teachers (9.5 percent) changed from one extreme to the other (versus 13.0 percent expected by chance). A noteworthy aspect of the teachers who moved to richer schools, as would be anticipated from repeated measures analysis of variance, is that these teachers were more likely than those in other categories to show an increase in effectiveness after the move (10 of the 12 who moved between extreme categories went from below average to above average). However, for all three categories of teachers who changed schools, the pattern is similar, with a higher percentage than expected by chance staying in the same category and a lower percentage than expected moving between extreme categories. This suggests that teacher effectiveness is, to a large extent, a characteristic that remains with the teacher rather than being attributable to the school environments in which teachers find themselves.

These results suggest that if policies are enacted to create incentives for teachers to move to schools that are underrepresented with highly effective teachers, using one-year teacher estimates with TEI values of +1 or greater, the likelihood of selecting a relatively ineffective teacher is small. When two or more years of teacher effect estimates are available, then the likelihood of selecting an ineffective teacher is even less, because the combined estimate becomes more stable, indicating a reduced risk of making a faulty decision. In specific terms, the repeatability of estimates goes from approximately 0.5 for a one-year estimate to approximately 0.6 for a two-year estimate and to about 0.7 for a three-year estimate. These point estimates have come from estimating the repeatability of the teacher effects over many years and grades. These estimates will be realistic for math but less so for reading, with estimates for the other subjects being less reliable.

Further confirmation of the above conclusion was sought with additional analyses. Specifically, analyses of covariance were conducted, using only the teachers who changed schools, with TEI before the move (TEI in year 1) as the predictor variable (covariate) and mobility group as the classification variable. Two dependent variables were used: TEI year 2 (that is, relative year = move) and TEI year 3 (relative year = post-move). Additionally, the set of analyses were completed using all 366 of the teachers for the state, and separate analyses were then con-

Table 8-7. *Analyses of Covariance Using Only Teachers Who Moved*[a]

Predictor variables	DF	SS	MS	F	Pr > F
Whole state					
TEI year 2					
TEI year 1	1	66.7	66.7	26.5	<.0001
Mobility group	2	30.7	15.4	6.1	0.0025
Residual	362	910.6	2.5	...	...
TEI year 3					
TEI year 1	1	111.7	111.7	41.0	<.0001
Mobility group	2	45.9	22.9	8.4	0.0003
Residual	362	986.6	2.7	...	...
Four urban districts					
TEI year 2					
TEI year 1	1	38.9	38.9	12.9	0.0004
Mobility group	2	23.3	11.6	3.9	0.0231
Residual	148	445.4	3.0	...	...
TEI year 3					
TEI year 1	1	85.7	85.7	25.6	<.0001
Mobility group	2	22.4	11.2	3.3	0.0383
Residual	148	496.1	3.4	...	...

a. DF = degrees of freedom; SS = sum of squares; MS = mean squared; F = F-statistic; and Pr > F = p-value of F-statistic.

ducted using only the 152 teachers from the four largest urban districts. Initial analyses (not shown) found no significant differences in the slopes of the within-group regression lines (with p values ranging from 0.41 to 0.96).[23] The lack of interaction in the analysis of covariance (that is, the parallelism of the regression lines in the three mobility groups) implies that the ability of the pre-move TEI to predict the post-move TEI holds equally for all three mobility groups. In particular, it can be inferred to hold for the teachers who moved to poorer schools even though the number of teachers in that group is relatively small. The final results, using parallel slopes, are presented in table 8-7.

The relationship between the response and the covariate was found to be higher with the second year after the move than with the first year after the move. This suggests that there may be a period of adjustment in the first year after the move regardless of the mobility group. While there were significant effects of mobility group not accounted for by adjustment for the covariate, the relative magnitude of the relationship (as shown by the relative magnitudes of the mean squares in the "MS" column of table 8-7) indicates that most of the variation explained was attributed to a teacher's effectiveness scores before the move. This suggests that the differences among classrooms are primarily attributable to the effectiveness of the individual teacher—not the specific environment in which the teacher works.

Discussion

In the repeated measures analysis, a significant positive effect in teacher effectiveness estimates was found when teachers moved from higher-poverty to lower-poverty schools. However, the magnitude of this effect was not sufficient to overpower the relationship between the measure of teaching effectiveness before the move to a lower-poverty school and the subsequent effect after the move, as shown in the analyses of covariance and the cross-tabulation tables. Another important observation is that the magnitude of the relationship between the teacher effectiveness measures before and after the move was higher with the second year after the move than with the year of the move. Perhaps this is the result of teachers' adjusting to their new surroundings and the achievement levels of their students.

Even though the number of teachers who had moved from a richer to a poorer school was small, the lack of interaction in the analysis of covariance (that is, the parallelism of the regression lines) indicates that the same relationship that holds for those who moved to a poorer school holds as well for the larger number of teachers who moved to a richer school or a school with a similar percentage of students eligible for free and reduced-price lunch. In short, the strongest predictor of teacher effectiveness after a move is teacher effectiveness before the move. These findings suggest that policymakers should not be dissuaded as they attempt to develop strategies for creating incentives for highly effective teachers to either move to or remain in schools with the greatest student academic needs. It is also important to note that this study used only individual teachers' one-year estimates. If a policy is implemented to identify candidates to be recruited and offered incentives to move to schools with greater needs, then two- or three-year estimates for each teacher will add even more reliability to the estimates and will further minimize the risk of faulty hiring or retention decisions. Even if one-year estimates are used to identify a pool of candidates with a TEI of +1 or greater who would be offered incentives to move to a school with the greatest academic need, then the likelihood of selecting a below-average teacher after the move is estimated from this study to be less than 0.3.

Where available, appropriately determined value added measures of teacher effectiveness should be included as a major component in determining which teachers are to be offered incentives to move to high-needs schools. Teachers selected on the basis of a policy that heavily weights prior value added estimates are more likely to be effective in facilitating academic growth for students, after moving to a new school, than teachers who are selected based upon traditional credentials.

Notes

1. Eric A. Hanushek, John F. Kain, and Steven G. Rivkin, "Teachers, Schools, and Academic Achievement," *Econometrica* 73, no. 2 (2005): 417–58.
2. Ibid.; Daniel Aaronson, Lisa Barrow, and William Sanders, "Teachers and Student Achievement in the Chicago Public High Schools," *Journal of Labor Economics* 25, no. 1 (2007): 95–135.
3. Cynthia D. Prince, *Higher Pay in Hard-to-Staff Schools: The Case for Financial Incentives* (Lanham, Md.: Scarecrow Press, 2003); Heather G. Peske and Kati Haycock, *Teaching Inequality: How Poor and Minority Students Are Shortchanged on Teacher Quality* (Washington: Education Trust, 2006); Brian A. Jacob, "The Challenges of Staffing Urban Schools with Effective Teachers," *Future of Children* 17, no. 1 (2007): 129–53; Jennifer Imazeki, "Attracting and Retaining Teachers in High-Need Schools: Do Financial Incentives Make Financial Sense?" San Diego State University, November 2007; Anthony T. Milanowski and others, *Recruiting New Teachers to Urban School Districts: What Incentives Will Work* (Seattle, Wash.: Center on Reinventing Public Education, 2007).
4. Historical trends in district implementation reflect a willingness among local policymakers to experiment with financial incentives to recruit and retain teachers. Using data from multiple waves of the National Center for Education Statistics' Schools and Staffing Survey, a large nationally representative sample of teachers, schools, and districts, Michael Podgursky and colleagues have examined the diffusion of incentive programs over time. One set of analyses finds that fewer than 8 percent of U.S. public school districts (employing 11.3 percent of teachers) provided recruitment incentives in the 1987–88 school year. The prevalence of these incentive programs climbed to 12 percent of districts (employing 25.0 percent of teachers) in the 2003–04 school year. For more information, see Michael J. Podgursky and others, "The Diffusion of Teacher Performance Pay: Evidence from Multiple Waves of SASS," Working Paper (Nashville, Tenn.: National Center on Performance Incentives, November 2007).
5. Anecdotal evidence from an interim evaluation report on the PayPLUS program in Butler County, Alabama, suggests that differentiated compensation systems may help improve a district's appeal when it is trying to recruit teachers. As an elementary school principal notes, "Sometimes in this business as an administrator I guess the biggest elephant in the room in rural areas like this is finding highly qualified people. How can we compete? We have a tool now, PayPLUS." See James W. Guthrie, Peter J. Witham, and Jessica L. Lewis, *Evaluation of Butler County's PayPLUS Salary Augmentation System: Early Findings about Program Implementation* (Davis, Calif.: Management Analysis and Planning, 2008), p. 27.
6. Charles T. Clotfelter and others, "Do School Accountability Systems Make It More Difficult for Low-Performing Schools to Attract and Retain High-Quality Teachers?" *Journal of Policy Analysis and Management* 23, no. 2 (2004): 251–71; Edward Liu, Susan Moore

Johnson, and Heather G. Peske, "New Teachers and the Massachusetts Signing Bonus: The Limits of Inducements," *Educational Evaluation and Policy Analysis* 26, no. 3 (2004): 217–36; Imazeki, "Attracting and Retaining Teachers in High-Need Schools."

7. Eric A. Hanushek, John F. Kain, and Steven G. Rivkin, "Why Public Schools Lose Teachers," *Journal of Human Resources* 39, no. 2 (2004): 326–54.

8. Donald Boyd and others, "Explaining the Short Careers of High-Achieving Teachers in Schools with Low-Performing Students," *Proceedings of the American Economic Association* 95, no. 2 (2005): 166–71; Donald Boyd and others, "The Draw of Home: How Teachers' Preferences for Proximity Disadvantage Urban Schools," *Journal of Policy Analysis and Management* 24, no. 1 (2005): 113–32.

9. Podgursky and others, "The Diffusion of Teacher Performance Pay."

10. See Lynn Cornett, *Teacher Supply and Demand in Tennessee* (Atlanta, Ga.: Southern Regional Education Board, 2001).

11. Tennessee Department of Education, *Annual Statistical Report, 2006–2007* (Nashville, 2007).

12. See also Southern Regional Education Board, *Focus on Teacher Pay and Incentives: Recent Legislative Actions and Update on Salary Averages,* focus report, May 2007.

13. Tennessee Department of Education, *Teacher Equity Plan,* September 2006. For more information on teachers' motivations for moving to different school districts, see Tennessee Advisory Commission on Intergovernmental Relations, *Teacher Mobility among Tennessee School Districts: A Survey of Causes,* February 2000.

14. Federal law stipulates that teachers who seek to be recognized as highly qualified must hold a bachelor's degree and full state certification or licensure and be able to prove their competency in each subject they teach in the classroom. Teachers are determined to be *highly qualified* on the basis of their educational background and job certifications, whereas teachers are frequently observed to be *highly effective* on the basis of standardized test results or other measures of educational outcomes. A core assumption of this chapter is that teacher effectiveness may be measured on the basis of test-score gains, but many practitioners recognize the validity of other means of comparison as well.

15. Tennessee Department of Education, *Teacher Equity Plan.* The U.S. Department of Education requires all states to submit a teacher equity plan in compliance with the teacher quality provisions of No Child Left Behind. The teacher equity plan requirement calls for each state to name the specific steps it will take to ensure that poor and minority students are not taught by inexperienced, unqualified, or out-of-field teachers at higher rates than other children.

16. The state report does not specifically define what constitutes high- and low-poverty schools. Novice teachers are defined as instructors with three years or less of experience, and inexperienced teachers are defined as instructors with five years' experience or less.

17. Tennessee Department of Education, "Tennessee's Most Effective Teachers: Are They Assigned to the Schools That Need Them the Most?" research brief, March 2007.

18. The state report defines high-poverty–high-minority schools as those in which at least 75 percent of students qualify for free or reduced-price lunch and at least 75 percent of students are African American, American Indian–Alaska Native, Asian–Pacific Islander, or Hispanic-Latino. Low-poverty–low-minority schools are those that enroll less than 25 percent students who qualify for free or reduced-price lunch and less than 25 percent students who are African American, American Indian–Alaska Native, Asian–Pacific Islander, or Hispanic-Latino.

19. For more information on the Tennessee Value-Added Assessment System, see William Sanders, Arnold M. Saxton, and Sandra P. Horn, "The Tennessee Value-Added Assessment System: A Quantitative Outcomes-Based Approach to Educational Assessment," in *Grading Teachers, Grading Schools: Is Student Achievement a Valid Evaluation Measure?* edited by Jason Millman (Thousand Oaks, Calif.: Corwin Press, 1997), pp. 137–62. Other important studies include William L. Sanders and June C. Rivers, "Cumulative and Residual Effects of Teachers on Future Student Academic Achievement: Tennessee Value-Added Assessment System (TVAAS)," research paper, University of Tennessee Value-Added Research and Assessment Center, 1996, pp. 1–14; S. Paul Wright, Sandra P. Horn, and William L. Sanders, "Teacher and Classroom Context Effects on Student Achievement: Implications for Teacher Evaluation," *Journal of Personnel Evaluation in Education* 11, no. 1 (1997): 57–67.

20. The hypothetical figure and discussion used in this paragraph are based on Dale Ballou, William Sanders, and Paul Wright, "Controlling for Student Background in Value-Added Assessment of Teachers," *Journal of Educational and Behavioral Statistics* 29, no. 1 (2004): 37–65.

21. Academic and policy researchers view value added models as a promising avenue for measuring teacher performance on the job. See Robert Gordon, Thomas J. Kane, and Douglas O. Staiger, "Identifying Effective Teachers Using Performance on the Job," Hamilton Project Discussion Paper 2006-01 (Brookings, 2006).

22. Sanders, Saxton, and Horn, "The Tennessee Value-Added Assessment System."

23. These preliminary calculations are available on request from the authors.

9

Teacher-Designed Performance-Pay Plans in Texas

Lori L. Taylor, Matthew G. Springer, and Mark Ehlert

M any localities and states are experimenting with teacher pay for performance. In 2006 the U.S. Congress appropriated $99 million a year for
five years to provide Teacher Incentive Fund grants to schools, districts, and states
to develop and evaluate administrator and teacher pay-for-performance plans. Pay
for performance is part of teacher compensation packages in the Dallas, Denver,
Houston, and New York City public school systems. Educators deemed to be high
performing across the states of Florida, Minnesota, and Texas claim their shares
of more than $550 million in incentives each year.[1]

This project was supported by the Texas Education Agency and the National Center on Performance Incentives, which is funded by the U.S. Department of Education's Institute of Education Sciences (R305A06034). We appreciate helpful comments and suggestions from
Catherine Gardner, Warren Langevin, Jessica Lewis, Andrew Moellmer, Ellen Montgomery,
Michael Podgursky, Amie Rapaport, Herb Walberg, and many others at the Texas Education
Agency and participants at the National Center on Performance Incentives' 2008 research to
policy forum and the Thirty-Third Annual Meeting of the American Education Finance Association. The views expressed in this paper do not necessarily reflect those of sponsoring agencies or individuals acknowledged.

Despite all the activity, however, there is still relatively little evidence on the characteristics of optimal incentive pay plans for teachers. Some of the economics literature indicates that winner-take-all plans, wherein only a few workers receive large awards, are the most effective at motivating workers. Other studies support provision of a broad array of bonus awards to individual employees. Still others suggest that group-based incentives are the most effective strategy when teamwork and cooperation are integral to the production process—as is arguably the case in education.

This chapter describes the teacher pay-for-performance plans designed and implemented by the public schools participating in the Governor's Educator Excellence Grant program (GEEG) in Texas. The GEEG program was a federally funded program that awarded noncompetitive grants to ninety-nine Texas public schools. Participating schools were required to develop their own pay-for-performance plans and to demonstrate significant teacher involvement in the design and approval of those plans.[2]

Schools participating in the GEEG program took advantage of their considerable discretion to design incentive plans exhibiting an array of differences on several key plan variables. Such variation provides a unique opportunity for analysis. This study explores the following research questions:

—How did schools propose to distribute awards to teachers, and how did a GEEG school's proposed award distribution plan play out in practice?

—What is the relationship between teacher characteristics and the dollar amounts awarded to teachers as part of their school's GEEG plan?

—What are the determinants of GEEG plan characteristics and the distribution of awards?

Because of the variation in plan designs and the prominent role that teachers played in designing and approving the incentive pay plans, the analysis in this chapter can offer important insights into the nature of compensation reforms that educators perceive to be acceptable. Identifying the features that make pay-for-performance plans attractive to teachers is crucial for future compensation reform efforts because the failure of many previous programs has been attributed to a lack of teacher engagement and buy-in around plan design.[3] Furthermore, knowing whether teacher and school characteristics are associated with particular GEEG plan characteristics could help policymakers and other education stakeholders better understand how different groups may perceive various design features of a teacher compensation reform proposal.

Governor's Educator Excellence Grant Program

Texas's Governor's Educator Excellence Grant program identified the 100 highest-poverty high-performing schools in the state and awarded them noncompetitive grants, ranging from $60,000 to $220,000 each year for three years. Schools were first notified of their eligibility for the program during the 2005–06 school year and were required to develop and submit their incentive plan proposals by the end of that school year. Because one school never finalized the design of its GEEG plan with the Texas Education Agency, a total of 99 schools participated in the program.

The GEEG award amounts were substantial. Most schools received between $150 and $200 per pupil for each of three years, which was equivalent to between 2.6 and 16.5 percent of a recipient school's instructional payroll. The average grant amount was 5.1 percent of instructional payroll.

Program Eligibility

To be eligible for the program, schools had to be in the top third of Texas schools with respect to the share of economically disadvantaged students during the 2004–05 school year. Eligibility for the program was determined separately for elementary, middle, high, and mixed-grade schools: elementary schools had to be in the top third of the poverty distribution for elementary schools, middle schools had to be in the top third of the distribution for middle schools, and so on. The identification strategy resulted in economically disadvantaged student thresholds of 81.3 percent for elementary schools, 65.4 percent for middle schools, 55.8 percent for high schools, and 70.5 percent for schools that serve mixed-grade configurations.

Roughly half of the eligible schools were classified as high performing. High-performing schools were those that had attained one of the two highest ratings in the Texas Accountability System—recognized or exemplary—for the 2004–05 school year.[4] Among other things, a "recognized" rating in 2004–05 meant that for every subject and every student subgroup at least 70 percent of the tested students had passed the state's high-stakes assessment, the Texas Assessment of Knowledge and Skills (TAKS).[5] An "exemplary" rating elevated this standard, requiring that at least 90 percent of the tested students in each subject and subgroup had passed the TAKS. Ultimately, all public schools with an exemplary rating in the 2004–05 school year that were also in the top third with respect to student poverty were GEEG eligible, as were the recognized schools with the highest shares of economically disadvantaged students in each grade category.

The remaining GEEG schools were high-improving schools, defined as being in the top quartile on the comparable improvement rankings in either math or reading and language arts in 2004–05. The Texas Education Agency (TEA) determines these rankings by matching each Texas public school annually with forty other Texas public schools on the basis of student demographics. The agency then calculates the average change in student test scores from one year to the next and places schools into quartiles based on their position relative to the forty comparable schools. A school in the top quartile of comparable improvement rankings has an average gain in TAKS scores at least equal to the tenth largest gain among the forty schools in its reference group.

Program Guidelines

The TEA established a set of guidelines for schools to reference when designing their pay-for-performance plans. Those guidelines divide GEEG program funding into two parts. Part 1 funds were to be used for awards paid directly to full-time teachers (those who teach four or more hours during the typical academic day). Part 2 funds were to be used to provide awards to other school personnel or to fund professional development programs for teachers, induction programs for teachers, or other professional growth opportunities. Seventy-five percent of the total GEEG awards were dedicated to part 1 incentives, while the remaining 25 percent were dedicated to funding part 1 or part 2 activities.

The TEA guidelines further stipulate that part 1 fund awards must be based on two criteria: success in improving student achievement (as evidenced by an objective performance measure) and a teacher's collaboration with faculty and staff. Although both student achievement and collaboration are required criteria of a school's GEEG plan, schools had a great deal of flexibility when it came to defining the actual performance measures and benchmarks used to evaluate teachers' performance. As illustrated in the top panel of table 9-1, the most common measures of student achievement were student assessments, and most schools chose more than one indicator to evaluate this criterion.

Schools also had the option of including two additional criteria for evaluating teacher performance with respect to their part 1 funds. First, they could reward a teacher's ongoing initiative, commitment, and professional involvement in activities that directly affect student achievement.[6] Second, they could reward a teacher for working in a hard-to-staff subject area (defined as an area that was experiencing a critical shortage of teachers or has had a high turnover rate).[7] As illustrated in the bottom panel of the table, forty-five of the ninety-nine schools developed GEEG plans based exclusively on the two required criteria, and thirty-nine

Table 9-1. *Characteristics of GEEG Pay-for-Performance Plans*[a]

Indicators of student performance	n
Comparable Improvement	5
Drop-out rate	5
Adequate Yearly Progress	6
Teacher attendance	6
Student attendance	7
Other	16
Texas Education Agency campus ratings	45
Student assessments	80
Performance criteria for rewarding teachers	
Required + hard-to-staff areas	1
Required + teacher initiative + hard-to-staff areas	14
Required + teacher initiative	39
Student performance + teacher collaboration (required)	45

Source: Data from Matthew G. Springer and others, *Governor's Educator Excellence Grant (GEEG) Program: Year One Evaluation Report* (Nashville, Tenn.: National Center on Performance Incentives, 2007).
a. Ninety-nine observations (schools).

schools used a measure of teacher initiative in addition to the two required performance criteria. The remaining schools proposed plans that relied on the two required performance criteria and the hard-to-staff criteria, with or without a measure of teacher initiative.

The TEA guidelines recommend that part 1 awards should be at least $3,000 and no more than $10,000 for each teacher. However, an eligible school could opt out of this proviso by offering a brief justification in its application in favor of an alternative award distribution plan. Most GEEG schools designed and implemented pay-for-performance plans that offered minimum and maximum awards of less than $3,000 a teacher. The proposed and actual distribution of GEEG awards are discussed in greater detail later in this chapter.

The GEEG program guidelines stipulate that part 2 funds may be spent on incentives for school personnel who contributed to improving student performance and who did not receive part 1 awards.[8] Part 2 funds could also be used for professional development activities, signing bonuses, teacher mentoring programs, new teacher induction programs, funding for feeder schools, or any other professional program that directly contributed to improving student performance. Fifty-seven GEEG schools used some or all of their part 2 funds to provide awards to teachers eligible for part 1 bonuses, thus making available to eligible teachers a larger pot of award money.

Data and Sample

The data for this study come from three primary sources. Information on characteristics of schools' GEEG plans were obtained from data collected and maintained by the National Center on Performance Incentives at Vanderbilt University as part of its contract with the TEA to evaluate the GEEG program. The center's research team reviewed GEEG plans described in applications submitted to the TEA by each of the ninety-nine participating schools and recorded information on the amount of total school grant, proposed minimum and maximum award amounts for individual teachers, indicators used to measure teacher performance, and models used to distribute teacher awards. All applications were independently reviewed and coded by two research assistants and subsequently checked by a third person to ensure accuracy. The performance center also surveyed all GEEG schools to collect data on the processes schools used to develop and approve plans, as well as supplemental information about plan features that were not clearly described in applications schools submitted to the Texas Education Agency.

Data on the distribution of actual bonuses awarded to teachers were collected by the TEA using a secure, online data upload system. Following the distribution of teacher awards in fall 2006, schools recorded the actual amounts awarded to each teacher. These data were extensively audited by researchers at both the TEA and the National Center on Performance Incentives and then match merged with administrative personnel records in Texas's Public Education Information Management System.

Eighty-five of the ninety-nine GEEG schools provided information on actual award amounts distributed to teachers that fall. Five elementary schools, six middle schools, and three secondary schools did not submit data on award amounts distributed to teachers despite repeated reminders from both the TEA and performance incentive center staff. Nonrespondent schools are not systematically different from respondents with respect to student ethnicity or student socioeconomic status, nor are there significant differences in response rates between high-performing and high-improving schools. Furthermore, respondent schools do not systematically differ from nonrespondents with respect to any of the specific program characteristics considered in this analysis. However, nonrespondent schools are significantly larger, on average, than respondent schools.

Data on school, teacher, and student characteristics were extracted from Texas's Academic Excellence Indicator System and confidential Public Education Information Management System files maintained by the TEA. Data from the excellence indicator system and the information management system cover GEEG schools, schools participating in other state-funded teacher pay-for-performance programs, and schools that are not participating in a state-funded pay-for-performance program.[9]

Governor's Educator Excellence Grant schools are systematically different from other schools in Texas with respect to student characteristics and school locations. By design, GEEG schools serve a higher share of economically disadvantaged students. Coincidentally, they also serve a student population that is disproportionately urban and Hispanic.[10] Twenty-eight of the ninety-nine GEEG schools are located in three large urban school districts—Houston, Brownsville, and Dallas.

However, GEEG schools are remarkably similar to other public schools in Texas with respect to observable characteristics of the teacher workforce. Teachers in GEEG schools had similar average years of experience (11.0 years) to other teachers in the state (11.5 years). Teachers in GEEG schools were slightly less likely to hold advanced degrees (19.3 percent versus 22.0 percent), and the campus-level teacher turnover rate was somewhat lower in GEEG schools (17.6 versus 21.3 percent) than in other schools in the state.[11] Average teacher salaries are about $750 a year higher in GEEG schools ($43,737 versus $42,992), which may reflect the fact that GEEG schools are disproportionately urban.

The Characteristics of Teacher-Designed Incentive Plans

Schools adopted more than twenty indicators to evaluate a teacher's performance on the two criteria required by GEEG program guidelines (student achievement and teacher collaboration). In exploring the plans implemented as part of the GEEG program, we focused on the units of accountability for evaluating teacher performance, the approaches identified in GEEG grant applications for measuring student performance, and the proposed and actual distributions of teacher awards.

Units of Accountability and Measures of Student Performance

Although GEEG program guidelines favor individual incentives over group incentives, the empirical literature on optimal incentives is mixed on the subject. Richard Freeman and Alexander Gelber conclude that individual incentives are systematically more effective than group incentives, while Ottorino Chillemi finds that group incentives are more effective than individual incentives when workers care about their co-workers' material benefit.[12] William Encinosa, Martin Gaynor, and James Rebitzer find that individual incentives

Table 9-2. *Measures of Student Performance, by Unit of Accountability*[a]

Unit of accountability	Attainment	Gain	Attainment + gain
Campus	21	3	8
Teacher	28	6	12
Grade level or subject matter team	2	0	0
Campus + teacher	7	2	6
Campus, teacher, + team	2	0	0

Source: Data from Matthew G. Springer and others, *Governor's Educator Excellence Grant (GEEG) Program: Year One Evaluation Report* (Nashville, Tenn.: National Center on Performance Incentives, 2007).

a. Ninety-seven observations (schools). Two schools are not included because of incomplete information in their program application.

induce greater work intensity than do group incentives for large groups but not for small ones.[13]

The GEEG plans are also mixed. Most GEEG schools designed plans that relied, at least in part, on individual incentives. Table 9-2 reports on the units of accountability and the measures of student performance for ninety-seven of the ninety-nine schools participating in the GEEG program. (Two schools are not included because of incomplete information in their program application.) Units of accountability indicate the type of incentives provided by the plan. Plans are classified according to whether they provide campus-wide incentives, team incentives, individual teacher incentives, or some combination of campus, team, and individual incentives. Measures of student performance are reported as student attainment, student growth, or a combination of the two.

As table 9-2 illustrates, forty-six schools considered student performance exclusively at the teacher level when determining GEEG awards. Another seventeen schools used both the teacher unit and a more aggregate unit (grade or school) to evaluate whether a teacher or a set of teachers received an award. Slightly less than one-third of schools participating in the GEEG program relied exclusively on group performance for determining teacher awards.

As the table also illustrates, most GEEG schools devised incentive plans that rewarded teachers for student performance levels. Nearly two-thirds provided incentives to teachers whose students reached designated performance levels, without any explicit consideration of gains. Only eleven of the ninety-seven schools designed plans that exclusively rewarded gains in student performance.

Table 9-3 uses a similar taxonomy to describe other domestic and international pay-for-performance programs. The list is restricted to programs that have been studied using a conventional treatment and control evaluation design, with pre-treatment data on student performance for both groups.[14] As in table 9-2, the

Table 9-3. *Characteristics of Pay-for-Performance Programs in the United States and Abroad*

Program	Period	Unit of accountability	Measures of student performance	Award amount (dollars)		% Monthly salary
				Minimum	Maximum	
United States						
Dallas, Texas, School Incentive Program	1992–95	School	Multiple indicators, including student test score gains, student achievement levels, student attendance, student promotion, and accelerated course enrollments	450	1,000	≈ 10%–22%
Merit Pay Program (Michigan)	1996–97	Teacher	Student retention and student evaluation of teacher	1,000	≈ 5,000	≈ 12.5%– 62.5%
Little Rock, Arkansas, Achievement Challenge Pilot Project	2005–07	Teacher	Student test score gains	350	7,600	≈ 8%–174%
Teacher Advancement Program	1999–present	Teacher and school	Student test score gains	2,500	12,000	≈ 45%–216%
Texas Educator Excellence Grant Program	2007–present	Teacher, team, or school	Multiple indicators, including student achievement levels, student test score gains, and student and teacher attendance	250	10,000	≈ 4.5%–180%

(continued)

Table 9-3. *Characteristics of Pay-for-Performance Programs in the United States and Abroad (continued)*

	Period	Unit of accountability	Measures of student performance	Award amount (dollars) Minimum	Maximum	% Monthly salary
International						
Israel, Ministry of Education, School Performance Program	1996–97	School	Number of credit units per student, student receiving a matriculation certification, and school drop-out rate	1,000	2,500	≈ 10%–40%
Kenya, International Christelijk Steuenfonds Incentive Program	1998–99	School	Student test score gains and student achievement levels	26	51	≈ 21%–43%
Israel, Teacher-Incentive Experiment	2001	Teacher	Student achievement levels	1,750	15,000	≈ 10%–86%
Andhra Pradesh Randomized Evaluation Project	2006–present	Teacher or school	Student test score gains	2.25	450	≈ 1%–200%

Sources: C. Clotfelter and H. Ladd, "Recognizing and Rewarding Success in Public Schools," in *Holding Schools Accountable: Performance-Related Reform in Education*, edited by Helen Ladd (Brookings, 1996); P. Glewwe, N. Ilias, and M. Kremer, "Teacher Incentives in the Developing World," mimeograph, Harvard University, Cambridge, Mass., 2008; Helen Ladd, "The Dallas School Accountability and Incentive Program: An Evaluation of Its Impacts on Student Outcomes," *Economics of Education Review* 18, no.1 (1999): 1–16; V. Lavy, "Evaluating the Effect of Teachers' Group Performance Incentives on Pupil Achievement," *Journal of Political Economy* 110, no. 6 (2002): 1286–317; V. Lavy, "Performance Pay and Teachers' Effort, Productivity and Grading Ethics," NBER Working Paper 10622 (Cambridge, Mass.: National Bureau of Economic Research, 2004); K. Muralidharan and V. Sundararaman, "Teacher Incentives in Developing Countries: Experimental Evidence from India," Working Paper (Nashville, Tenn.: National Center on Performance Incentives, 2008); M. G. Springer, D. Ballou, and A. Peng, "The Impact of the Teacher Advancement Program on Student Test Score Gains: Findings from an Independent Appraisal," CESifo/PEPG Conference on Economic Incentives: Do They Work in Education? Insights and Findings from Behavioral Research, May 17. Munich, Germany: Center for Economic Studies Information and Forschung/Program on Education Policy and Governance, 2008. M. Springer and others, *Texas Educator Excellence Grant (TEEG) Program: Year Two Evaluation Report* (Nashville, Tenn.: National Center on Performance Incentives, 2008); M. Winters and others, *An Evaluation of Teacher Performance Pay in Arkansas*, University of Arkansas, Department of Education Reform, 2006.

units of accountability include teacher, team, school, or some combination of the three. The measures of student performance for evaluating teachers include student test-score gains and attainment as well as a number of other indicators such as teacher and student absenteeism, student promotion, and student participation in advanced courses. A comparison between tables 9-2 and 9-3 quickly demonstrates that GEEG program schools represent the full range of previously analyzed program types.

Proposed Distribution of Teacher Awards

Figure 9-1 shows the range of award amounts specified in GEEG grant applications submitted to the Texas Education Agency. Each vertical bar represents a single school. The lower end of each bar is the minimum designated award under that school's GEEG plan, while the upper end of the bar indicates the maximum award proposed by that school. The minimum award amount is defined as any value other than $0 that a teacher can earn as part of his or her school's GEEG program; that is, if a teacher met the criteria for earning only the minimum award identified in the school's grant application, that teacher would receive the designated minimum award amount. The maximum represents the total award amount that a teacher could earn if he or she met all possible award criteria laid out in the GEEG plan. Six schools are not represented in the figure because we

Figure 9-1. *Range of Proposed Award Amounts, GEEG Schools, 2006*

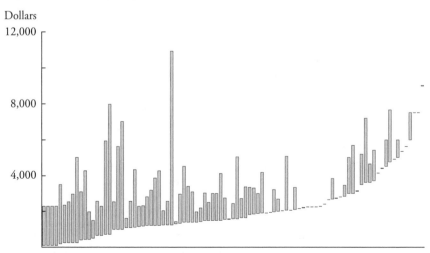

Source: Proposed GEEG teacher award information collected during fall 2006 by coding GEEG plan applications submitted to the Texas Education Agency.

could not reliably determine the minimum and maximum awards proposed by those schools.

As the figure illustrates, the distribution of awards proposed in GEEG grant applications varies considerably, both within and between schools. Twenty-two schools designed GEEG plans wherein the maximum plan award equals the minimum plan award, meaning a teacher who reaches a predetermined performance threshold receives the same award regardless of the degree to which he or she performed above that standard. Six schools proposed minimum and maximum award amounts that had a range of more than $4,000, one of which exceeded $9,600. The average difference between the proposed minimum and maximum awards in GEEG plans is $1,615.

Figure 9-1 also indicates that most schools proposed an award distribution structure that does not align with the minimum and maximum dollar amounts recommended in GEEG program guidelines. The Texas Education Agency guidelines advise that part 1 incentives should be at least $3,000 and no more than $10,000 per teacher, apparently under the assumption that the minimum award should be large enough to elicit a response to the incentive plan. However, seventy-five schools proposed a minimum award of less than $3,000 in their GEEG grant application, and almost half of all schools proposed a maximum award of less than $3,000.

Although most acknowledge a monetary performance award must be perceived as large enough to motivate teachers, there is little definitive evidence to guide decisionmakers on the optimal size of awards. The experimental economics literature, for example, suggests higher award payoffs lead to greater effort but also that multiple prizes can be more effective than a single large prize that most employees have little chance of winning.[15] Furthermore, the optimal incentive structure appears sensitive to the amount of information workers have about their performance relative to other workers. When workers are not aware of the abilities of other participants, a larger prize is more likely to elicit the greatest effort among employees. However, if workers have a chance to observe other potential recipients in action, some workers may reasonably conclude that they have little or no chance of winning and therefore will not respond to a winner-take-all incentive, no matter how large. Under those conditions, the optimal incentive system needs to include an array of intermediate awards to elicit more total effort from employees.

Since the range between the minimum award and the maximum award can be misleading if there are teachers who do not receive an award under a school's GEEG plan, we turn to the Gini coefficient to measure the dispersion of GEEG awards. A Gini coefficient, a common ratio measure of income inequality, ranges from zero to one. A value of zero means all teachers receive exactly the same award (that is, the distribution is perfectly equal), while a value of one means only one teacher receives an award (that is, the distribution is perfectly unequal).

We calculate a Gini coefficient for the proposed distribution of part 1 funds. This "plan Gini" corresponds to the most unequal distribution of awards possible, given the award parameters identified in the plan application a school submitted to the Texas Education Agency and the total amount of part 1 funds the TEA awarded to that school. The most unequal distribution that exhausts part 1 funds occurs when total part 1 funds are distributed across teachers so that as many teachers as possible receive the maximum designated award, one teacher receives any residual part 1 funds (which would necessarily be less than the maximum award), and the remaining teachers received no award at all.[16]

Figure 9-2 displays the distribution of plan Gini coefficients for the ninety-four GEEG schools for which it was possible to determine a maximum proposed award for teachers.[17] The sample mean for plan Gini coefficients is 0.34, with the highest value of a plan Gini coefficient being 0.77. Three schools have plan Ginis of

Figure 9-2. *Distribution of Plan Gini Coefficients, by Number of Schools, 2006*

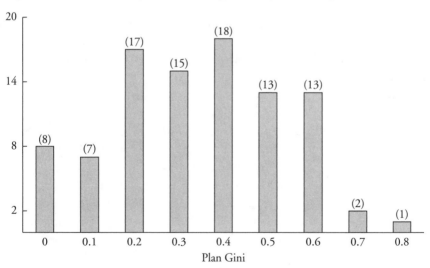

Source: Plan Gini derived from proposed GEEG teacher award information collected during fall 2006 by coding GEEG plan applications submitted to the Texas Education Agency.

0.00 (that is, perfect equality), meaning that every teacher could receive the maximum proposed award.

The distribution of plan Ginis suggests that the maximum potential inequality of GEEG award plans is less than the inequality of the distribution of income in the United States (0.42 in 2005)[18] but markedly greater than the inequality of teacher salaries within the ninety-nine schools participating in the GEEG program. (Gini coefficients for the distribution of total teacher pay in the 2005–06 school year in GEEG schools ranged from 0.04 to 0.16, with a mean of 0.09.) Only nine GEEG schools (seven elementary schools and two high schools) had plan Ginis that were lower than their Gini coefficients for teacher pay, meaning that the award distribution plan identified in their GEEG grant application is more egalitarian than the base teacher salaries within their school.

The award distribution schemes proposed in GEEG grant applications further indicate that a handful of schools may be unable to fully implement their plan as originally conceptualized.[19] None of the twenty-two GEEG schools with a proposed award range of zero had a plan Gini of 0.00, meaning that no school in which the minimum proposed award equals the maximum proposed award had sufficient funding to give all teachers an award if all teachers met those plans' predetermined performance thresholds. Similar flaws in the design and management of pay-for-performance systems have compelled schools and school systems to abandon teacher compensation reforms owing to a lack of confidence in the program among stakeholders.[20] A fixed-tournament incentive system, wherein the winner or winners take all, can mitigate unknown financial exposure, though this type of system is believed to threaten team production by reducing teacher cooperation because teachers within a school may be competing for a limited number of awards.[21]

Actual Distribution of Teacher Awards

The timing of implementation of the GEEG program meant teacher awards were retroactive during the first year of the three-year program. Program plans submitted to the TEA were approved at the end of the 2005–06 school year, the same school year in which teacher performance was evaluated to determine their eligibility for the first round of awards. Thus the actual distribution of awards in the first award cycle should largely reflect the GEEG plans that teachers designed for themselves and should not be confounded by behavioral responses to the plan itself.

Figure 9-3 displays the distribution of part 1 awards pooled across all teachers and schools, conditional upon a teacher receiving an award for his or her per-

Figure 9-3. *Distribution of Part 1 Funding, by Award Amount, 2006*

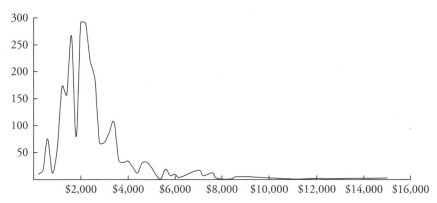

Source: GEEG teacher award information collected during fall 2006 using an online, secure data upload system.

formance during the 2005–06 school year. Fourteen schools did not provide the actual award amounts distributed to teachers; thus information displayed in figure 9-3 includes actual award data for 85 percent of schools participating in the GEEG program. Awards ranged from a low of $75 to a high of $15,000, with most teachers awarded between $1,000 and $3,000. Almost 80 percent of the teachers who earned an award from part 1 funds received less than $3,000.

Forty-three percent of GEEG schools distributed awards from part 1 funds that exceeded the maximum dollar amount specified in their application submitted to the TEA. For example, although the proposed maximum award in one high school was less than $11,000, three teachers in that school received $15,000 each, while the other eight full-time teachers did not receive an award. This pattern suggests some schools, if too few of their teachers had qualified for a bonus, resorted to contingency plans to distribute grant balances among those teachers meeting the performance criteria thresholds. Contingency plans are a required element of the GEEG program, since grants awarded to schools must be spent before the close of the fiscal year. Schools may turn to a contingency plan for a number of reasons, for example, if the performance standard was set too high or the minimum and maximum bonuses were set too low.

Among the eighty-five GEEG schools that provided awards data, the share of teachers who received a performance award from part 1 funding in fall 2006 ranged from 36 to 100 percent, with a sample mean of 78 percent. Interestingly, 70 of the 624 full-time teachers who were new to a GEEG school in the fall of 2006 received part 1 awards (thirty campuses made such awards), even though awards were based on evaluations of the prior year's accomplishments. Although awarding a teacher new to the school was permitted under program guidelines, the actual distribution of awards may be suggestive of an egalitarian view toward pay-for-performance policies in these schools. On the other hand, awarding a teacher new to the school may speak to the many complexities associated with designing, implementing, and managing a pay-for-performance program.[22]

We also studied the relationship between a school's proposed and actual distribution of part 1 funds by calculating the school's "actual Gini" and comparing their plan Gini coefficient with their actual Gini coefficient. The actual Gini coefficient summarizes the distribution of part 1 awards among teachers who could have qualified for a part 1 award because they taught full-time in a GEEG school during the first year of the program (the 2005–06 school year).

As illustrated in figure 9-4, the actual distribution of awards had higher Gini coefficient values than Gini coefficient values for the proposed distribution of awards in forty-nine of the eighty schools for which we have data on both the proposed and actual distribution of GEEG awards.[23] This indicates that the distribution of actual awards in about 61 percent of schools is less egalitarian than the

Figure 9-4. *Plan and Actual Gini Coefficients for Awards, 2006*

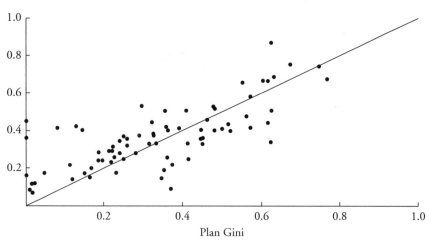

Source: Plan Gini derived from proposed GEEG award information collected during fall 2006 by coding GEEG plan applications submitted to the Texas Education Agency. Actual Gini derived from GEEG teacher award information collected during fall 2006 using an online, secure data upload system.

least egalitarian plan possible, given the GEEG grant applications submitted to the TEA.

Comparison with Award Amounts of Other Programs

The dollar amounts of the awards individual teachers received as part of their school's GEEG plan are, on average, comparable to those of the average performance award distributed to a teacher working in the average public school district offering some type of performance-based financial award. Roughly 13 percent of public school districts in the United States operated some form of performance incentive program during the 2003–04 school year, and the average size of an award payment was $2,005 for a traditional public school teacher, or the equivalent to 4.6 percent of the average base salary. While the actual dollar amounts of award payments are virtually identical for the average public charter school teacher ($2,024), award payments in charter schools account for a modestly larger percentage of the average charter school teacher's base annual salary (5.7 percent).[24]

The small average awards and wide range of minimum and maximum awards found in GEEG program plans also appear to be consistent with those of previously evaluated pay-for-performance programs. As displayed in table 9-3, award payments in the United States tend to be below $3,000, with minimum awards ranging from $250 to $2,500 and maximum awards ranging from $1,000 to $12,000. International programs follow a similar pattern, as becomes evident when one examines the size of awards as a percentage of monthly salary.

Pay-for-performance programs in which the unit of accountability is set at the school level typically report a smaller maximum award than those programs using a teacher or team of teachers as the evaluation unit. This may speak to the diseconomies of scale that result when awards are granted to individuals rather than groups of individuals. An exception is the random-assignment study in the Indian state of Andhra Pradesh evaluated by Karthik Muralidharan and Venkatesh Sundararaman, in which teachers evaluated based on group performance were eligible for similar bonus amounts as teachers evaluated on their individual performance to permit valid comparison of incentive effects between team- and individual-level conditions.[25] Ultimately, the authors find that the group incentive program had a smaller positive effect than the individual-level incentive condition, though both incentive conditions outperformed comparison schools that received no incentives and schools that received additional paraprofessional teachers and school grants for spending on school resources. Among GEEG schools, there was no significant difference in maximum awards, whether proposed or realized, between schools for which the unit of accountability was the school and those for which the unit of accountability was the teacher.

Relationship between Teacher Characteristics and Amount of Award

To explore the relationship between observable teacher characteristics and the dollar amount awarded to teachers, we estimate probit, ordinary least squares (OLS), and tobit models of the individual teacher awards. The probit analysis estimates the probability that a teacher received an award, while the OLS and tobit analyses examine the size of such awards. The dependent variable for the probit analysis is a binary variable indicating whether a teacher received a part 1 GEEG award at all. The dependent variable for both the OLS and tobit models is the dollar amount of the teacher's actual part 1 award.[26] The regression sample was made up of eighty-five GEEG schools and 3,245 full-time teachers employed in those schools during the 2005–06 school year.

Probability a Teacher Receives a GEEG Award

The first model reported in table 9-4 presents results from a probit analysis on the probability that a teacher received a GEEG award. For ease of exposition, the table reports marginal effects. Thus a coefficient estimate of –0.448 indicates that the probability of receiving a part 1 GEEG award is 44.8 percentage points lower for a teacher who was new to the building than for a teacher who was not new to the building, all other things being equal. In other words, teachers who were new to the school during the 2005–06 school year were significantly less likely to receive an award than were teachers who had worked in the school during the 2004–05 school year (that is, the school year in which GEEG eligibility was determined). The lower probability that a newly arrived teacher will receive a GEEG award does not appear to reflect bias against newly minted teachers, however. Less than half of the teachers who were new to a GEEG school were also new to teaching, and there is no relationship between years of experience and the probability of receiving an award.[27]

The values on the coefficients from the probit model show that teachers in bilingual education and English as a second language (ESL) programs, language arts teachers, and teachers with self-contained classrooms were significantly more likely to receive GEEG awards.[28] Because student assessment measures are not available in all grades and subjects, particularly in fine arts and vocational courses, it is possible that some teachers are not eligible to receive part 1 bonuses in a school's GEEG plan. Furthermore, some schools implemented multiple measures

Table 9-4. *Teacher Characteristics as Determinants of Teacher Award Distribution*

Item	Probit	OLS	Tobit
Years of experience	0.001	4.154	4.179
	(0.00)	(14.28)	(18.46)
Experience squared	0	−0.110	−0.072
	(0.00)	(0.46)	(0.58)
Experience missing	−0.037	207.666	200.937
	(0.05)	(142.58)	(171.73)
B.A.	0.124	9.230	326.425
	(0.15)	(533.61)	(977.57)
M.A.	0.067	−60.025	187.806
	(0.13)	(531.86)	(984.54)
Ph.D.	−0.008	129.136	283.820
	(0.20)	(731.68)	(1,232.34)
New to building	−0.448	−1,317.390	−2,268.300
	(0.053)***	(132.980)***	(317.541)***
Teaching assignment			
Language arts	0.086	292.414	433.609
	(0.027)***	(87.800)***	(116.424)***
Math	0.037	326.967	405.267
	(0.020)	(82.250)***	(96.372)***
Science	0.002	−273.288	−305.438
	(0.020)	(113.608)**	(130.200)**
Foreign language	0.025	79.468	121.649
	(0.05)	(158.49)	(230.01)
Fine arts	−0.111	−363.611	−611.781
	(0.045)**	(99.383)***	(157.546)***
Vocational/technical	−0.097	−88.387	−254.122
	(0.09)	(233.71)	(383.23)
Special education	0.008	211.960	224.161
	(0.04)	(154.61)	(211.39)
Bilingual	0.127	387.162	573.781
	(0.037)***	(94.773)***	(100.203)***
TAKS self-contained	0.117	773.820	976.561
	(0.031)***	(127.558)***	(172.526)***
Constant	...	1,379.94	661.851
	...	(549.165)**	(1,000.020)
Summary statistic			
R^2	...	0.18	...
N	3,245	3,245	3,245

Source: Authors' calculations.

a. Robust standard errors in parentheses. For ease of interpretation, the probit coefficients and standard errors have been transformed into marginal effects at the mean.

*Significant at 10 percent; **significant at 5 percent; ***significant at 1 percent.

for evaluating a teacher's impact on student performance, some of which are more easily applied to all teachers regardless of their specialization (for example, student dropouts, student attendance, and teacher absenteeism) than are student achievement results from a standardized assessment.

The value on the mathematics coefficient from the probit model is an anomaly to this characterization. Even though a mathematics assessment is administered to students annually in grades 3 to 11, math teachers are no more likely than other teachers to receive a GEEG award, holding all other things equal. However, there may be insufficient variation in the data to detect an independent effect for math teachers since all but 8 of the 518 math teachers in GEEG schools are also either bilingual or ESL teachers, language arts teachers, or teachers in self-contained TAKS classrooms.

Award Amounts Received by Teachers

The second and third models in table 9-4 report results on the relationship between observed teacher characteristics and award amounts received by a teacher. Tobit analysis is more appropriate for censored data, so it is the preferred specification for this set of analyses.[29] Nonetheless, as displayed in table 9-4, the results from both the OLS and tobit analyses are qualitatively similar to one another and reinforce the general conclusions of the probit analysis.

Results from the OLS and tobit models indicate that teachers who were new to a GEEG school during the 2005–06 school year received less than other teachers with similar educational attainment and experience. Similar to the probit model, however, this pattern does not appear to reflect a bias against beginning teachers. There is no evidence that highly experienced teachers received higher awards than less experienced teachers.[30] Furthermore, there is no evidence that teachers with advanced degrees earned larger awards than other teachers.[31]

Estimates based on the dollar value of the individual awards reveal more about the relationship between teaching assignments and the GEEG award distribution than is evident from the probit analysis. The analysis of award amounts confirms that teachers in tested grades and subjects received significantly larger awards than other teachers. Teachers with self-contained classrooms in TAKS grades received by far the largest GEEG awards, all other things being equal. Teachers in language arts, bilingual education and ESL, and mathematics received significantly higher incentive awards than other teachers but significantly less than those received by TAKS teachers. On average, the 270 fine arts teachers in the analysis received the smallest GEEG awards.

Intriguingly, the models suggest that math teachers received higher awards than other teachers but had no greater probability of receiving an award. This implies that when math teachers qualified for a GEEG award, the average size of their award was larger than those of their peers.

Taken as a whole, the relationship between observable teacher characteristics and the dollar amount awarded to teachers in GEEG schools appears to reflect factors other than those rewarded by the traditional single salary schedule. The single salary schedule rewards teachers based on years of experience and degrees held. However, those two factors—separately or jointly—have no influence on the probability that a teacher receives a GEEG award or the size of the award that a teacher receives.

Plan Characteristics and the Distribution of Teacher Awards

To investigate determinants of GEEG plan characteristics and the distribution of awards, we draw on the literature to identify a number of teacher and school characteristics that could be associated with the GEEG plan adopted at a particular school. We then explore whether these observable characteristics explain the variation in three key aspects of GEEG plans: the unit of accountability for determining a teacher's award eligibility, the approaches for measuring student performance, and the equality of proposed and actual teacher awards. Each subsection briefly describes the dependent variables and basic modeling strategy and then reports on key findings.

Likely Determinants

We incorporate several school, teacher, and GEEG plan characteristics into our analysis of the determinants of each school's GEEG plan. The school determinants are the share of economically disadvantaged students, school type (elementary and secondary), and school size. The teacher determinants are the average years of teacher experience, the share of teachers who are male, the share of teachers who are new to the building, and a Gini coefficient for teacher salaries. The salary Gini summarizes the distribution of teacher base pay and therefore indicates the homogeneity of the teacher corps with respect to the determinants of base pay—experience and educational attainment. When all the teachers share the same step on the salary scale, the salary Gini equals zero. As teacher characteristics become more dispersed, the salary Gini increases. The GEEG plan determinants are the level of GEEG funding per pupil and an indicator for whether the school was eligible for GEEG designation as a high-improving school.

Individualistic incentive plans are less likely where individual performance is difficult to measure. Within-school variations in student characteristics can make it more difficult to measure the effectiveness of individual teachers, so schools in which the student body is more diverse should be less likely to adopt individualistic incentive plans. To capture this effect, we include the share of economically disadvantaged students in all models. Although all GEEG schools are high-poverty schools, the share of economically disadvantaged students ranges from 42.9 to 100 percent, and schools in which all or nearly all of the students are economically disadvantaged are much less diverse than other GEEG schools with respect to an important determinant of student performance. However, economically disadvantaged students make up a greater share of elementary school students than of secondary school students, and recent surveys suggest that elementary schoolteachers are less supportive of teacher pay-for-performance plans than are secondary-level teachers.[32] Therefore, we also include indicators for elementary and secondary schools.

We include variables for school size and a measure of teacher homogeneity (the teacher salary Gini coefficient) because studies suggest that small groups are more likely than large groups to adopt egalitarian incentive structures[33] and that the median teacher would reasonably prefer a more egalitarian structure if he or she had full information about the abilities of other teachers (as would be more likely in a small school) and if there were significant variation in those abilities.[34] The salary Gini is intended to capture the potential for such variations.

We include both the share of teachers who are male and the average years of teaching experience because the literature suggests that perspectives on pay-for-performance plans vary by gender and experience.[35] For example, Muriel Niederle and Lise Vesterlund find that even when there are no gender differences in performance, men are twice as likely as women to choose an incentive scheme that rewards individual performance.[36] Self-report data from teachers further indicate that female teachers have more negative impressions of pay-for-performance programs than do male teachers.[37] In addition, several studies on teacher attitudes toward performance-pay policies conclude that beginning teachers are more accepting of performance pay than are more experienced, veteran teachers.[38]

We include the share of teachers who are new to the building because those characteristics are strong predictors of individual teacher awards; schools with a large number of new teachers may therefore have more individualistic award schemes. We include GEEG funding per pupil to allow for the possibility that schools with more generous per capita funding might be more willing to spread the wealth around. Finally, we include an indicator for high-improving schools because such schools arguably have more room for improvement than high-performing schools and might adjust their incentive plans accordingly.

Units of Accountability

To predict whether teacher and school characteristics are associated with the units of accountability identified in GEEG plans for determining a teacher's award eligibility, we categorize GEEG schools into three groups: those that use campus-level performance only, those that use teacher-level performance only, and those that use some combination of the two. Schools using teams as a unit of accountability are categorized into the latter category, while those that use campus-level performance only are the referent group in the multinomial logit model. In total, our sample contains thirteen schools that use campus-level performance only, forty-seven schools that use teacher-level performance only, and fifty schools in the combined performance group.

Table 9-5, panel A, presents results when teacher and school characteristics are associated with the unit of accountability. The evidence suggests that as teachers in a school become more dissimilar (at least with respect to salary and its determinants) there is an increasing probability that the school's plans will incorporate incentives for individual teachers. The model predicts that schools in which teachers' characteristics are highly similar (that is, schools with a teacher salary Gini at or below 0.065, which is the 10th percentile for this indicator) are more than three times more likely to rely exclusively on campus-level incentives than are schools in which the teachers are highly dissimilar (that is, with a teacher salary Gini at or above 0.127, which is the 90th percentile for this indicator).[39]

There are no systematic differences across the three accountability categories with respect to the other determinants in the model. Given teacher homogeneity, there is no evidence of differences across school type (elementary, secondary, and other) or school size with respect to the chosen units of accountability. High-improving schools, schools with more experienced teachers, and schools with a higher share of teachers who are new to the building are also no more likely than other schools to favor incentives for individual teachers.

Measuring Student Performance

A second set of analyses categorizes schools into three groups according to the approaches for measuring student performance proposed in their GEEG grant application: those that use performance growth only, those that use performance levels only, and those that use both performance growth and performance levels.

Table 9-5. *Determinants of Plan Characteristics and the Distribution of Teacher Awards*[a]

Item	A: Units of accountability		B: Measuring student performance		C: Equity of proposed and actual awards		
	Teacher and campus	Teacher only	Growth only	Levels only	Plan Gini	Actual Gini	Percent teachers no award
Percent economically disadvantaged students	0.069	0.003	-0.100	-0.015	-0.006	-0.003	-0.003
	(0.05)	(0.04)	(0.07)	(0.03)	(0.002)**	(0.000)	(0.002)*
Average teacher experience	-0.116	-0.070	-0.311**	-0.065	-0.009	-0.016	-0.012
	(0.10)	(0.10)	(0.14)	(0.08)	(0.010)	(0.007)**	(0.005)**
Teacher salary Gini	27.006*	31.390**	-15.548	2.890	2.808	2.342	2.042
	(14.86)	(14.31)	(26.76)	(13.10)	(0.806)***	(0.904)**	(0.784)**
School size	-0.117	0.968*	0.102	0.012	0.084	0.022	-0.039
	(0.92)	(0.55)	(1.36)	(0.65)	(0.030)**	(0.03)	(0.02)
GEEG funding per pupil	-2.397	2.541	2.422	-0.266	0.031	-0.147	-0.245
	(3.79)	(2.00)	(5.80)	(3.43)	(0.090)	(0.081)*	(0.096)**
Share of teachers new to campus	0.504	0.485	-6.734	-2.273	0.119	0.278	0.258
	(3.65)	(2.47)	(4.34)	(2.27)	(0.170)	(0.149)*	(0.180)

Share of teachers male	3.309	2.002	3.610	−2.425	0.065	−0.070	−0.160
	(2.29)	(2.65)	(5.64)	(2.74)	(0.15)	(0.14)	(0.14)
Elementary school	−0.279	0.854	2.020	−0.808	−0.056	−0.068	−0.052
	(0.93)	(0.73)	(2.70)	(0.56)	(0.050)	(0.035)*	(0.040)
Secondary school	0.908	0.182	−0.973	−1.032	−0.099	0.049	0.058
	(1.19)	(1.14)	(1.42)	(0.95)	(0.058)*	(0.040)	(0.050)
High-improving school	−0.942	0.052	1.659	−0.242	−0.003	0.042	0.037
	(0.73)	(0.56)	(1.25)	(0.43)	(0.04)	(0.03)	(0.03)
Constant	−7.315	−9.588*	9.679	4.463	0.191	0.480	0.745
	(7.82)	(4.96)	(13.25)	(6.86)	(0.340)	(0.330)	(0.226)***
Summary statistic							
N	97		97		94	84	84
Wald chi^2 (20)	48.46		117.08		…	…	…
Probability of a greater chi^2	0.0004		0		…	…	…
Pseudo R^2	0.1002		0.1593		…	…	…
R^2	…		…		0.3	0.42	0.51

Source: Authors' calculations.

a. Robust standard errors in parentheses.

*Significant at 10 percent; **significant at 5 percent; ***significant at 1 percent.

Fifty-three schools relied exclusively on performance levels. Another twelve schools rewarded exclusively growth. The remaining twenty-six schools rewarded both performance levels and performance gains. Schools that rewarded both student achievement levels and student achievement growth are the referent group.[40]

As illustrated in panel B of table 9-5, average teacher experience has a significant influence on the probability that a GEEG plan rewards student growth rather than achievement level. The evidence suggests that the lower the average teacher experience, the more likely that the school relies solely on measures of student gains and the less likely the plan incorporates achievement-level measures. For example, the model predicts that a school in which the average teacher has five years of experience is nearly seven times more likely to design a plan that rewards only growth than is a school in which the average teacher has fifteen years of experience. (The predicted probabilities are 28.3 and 4.1 percent, respectively.)

There is no evidence that the other determinants in the model have a significant influence on the plan's measure of student performance. Given the high degree of collinearity between the percentage of economically disadvantaged students and the grade levels taught in a school, we examine student socioeconomic status and grade level jointly. We find no evidence that differences in these indicators change the probability that a school rewards achievement levels rather than measures of improvement. Similarly, there is no indication that school size or GEEG funding per pupil has any influence on performance analysis strategies in use by schools.

EQUALITY OF PROPOSED AND ACTUAL AWARDS

The final set of analyses investigated determinants of award equality using a simple regression model identified in the economics literature on optimal incentives. We use three indicators of award equality: the plan Gini coefficients, the actual Gini coefficients, and the share of teachers receiving no award. Panel C of table 9-5 displays results from examining the issue using each of these three indicators of award equality.

In all three cases, the share of economically disadvantaged students is jointly significant at the 10 percent level with the indicators for school type. Results reported in panel C further suggest that schools with more economically homogeneous student bodies have more egalitarian award plans. Contrary to expectations based on the survey literature, the analysis provides no evidence that a relative distaste for performance pay among elementary school teachers leads to systematically more egalitarian GEEG plans in elementary schools.

The literature also implies that teachers will favor more egalitarian plans when they have a reduced expectation of winning a winner-take-all tournament—as would be the case where a greater variation in abilities exists. If this is true, then the evidence suggests that a variation in teacher salaries does not signal a greater variation in teacher abilities. As displayed in table 9-5 (panel C), schools in which teachers are more homogeneous with respect to salary devise GEEG award distribution models with greater equality than their counterparts.

Larger schools also have less egalitarian plans than small schools, although the evidence is less transparent. School size is highly and inversely correlated with GEEG funding per pupil. School size and school funding per pupil are jointly significant in all three models, and in all three cases a marginal increase in school size significantly increases the inequality of the awards distribution across a range of school sizes.[41]

As the literature would predict, our analyses find that schools with more-experienced teachers are likely to have more-egalitarian incentive plans, although the effect is not significant for the plan Gini. However, contrary to the predictions of the literature, there is no evidence that schools with a higher share of male teachers adopt more individualistic incentive plans.

The share of newly hired teachers is entered into the regressions to capture the possibility that schools with a greater share of newly hired teachers might reasonably be expected to distribute their awards less evenly. The evidence in panel C provides mixed support for this hypothesis. The share of new teachers had a significant and positive influence on the actual Gini but not on the other two indicators. In addition, we find no evidence that schools eligible for GEEG based on high accountability ratings design more-egalitarian plans than those eligible by comparable improvement rankings.

Conclusion

This study focused on characteristics and determinants of teacher pay-for-performance plans implemented at ninety-nine traditional public and public charter schools in Texas participating in the GEEG program. The GEEG program provides an ideal setting to study the nature of compensation reforms that educators perceive to be acceptable. We found that GEEG plans varied considerably in terms of the criteria used to identify high-performing educators as well as the level at which teachers were held accountable (that is, individual, team, school, or some combination thereof) and the degree of equality in their distribution of awards.

There was a striking commonality among plans, however. Most of the incentive plans rejected TEA guidelines, which favor a small number of relatively large awards. Nearly 80 percent of eligible teachers in GEEG schools received an incentive award, and most of those received an award substantially less than the $3,000 minimum award recommended by the Texas Education Agency. The average award received by a GEEG teacher was strikingly similar in magnitude to the average incentive award reported nationwide by participants in the Schools and Staffing Survey for the 2003–04 school year.

Our analysis of the GEEG program plans suggests that teachers tend to design relatively egalitarian incentive plans for themselves. In turn, this observation suggests a possible policy tension between incentives that are strong enough to elicit a behavioral response from teachers and the need for teacher acceptance and participation in such plans. Future research on teacher pay-for-performance plans needs to explore more fully the behavioral changes caused by differing levels of a monetary award, similar to dose-response studies in the medical literature.

Our results suggested that bilingual education and ESL teachers, language arts teachers, and teachers with self-contained classrooms in TAKS-tested grades were significantly more likely to receive GEEG awards, and those teachers in grades and subjects covered by the TAKS test received significantly larger awards than other teachers. The reason for this, we presume, is that student assessment measures are not available in all subjects, and some teachers may therefore have found it difficult to provide objective evidence of improving student performance, as required by the TEA program guidelines. This finding may suggest a limitation frequently noted about the current state of knowledge on performance-pay plans in the education sector, that is, the present capacity for designing plans that include multiple means of measuring performance so that all educators have the opportunity to earn an award regardless of the subject or grade they teach or position they hold within a school.

Several teacher and school characteristics are associated with GEEG plan characteristics and the distribution of awards. In particular, the distribution of teacher experience and the level of teacher experience had a significant influence on plan design. The more dissimilar the composition of teachers within a school (at least with respect to teacher salary), the less likely their GEEG plan awards teachers based on campus-level performance and the more unequal the distribution of incentive awards. Schools in which average teacher experience is lower had less egalitarian incentive plans and were more likely to implement pay-for-performance plans that reward teachers for student growth as opposed to attainment. This influence of schoolwide measures of teacher experience on plan design is particularly striking given that we find no evidence that the experience or education attainment of individual teachers had any impact on the probability they received an award or the magnitude of that award.

Policymakers have become more and more focused on teacher compensation reform to enhance academic opportunities and outcomes of public elementary and secondary school children in the United States. However, research on the topic frequently notes that, in the absence of teacher engagement and participation in plan design, teacher compensation reforms are often short lived. While failure to successfully implement and sustain teacher compensation reforms could also be attributed to other factors, this study offers important insight into design features of performance-pay plans that educators may perceive to be reasonable. We also examined the association between teacher and school characteristics and the characteristics of the GEEG plan implemented at a particular school to better understand whether some groups of educators perceive particular design features of performance-pay plans as more attractive. This information may prove useful as practitioners, researchers, and policymakers explore the use of teacher pay for performance policy to improve administrator and teacher productivity, recruit more-qualified teaching candidates, and enhance learning opportunities.

Notes

1. For a comprehensive overview of teacher pay-for-performance programs, see the state-by-state resource map hosted by the National Center on Performance Incentives (www.performanceincentives.org/statebystate_resources/index.asp [March 2, 2009]).
2. The GEEG application guidelines note, "Grant applications must validate significant teacher involvement in the development of the incentive program; valid examples of teacher involvement include attendance records, meeting minutes, or other evidence that indicates significant teacher involvement in the creation of the incentive program. Additionally, each application must include no less than three letters from teachers, outlining their involvement in the process and their support for the program." A school's application also had to be approved by the local education agency and the local school board.
3. Richard J. Murnane and David K. Cohen, "Merit Pay and the Evaluation Problem: Why Most Merit Pay Plans Fail and a Few Survive," *Harvard Educational Review* 56, no. 1 (1986): 1–17; Michael J. Podgursky and Matthew G. Springer, "Teacher Performance Pay: A Review," *Journal of Policy Analysis and Management* 26, no. 4 (2007): 1–52.
4. A registered alternative-education campus could also be considered high performing if it had high passing rates on the Texas Assessment of Knowledge and Skills (TAKS) test. It did not have to meet the dropout rate standards required for recognized or exemplary status.
5. A school could also be considered recognized if 65 percent of the students passed in each subject and subgroup and the school showed "required improvement." For more on state

accountability ratings, see Texas Education Agency, *2005 Accountability Manual* (Austin: Texas Education Agency, 2005).

6. The GEEG program guidelines further define teacher initiative as "a teacher's demonstration of ongoing initiative, commitment, personalization, professionalism, and involvement in other activities that directly result in improved student performance, for example, working with students outside of assigned class hours, tutoring, creating programs to engage parents, and taking initiative to personalize the learning environment for every student."

7. Subjects identified include "math, science, special education, technology, bilingual/English as a second language, foreign language, literacy instruction, or areas of need specific to the district." See Texas Education Agency, "Creating a High-Quality Texas Educator Excellence Grant Plan" (Austin: Texas Education Agency, 2006).

8. Athletic coaches cannot receive part 2 funds.

9. There are two other state-funded pay-for-performance programs, the Texas Educator Excellence Grants program (TEEG) and the District Awards for Teacher Excellence program. The former was initiated during the 2006–07 school year and provided funding for pay-for-performance plans to be implemented in more than a thousand additional Texas schools. Eligibility criteria were similar to those for the Governor's Educator Excellence Grants program: the schools must serve high percentages of economically disadvantaged students, and they must be rated as high achieving or high improving on the Texas accountability rating system. For more information on the TEEG program, see Matthew G. Springer and others, *Texas Educator Excellence Grant (TEEG) Program: Year One Evaluation Report* (Nashville, Tenn.: National Center on Performance Incentives, 2008).

10. For more on the differences between Governor's Educator Excellence Grant schools and other Texas schools, see Matthew G. Springer and others, *Governor's Educator Excellence Grant (GEEG) Program: Year One Evaluation Report* (Nashville, Tenn.: National Center on Performance Incentives, 2007).

11. The turnover rate is defined as the fraction of teachers in the 2005–06 school year who are not serving as teachers in the same school in the 2006–07 school year.

12. Richard B. Freeman and Alexander M. Gelber, "Optimal Inequality/Optimal Incentives: Evidence from a Tournament," Working Paper W12588 (Cambridge, Mass.: National Bureau of Economic Research, 2006); Ottorino Chillemi, "Competitive versus Collective Incentive Pay: Does Workers' Mutual Concern Matter?" *Economic Theory* 35, no. 1 (2008): 175–86.

13. William E. Encinosa III, Martin Gaynor, and James B. Rebitzer, "The Sociology of Groups and the Economics of Incentives: Theory and Evidence on Compensation Systems," *Journal of Economic Behavior and Organization* 62, no. 2 (2007): 187–214.

14. Table 9-3 does not include David Figlio and Lawrence Kenny's national study on the impact of individual teacher performance incentives on student test-score gains because the characteristics of the incentive programs vary considerably. See David N. Figlio and Lawrence W. Kenny, "Individual Teacher Incentives and Student Performance," *Journal of Public Economics* 91, nos. 5–6 (2007): 901–14.

15. See, for example, Freeman and Gelber, "Optimal Inequality/Optimal Incentives"; Donald Vandegrift, Abdullah Yavas, and Paul M. Brown, "Incentive Effects and Overcrowding in Tournaments: An Experimental Analysis," *Experimental Economics* 10, no. 4 (2007): 345–68; Christine Harbring and Bernd Irlenbusch, "An Experimental Study on Tournament Design," *Labour Economics* 10, no. 4 (2003): 443–64.

16. The Gini coefficient for school k equals

$$G = 1 + \frac{1}{N} - \left[\frac{2}{mN^2}\right]\sum_{i=1}^{i=n}(N - i + 1)y_i,$$

where N is the number of teachers in school k, m is the average award per teacher in school k, y_i is the individual award of teacher i in school k, and the teachers in school k have been sorted from the teacher with the lowest GEEG award or no GEEG award (y_1) to the teacher with highest GEEG award (y_N). To illustrate further, consider a scenario in which a school has eleven full-time-equivalent teachers and received $45,000 in part 1 funds to implement its GEEG plan, with a maximum possible award of $6,000. If seven teachers receive the maximum possible award, enough award money remains to give one teacher an award of $3,000 (45,000 − 7[6,000] = 3,000). The remaining three teachers receive nothing. The plan Gini coefficient for this school would be 0.3151.

17. Evaluators could not reliably calculate a plan maximum award for four schools. Data from the Public Education Information Management System on the total number of teachers in the school were not available for the fifth school.

18. U.S. Census Bureau, Current Population Survey, 2004 and 2006 Annual Social and Economic Supplements.

19. We also found that three schools with a zero award range have above-average plan Ginis, indicating the proposed award distribution plan is in fact less egalitarian than that of the average school in our sample.

20. Keung Hui and Samiha Khanna recently reported that "teachers at 82 percent of the schools across [North Carolina] are eligible for bonuses this year because their schools met or exceeded expectations in the state's ABCs of Public Education testing and accountability program. . . . But the number of eligible teachers so exceeds the thinner pot of money provided by the General Assembly that the State Board of Education reduced individual payouts this year by as much as $447." See T. Keung Hui and Samiha Khanna, "Teachers Excel, but Bonus Cut," *Raleigh (N.C.) News and Observer,* August 8, 2008 (www.news observer.com/news/education/story/1169139.html). Additionally, the Houston Independent School District mistakenly allocated about $73,700 to ninety-nine employees. See Jennifer Radcliffe, "HISD Tying Teacher Bonuses to Teamwork," *Houston Chronicle,* August 24, 2007 (http://www.accessmylibrary.com/coms2/summary_0286-32709685_ITM).

21. Edward Lazear, *Modern Personnel Economics for Managers* (New York: Wiley, 1997). Victor Lavy reports findings from two rank-order tournaments in Israel. See Victor Lavy, "Evaluating the Effect of Teachers' Group Performance Incentives on Pupil Achievement," *Journal of Political Economy* 110, no. 6 (2002): 1286–317; Victor Lavy, "Performance Pay and Teacher's Effort, Productivity, and Grading Ethics," Working Paper W10622 (Cambridge, Mass.: National Bureau of Economic Research, 2004).

22. Many chapters in this volume address complexities associated with designing, implementing, and managing a performance incentive system. See, for example, chapters 5, 6, and 7. The Center for Educator Compensation Reform also posts useful information on implementing teacher compensation reforms on its website (www.cecr.ed.gov/guides/compReform.cfm [March 3, 2009]).

23. We could not reliably calculate a plan maximum award for five of the eighty-five schools that provided data on their award distributions.

24. This information comes from the authors' own calculations using the Schools and Staffing Survey, conducted by the U.S. Department of Education's National Center for Education Statistics. The Schools and Staffing Survey is a nationally representative sample of roughly 8,000 public schools and 43,000 public schoolteachers. There have been five waves of the survey, associated with five school years: 1987–88, 1990–91, 1994–95, 1999–2000, and 2003–04. A sixth administration is currently in the field (2007–08). For more information about trends in teacher pay based on Schools and Staffing Survey data, see chapter 4 in this volume; and Michael J. Podgursky and others, "The Diffusion of Teacher Pay Policies: Evidence from Multiple Waves of the Schools and Staffing Survey," Working Paper 2008-25 (Nashville, Tenn.: National Center on Performance Incentives, 2008). An insightful comparison of personnel policy, wage setting, and teacher quality in traditional public, public charter, and private schools can be found in Michael J. Podgursky, "Teams versus Bureaucracies," in *Charter School Outcomes,* edited by Mark Berends, Matthew G. Springer, and Herbert J. Walberg (New York: Taylor and Francis Group, 2007): 61–84.

25. Karthik Muralidharan and Venkatesh Sundararaman, "Teacher Incentives in Developing Countries: Experimental Evidence from India," Harvard University, Department of Economics, 2006.

26. Teachers who did not receive an award were coded as receiving an award of zero dollars. Because there may be a correlation in the residuals between two schools from the same school district, we report robust standard errors clustered by school district for all three models. The tobit methodology does not accommodate clustered standard errors, so the standard errors for the tobit model have not been clustered.

27. When examining the actual distribution of GEEG awards we also found that nearly one-third of GEEG schools awarded part 1 funds to teachers who had taught at the school during the 2004–05 school year but were no longer working at the school. Some GEEG schools may have retroactively rewarded these teachers since a school's performance during the 2004–05 school year was used to determine which schools were selected to be part of the GEEG program.

28. We consider bilingual education and ESL teachers to be part of the state's testing system because the No Child Left Behind Act of 2001 requires schools to report separately on the adequate yearly progress of students with limited English proficiency.

29. Takeshi Amemiya, "Regression Analysis When the Dependent Variable Is Truncated Normal," *Econometrica* 41, no. 6 (1973): 997–1016; James Tobin, "Estimation for the Relationships with Limited Dependent Variables," *Econometrica* 26, no. 1 (1958): 24–36.

30. The hypothesis that the coefficients on the three experience variables are jointly equal to zero cannot be rejected at the 10 percent level.

31. The hypothesis that the coefficients on the three educational attainment variables are jointly equal to zero cannot be rejected at the 10 percent level.

32. Dan Goldhaber, Michael DeArmond, and Scott DeBurgomaster, "Teacher Attitudes about Compensation Reform: Implications for Reform Implementation," Working Paper 20 (Seattle, Wash.: Center for Reinventing Public Education, School Finance Redesign Project, 2007); Brian Jacob and Matthew G. Springer, "Teacher Attitudes on Pay for Performance: A Pilot Study," National Center on Performance Incentives, 2007.

33. Encinosa, Gaynor, and Rebitzer, "The Sociology of Groups and the Economics of Incentives," find that small groups are more likely to adopt equal-sharing rules than are large

groups but that when mutual assistance is important, large groups must offer weaker incentives to achieve the same level of mutual aid.

34. See Freeman and Gelber, "Optimal Inequality/Optimal Incentives."

35. The share of male teachers in GEEG schools ranges from a minimum of zero to a maximum of 63 percent, with a sample mean of 26 percent.

36. Muriel Niederle and Lise Vesterlund, "Do Women Shy Away from Competition? Do Men Compete Too Much?" *Quarterly Journal of Economics* 122, no. 3 (2007): 1067–101. For other work on gender preferences in incentive pay plans, see Dale Ballou and Michael Podgursky, "Teacher Attitudes toward Merit Pay: Examining Conventional Wisdom," *Industrial and Labor Relations Review* 47, no. 1 (1993): 50–61; Goldhaber, DeArmond, and DeBurgomaster, "Teacher Attitudes about Compensation Reform"; Catherine Eckel and Philip Grossman, "Sex Differences and Statistical Stereotyping in Attitudes toward Financial Risk," *Evolution and Human Behavior* 23, no. 4 (2002): 281–95.

37. Ballou and Podgursky, "Teacher Attitudes toward Merit Pay"; Goldhaber, DeArmond, and DeBurgomaster, "Teacher Attitudes about Compensation Reform."

38. Ballou and Podgursky, "Teacher Attitudes toward Merit Pay"; Goldhaber, DeArmond, and DeBurgomaster, "Teacher Attitudes about Compensation Reform"; or Jacob and Springer, "Teacher Attitudes on Pay for Performance."

39. The predicted probabilities are 48.2 and 13.9 percent, respectively. The predicted probabilities are calculated using the method of recycled predictions, holding all other variables in the model constant at their means.

40. Eight schools are excluded because of incomplete data.

41. The marginal effect of school size is a nonlinear function of enrollment. For the plan Gini and actual Gini analyses, the marginal effect is positive for all school sizes and statistically significant (at the 10 percent level) for all but a handful of schools. For the share of teachers with no award, the marginal effect is significant and positive for some schools and insignificant for the rest.

PART THREE

Informing Teacher
Incentive Policies

10

Teacher Salary Bonuses in North Carolina

Jacob L. Vigdor

W hat would happen if teacher salary schedules rewarded performance, as measured by standardized test-score outcomes, rather than the acquisition of credentials? Would student test scores improve? Would these improvements be distributed in an equitable way, or would the program encourage teachers to abandon difficult-to-educate students, either by changing jobs or changing the way they teach? Are there any companion policies that could offset potentially regressive impacts?

Starting in the 1996–97 school year, the state of North Carolina implemented a system of performance incentives for all teachers in all public schools. While the specific details of the bonus program have changed over time, the general structure has not. All teachers in a given public school are awarded cash bonuses of up to $1,500 each year depending on how the students in that school perform on the state's end-of-grade examinations in math and reading or on high school end-of-course exams. The performance standard has always been based on the amount of improvement shown by students from one year to the next, rather than on proficiency levels. In theory, at least, the experience of North Carolina public schools over the past ten years could provide valuable information on the empirical questions raised above.

The North Carolina Accountability Program

In the 1996–97 school year, the North Carolina accountability program, known formally as the ABCs (*A*ccountability; teaching the *B*asics of reading, writing, and mathematics; and increasing *C*ontrol of schools at the local level) of Public Education, began awarding salary bonuses to teachers in schools that met specific targets for test-score improvement in their student body. In the initial year of implementation, teachers in elementary and middle schools were awarded the amount of $1,000 if the mean year-over-year test-score gains in the school exceeded a threshold for "exemplary" growth. In the following year, the bonus program was extended to high schools, and the bonus was altered to have a two-tiered structure, with teachers in schools meeting "exemplary" growth receiving $1,500 and teachers in schools meeting "expected" growth receiving $750. This basic structure has been in place ever since, though the formula for computing the bonus eligibility threshold has changed, and the label "exemplary" was replaced in 2001–02 with the term "high."

The practice of awarding bonuses to teachers on the basis of the entire school's performance has a theoretically ambiguous effect on the strength of incentives present to improve test scores. On the one hand, tying bonus payments to group performance dilutes the impact of an individual teacher's effort on the probability of receiving a reward. This introduces a potential "free rider" problem, whereby teachers reduce their effort because the ultimate outcome is largely beyond their personal control. The existence of a free rider produces the theoretical prediction that the bonus program should have had a stronger impact in smaller schools.

On the other hand, to the extent that improving test scores requires cooperation among the teachers in a school, the use of group-level incentives could encourage good habits. Moreover, the use of school-level performance sidesteps concerns about how to create effective incentives for teachers in untested grades (K–2) or in untested subjects (anything other than math and reading in middle schools).

The Initial Model for Computing Bonus Eligibility Thresholds

Before the 2005–06 school year, North Carolina elementary and middle schools, serving grades 3 through 8, were evaluated on the basis of their ability to improve students' test scores from one year to the next by more than a predetermined mean amount. The state used a simple formula of the form

$$\Delta y_{igst} = \Delta \bar{y}_{gs94} + b_1 ITP_{igt} + b_2 IRM_{igst},$$

where Δy_{igst} represents the target threshold for the year-to-year change in test scores in subject s for students in grade g in year t at school i and $\Delta \bar{y}_{gs94}$ is the average change in test score for a student in grade g anywhere in North Carolina at the end of the 1993–94 school year, relative to that same student's score in grade $g - 1$ at the end of the 1992–93 school year.[1] These were the first two years in which North Carolina administered statewide end-of-grade tests in reading and math. North Carolina's standardized tests employ a developmental scale, which permits scores from consecutive grades to be directly comparable to one another. Ignoring the second and third terms on the right-hand side of the equation for a moment, the basic model rewarded teachers when average test-score gains in their school exceeded the statewide average between 1992–93 and 1993–94.

The second and third terms in the equation are "correction" factors. The term ITP_{igt} represents the index of true proficiency for students in grade g at school i in year t. The index of true proficiency does not vary by subject. It is obtained by subtracting the 1994–95 state average scale scores from the average scores of students in grade $g - 1$ at school i in year $t - 1$. The coefficient b_1 varies by grade and subject but is universally positive.[2] Thus schools with students who achieved higher test scores in grade $g - 1$ in year $t - 1$ had to attain a greater degree of growth to be eligible for bonus payments, other things equal. The rationale for including this correction factor was the premise that higher-achieving students should have greater test-score improvement over time. This premise is debatable: it may be more difficult to produce significant gains from high-achieving students. However, the higher standard imposed on high-achieving students by this correction factor was in practice offset by the second.

The second correction factor, IRM_{igst}, was intended to account for statistical noise in standardized test scores. Students who score unusually well in subject s in grade g in year t are more likely to exhibit slower test-score improvement over the subsequent year, simply because their initial test score was more likely to have been high for idiosyncratic reasons. Some high-scoring students, for example, may simply have guessed a number of correct answers on multiple-choice tests. Similarly, some low-scoring students may have guessed poorly or may have been negatively affected by poor health or other distractions on the day of the exam. When aggregated to the school level, concerns about mean reversion are lessened, as the idiosyncratic factors producing noise in test scores cancel each other out at least to some extent. The degree of canceling out rises in proportion to the size of the school.[3] For this reason, a rational correction for mean reversion would have treated schools of different sizes differently. Small schools with an unusually high mean for the previous year should have received a greater discount on their growth threshold than large schools with similarly high test scores.

The North Carolina formula did not use a rational correction for mean reversion. Instead, the index of mean reversion used, calculated separately by subject, was nothing more than the difference between the average score of school i students in subject s in grade $g-1$ in year $t-1$ and the statewide average on the same test in 1994–95. The coefficient b_2 varies by grade and subject but is always negative.[4] Moreover, the coefficient b_2 is universally greater in absolute value than the coefficient b_1. Thus in a comparison of any two schools with equal reading test scores, the school with higher math test scores faced a lower threshold for test-score improvement over the subsequent year.

Does this imply that the system used before 2005–06 penalized schools serving students with low initial performance? This question turns out to be very difficult to answer. It may well be the case that it is easier to produce test-score gains with lower-performing students. Evidence that more-disadvantaged schools were less likely to cross the bonus threshold could be taken as evidence that the playing field was tilted against them but might also reflect a lower quality of instruction at those schools. What is less controversial is that this system incorporated a feedback mechanism. Schools that achieved high growth in year t not only received bonus payments but also were rewarded by having a lower threshold set for the subsequent year.

Regardless of where thresholds were set, schools faced a straightforward incentive to increase the mean test score in reading and math. For a school with G tested grades, a set of $2G$ mean test scores were produced every year, to be compared with the set of $2G$ bonus thresholds. To reduce this information to a single indicator of bonus eligibility, the differences between actual test-score gains and the target threshold were standardized (by dividing by the standard deviation of this difference across all schools in the state) and averaged, with the average weighted by the number of students taking each test. If this weighted average, the "expected growth composite," exceeded zero, teachers in the school were eligible for bonus payments of $750.[5] A second composite measure was computed by multiplying each of the $2G$ growth thresholds by 1.1, then executing a similar procedure of subtracting the second threshold from the actual test-score improvement in each grade and subject, standardizing the result, and taking the weighted average. If this second weighted average exceeded zero, teachers in the school were eligible for bonus payments of $1,500.

The procedure for evaluating high schools differed in this model. Students stop taking uniformly scaled end-of-grade standardized tests in eighth grade. In high school, students take end-of-course examinations in a limited number of subjects. The threshold for bonus eligibility is based on student performance on these end-of-course tests as well as information on dropout rates and student performance on tenth-grade school-wide exams. Beginning in 2000–2001, thresholds for performance on end-of-course exams were computed in a manner analogous to the end-of-grade growth formulas. The threshold was set at the state average score on each test plus a correction factor based on the eighth-grade test performance of students enrolled in the course. The threshold for eligibility was generally set higher for schools serving students who scored better on the relevant eighth-grade test. As in K–8 schools, teachers received a $750 bonus when the weighted average of differences between actual performance and subject-specific thresholds exceeded zero and $1,500 bonuses when the weighted average difference between actual performance and slightly higher subject-specific thresholds exceeded zero.

The Current Model for Computing Bonus Eligibility Thresholds

The accountability system was evaluated during the 2003–04 state legislative session, and several flaws were noted. Among other things, the formula proved difficult to adapt to changes in the underlying standardized tests. Although not explicitly stated in official reports, the system could also be criticized for poorly addressing the concern of mean reversion and for using a formula that rewarded schools whose large test-score gains were concentrated among a small minority of students. In response to these flaws, the North Carolina Department of Public Instruction modified the formulas for determining whether schools were eligible for bonus payments. The new formulas went into effect in the 2005–06 school year.

The primary change in the formula was to stop using the difference in developmental scale score as the main measure of a student's progress from grade $g-1$ in year $t-1$ to grade g in year t. Instead, the new formula effectively transforms each student's test score into a Z score, using a mean and standard deviation derived from the first year in which a given standardized test was used in North Carolina.[6] An individual student's academic change is then calculated according to the following formula:

$$\text{Academic change}_{gt} = Z_{gt} - d\left(Z_{(g-1)(t-1)}\big/2 + Z_{(g-2)(t-2)}\big/2\right).$$

The formula takes the average of the student's two prior Z scores, multiplies this average by a discount factor d, and subtracts them from the current-year Z score.[7]

The discount factor is used to address mean reversion: students with prior scores further away from the average are expected to move toward the average over time. The procedure using end-of-course test-score results for high school students is similar.

In elementary and middle schools, teachers are eligible for $750 bonuses if the average academic change, across all students in all subjects, is greater than zero. High school eligibility also factors in dropout rates, the results of tenth-grade competency exams, and the percentage of graduates in college preparatory tracks.

Eligibility for $1,500 bonuses is determined by a different method. Conditional on eligibility for a $750 bonus, schools in which the proportion of students with academic change greater than zero exceeds 60 percent receive the full $1,500. Thus schools that achieve strong test-score improvement by raising the performance of a limited number of students will generally not receive the full bonus.

The new method of computing bonus eligibility can still be criticized for employing a crude correction for mean reversion. Idiosyncratic factors, such as the quality of random guesses or a student's health the day of the test, can explain part of the variation in student test scores. When aggregated to the school level, however, many of these idiosyncratic factors cancel one another out, to an extent that varies systematically with the size of the school. Instead of employing a correction factor that makes use of this statistical regularity, the new formula continues to effectively set a higher bar for below-average schools and a lower bar for above-average schools. Schools that manage to hold mean achievement steady from one year to the next receive bonuses if the prior achievement was above the mean but do not if their prior-year achievement was below the mean. For the same reasons stated above in reference to the original bonus eligibility criterion, it is not possible to determine whether on net this formula penalizes or rewards low-performing schools. Clearly the new formula incorporates a feedback mechanism: by raising performance schools both receive rewards and make it easier to requalify in subsequent years.

Performance Bonuses in Practice

Figure 10-1 shows basic information on the proportion of schools that met their expected or exemplary growth standard in each academic year from 1996–97 to 2006–07. Data for the first two years reflect only the performance of elementary and middle schools; beginning in 1998–99 the data include all schools. In this graph, schools that met the standard for exemplary growth are also counted as having met the standard for expected growth. Schools that met the expected growth standard received only $750 bonus payments for each teacher; schools

Figure 10-1. *Share of Schools Meeting Growth Standards, North Carolina Public Schools, 1996–2007*

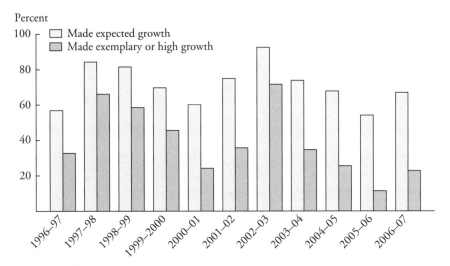

that also met the exemplary growth standard received payments of $1,500 for each teacher.

In each year, most schools in North Carolina qualified for some form of bonus. In three of the eleven years shown, most received the full $1,500 bonus payment. Thus bonus payments were relatively common but far from universal. There is no evidence of a steady trend in the rate of bonus receipt over time. Bonus receipt peaked in the second year of the program, then declined over the next three years. The structure of the bonus program may have contributed to the persistence of trends over time, as schools performing poorly in a given year were assigned higher thresholds for bonus receipt in the following year. Bonus receipt rates bottomed out in 2000–01, peaked again in 2002–03, then bottomed out at an even lower level in 2005–06.

Is it reasonable to think that the quality of instruction in North Carolina public schools varies so dramatically from year to year and follows such cyclical patterns? There is a considerable amount of stability in the public school system. The great majority of students and teachers continue in the same school from one year to the next. Instructional practices do not vary much from year to year. It seems more likely that these fluctuations in bonus receipt rates are artifacts of the structure of the bonus program itself, statistical noise inherent in standardized testing, or possibly consequences of minor alterations to the bonus program over time.

There is also evidence, however, that the bonus program was more than a system of randomly assigning rewards to teachers. Table 10-1 shows the distribution

Table 10-1. *Distribution of Schools, by Frequency of Bonus Receipt, 2002–07*[a]

Exemplary growth ($1,500 bonus)	Expected growth ($750 bonus)					
	0 times	1 time	2 times	3 times	4 times	5 times
0 times	169	152	98	59	70	50
1 time	...	145	190	248	198	130
2 times	...	...	75	133	166	206
3 times	...	...	...	29	92	175
4 times	...	...	...	...	25	112
5 times	...	...	...	...	...	66
n	169	297	363	469	551	739
Share of total (percent)	7	11	14	18	21	29

a. $N = 2,588$. Sample consists of all schools with five observations on expected or exemplary growth over the span from 2002–03 to 2006–07.

of schools by the number of times they qualified for $750 and $1,500 bonuses over the five-year span from 2002–03 to 2006–07. During this period, about 70 percent of schools received bonus payments in a typical year. If distributed randomly, about 17 percent of schools would have received a bonus in all five years, less than 1 percent would have never received a bonus, and about 3 percent would have received the bonus exactly once. As shown in the bottom row of the table, the proportion of schools in the extreme categories exceeds these benchmark figures, indicating that there is at least some persistence in bonus receipt. The proportion of schools receiving a bonus either one or zero times in five years is 18 percent rather than 4 percent, and 29 percent rather than 17 percent receive a bonus in each year. The actual distribution is thus less consistent with random bonus awards and more consistent with persistent performance differences across schools.

Evidence suggests that the process by which a school receives a $1,500 rather than $750 bonus is essentially random. Among schools that received a bonus only once in five years, almost half received the $1,500 bonus rather than the $750 bonus. Among schools receiving bonuses in multiple years, statistics show that the higher bonus amount was awarded half or slightly less than half the time. There is some evidence of persistence: the number of schools receiving the full $1,500 five times is higher than would be expected if the larger amount were awarded randomly to 50 percent of schools receiving any bonus. Overall, though, that a school received a $1,500 rather than a $750 bonus appears much less meaningful than that a school received any bonus at all.

As mentioned previously, that schools serving disadvantaged populations were less likely to receive the bonus could imply that instruction quality truly is lower in those schools or that the bonus program itself imparted a bias against those schools. Table 10-2 shows summary statistics for school and year observations in the interval from 2002–03 to 2006–07 by whether the school received any bonus in the given year and, if so, the amount of the bonus. As expected, given the finding just mentioned, schools that received no bonus payment served a higher proportion of black and Hispanic students and a higher proportion of students participating in the federal free and reduced-price lunch program. Consistent with the notion that the distinction between schools receiving $750 and $1,500 bonuses is largely random, schools in these two categories are largely indistinguishable along these three dimensions.

Given the collective nature of the bonus program, one might expect a stronger response in smaller schools, where the free rider problem is easier to overcome. In fact, this is not the observed pattern. The schools receiving no bonus payments tend to be smaller than those that do. This may reflect the fact that smaller schools tend to be located in rural areas of the state, which are generally poorer than the state's urban areas. As virtually all cities in North Carolina are served by county-wide school districts, high-poverty inner-city schools are relatively uncommon. It is interesting to note that among schools that received a bonus, those qualifying for the full $1,500 were on average 10 percent smaller. This pattern may be an

Table 10-2. *Summary Statistics for School and Year Observations, by Bonus Eligibility Status, 2002–07*[a]

Variable	No bonus	$750 bonus	$1,500 bonus
Share free and reduced-price lunch	47.80	36.90	34.40
Share black	41.30	30.70	30.30
Share Hispanic	7.70	6.90	6.70
Enrollment	518	631	570
	(280)	(403)	(334)
Share elementary school	37.40	42.80	53.80
Share middle school	23.10	15.00	12.50
Share high school	10.00	20.00	14.60

a. Unit of observation is the school and year. Standard deviations in parentheses, where appropriate. Sample consists of school years between 2002–03 and 2005–06, inclusive. Means and proportions are unweighted. The sample size ranges from 8,019 (free and reduced-price lunch) to 8,747 (enrollment). Reductions in sample size can be attributed to missing data in the Common Core. The omitted category of school serves a nontraditional assortment of grades.

artifact of the free rider problem, but it is also consistent with the view that the process of reaching the higher bonus threshold is effectively random. If schools receive the $1,500 bonus only when their average test scores are unusually high, the higher variance of average test scores in smaller schools would produce this pattern.

Middle schools were disproportionately unlikely to receive bonus payments in any given year. The difficulties faced by middle school students in North Carolina and elsewhere have been widely established and discussed.[8] Moreover, middle schools tend to have high rates of teacher turnover, which would support the hypothesis that instruction quality tends to be lower in those schools.[9] Schools serving a wider range of students, for example grades K–8 or 6–12, are also disproportionately represented in the no-bonus category, which is unsurprising since these configurations almost always contain middle grades as well. Among the schools that received at least some bonus, elementary schools were more likely to receive the full $1,500. This pattern may to some extent reflect the previously noted tendency for smaller schools to receive a larger bonus, since elementary schools tend to be smaller than secondary schools.

Evaluating the Bonus Program: Time-Series Evidence

Have North Carolina's bonus payments, offered to most of the state's teachers in many years, improved student performance on standardized tests? This question is inherently difficult to answer. The effects of incentives such as this are systemic in nature: they should have increased teachers' efforts regardless of the ultimate outcome.[10] Moreover, the incentive system was put into effect simultaneously across the state, leaving no reliable control group to aid in the identification of treatment effects. Finally, the bonus program was implemented along with a more comprehensive system of school ratings. Schools are assigned one of several ratings each year based on the overall proficiency level attained by students in that year. It is therefore impossible to ascertain whether any purported effects of the accountability system are attributable to the bonus payments or to the broader system of school ratings.

Some basic time-series evidence on student proficiency rates in North Carolina yields helpful information. If the bonus program had a positive impact on student test scores, proficiency rates would be expected to grow over time as cohorts exposed to the program for at most a brief period of time are replaced by cohorts for whom the bonus program has always been in effect. These across-cohort comparisons are hampered by additional trends in North Carolina public schools, most notably the rapid growth of the Hispanic population. Hispanic students generally attain lower scores on standardized tests in North Carolina, although they show some progress if they remain in the public school system for multiple years.[11]

This is not the first attempt to estimate the impact of performance incentives on student outcomes. Previous studies have generally focused on much smaller programs, however. Randall Eberts, Kevin Hollenbeck, and Joe Stone evaluate a program implemented by a single high school.[12] David Figlio and Lawrence Kenny evaluate numerous programs implemented by public and private schools nationwide, lumping various programs into categories on the basis of the strength of the incentive.[13] Programs similar to North Carolina's, implemented in Dallas, Israel, and Kenya, have been previously evaluated, with mixed evidence on their effectiveness in raising test scores.[14]

Figure 10-2 illustrates the time-series trends in proficiency rates for eighth-grade students in North Carolina on two reading tests: the North Carolina end-of-grade tests used for purposes of determining bonus eligibility, and the lower-stakes National Assessment of Educational Progress (NAEP) test. Proficiency rates are shown beginning in 1998 and continuing through 2007. For students who were in eighth grade in 1997–98, the bonus program began in their seventh-grade year. The bonus program predates the entry into the public school system of students who were in the eighth grade in 2006–07. Thus even though this chart shows no variation attributable to a bonus program's being in place at the time of the test, the hypothesis that the bonus program's impact would

Figure 10-2. *Proficiency Rate in Eighth-Grade Reading, North Carolina Public Schools, 1998–2007*

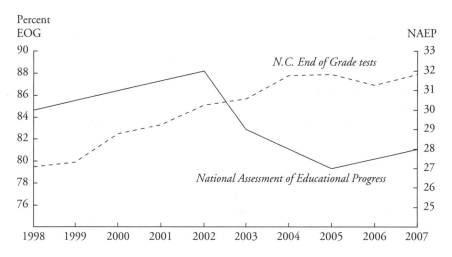

cumulate over time suggests that there should be some observable difference across cohorts.

According to North Carolina's own test results, there have been significant improvements in student reading over time. Across the cohorts shown here, proficiency rates increased from 80 percent to 88 percent on North Carolina's End of Grade test. The greatest gains occurred in the first few years, when each successive cohort represented an additional year's exposure to the bonus program. Proficiency rates leveled off in 2004; the four cohorts exposed to the bonus program since their first-grade year performed at nearly identical levels as eighth-graders.[15] Taken in isolation, this pattern suggests that the implementation of the bonus program raised proficiency rates, with an extra year's worth of exposure to the program associated with a 1 percentage point increase in proficiency.

The second time series displayed on this graph suggests that North Carolina's own test results should not be considered in isolation. Reading scores on the NAEP test were generally much lower for North Carolina eighth-graders, with recent proficiency rates hovering around 30 percent rather than above 80 percent. Moreover, while there is some evidence of an uptick in proficiency ratings among earlier cohorts, later NAEP results have been comparatively poor, with the most recent results (2007) indicating a proficiency rate of 28 percent, relative to a rate of 30 percent for the 1998 cohort. Overall, the bonus program appears to have led schools to improve performance on the high-stakes test, with at best no impact on performance as measured by a more impartial test.[16] This pattern has been observed in other studies comparing student gains on high-stakes and low-stakes tests.[17]

Figure 10-3 presents analogous evidence on trends in eighth-grade math proficiency ratings using both North Carolina end-of-grade tests and the NAEP. Here, the evidence is more consistent. According to the N.C. End of Grade test results, proficiency rates increased from 76 percent to 88 percent from 1998 to 2007.[18] As with the reading results, most of the increase had occurred by 2004, although the 2007 cohort appears to have made significant progress relative to its predecessors. In this case, the NAEP scores follow a similar pattern of improvement, with proficiency increasing from 27 percent to 34 percent from 2000 to 2007. Overall, then, the time-series evidence is less ambiguous in the case of math than in that of reading.

EVALUATING THE BONUS PROGRAM: CROSS-SECTIONAL EVIDENCE

As noted above, there are clear limitations to time-series analysis of the impact of North Carolina's bonus program. There is no cross-sectional variation in exposure to the bonus program across public schools. There is, however, variation in

Figure 10-3. *Proficiency Rate in Eighth-Grade Math, North Carolina Public Schools, 1998–2007*[a]

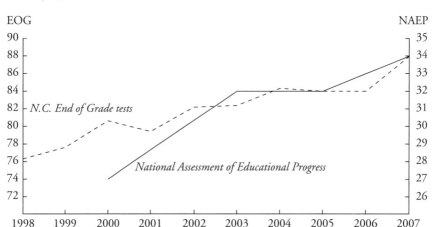

a. Estimates for N.C. End of Grade tests for 2006 are based on seventh-grade test results and for 2007 on sixth-grade test results.

the actual receipt of bonus payments. The expectation is that the initiative to change teaching practices or personnel is particularly strong in schools that do not receive a bonus in a particular year. The question of whether failure to receive a bonus leads to some improvement in instructional quality, though perhaps of less ultimate interest from a policy perspective, is easier to answer, particularly given the 2005–06 revisions to the structure of the bonus program. After 2005–06, the implementation of a strict standard for bonus eligibility, coupled with the reporting of the criterion variable in state reports, enables a regression-discontinuity analysis of the impact of failure to receive a bonus on subsequent student performance. The regression-discontinuity analysis takes advantage of the fact that schools with criterion variables that are nearly identical, but just on either side of the eligibility threshold, are treated very differently. One group receives a bonus, the other does not. The analysis presented here examines whether schools that just missed bonus eligibility in one year are more or less successful the following year, relative to schools that barely qualified.

As previously described, the post-2005 bonus criterion variable is a modified version of the mean change in Z score for students with at least one prior year's test score in a given subject. The modification deflates the change in Z score for students initially below the mean and inflates it for students initially above the mean, to account for mean reversion. Schools receive a bonus if the mean modified change in Z score, hereafter referred to as DZ, exceeds zero. Beginning in the 2005–06 school year, the state of North Carolina began reporting this DZ on school report cards, along with information on whether schools met "expected growth," the standard for receiving a $750 bonus. Examination of these school report cards reveals only a handful of anomalies, cases in which school bonus receipt was not perfectly predicted by the positive or negative sign of DZ.

Regression discontinuity is a viable identification strategy under the assumption that all potential covariates influencing the outcome of interest vary smoothly over the interval containing the discontinuity. Basic analysis of the relationship between the 2005–06 DZ and three school-level covariates— percentage black, percentage Hispanic, and percentage receiving free or reduced-price lunch—reveals little evidence that schools on one side of the threshold are different from those on the other. There is some marginally significant evidence that schools just above the threshold for receiving a bonus payment are more disadvantaged than those just below. For this reason, results reported below include specification checks that control for potentially complex nonlinear relationships between the proportion of students receiving free or reduced-price lunch and DZ.

Figure 10-4 shows the basic results of the analysis. The horizontal axis displays the assignment variable, DZ, for the 2005–06 school year. The vertical axis measures the same variable for the 2006–07 school year. The figure permits a direct assessment of whether schools that barely missed qualifying for a bonus

Figure 10-4. *Bonus Receipt in 2005–06 and Test Outcomes in 2006–07*[a]

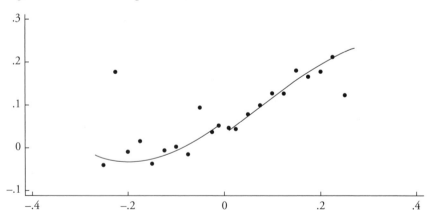

a. The x-axis presents the mean modified change in Z score in 2005–06; the y-axis presents the mean modified change in Z score in 2006–07.

in 2005–06 performed better the following year relative to schools that barely qualified. Data points are collapsed into bins of width 0.025, and the fitted curve represents a cubic in 2005–06 DZ augmented with an indicator for whether that variable was positive.[19]

Before the result of interest is discussed, note that most of the data points lie above zero on the vertical axis. This may indicate that the quality of instruction improved in 2006–07 relative to 2005–06 or that teachers and administrators learned more about the new incentive system after its first year of implementation and restructured their efforts to improve the likelihood of receiving a bonus. A general increase in the probability of bonus receipt between the two years is also seen in figure 10-1.

The evidence in this case points to a clear and statistically significant discontinuity at the bonus threshold for 2005–06. Among schools above the threshold in the initial year, there is a prominent, nearly linear relationship between DZ for 2005–06 and the same variable for 2006–07. At the threshold itself, this relationship weakens considerably. The three data points immediately to the left of the discontinuity are roughly equivalent to the three data points immediately to the right, whereas these latter three points are considerably lower than the three points to their right. The underlying regression specification indicates that failure to receive a bonus in 2005–06 is associated with a 0.028 increase in DZ for 2006–07. In other words, relative to the cubic trend, schools below the threshold improved enough to move themselves into the next highest bin. The estimated effect is significant with a p value of 0.03.

To assess the robustness of this finding to a potential discontinuity in percentage of students receiving free and reduced-price lunch, the regression equation was reestimated with a set of ninety-eight indicator variables separating schools into percentage free and reduced-price lunch bins of width 0.01. In this specification, the estimated magnitude of the discontinuity effect is reduced by about one-fourth, to 0.023, with a p value of 0.095. With a more conventional linear control for percentage receiving free and reduced-price lunch, the estimated effect is 0.025, with a p value of 0.047. Overall, then, the results suggest that the failure to receive a bonus spurs teachers and administrators to alter their practices in ways that produce an average gain of 2 to 3 percent of a standard deviation for each student in each course.

ACHIEVEMENT GAPS AND BONUS PROGRAMS

While one goal of the North Carolina school accountability program has been to increase test scores across the board, a second goal has been to reduce achievement gaps between students of different races and between students of varying socioeconomic status. Inferring the program's impact on these outcomes is rendered difficult by the same factors that complicate the analysis of the policy's overall effect.[20]

A basic examination of trends in NAEP reading scores by race or by eligibility for free and reduced-price lunch shows no evidence of a narrowing of the gap across these cohorts; if anything, the mean difference between disadvantaged and advantaged populations has increased. The average score for white students, or for students not eligible for subsidized lunches, has remained constant, while the average score for blacks and students receiving subsidized lunches has declined slightly.

The gaps in NAEP math test scores between disadvantaged and advantaged students do not noticeably decline over time. For both blacks and students eligible for free and reduced-price lunch, there is a broad improvement in test scores over time. It may be possible that society values test-score improvements at the bottom end of the NAEP scale more than equivalent improvements at the high end of the scale. The data on math test-score gaps are thus best described as inconclusive. Reading test-score gaps, on the other hand, can be assessed more confidently, since scores remained constant for the advantaged groups and declined for disadvantaged groups. Even if the importance of two increases cannot be ranked, stasis is clearly preferable to decline.

The failure of the North Carolina bonus program to demonstrably close test-score gaps may reflect a pattern of teacher responses to the program documented by Charles Clotfelter and his colleagues.[21] This study analyzes teacher turnover in North Carolina public schools before and after the implementation of the bonus program. The introduction of the bonus program is associated with a significant increase in the rate of teacher departure from lower-performing schools. Figure 10-5, reprinted from the original study, shows that the retention rate of teachers beginning employment at low-performing schools in 1996–97 is lower than that of teachers who began in comparable schools two years earlier.

Earlier studies have documented a broad tendency for teachers to leave jobs in lower-performing schools to take positions at more advantaged campuses, often at the same or lower salary.[22] The North Carolina bonus program, which as demonstrated above tended to steer rewards away from lower-performing schools, created yet another reason for teachers to prefer jobs in higher-performing schools. The intention of the bonus program was to spur teachers and administrators to exert greater effort to increase student test scores. The program appears to have had the unintended consequence of spurring teachers to abandon schools that serve lower-performing students. Differences in expected salary brought about directly by the bonus program most likely explain some of this effect; teachers may

Figure 10-5. *Teacher Retention Rates in Low-Performing Schools, 1995 and 1997*[a]

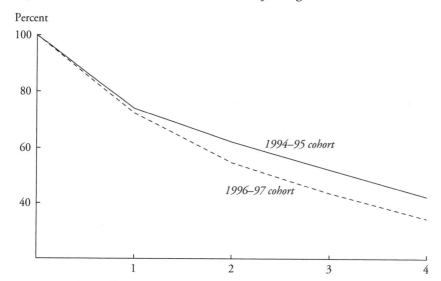

Percent

Source: Charles T. Clotfelter and others, "Do School Accountability Systems Make It More Difficult for Low Performing Schools to Attract and Retain High Quality Teachers?" *Journal of Policy Analysis and Management* 23, no. 2 (2004): 251–71.

a. *Low-performing schools* are defined as schools more than half of whose students are below grade level in the initial year. The horizontal axis refers to the number of years since the initial year for each cohort.

also have sought to avoid positions with a strong emphasis on preparing students for standardized tests.

TEACHER TURNOVER AND BONUS PROGRAMS

Teachers generally avoid jobs in disadvantaged schools; this preference appears to be strengthened when disadvantage translates into a lower likelihood of receiving merit-based bonus payments. The most obvious potential policy lever for counteracting this preference is salary. The question of whether teachers would be more willing to work in a disadvantaged school if they were offered a higher salary is in practice difficult to answer. Suppose, for example, that teacher turnover rates are uncorrelated with salaries among schools with similar observed working conditions. One explanation for this pattern is that higher salaries do not reduce turnover rates. It is also possible, however, that the schools offering higher salaries for equivalent observed working conditions offer inferior unobserved working conditions. Student socioeconomic status, for example, is easy to measure, but it is more difficult to quantify the degree of parent involvement in a school or the competence of the district administration.

A recent study by Clotfelter and colleagues uses a second North Carolina bonus program to address this important but difficult question.[23] For a three-year period beginning in 2001–02, the state offered annual bonuses of $1,800 to certified teachers of math, science, and special education who took and remained in jobs in middle or high schools that met one of two criteria: high rates of participation in the free or reduced-price lunch program and high rates of failure on end-of-course examinations in algebra and biology. The program thus created within-school variation in salaries, breaking the potential correlation between salary levels and unobserved working conditions (as long as working conditions within a school do not vary substantially across teacher subject area). The analysis by Clotfelter and colleagues compares turnover rates of teachers before and after the implementation of the bonus program, across eligible and ineligible subjects, and between eligible and barely ineligible schools, a methodology often referred to as differences-in-differences-in-differences.

Table 10-3 shows the study's basic results, derived from a statistical model predicting the probability of a teacher's departure after year t of a period of continuous employment at a single school, conditional on staying through year t.[24] Table entries are hazard ratios. When less than 1, the hazard ratio indicates a factor that reduces the likelihood of departure. The basic estimate here indicates that the bonus program reduced the likelihood of departure by 15 percent. More refined estimates, presented in Clotfelter and colleagues, tend to indicate an even larger effect on teacher turnover.[25] Converted into an elasticity, this estimate suggests that a 1 percent increase in salary at low-performing schools would lead to a 3 to 4 percent reduction in turnover rates.

It should be emphasized that the math, science, and special education bonus program was not performance based. There were no provisions to ensure that bonus payments were made to the most effective teachers, except that uncertified teachers were not eligible to receive them. Clotfelter and colleagues report that the program had the highest proportional impacts on experienced teachers, who have repeatedly been associated with greater effectiveness at improving student test scores relative to novices.

Conclusions

North Carolina's accountability bonus program is the nation's largest, and perhaps its longest-running, initiative to reward teachers for producing gains in stu-

Table 10-3. *Basic Estimate of the Math, Science, and Special Education Bonus Program's Impact*[a]

Teacher receives a bonus payment	0.848**
	(–0.057)
Teacher is certified in math, science, or special education and is employed by an ever-eligible school	1.005
	(–0.062)
Teacher is employed by a currently eligible school	0.802**
	(–0.034)
Teacher is certified in math, science, or special education in a post-program year	1.114*
	(–0.07)
Teacher is certified in math, science, or special education	0.996
	(–0.054)
Teacher is employed by an ever-eligible school	1.286**
	(–0.041)
Year is 2000	1.141**
	(–0.05)
Year is 2001	1.560**
	(–0.07)
Year is 2002	1.907**
	(–0.076)
Summary statistic	
N	29,562
Log likelihood	59,123.93

Source: Charles T. Clotfelter and others, "Would Higher Salaries Keep Teachers in High-Poverty Schools? Evidence from a Policy Intervention in North Carolina," *Journal of Public Economics* 92, nos. 5–6 (2008): 1352–70.

a. Table entries are hazard ratios, with standard errors in parentheses. The hazard refers to the probability of exiting a school after period t, conditional on remaining in that school until period t. Unit of observation is the teacher/school/year.

**Denotes a hazard ratio significantly different from 1 at the 5 percent level; *denotes a hazard ratio significantly different from 1 at the 10 percent level.

dent test scores. Over the past decade, the program has paid millions of dollars in bonuses to tens of thousands of teachers throughout the state. The creators of the bonus program can be praised for certain aspects of its design, particularly the focus on test-score improvements rather than on straight proficiency espoused by the No Child Left Behind Act. Repeated tinkering with the incentive system also reflects a willingness to address concerns as they are raised. It is also clear, however, that certain aspects of the bonus program are statistically perplexing, threaten to place disadvantaged schools at a further disadvantage, or weaken the program's potential incentive effect.

The bonus program has always based rewards on the performance of a school rather than that of an individual teacher. Economic theory suggests that this emphasis on collective outcomes will lead to a free rider program, as any one teacher's effort has only a small impact on the school as a whole. Moving to a teacher-level incentive system, however, is not necessarily advisable, given the statistical noise in standardized tests and the demonstrated failure of many public schools to allocate students in a fair or even way across classrooms.[26] There clearly are trade-offs between rewarding individual teachers and rewarding teachers who work at a high-performing school. Further research is necessary to quantify these trade-offs and indeed to determine whether the flaws are sufficient to warrant abandoning efforts to present incentives to teachers.

Beyond this trade-off, perhaps the most glaring flaw in the design of North Carolina's program has been its treatment of mean reversion. Mean reversion is a real concern; however, unless noise in student test scores can be attributed entirely to school-level shocks, the proper correction for mean reversion should take account of school size. The state's crude efforts to address mean reversion likely have the unintended effect of penalizing low-performing schools, though the magnitude of the effect is impossible to identify.

There is at least some evidence that the bonus program has led to an improvement in test scores, though the evidence presented here should be considered less than definitive. Math proficiency rates have increased both on the high-stakes test used to determine bonus eligibility and on the lower stakes NAEP exam. Reading proficiency rates have improved only on the state's own examination. The regression discontinuity analysis of failure to receive a bonus suggests that following a negative outcome schools do implement changes that lead to improvements.

Hopes that the bonus program would help ameliorate racial or socioeconomic differences in achievement have not been realized, quite possibly because teachers have reacted to the uneven playing field by leaving disadvantaged schools in increased numbers. According to NAEP results, achievement gaps in 2007 were as wide as or wider than they had been a decade earlier.

What lessons does the North Carolina experience offer to other states, districts, or individual schools seeking to improve teacher effort by offering incentives? Above all else, the results discussed here suggest that incentive programs, when adopted in an effort to raise the performance of disadvantaged students, can be a two-edged sword. If teachers perceive bonus programs as yet another factor making jobs in advantaged schools more attractive, increased turnover rates in low-performing schools are a predictable consequence. This unintended side effect could be avoided as long as teachers perceived the bonus program as a fair reward for their effort, rather than as a reward for student background or other inputs over which teachers have no direct control.

This implication, in turn, suggests a fruitful avenue for further policy-relevant research. To craft a bonus program that presents a truly level playing field, policymakers need evidence on the expected test-score gains of individuals at varying points in the achievement distribution under constant instructional quality. Such evidence could be based on within-class empirical models, based solely on students enrolled in the same classroom, under the assumption that instructional quality does not vary within classrooms. If instructional quality varies within classrooms, however, more sophisticated methods will be required to derive these estimates.

Finally, given the political controversy surrounding the use of performance bonuses in public schools, it should be noted that the accountability bonus program enjoys broad support in North Carolina. The state does not have a teachers' union with collective bargaining power, which undoubtedly eased the path toward implementing the bonus program, but there is a professional association of teachers, the North Carolina Association of Educators, which engages in policy advocacy on a number of fronts. In its published agenda for the 2007–08 legislative session, there is no opposition to the bonus program. In fact, the teacher association explicitly advocates maintaining the bonus program and expanding it to certain state-run schools that do not currently participate. The association's stated policy stances may reflect political reality as much as teachers' own preferences, but their expression of explicit support, rather than tacit acceptance, is noteworthy. While there is some evidence of effectiveness in spite of its flaws, it is the sheer popularity of the bonus program that provides the most heartening evidence to jurisdictions contemplating similar initiatives.

Notes

1. Test-score gains for third-graders are computed by comparing their end-of-grade reading and math test scores to scores on a pretest in the same subjects. The pretest is administered at the beginning of the school year. The benchmark average growth for third-graders was initially based on the results of pretests and end-of-grade tests administered in the 1996–97 school year. This benchmark was later replaced with results from the 2000–01 school year.
2. In the 2003–04 school year, for example, the coefficient b_1 was 0.22 for reading in all grades except third, where it was 0.47. In math, the coefficient was 0.26 in all grades except third, where it was 0.20.
3. Statistically speaking, if one student's test score equals his or her true achievement plus an error term with mean zero and variance σ^2, then the mean test score in a school with n students is equal to the mean true achievement plus an error term with mean zero and variance σ^2/n, as long as the students' error terms are independent of one another. If student

errors are perfectly correlated with one another—an unlikely scenario—then the school-level error term is independent of size.

4. In the 2003–04 school year, the coefficient was –0.58 for math in all grades, –0.60 in reading for all grades except third, and –0.98 for third-grade reading.

5. Schools meeting this criterion were ruled ineligible for bonus payments if they claimed an "excessive" number of exemptions from testing or tested fewer than 98 percent of all eligible students.

6. A Z score is the difference between any one observation of a variable, such as a test score, and the mean of that variable, expressed in units of standard deviation. For example, on a test with mean 100 and standard deviation 10, a score of 90 would translate into a Z score of –1.

7. In cases in which only one prior-year test score is available for a student, that single score is used in place of the average of the previous two. The discount factor is 0.92 when two years' worth of previous test scores are available and 0.82 when a single year's data is available.

8. See, for example, Philip J. Cook and others, "The Negative Impacts of Starting Middle School in Sixth Grade," *Journal of Policy Analysis and Management* 27, no. 1 (2008): 104–21.

9. Charles T. Clotfelter and others, "Would Higher Salaries Keep Teachers in High-Poverty Schools? Evidence from a Policy Intervention in North Carolina," *Journal of Public Economics* 92, nos. 5–6 (2008): 1352–70.

10. One potential strategy for identifying the impact of the bonus program would be to exploit the free rider hypothesis, which predicts that the impact of school-wide incentives would be smaller in large schools. Some preliminary evidence, presented in table 10-2, suggests that the free rider problem has been a factor in North Carolina. A test based on the free rider problem would be weak in one critical respect: a failure to find that performance in small schools improved relative to larger schools could be taken as evidence either that the incentives had no impact or that the free rider problem was unimportant. North Carolina's crude implementation of corrections for mean reversion also threaten such an identification strategy. Other things being equal, large low-performing schools faced a higher hurdle for bonus qualification, while large high-performing schools faced a lower hurdle.

11. Charles T. Clotfelter, Helen F. Ladd and Jacob L. Vigdor, "The Academic Achievement Gap in Grades 3 through 8" *Review of Economics and Statistics* (forthcoming).

12. Randall Eberts, Kevin Hollenbeck, and Joe Stone, "Teacher Performance Incentives and Student Outcomes," *Journal of Human Resources* 37, no. 4 (2002): 913–27

13. David N. Figlio and Lawrence W. Kenny, "Individual Teacher Incentives and Student Performance," *Journal of Public Economics* 91, nos. 5–6 (2007): 901–14.

14. Helen F. Ladd, "The Dallas School Accountability and Incentive Program: An Evaluation of Its Impacts on Student Outcomes," *Economics of Education Review* 18, no. 1 (1999): 1–16; Victor Lavy, "Evaluating the Effect of Teachers' Group Performance Incentives on Pupil Achievement," *Journal of Political Economy* 110, no. 6 (2002): 1286–1317; Paul Glewwe, Nauman Ilias, and Michael Kremer, "Teacher Incentives," Working Paper 9671 (Cambridge, Mass.: National Bureau of Economic Research, 2003).

15. It is interesting to note that these four cohorts do vary in their exposure to the No Child Left Behind program, which more directly targets proficiency as the basis for school sanctions. This basic evidence thus suggests that the system of transfers, supplemental tutoring, and school restructuring imposed on poorly performing schools in the No Child Left Behind regime has had little impact on the proficiency of eighth-grade students.

16. This contrast is more striking in light of the purported similarity between the stated criteria used both by the state of North Carolina and the NAEP to judge proficiency in reading for eighth-grade students. Published criteria in both cases refer to the ability to make inferences and draw conclusions from text and to identify and evaluate literary devices.

17. David N. Figlio and Cecilia E. Rouse, "Do Accountability and Voucher Threats Improve Low-Performing Schools?" *Journal of Public Economics* 90, nos. 1–2 (2006): 239–55; Brian A. Jacob, "Test-Based Accountability and Student Achievement: An Investigation of Differential Performance on NAEP and State Assessments," Working Paper 12817 (Cambridge, Mass.: National Bureau of Economic Research, 2007).

18. Effective in 2005–06, North Carolina redefined the proficiency standard in mathematics, resulting in a drop in reported proficiency rates on N.C. End of Grade program tests. The proficiency rates shown for the 2005–06 and 2006–07 cohorts are extrapolated from proficiency rates on program math tests for seventh- and sixth-grade students, respectively.

19. The sample is trimmed to exclude the lowest-performing twenty-five schools and the highest-performing fifty schools, which as outliers have the potential to unduly influence the regression discontinuity analysis. These schools represent just over 3 percent of all potential observations. The specific criterion for exclusion is a 2005–06 *DZ* value above 0.25 in absolute value.

20. In theory, the regression discontinuity design could be applied to the study of achievement gaps.

21. Charles T. Clotfelter and others, "Do School Accountability Systems Make It More Difficult for Low Performing Schools to Attract and Retain High Quality Teachers?" *Journal of Policy Analysis and Management* 23, no. 2 (2004): 251–71.

22. Susanna Loeb and Marianne E. Page, "Examining the Link between Teacher Wages and Student Outcomes: The Importance of Alternative Labor Market Opportunities and Non-Pecuniary Variation," *Review of Economics and Statistics* 82, no. 3 (2000): 393–408; Eric A. Hanushek, John F. Kain, and Steven G. Rivkin, "Why Public Schools Lose Teachers," *Journal of Human Resources* 39, no. 2 (2004): 326–54.

23. Clotfelter and others, "Would Higher Salaries Keep Teachers in High-Poverty Schools?"

24. The statistical model is a Cox proportional hazard model. Clotfelter and others, "Would Higher Salaries Keep Teachers in High-Poverty Schools?" also presents results derived from parametric hazard models.

25. Ibid.

26. Charles T. Clotfelter, Helen F. Ladd, and Jacob L. Vigdor, "Teacher-Student Matching and the Assessment of Teacher Effectiveness," *Journal of Human Resources* 41, no. 4 (2006): 778–820.

11

Teacher Effectiveness, Mobility, and Attrition in Florida

Martin R. West and Matthew M. Chingos

Although the impacts of per pupil spending, class size, and other school inputs on student achievement continue to be debated, there is a strong consensus that teacher quality is hugely important and varies widely, even within schools.[1] Hiring and retaining more-effective teachers thus has enormous potential for raising overall levels of student achievement and reducing achievement gaps along lines of race and class. Indeed, it is no stretch to conclude, as Robert Gordon and colleagues put it, that "without the right people standing in front of the classroom, school reform is a futile exercise."[2] It is hardly surprising, then, that recent years have seen a surge in interest among researchers and policymakers in measures intended to improve the quality of the teaching workforce.[3]

Among the most controversial strategies now under consideration is the introduction of performance-pay plans that would tie teachers' compensation directly

We thank former Commissioner John Winn and other officials at the Florida Department of Education for supplying the data used in this analysis. Lawrence Katz, Cynthia Prince, Matthew Springer, John Tyler, and seminar participants at Harvard University and Vanderbilt University provided helpful comments on previous drafts. Jonah Rockoff generously shared programming code used in one portion of the analysis. Financial and administrative support was provided by the Searle Freedom Trust and the Program on Education Policy and Governance at Harvard University.

to their students' academic progress. Arguments for performance pay in K–12 education typically emphasize the incentives they would create for current educators to make pedagogical or organizational changes to foster student learning. An equally important rationale for such policies, however, could be the recruitment and retention of teachers who are already effective in the classroom. Existing teacher compensation systems, which reward teachers based primarily on seniority and degree completion, offer no special inducement for more-effective teachers to enter or remain in the profession. In fact, to the extent that good teachers have superior earnings opportunities in other fields, the current system of compensation may create a disincentive for them to continue teaching. As a result, there is widespread concern that the best teachers are leaving the schools where they are most needed for more affluent schools or more lucrative occupations.

There is a substantial literature on the correlates of teacher retention but far less research on the link between retention and effectiveness. Indeed, to our knowledge, only three studies have examined the relationship between mobility and attrition patterns and teacher quality using direct measures of teachers' classroom effectiveness.[4] Each finds that teacher effectiveness is in fact positively associated with retention in either specific schools or the profession—a finding that might be interpreted as discrediting the concern that public schools are losing their best teachers. However, this interpretation ignores the possibility that the optimal pattern may be high attrition rates among the least effective teachers and low attrition rates among the most effective teachers. While it is sensible to measure overall differences in attrition and mobility rates by effectiveness, it is also important to consider the absolute attrition rates for different groups of teachers and whether they could (and should) be higher or lower.

This chapter, which presents a descriptive analysis of the early career paths of new elementary school teachers in the state of Florida from 2001–02 to 2005–06, extends this emerging line of research in several ways. Specifically, we address three questions:

—How do patterns of mobility across schools and attrition from the profession differ for new fourth- and fifth-grade teachers in Florida who are more and less effective, as measured by their students' academic progress on state tests?

—Do these patterns differ for schools serving more advantaged students and for schools with high-performing students?

—For teachers switching schools, how did their schools and salaries change when they moved?

Although we do not find evidence that Florida elementary schools are disproportionately losing their most effective early-career teachers, our data nonetheless suggest that schools have considerable room to raise student achievement and close achievement gaps through targeted policies aimed at retaining only their most effective performers. A clear majority of the state's most effective teachers leave their initial schools only four years into their careers, and these same teachers are no less likely than the least effective to leave the state's public school system altogether. We also find that some schools—namely, those with the highest-performing students—already do a far better job than most of retaining their most effective teachers and dismissing the least effective.

Teacher Policy and Mobility in Florida

In recent years, the combination of population growth and class-size reduction policies has dramatically increased the demand for teachers in Florida. The school-age population in the state increased by 6 percent (from 2,708,000 to 2,869,000) between 2000 and 2005, while the national school-age population grew by only 0.02 percent.[5] Perhaps more important, in November 2002 voters approved an amendment to the Florida constitution establishing maximum class sizes of eighteen students in grades K–3, twenty-two students in grades 4–8, and twenty-five students in high school, to be attained by the 2010–11 school year. Implementing legislation passed in 2003 mandated a reduction of two students a year in district average class sizes from 2003–04 until 2005–06; a two-student reduction in school average class size during the 2006–07 and 2007–08 school years; and a two-student reduction in individual classroom averages in 2008–09 until goals are reached before or during the 2010–11 school year. As a consequence, average class sizes statewide decreased by 6.12 students in grades K–3 and 4.75 students in grades 4–8 between the 2003–04 and 2006–07 school years.

In response to the hiring pressures stemming from these developments, the state legislature established two innovative programs that provide alternative routes into teaching: educator preparation institutes at community colleges and district-based alternative certification programs. The state's department of education also invested considerable resources in recruiting out-of-state teachers and proposed legislation that would encourage former military personnel and military spouses to enter the classroom. However, there remains an urgent need to increase the supply of teachers entering Florida's classrooms that presumably also creates strong incentives for schools and districts to retain their current teachers.

While the Florida legislature has, since 2006, passed two landmark laws mandating that each of its sixty-seven school districts adopt plans that would make teachers eligible for bonuses based on their students' academic progress, the use of performance pay in Florida during the time period we examine was limited, especially for elementary school teachers.[6] The most important exception is the School Recognition Program, which since 2002 has offered awards of $100 per full-time-equivalent student to each school that improves its grade on the state's accountability system or maintains its ranking in the highest category. Although most recognized schools distribute the bulk of these funds to their employees, they typically do so relatively evenly among teachers and staff. As a result, the one-year bonuses for classroom teachers typically amount to less than $1,000 per teacher.[7] The state also offers bonuses to teachers who have attained certification from the National Board for Professional Teaching Standards and for teachers whose students pass advanced placement exams, but these programs are generally not relevant for early-career teachers in the elementary grades. Finally, the use of bonuses to recruit and retain teachers in hard-to-staff schools and subjects is not widespread in the state. There is little reason, then, to think that Florida's tentative early steps toward differentiated compensation for teachers had a measurable impact on the attrition and mobility patterns documented below.

The database we draw upon in this chapter enables us to track all 11,076 fourth- and fifth-grade regular classroom teachers in the 2001–02 through 2005–06 academic years, the most recent for which data are available. Eighty-two percent of teachers in these grades remained in the same school after one year, but this figure dropped to around 50 percent by the fifth year. Most of the movement of teachers across schools in Florida occurs within districts rather than between districts. By the 2002–03 academic year, 7 percent of teachers were employed by another school within the same district in which they had taught the previous year, while only 1 percent had moved to another district. By 2005–06, these figures had increased to 18 and 4 percent, respectively. But teachers who leave the Florida public schools altogether consistently outnumber the combined share of teachers who switch schools either within or between districts. The share of 2001–02 teachers no longer employed in any public school in Florida rose from 10 percent in 2002–03 to 27 percent in 2005–06. Interestingly, the one-year mobility and attrition rates we observe in Florida in 2003–04 are remarkably close to the national average for elementary school teachers that same year: by the 2004–05 school year, 83 percent of all teachers remained in the same school, 9 percent had moved to a different school, and 8 percent had left the profession.[8]

Figure 11-1. *Status of New Teachers over Time, Florida Public Schools, 2001–06*

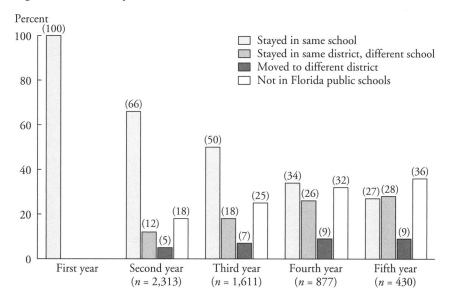

Figure 11-1 provides an overview of mobility and attrition among the 2,313 fourth- and fifth-grade teachers who entered the profession from 2001–02 to 2004–05, the group that is the focus of our analysis. Rather than organize the data by chronological year, we instead track each teacher's movements relative to his or her first year of teaching. Because we can follow teachers only through 2005–06, we observe the cohorts of teachers entering after 2001–02 for fewer than five years. The size of the samples on which each data point is based therefore grows smaller with each successive year. The figure confirms that this group of new teachers is much more mobile than the full sample of teachers in the same grades, much as one would expect of any worker early in his or her career. Only 66 percent of new teachers remained in the same school for a second year, and by the fifth year more have left the profession than remain at the same school. As with the full group of teachers described above, most of the movement of new teachers among schools occurs within districts rather than between districts.

Of course, when a new teacher switches schools but does not exit the profession, one school's loss is another school's gain. From a system-wide standpoint, the movement of teachers across schools could have a negligible impact on student achievement if it does not interfere with staff cohesion and if a year of experience in a school will prepare the teacher for a different school just as well as a

Figure 11-2. *Retention of New Fourth- and Fifth-Grade Teachers,*
by School Racial Makeup, Florida Public Schools, 2001–06[a]

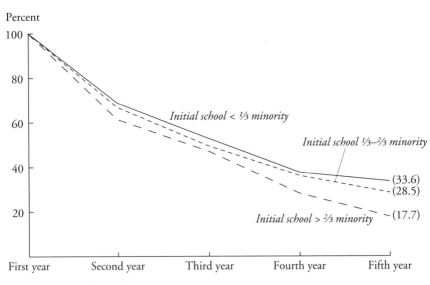

a. See figure 11-1 for *n* values.

year of experience in the new school would have. Teacher mobility could even
be beneficial for student achievement if teachers sorted themselves into school
environments in which they are more effective. Of course, another plausible
equilibrium is one in which the best teachers drift toward the schools with the
best salaries and most-favorable working conditions (for example, good neighborhood, students from affluent families, and so forth) where they instruct the
students who arguably need them the least. One might expect this to occur if
salary differences are small across schools (so only compensating differentials
affect job choice) or if schools with wealthier families are able to offer higher
salaries to attract high-quality teachers. In Florida, school districts (which are
coterminous with counties) are very large, so the former hypothesis is likely more
relevant than the latter.

   Figure 11-2 offers some basic evidence as to how the mobility of new fourth-
and fifth-grade teachers varies according to the racial distribution of their schools'
student bodies. There are substantial differences in the rate at which new teachers remain in their initial schools, and teachers in schools serving less than one-
third minority students are more likely to stay in their schools than teachers in
high-minority schools. A virtually identical pattern emerges when we group

schools according to the share of students eligible for the free or reduced-price lunch program, a standard indicator of poverty. This constitutes suggestive evidence, based on the link between teacher experience and effectiveness, that teacher attrition may have a larger negative impact at schools that serve primarily disadvantaged students. It could, however, be that the difficult working conditions of urban schools more efficiently weed out ineffective teachers and thus that higher teacher attrition at these schools is actually beneficial for student achievement. In short, to truly understand the implications of teacher mobility for student achievement, it is essential to examine the relationship between mobility and effectiveness.

Analytic Strategy and Data

Most research on teacher quality has used observed teacher characteristics (for example, experience, graduate degrees, college selectivity, or certification test scores) as proxies for unobserved ability. Recent findings, however, cast considerable doubt on the relationship between these indicators and classroom effectiveness.[9] We use the terms *effectiveness* and *quality* interchangeably in this chapter to refer only to the effect that a teacher has on his or her students' test scores. Of course, teacher quality has other dimensions, most of which are difficult to measure and all of which are outside the scope of our analysis. The value of the findings presented below hinges on the assumption that the test instruments used are, on average, a reasonable measure of students' overall academic development.

Measuring Teacher Effectiveness

We begin our analysis of the relationship between teacher effectiveness and mobility by computing a value added measure of effectiveness for each teacher. Specifically, we regress students' math and reading test scores separately on their prior-year test scores (including squared and cubed terms of the prior-year scores in order to allow for nonlinearities in the relationship between prior and current achievement); vectors of student, classroom, and school characteristics; dummy variables for teacher experience; and grade-by-year fixed effects.[10] Our student-level control variables (in addition to prior-year test scores) are the number of days absent the previous year and dummy variables for race, gender, limited English proficiency status, special education status, migrant status, whether the student was in a different school the previous year, and free or reduced-price lunch eligibility. Classroom- and school-level control variables include all of the student-level characteristics aggregated to the appropriate level. In addition, they include class size and the percentage of students in the classroom and school who were repeating a grade. The model, then, is

$$A_{it} = \omega A_{i,t-1} + \beta X_{it} + \gamma C_{it} + \phi S_{it} + \delta W_{it} + \pi_{it} + \varepsilon_{it},$$

where A_{it} is the test score of student i in year t (standardized by grade and year to have a mean of zero and standard deviation of one); $A_{i,t-1}$ is the student's prior-year test scores in both subjects (and their squared and cubed terms); X, C, and S are student-, classroom-, and school-level characteristics; W is a vector of teacher experience dummy variables; π is a vector of grade-by-year fixed effects, and ε is a standard zero-mean error term. We estimate this equation separately by subject (reading and math) and average the residuals by teacher and year to construct a single value added measure of teacher effectiveness.[11]

Although they are now widely used by researchers, the reliability of this kind of value added model of teacher effectiveness using nonexperimental data continues to be debated.[12] The key potential confounding factor is the nonrandom matching of students and teachers both across and within schools. For example, families choose where to live based in part on the quality of local schools, and they pay a premium for better schools through higher house prices and property taxes. At the within-school level, motivated parents could pressure the school to assign their children to teachers they perceive as better, senior teachers may be rewarded with classes that have fewer students with behavior problems, or administrators may simply try to match students with the most appropriate teacher. Any of these potential sources of nonrandom sorting would bias our estimates of teacher quality if there are unobserved differences across students that cannot be controlled for using the variables described above.[13]

Fortunately, a recent validation study confirms that value added estimates of teacher effectiveness are highly correlated with estimates based on experimental data in which teachers and students are randomly paired, providing strong evidence that they are in fact reliable.[14] Moreover, it is unclear whether and in what direction any nonrandom matching would bias our analyses. The nonrandom matching of students and teachers based on unobserved characteristics should increase measurement error in our teacher effectiveness ratings, thereby attenuating differences in mobility patterns between teachers in different segments of the effectiveness distribution. It is not obvious a priori, however, whether the additional error would be systematically related to teacher mobility. In short, while our analysis is not based on experimental estimates of teacher effectiveness, there is little reason to expect that this is an important limitation in this context.

The Florida Database

The information with which we implement this approach comes from the K–20 Education Data Warehouse assembled by the Florida Department of Education. Our data extract contains observations on every student in Florida who took the state assessment tests from 1998–99 to 2005–06, and each student in the database is linked to his or her teacher (or teachers) for 2001–02 through 2005–06.[15] The data include test-score results from the Florida Comprehensive Assessment Test (FCAT), the state accountability system's "high-stakes" test, and the Stanford Achievement Test, a nationally norm-referenced test that is administered to students at the same time as the FCAT but is not used for accountability purposes. Beginning in 2000–01, students in grades 3 through 10 were tested every year in math and reading. Thus annual gain scores can be calculated for virtually all students in grades 4 through 10 beginning in 2001–02. The data also contain information on the demographic and educational characteristics of the students, including gender, race, free or reduced-price lunch eligibility, limited English proficiency status, special education status, days in attendance, and age.

Our teacher data files contain detailed information on individual teachers, including demographic information, experience, and compensation. We use the employment data (the course enrollment file that matches students and teachers) to track where teachers are employed each year and to link them to their students. We use the experience data to identify the cohorts of fourth- and fifth-grade teachers that entered the teaching profession from 2001–02 and 2004–05.[16] The teacher experience variable we construct is made up of all years the teacher has spent in the profession, including both public and nonpublic schools in both Florida and other states.

The measure of teacher effectiveness used in the analysis presented below is based on FCAT math and reading test scores only. Because the FCAT is the test for which schools are held accountable, schools should have a particularly strong incentive to retain those teachers who are effective in raising student achievement on that test. The choice of which test to use, however, makes little difference to our results. The effectiveness of teachers as measured by their students' FCAT performance is modestly correlated with their effectiveness as measured by the Stanford Achievement Test ($r = 0.64$), and the attrition and mobility patterns documented below are similar regardless of which test we use to gauge effectiveness.

Students who repeated or skipped a grade are excluded from our analysis because their prior-year test scores are not directly comparable to those of their classmates.[17] We limit our analysis to fourth- and fifth-grade students and their teachers, as these students typically have only one teacher for primary math and reading (their regular classroom teacher). Students who had more than one class-room teacher or are in a classroom of fewer than ten or more than fifty students are dropped from this analysis.[18] The data on which this analysis is based span from 2001–02, the first year for which we can calculate gain scores for fourth- and fifth-graders in both reading and math, to 2005–06, the most recent year for which data are currently available.

Results

The estimates based on our value added model of teacher effectiveness are consis-tent with previous findings on both returns to experience and variation in teacher effectiveness. In math, the students of first- and second-year teachers have test scores about 4 and 1 percent of a standard deviation lower, respectively, than stu-dents of the most experienced teachers (those with more than twenty years of experience). Teachers between the third and twentieth year of experience are all about as effective as teachers with more than twenty years of experience. In read-ing, the test scores of students of first- and second-year teachers are about 5 and 4 percent of a standard deviation lower, respectively, than the most experienced teachers. Students of teachers in their third through tenth years of teaching also score about 2 to 3 percent of a standard deviation lower in reading than do those of the most experienced teachers.

The standard deviation of our teacher effectiveness measures, once adjusted for sampling error, is also similar to that found in previous work. After using the cor-relation of individual teacher's ratings across years to separate the persistent and nonpersistent components of our teacher effectiveness measure, we estimate a standard deviation of the persistent component of 0.11 in math and 0.05 in read-ing.[19] In other words, the effectiveness of fourth- and fifth-grade teachers in the state of Florida as measured by their students' academic progress varies enormously, as has been the case in every context in which this question has been examined.

Mobility and Attrition by Effectiveness Tercile

We use the results of the same model to divide all teachers in Florida who were in charge of a fourth- or fifth-grade classroom from 2001–02 to 2005–06 into thirds based on their average effectiveness score in both math and reading dur-ing the time they were employed at the school in which they taught during their first year.[20] The differences in the average effectiveness of teachers in each of these terciles are substantial. Students assigned to a teacher in the lowest third could expect to make gains of 0.20 standard deviations less on the math FCAT than had they been assigned to a teacher in the middle third; students assigned to a teacher in the top third could expect to make gains that were 0.20 standard deviations greater. On the reading FCAT, the expected gains for students of bottom-third and top-third teachers would be –0.09 and 0.09 standard deviations, respectively.[21]

We then focus on the 2,313 of these teachers who entered the profession from 2001–02 to 2004–05. These teachers are somewhat clustered in the bottom of the effectiveness distribution, with just over 40 percent falling in the bottom third, 28 percent in the middle third, and 31 percent in the top third. The concentration of new teachers among the least effective could reflect either a cohort effect (that is, teachers entering the Florida school system are less effective than previous entrants) or imperfections in our adjustment for the effects of experience.[22] Fortunately, neither possibility is a problem for our analysis of early-career mobility and attrition across the three groups.

Figures 11-3 and 11-4 track the mobility of new teachers separately within each of these terciles. Mobility behavior is described by two binary variables: whether the teacher was still in the same school (figure 11-3) and whether the teacher was still in the profession (figure 11-4). It is important to keep in mind that our data do not allow us to distinguish between voluntary and involuntary movement among teachers—that is, between involuntary transfers and dismissals and voluntary decisions to seek out a new school or leave the teaching profession. Conventional wisdom, however, would suggest that most mobility and attrition is voluntary, even among new teachers, and the patterns we observe generally provide no strong reason to think otherwise.

Contrary to common preconceptions (but consistent with previous research), we find that the most effective teachers are actually more likely to remain in their original schools than are teachers in the bottom third of the effectiveness distribution. The differences are especially pronounced in the first three years. By the second year of teaching, only 59 percent of bottom-third teachers remain in their original schools, as compared with roughly 70 percent of both middle- and top-third teachers. These differences in retention rates narrow somewhat over time but remain evident by year 5 (although the difference in retention rates for the middle- and bottom-third teachers is only statistically significant at the 85 percent level).

At the same time, figure 11-3 also suggests that schools would be well served by doing more to retain their most effective teachers—as only 30 percent remain in their original school by year 5—and by dismissing more of the worst teachers

Figure 11-3. *New Teacher Retention in Same School, by Teacher Effectiveness, Florida Public Schools, 2001–06*[a]

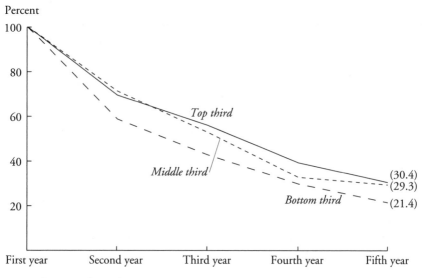

Percent

First year   Second year   Third year   Fourth year   Fifth year

a. See figure 11-1 for *n* values.

before they are granted tenure, which in Florida generally occurs between the third and fourth years of teaching. The fact that there is no sharp drop in retention rates at this point, either overall or for the least effective teachers, suggests that schools are not using the tenure decision process to weed out probationary teachers who have been ineffective in the classroom. The markedly higher mobility rates of bottom-third teachers in the first three years, however, could indicate that schools are counseling out their worst performers.

Figure 11-4, which examines the rate at which teachers remain in any public school in Florida, paints a somewhat different picture. While teachers in the bottom third of the distribution are still less likely to remain in the profession through the second year of teaching, the differences across terciles are small and disappear altogether by year 4. By year 5, only 61 percent of the top-third teachers remain in Florida schools, again suggesting the potential value of targeted policies to increase retention for this group. The clear difference between the school-level and statewide retention patterns suggests that the least effective teachers, though they are more likely to leave their initial schools, are often successful in gaining employment elsewhere in the Florida public school system.

Figure 11-4. *New Teacher Retention in Profession in State, by Teacher Effectiveness, Florida Public Schools, 2001–06*[a]

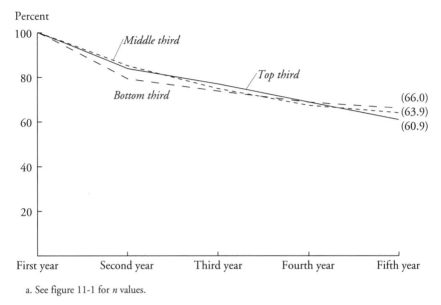

Percent

a. See figure 11-1 for *n* values.

School Characteristics and Mobility by Effectiveness Tercile

Of course, it is possible that the relationship between teacher mobility and teacher effectiveness varies according to the characteristics of the school. For example, it may be the case that schools serving disadvantaged students lose their most effective teachers to schools with more desirable teaching environments and are left with only their worst performers. Figure 11-5 explores this issue by tracking the mobility of new teachers out of schools with large (more than two-thirds) shares of minority students. As above, we find that overall levels of attrition are substantially higher in high-minority schools than in schools statewide (compare figure 11-3). The relative attrition rates of the most and least effective teachers, however, are quite similar to the patterns elsewhere. Specifically, teachers in the bottom third of the distribution are roughly 10 percentage points more likely than those in the middle or top third to leave their original schools in the first two years of teaching . These schools do appear to suffer from a sharp drop-off in retention rates among the most effective teachers in year 5, but this result should be interpreted cautiously because it is based on data from only a single cohort of new teachers. The patterns for high-poverty schools (not shown) essentially parallel

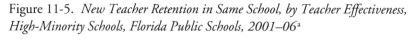

Figure 11-5. *New Teacher Retention in Same School, by Teacher Effectiveness, High-Minority Schools, Florida Public Schools, 2001–06*[a]

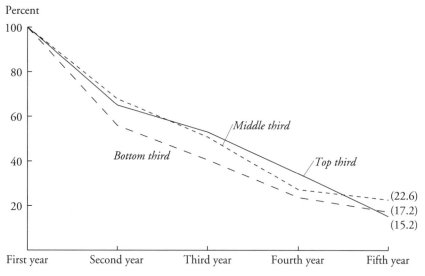

a. See figure 11-1 for *n* values.

those for high-minority schools, with the exception of the year-5 decline in reten-tion among the most effective teachers.

Figure 11-6 looks separately at teacher mobility in the 273 elementary schools with at least one teacher in our sample in which more than two-thirds of students score at proficient levels in both math and reading on the FCAT. Interestingly, at these relatively high-performing schools, the retention rates of the most and least effective teachers appear to diverge sharply, especially in years 4 and 5. By year 4, only 27 percent of the least effective teachers remain in their initial school, as com-pared with more than 45 percent of the most effective teachers. By year 5, fewer than 10 percent of the bottom-third teachers remain in their school. This pattern, which contrasts sharply from what is observed for the state's schools as a whole, suggests that the most successful schools in the state do a better job of selectively retaining their strongest teachers. And although we still cannot distinguish between teacher dismissals and voluntary departures, the extremely small share of ineffec-tive teachers remaining in schools that we would expect to have more desirable teaching environments suggests that they are also more aggressive in weeding out poorly performing teachers early in their careers. Both of these factors may play a role in these schools' overall success.

Figure 11-6. *Teacher Retention in Same School, by Teacher Effectiveness, High-Scoring Schools, Florida Public Schools, 2001–06*[a]

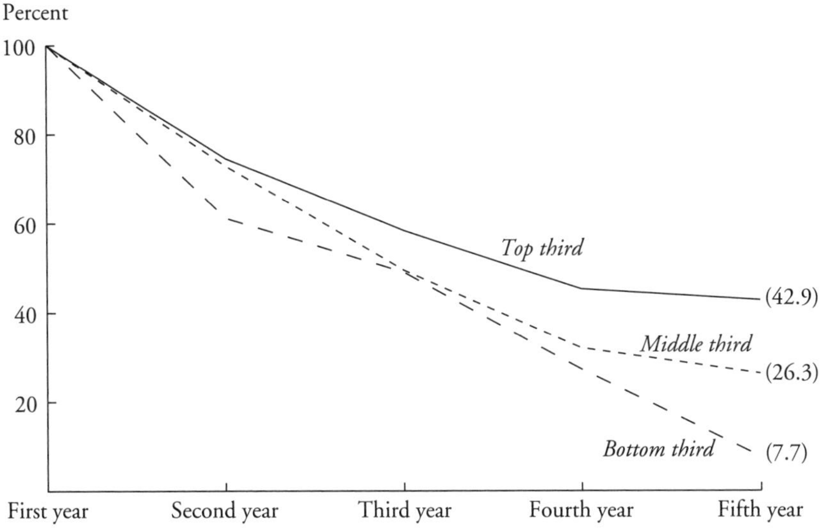

Percent

Top third

(42.9)

Middle third

(26.3)

Bottom third   (7.7)

First year   Second year   Third year   Fourth year   Fifth year

a. See figure 11-1 for *n* values.

Characteristics of New and Old Schools for Switchers

The results presented thus far confirm that fourth- and fifth-grade teachers in Florida are highly mobile in the early years of their careers and that much of that mobility appears to be voluntary. Some insight can be gained into the factors influencing the movement of teachers among schools and districts and its conse-quences for students by comparing the characteristics of teachers' original schools before and after each move. It is important to keep in mind that this analysis is purely descriptive. We have no basis for drawing strong causal inferences about the effects of particular school characteristics on teacher mobility. Nonetheless, the patterns we observe are consistent with the notion that school working con-ditions, as reflected in the demographic and educational characteristics of their student bodies, play a major role in teachers' decisions about where to teach.

Table 11-1 compares the characteristics of the old and new schools of teachers who left their initial school but continued to teach in the state of Florida. It pro-vides clear evidence that teachers who switch schools tend to move into higher-performing schools with more advantaged student bodies. Among those who remained in the same district, teachers who changed schools experienced on

Table 11-1. *Characteristics of Old and New Schools*[a]
Percent, except as indicated

Item	Old	New	Δ	%Δ	Sig.
	Same district (N = 494)				
Black	32.7	25.6	–7.1	–21.8	**
Hispanic	23.5	25.7	2.2	9.3	*
Eligible for free lunch	61.3	53.3	–7.9	–12.9	**
Special ed	17.2	16.2	–1.0	–5.6	*
Proficient in math	50.9	58.7	7.7	15.2	**
Proficient in reading	55.8	61.8	6.0	10.7	**
School grade	2.83	3.07	0.24	8.5	**
Base salary	$27,418	$31,396	$3,978	14.5	**
	Different district (N = 189)				
Black	35.4	24.5	–10.9	–30.8	**
Hispanic	17.4	14.7	–2.7	–15.4	
Eligible for free lunch	61.6	49.0	–12.6	–20.5	**
Special ed	18.5	16.4	–2.1	–11.6	**
Proficient in math	50.6	61.8	11.1	22.0	**
Proficient in reading	56.2	65.2	9.0	15.9	**
School grade	2.81	3.21	0.40	14.2	**
Base salary	$26,403	$32,857	$6,454	24.4	**

Source: Authors' calculations from Florida's K–20 Education Data Warehouse.

a. Statistical significance of the difference between old and new schools at the 5 percent level is indicated by * and at the 1 percent level by **.

average a 22 percent decline in the share of students who were black and a 13 percent decline in the share eligible for the free or reduced-price lunch program. The new schools also had larger shares of students who were proficient on the FCAT in math and reading and received better overall scores on the state's highly visible school grading system, half of which is based on students' annual gains in achievement.

These changes in school characteristics were even more pronounced for teachers moving between districts. These teachers experienced a 31 percent decline in the share of black students, a 21 percent decline in the share of students eligible for the free lunch program, and increases of 22 percent and 16 percent, respectively, in the percentage of students proficient in math and reading. District switchers also saw a jump in their annual base salaries of 24 percent, or more than $6,400. The average salary increase of $4,000 experienced by within-district movers, who typically remained on the same salary schedule, provides a rough benchmark for evaluating this jump and suggest that district switchers do tend to choose systems with higher overall salary levels.

Table 11-2 looks separately at the changes experienced by switchers within each of the three effectiveness levels, combining the data from both within- and between-district switchers for all characteristics except base salary because of the relatively small number of between-district moves in each group. These data confirm that the tendency of teachers to move to schools with less disadvantaged student bodies is not unique to teachers in the top or middle third of the effectiveness distribution. If anything, teachers in the bottom third experience larger declines in the share of students who are black and larger increases in student academic performance as they move between schools. This may reflect the fact that these teachers tend to start out in schools that have somewhat more disadvantaged and lower-performing student bodies, a reminder that it is important to pay attention to the initial distribution of teachers as well as to their mobility.

In sum, it is clear that effective and ineffective teachers alike tend to migrate in the early years of their career toward higher-performing schools with more-advantaged student bodies. This pattern suggests that schools that attract experienced applicants may not do a very good job of selecting only those teachers with a successful track record in the classroom, at least as measured by the academic progress of the students under their care.

Implications for Policy

The United States currently faces the daunting challenge of hiring large numbers of new teachers while simultaneously improving the quality of its teaching workforce. These pressures are particularly acute in Florida because of the state's commitment to dramatic reductions in class size by the end of this decade. The difficulty of predicting the effectiveness of teachers based on what is known about them before they enter the profession—the kind of information included on their resumes—means that retaining those teachers who have demonstrated their effectiveness in the classroom is essential to accomplishing the task.

How are schools faring in this regard? Is the teacher labor market glass half empty or half full? The answers to these questions will depend in part on prior expectations. If we suspect that the nation's most effective teachers are fleeing the classroom in droves, then even a finding that leavers are little different than those

Table 11-2. *Characteristics of Old and New Schools, by Teacher Effectiveness in Old School*[a]

Percent, except as indicated

Item	Old	New	Δ	%Δ	Sig.
	Bottom third ($N = 316$)				
Black	38.7	27.2	−11.5	−29.7	**
Hispanic	21.1	22.1	1.0	4.5	
Eligible for free lunch	64.0	54.6	−9.4	−14.7	**
Special ed	17.7	16.7	−1.0	−5.6	
Proficient in math	46.4	57.3	10.9	23.4	**
Proficient in reading	52.0	60.7	8.7	16.8	**
School grade	2.48	2.97	0.49	19.7	**
Base salary (within district; $n = 230$)	$26,895	$31,039	$4,144	15.4	**
Base salary (between districts; $n = 89$)	$25,698	$33,060	$7,362	28.6	**
	Middle third ($N = 191$)				
Black	27.2	25.2	−2.0	−7.4	
Hispanic	22.5	22.3	−0.2	−1.0	
Eligible for free lunch	58.4	52.3	−6.1	−10.5	**
Special ed	18.2	16.0	−2.1	−11.7	**
Proficient in math	54.9	60.5	5.6	10.2	**
Proficient in reading	59.7	64.1	4.3	7.2	**
School grade	3.09	3.21	0.13	4.2	
Base salary (within district; $n = 132$)	$28,468	$33,191	$4,723	16.6	**
Base salary (between districts; $n = 59$)	$25,822	$33,229	$7,406	28.7	**
	Top third ($N = 176$)				
Black	30.9	22.0	−8.9	−28.8	**
Hispanic	22.4	24.1	1.8	7.9	
Eligible for free lunch	59.8	47.6	−12.2	−20.3	**
Special ed	16.6	15.7	−0.9	−5.4	
Proficient in math	54.5	62.6	8.1	14.8	**
Proficient in reading	58.9	64.9	6.1	10.3	**
School grade	3.13	3.26	0.13	4.0	
Base salary (within district; $n = 132$)	$27,256	$30,196	$2,940	10.8	
Base salary (between districts; $n = 44$)	$28,538	$31,961	$3,423	12.0	

Source: Authors' calculations from Florida's K–20 Education Data Warehouse.

a. Within- and between-district switches pooled for all characteristics except for base salary. Statistical significance of the difference between old and new schools at the 5 percent level is indicated by * and at the 1 percent level by **.

who stay may be seen as reassuring, however odd such a pattern would appear in other sectors of the economy.

At least in the case of Florida, our results also suggest that the answer will depend on the level at which one conducts the analysis. When we compare the mobility rates of the most and least effective teachers at specific schools, we find that the least effective are actually somewhat more likely to leave in the first years of their careers. And schools with high-performing students are able to retain a bare majority of their most effective teachers while dismissing all but a handful of their worst performers. Comparing the average effectiveness of those who have stayed in their school and those who have moved on by year 4 confirms that those who stay do tend to be modestly more effective than those who leave—by about 4 percent of a standard deviation. Looking at the state public school system as whole, however, the pattern is less encouraging. There is essentially no difference whatsoever in the effectiveness of those who remain in Florida public schools and those who leave. The disparity between mobility and attrition patterns in the state is consistent with the notion that many public schools engage in a "dance of the lemons," in which poorly performing teachers are passed from one school to another rather than being dismissed.

Perhaps surprisingly, we find little evidence that schools serving disadvantaged students are particularly likely to lose their best teachers. Rather, the tendency of teachers to drift to schools with more favorable student characteristics is evident among both low and high performers. It is important to emphasize that this does not imply that schools serving more disadvantaged students are not adversely affected by current mobility patterns among new teachers. Indeed, given the value of classroom experience, the higher overall attrition rates at these schools should be a matter of considerable concern. But policies aimed at increasing retention in schools that serve disadvantaged students will be far more beneficial for students if they aim at retaining their most effective teachers, not just at lower turnover rates.

Discussions of differentiated compensation policies in education often treat financial incentives for performance and for teaching in hard-to-staff schools as separate issues. Proposed performance-pay schemes, including those recently enacted in Florida, would make all teachers eligible for bonuses based on their students' academic progress. Separate bonuses would be available for all qualified teachers accepting assignments in hard-to-staff schools. While much more research is needed on the extent to which teachers respond to the incentives created by such policies, combining the two approaches—for example, by offering larger performance incentives in hard-to-staff schools—may represent a

promising approach to improving both overall teacher quality and the allocation
of the most effective teachers across schools.

Notes

1. Eric A. Hanushek and others, "The Market for Teacher Quality," Working Paper 11154
   (Cambridge, Mass.: National Bureau of Economic Research, February 2005) shows that a
   student who has a teacher at the 85th percentile in terms of effectiveness can expect an
   annual achievement gain that is 0.22 standard deviations greater than a student with the
   median teacher. See also Jonah Rockoff, "The Impact of Individual Teachers on Student
   Achievement: Evidence from Panel Data," *American Economic Review* 94, no. 2 (2004):
   236–40; Barbara Nye, Spyros Konstantopoulos, and Larry V. Hedges, "How Large Are
   Teacher Effects?" *Educational Evaluation and Policy Analysis* 26, no. 3 (2004): 237–57; and
   Steven G. Rivkin, Eric A. Hanushek, and John F. Kain, "Teachers, Schools, and Academic Achievement," *Econometrica* 73, no. 2 (2005): 417–58.
2. Robert Gordon, Thomas J. Kane, and Douglas O. Staiger, "Identifying Effective Teachers
   Using Performance on the Job," Discussion Paper 2006-01 (Brookings, April 2006), p. 5.
3. Frederick M. Hess, Andrew J. Rotherham, and Kate Walsh, *A Qualified Teacher in Every
   Classroom: Appraising Old Answers and New Ideas* (Harvard Education Press, 2004).
4. Hanushek and others, "The Market for Teacher Quality"; John M. Krieg, "Teacher Quality and Attrition," *Economics of Education Review* 25, no. 1 (2004): 13–27; and Dan Goldhaber, Betheny Gross, and Daniel Player, "Are Public Schools Really Losing Their Best?
   Assessing the Career Transitions of Teachers and Their Implications for the Quality of the
   Teacher Workforce," Working Paper 12 (Washington: Urban Institute, October 2007).
5. U.S. Department of Education, *Digest of Education Statistics 2007* (U.S. Government
   Printing Office, 2007).
6. Eric A. Hanushek, "Teacher Compensation," in *Reforming Education in Florida,* edited by
   Paul E. Peterson (Stanford, Calif.: Hoover Institution Press, 2006), pp. 149–63; Richard
   Buddin and others, "Merit Pay for Florida Teachers: Design and Implementation Issues,"
   Working Paper WR-508-FEA (Santa Monica, Calif.: RAND, August 2007).
7. Our data on teacher compensation indicate that the median award for all Florida teachers
   receiving bonuses through the School Recognition Program is $920.
8. U.S. Department of Education, *Digest of Education Statistics 2007.*
9. For a recent review of this evidence, see Charles Clotfelter, Helen Ladd, and Jacob Vigdor,
   "Teacher-Student Matching and the Assessment of Teacher Effectiveness," Working Paper
   11936 (Cambridge, Mass.: National Bureau of Economic Research, January 2006).
10. We control for teacher experience using a dummy variable for each of the first twenty years
    of experience, so the omitted category includes all teachers with more than twenty years of
    experience.
11. This estimation approach is similar to the one used in Thomas J. Kane, Jonah E. Rockoff,
    and Douglas O. Stagier, "What Does Certification Tell Us about Teacher Effectiveness?
    Evidence from New York City," Working Paper 12155 (Cambridge, Mass.: National
    Bureau of Economic Research, April 2006). As a robustness check, we estimated teacher
    effects using models in which the dependent variable is a gain score standardized by decile
    of prior achievement, as in Hanushek and others, "The Market for Teacher Quality." The
    results, which are qualitatively similar to those reported here, are available upon request.

12. See, for example, Jesse Rothstein, "Teacher Quality in Educational Production: Tracking, Decay, and Student Achievement," Princeton University, May 2008.

13. One way to eliminate bias from nonrandom matching between schools is to focus on differences in teacher quality within schools through the inclusion of school fixed effects. We do not include school fixed effects in our preferred specification in order to allow for comparisons of teachers across schools. However, all of the results presented below are qualitatively similar to those found when we estimate teacher effectiveness conditional on school fixed effects.

14. Thomas J. Kane and Douglas O. Staiger, "Are Teacher-Level Value-Added Estimates Biased? An Experimental Validation of Non-Experimental Estimates," Harvard University, March 17, 2008.

15. We match students to their teachers using course records that clearly identify fourth- and fifth-grade classrooms. We also performed additional analyses that included teachers who appeared to be regular classroom teachers (for example, because they taught students both English and math, and those students were not listed in a clearly identified fourth- or fifth-grade classroom) but were not as clearly identified as such. The results of those analyses are qualitatively similar to those reported here.

16. Because the experience database does not reliably distinguish teachers with no experience and those with missing experience data, we define the cohort of new teachers in a given year as those who have missing or no experience that year and were not employed by a Florida public school in the previous year.

17. The number of students who skipped a grade is trivial, while the number who repeated a grade is substantial. The repeaters are included in the calculation of classroom- and school-level peer variables. We also calculate, and include in all regressions, variables indicating the percentage of students in each classroom and school who were repeating a grade.

18. A large and increasing number of elementary school students in Florida appear to have more than one regular classroom teacher, perhaps owing to an increase in the practice of team teaching. In future work we hope to develop effectiveness measures for this group.

19. We follow the variance decomposition method described in Kane, Rockoff, and Stagier, "What Does Certification Tell Us about Teacher Effectiveness?" They report standard deviations of teacher effectiveness of 0.13 in math and 0.10 in reading, using data from elementary schools in New York City.

20. In other words, any time spent at a school other than the one where a teacher worked in his or her first year of teaching does not contribute to that teacher's effectiveness measure. We take this approach because of our interest in whether schools are retaining teachers based on their observed performance in their initial school.

21. These calculations are based on the standard deviation of the persistent component of the teacher effectiveness measure calculated separately for math and reading, and thus the differences in expected student achievement in each subject are calculated by teacher effectiveness (tercile) in that subject. As stated earlier, the effectiveness terciles used in the rest of this analysis are based on the average of the effectiveness measures across the two subjects.

22. We find some suggestive evidence in support of the former possibility, as the effectiveness ratings of teachers who entered in 2003–04 and 2004–05, when the state's mandate regarding class-size reduction increased the number of new teachers hired in these grades, are especially low.

12

Student Outcomes and Teacher Productivity and Perceptions in Arkansas

Marcus A. Winters, Gary W. Ritter,
Jay P. Greene, and Ryan Marsh

In the United States, most public school teachers receive compensation according to a salary schedule that is almost entirely determined by number of years of service and highest degree attained. The wisdom of this system, however, has increasingly been questioned by policymakers and researchers in recent years. Several school systems have considered adding a component to the wage structure that directly compensates teachers based on the academic gains made by the students in a teacher's care, at least partly measured by student scores on standardized tests. Several public school systems, including those in Florida, New York City, and Texas, have recently adopted such performance-pay policies. Recent survey research suggests that nearly half of all Americans support performance pay for teachers whose students are making academic progress, while about a third of Americans directly oppose such a plan.[1]

Notwithstanding the level of support or opposition for teacher compensation reform, there is currently little definitive empirical evidence from the United States on the impact of teacher-level performance-pay plans on student outcomes. David Figlio and Lawrence Kenny independently surveyed schools that participated in the National Educational Longitudinal Survey (NELS) and then supplemented that survey's data with information on whether schools compensated teachers for their performance.[2] They found that test scores were higher in schools that individually rewarded teachers for their classroom performance.

Another recent study, conducted by Thomas Dee and Benjamin Keys, evaluated the impact of Tennessee's Career Ladder Evaluation System on student outcomes using data from the Tennessee Student Teacher Achievement Ratio (STAR) program, a random assignment study on the impact of class size on student achievement conducted in the early 1980s.[3] While the study cannot be considered a conventional random assignment experiment because teachers were not randomly assigned to participate in the career ladder program, the authors are able to eliminate many of the potential biases encountered when one estimates a treatment effect using observational data. They find that students instructed by teachers who were participating in the career ladder program made significant gains in math. The effects in reading were generally smaller and statistically insignificant.

This chapter aims to add to the research base by presenting evidence from a performance-pay program implemented in five Little Rock, Arkansas, elementary schools during the 2004–05 and 2006–07 school years. The program, called the Achievement Challenge Pilot Project (ACPP), is unique in that teachers received awards based entirely on year-to-year gains in student test scores. While most other evaluations of teacher pay-for-performance programs must account for multiple performance measures (that is, student test-score gains, peer evaluation, student attendance, teachers' professional development),[4] the Arkansas program allows us to estimate the effect of a teacher pay-for-performance plan on student outcomes aimed solely at measured gains in student achievement.

Using the ACPP as our backdrop, we address three questions:

—Does a pay-for-performance plan that rewards teachers for student achievement growth on standardized assessments lead to improved student test-score gains in math, reading, and language exams?

—Does the ACPP create larger-than-expected test-score gains for students enrolled in classrooms taught by the least effective teachers?

—Does the ACPP affect teacher perceptions, attitudes, and behaviors?

We find that students whose teachers were eligible for performance awards made substantially larger test-score gains in math, reading, and language than students taught by teachers not participating in ACPP. Furthermore, evidence suggests a negative relationship between the average performance of a teacher's students the year before the program was instituted and the additional gains made afterward. That is, ACPP appears to have improved student achievement, and students of teachers who were previously less effective at producing learning gains appear to have made larger-than-average improvement.

Teachers participating in the ACPP generally are supportive of the program. Results from the teacher surveys suggest that the pay-for-performance program does not negatively affect teacher collaboration, increase counterproductive competition, or encourage teachers to disproportionately focus effort on a particular subgroup of students. If anything, the ACPP may lead to greater salary satisfaction and a greater sense of effectiveness among teachers when compared with survey responses of teachers in a set of comparison group schools.

While the effects we uncovered were statistically significant and substantial, they are based on teachers in only three schools that participated for the first time in the ACPP in the 2006–07 school year. It is also possible that reported results could be driven by selection bias or influenced by random shocks in test scores. At the same time, the long-term impacts of a teacher pay-for-performance scheme may in fact be greater than what we describe here, as our study can only test for short-term motivational impacts. We cannot test for the potentially positive impacts that such a plan might have by attracting and retaining more talented individuals to the teaching profession.

Little Rock's Achievement Challenge Pilot Project

The Achievement Challenge Pilot Project was a teacher and staff performance-pay program operated within the Little Rock School District from the 2004–05 to 2006–07 school years. The purpose of the program was to motivate faculty and staff to bring about greater student achievement gains. The project used student improvement on nationally normed standardized tests as the basis for financial rewards to teachers, while staff bonuses were linked to the gains of the school as a whole.

The arrival of superintendent Roy Brooks in 2004 marked the introduction of teacher compensation reform in Little Rock. A veteran administrator from Florida, a state with a culture of acceptance of school accountability that had adopted the Special Teachers Are Rewarded pay-for-performance plan, Brooks initiated a number of educational and administrative reforms in Little Rock, including the ACPP. The Little Rock school board and the Little Rock Classroom Teachers Association supported almost none of his reforms, including teacher pay for performance.[5]

The Hussman Foundation, in partnership with the Public Education Foundation of Little Rock, provided financial support to implement the pilot project at

Meadowcliff Elementary School in the 2004–05 school year. The program expanded to Wakefield Elementary in the next school year, with financial support from the Hussman Foundation, while the Little Rock School District took over financial responsibility for the program at Meadowcliff Elementary School. The school district paid for the ACPP at both elementary schools in the third year of the program, and funding from the Hussman Foundation, the Walton Foundation, and the Brown Foundation supported its implementation at three more elementary schools—Geyer Springs, Mabelvale, and Romine. The five elementary schools targeted for participation served a large percentage of disadvantaged students with low student achievement.

Teachers in these schools also voted to allow the ACPP program to operate in their schools. It was agreed upon that the program could be implemented in each of these five schools only on the condition that at least 50 percent of the teachers, plus one additional teacher, voted in its favor. This was insisted upon by the Little Rock teachers union, 100 percent of whom voted in favor, when Meadowcliff Elementary School first adopted the program.

Bonus Distribution Mechanism

The ACPP provided bonuses directly to teachers based on the average spring-to-spring achievement gains of students in the teacher's class on the composite score of the Iowa Test of Basic Skills. The composite score includes student achievement on the math, reading, and language arts portion of the exam. For the purposes of performance rewards, student test scores were reported in normal curve equivalent units. Normal curve equivalent units rank the student on a normal curve compared with a nationally representative group of students who have taken the test. Normal curve equivalent scores are similar to percentile scores but differ in that they are equal-interval scaled, meaning that the difference between two scores on one part of the curve are equivalent to the difference of a similar interval on another part of the curve. Normal curve equivalent scores are scaled between 1 and 99, with a mean of 50.

Teachers whose students have an average growth in normal curve equivalent scores of 0 to 4 percent earn $50 for each student in their classes; teachers whose students have an average achievement growth between 5 and 9 percent earn $100 for each student; teachers whose students have an average achievement growth between 10 and 14 percent earn $200 per student; and teachers whose students have an average achievement growth over 15 percent earn $400 times the number of students in their classes.

Many education stakeholders argue strongly against the use of a single indicator to represent the overall contribution of a teacher to a student's learning growth. Opponents of plans like the ACPP maintain that teacher pay-for-performance plans should include multiple measures of performance, often incorporating indicators of professional development and assessments of pedagogical techniques alongside student achievement as measures of teacher performance. Alternatively, others argue that enhanced student achievement is the ultimate goal of any teacher and thus the only true measure of effectiveness.

Educators and staff members who did not work in single classrooms received performance awards based on schoolwide gains in achievement. The maximum size of these bonuses varied based on job classification. For example, principals could earn a $2,500 bonus for a schoolwide average gain of 0 to 4 percent, a $5,000 bonus for a gain of 5 to 9 percent, a $7,500 bonus for a gain of 10 to 14 percent, and a $10,000 bonus for a gain of 15 percent or more. Payouts for aides, by comparison, were $250 for a schoolwide average gain of 0 to 4 percent, a $500 bonus for a gain of 5 to 9 percent, a $750 bonus for a gain of 10 to 14 percent, and a $1,000 bonus for a gain of 15 percent or more.

Table 12-1 displays the average bonuses earned in the three schools included in our sample. Elementary students at Geyer Springs recorded an average gain in normal curve equivalent score of 8.5 percent, the highest gain of any of the participating schools, meaning the average level of student academic growth based on the Iowa Test of Basic Skills exceeded the academic growth of the national norm over the same period. Eleven of twelve Geyer Springs teachers earned bonuses ranging from $350 to $7,600, and the principal, teachers, educational coaches, and staff members shared incentives totaling $64,350 as a result of the school performance and individual classroom gains.

Table 12-1. *Performance Bonuses Awarded in Arkansas's Achievement Challenge Pilot Project, 2006–07*

School	Total bonus	Highest teacher bonus	Lowest teacher bonus	Average teacher bonus	Total enrollment	Average cost per pupil
Mabelvale	$39,550	$6,400	$450	$1,188	338	$117
Geyer Springs	$64,530	$7,600	$350	$2,846	333	$194
Romine	$12,450	$5,200	$450	$723	365	$34

Source: Bonus data were provided by the Public Education Foundation of Little Rock. School enrollment data were gathered from the Arkansas Department of Education website at http://arkansased.org/.

also displays bonus figures for Mabelvale Elementary and Romine ~y. The above-average performance of students at Mabelvale Elementary ~d in a bonus distribution of $39,550 to faculty, administrators, and staff ~mbers. Romine Elementary students recorded an average decrease in normal curve equivalent score of 4.1 percent, meaning the average level of student academic growth was less than the academic growth of the national norm over the same time period. While four of the fifteen teachers in the school received bonuses of up to $5,200 because of academic gains made in individual classrooms, as a result of the decrease in overall school performance, the principal and other staff members did not receive any monetary award.

Strengths and Weaknesses of the Program Design

The ACPP illustrates several characteristics that future teacher-compensation reforms should take into consideration. First of all, the project's reward scheme was straightforward and understandable to those eligible to receive a bonus. One of the key criticisms of merit-pay plans is that teachers often view them as based on "secret formulas" and have no idea why merit pay is awarded or not. If a pay-for-performance intervention is to influence the motivation of classroom teachers, it certainly must be clear to teachers how they might become eligible for an award.

Second, the ACPP rewards were allocated based on student achievement gains rather than on absolute attainment. It seems obvious that any plan that determines merit by absolute achievement levels will create the perverse incentive for teachers to leave behind students in low-performing schools or classrooms and seek placement in high-performing schools or classrooms in an effort to maximize their chances of receiving a bonus. The only way to improve the overall achievement of all students is to reward growth in student achievement.

Third, awards were allocated to teachers based on the extent to which they met their goals, regardless of how their peer teachers performed. That is, all teachers could receive an individual-level bonus regardless of other teachers' performance within the same school. Such a teacher pay-for-performance plan is preferred to one that allocates a fixed pool of rewards to a predetermined number of teachers. So-called "zero-sum" games or "fixed-tournament" bonus schemes may discourage teacher collaboration, a critical component of the teaching and learning environment. Moreover, in an effort to encourage a schoolwide ethos of cooperation and collaboration, the ACPP ensured that all school employees, from the principal to the custodians, were eligible for some level of bonus.[6]

Finally, as shown in table 12-2, the ACPP bonus payout scheme offered substantial rewards. Many have argued that the primary failure of low-paying plans

Table 12-2. *Sample Bonus Payout Scheme for Geyer Springs, Mabelvale, and Romine Schools, for 2006–2007 School Year*[a]
Dollars

Position	0–4 percent growth	5–9 percent growth	10–14 percent growth	15 percent or more growth	Maximum payout
Principal	2,500	5,000	7,500	10,000	10,000
Teacher[a]					
Grades 4–5	50	100	200	400	11,200
Grades 1–3	50	100	200	400	10,000
Kindergarten	50	100	200	400	8,000
Coach[b]	1,250	2,500	3,750	5,000	5,000
Specialist[c]	1,000	2,000	3,000	4,000	4,000
Music teacher	1,000	2,000	3,000	4,000	4,000
Special education	1,000	2,000	3,000	4,000	4,000
Physical examiner	500	1,000	1,500	2,000	2,000
Aide	250	500	750	1,000	1,000
Secretary	125	250	375	500	500
Custodian (full-time)	125	250	375	500	500

Source: Bonus data were provided by the Public Education Foundation of Little Rock.

a. Teacher payouts are on a per child basis, while all other payouts are for total payouts.

b. Coaches include literary, math, and instructional coaches.

c. Specialists include math and reading specialists, reading recovery specialists, gifted and talented instructors, library specialists, counselors, and preschool (four-year-olds) instructors.

is that teachers simply do not believe the perceived additional work is worth the potential bonus. However, teachers in ACPP schools with average annual salaries under $40,000 were eligible for bonuses of more than $10,000, and the top bonus paid to a teacher in the 2006–07 school year was $7,600. The potential award amounts for a range of other job types, including coaches, specialists, and custodians, are also significant. It is clear that potential payouts represent a significant portion of overall compensation.

At the same time, specific features of the ACPP were revised from one year to the next as education stakeholders in Little Rock gained a greater understanding of their pay-for-performance plan in action. For example, the bonus distribution formula in Meadowcliff school was different from that used in the other schools because the developers of the ACPP did not want to modify the rules in midstream. When the program was first implemented in Meadowcliff school in the 2004–05 school year, bonuses were awarded to teachers based on the number of students with test-score growth in each of the previously mentioned ranges (0 to 4 percent, 5 to 9 percent, and so on) rather than on the classroom averages. Upon eration, ACPP developers realized that this type of scheme, in which ere rewarded for students' improvement but were held harmless for stu- who declined, might encourage teachers to neglect some students. Thus for e schools entering the ACPP after the first year, the distribution formula was based on classroom averages so that the scores of all students would be reflected in the calculation of the merit award.

While this change was certainly reasonable, it did cause some confusion among teachers in later years. Another change that resulted in teacher discontent occurred in year 3, when the bonus distribution was based on test-score growth between the spring of 2006 and the spring of 2007 (previous rewards were based on the difference between fall and spring scores in the same academic year). Subsequent interviews with teachers revealed that many teachers believed that this change unfairly resulted in decreased bonuses.[7] These problems could well have been avoided with better communication between program staff and participating teachers.

Analytic Strategy and Data

This study examines the Achievement Challenge Pilot Project by asking whether students in project classrooms perform better than their peers on standardized assessments of math, reading, and language. We also assess the extent to which the program is particularly effective for students in classrooms of previously low-performing teachers.

Student-level administrative data for the study come from the universe of public school students enrolled in Little Rock, Arkansas, elementary schools in the 2004–05 through 2006–07 school years, providing two observations of student test-score gains. Our data set includes demographic information, test-score results from the Iowa Test of Basic Skills in math, reading, and language, an identifier for the student's classroom teacher, and a unique student identifier that allows us to track each student over time. Math, reading, and language subscores are reported in normal curve equivalent units.

Table 12-3 reports baseline descriptive information for all students in our sample, students never enrolled in an ACPP school, and students who were enrolled in an ACPP school for at least one year. About 63 percent of students who were never enrolled in an ACPP school qualified for the federal free and reduced-price lunch program, while 67 percent are African American. Students who were enrolled in an ACPP school for at least one year may be considered a more disadvantaged group of students than those students never enrolled. For example,

Table 12-3. *Baseline Descriptive Statistics*[a]

Variable	All		Never enrolled		Enrolled one year or more	
	Mean	SD	Mean	SD	Mean	SD
Black	0.69	0.46	0.67	0.47	0.88	0.33
Asian	0.02	0.12	0.02	0.13	0.00	0.00
Hispanic	0.04	0.19	0.04	0.19	0.06	0.23
Indian	0.00	0.06	1.00	0.06	0.00	0.05
Male	0.50	0.50	0.50	0.50	0.52	0.50
Eligible for free and reduced-price lunch	0.65	0.48	0.63	0.48	0.88	0.33
Baseline math	50.41	21.54	51.15	21.57	38.57	17.27
Baseline reading	50.16	21.53	51.12	21.55	40.53	18.87
Baseline language	49.87	21.13	50.88	21.18	40.21	18.02
Math gain 2006	1.94	14.37	2.14	14.25	−1.29	15.83
Reading gain 2006	1.83	14.51	1.89	14.53	1.19	14.29
Language gain 2006	0.00	16.07	0.18	15.90	−1.75	17.45
Number of students (math)	7,142		6,720		422	
Number of students (reading)	2,820		2,565		255	
Number of students (language)	4,255		12		402	

Source: Descriptive statistics on student sample are based on student-level administrative data provided by Little Rock School District for the universe of students in Little Rock elementary schools from 2004 to 2005 and from 2006 to 2007.

a. Only students included in the overall math regression are included in the summary statistics for demographic variables. Reading and language test descriptive statistics include only students used in those regressions.

88 percent qualify for the federal free and reduced-price lunch program and 88 percent are African American.

Table 12-3 further indicates that baseline scores in math, reading, and language of students in non-ACPP schools were substantially above those of students who were enrolled in ACPP schools. The difference in prior test scores is significant in all subjects. Finally, students never enrolled in an ACPP school made significantly and substantially larger improvements in these subjects the year before treatment took place. That students in schools that eventually received ACPP treatment had lower test scores and lower prior gains in these subjects suggests that regression to the mean could potentially drive any results. That is, students with very low scores are more likely to make academic gains, if only by randomness.

The analysis uses a differences-in-differences procedure to study the impact of the ACPP on student test-score gains. The analysis excluded students in two schools, Meadowcliff and Wakefield, that began the performance-pay treatment before the 2006–07 school year. The reason for this decision is that since these schools were treated in each year for which data are available, in the analysis they would become part of the comparison group. That is, if they were included in the model, schools that had always been in the program during the period for which scores are available would be lumped together with schools that had never been in the program. To isolate the effect of the program, the model needs to focus on schools that switch status from not having performance pay to having it, which restricts the analyses to three of the five elementary schools participating in the ACPP.

We use ordinary least squares regression to estimate a model taking the form

$$(1) \quad Y_{i,a,t} = \beta_0 + \beta_1 Y_{i,a,t-1} + \beta_2 \textbf{Student}_{i,t} + \beta_3 School_{i,t} + \beta_4 Year_t + \beta_5 Treat_{i,t} + \varepsilon_{i,t},$$

where $Y_{i,a,t}$ is the test score of student i in subject a in the spring of year t; **Student** is a vector of observable characteristics about the student; *School* is an indicator variable for the school that the student attended; *Year* is an indicator variable for the year; and ε is a stochastic term clustered by school.

Treat is an indicator variable for whether the observation occurred for a student attending the treatment school during the treatment year. That is, this variable is an interaction between *Year* = 2007 and the indicator variable for each school that was eventually treated. The coefficient for the *Treat* variable represents the impact of the performance-pay treatment after we account for the differences in the test scores that occur naturally over time and within the individual schools.

A second analysis estimates a model identical to the above equation 1 but controls for time-invariant characteristics of teachers, using a teacher fixed-effect estimator. A teacher fixed effect is a dummy variable for each teacher and is often used in the evaluation literature to account for the average impact of each teacher on student test-score gains. In essence, in the same way that a school fixed effect in the prior model controls for a child's being taught in a particular school, the teacher fixed-effect controls for a child's being taught by a particular teacher. Our second model takes the form

$$(2) \quad Y_{i,a,t} = \psi_0 + \psi_1 Y_{i,a,t-1} + \psi_2 \textbf{Student}_{i,t} + \psi_3 School_{i,t}$$
$$+ \psi_4 Year_t + \psi_5 Treat_{i,t} + \psi_6 Teacher_{i,t} + \rho_{i,t},$$

where *Teacher* is an indicator for the student's teacher, ρ is a stochastic term clustered by teacher, and all other variables are as previously defined.

Controlling for teacher fixed effects has the potential benefit of more clearly identifying the effect of offering teachers bonuses by controlling for how effective a teacher already was, on average. But this potential improvement in precision comes at a price. It means that those students whose teachers were not in those schools for more than one year are not used to identify the treatment effect. For example, this accounts for about a third of students in the math analysis. Adding dummy variables for every teacher reduces the degrees of freedom, giving the model less statistical leverage. For these reasons, our teacher fixed-effects analysis should not be viewed as the main analysis of interest; rather, we implement this second strategy to check the robustness of the first analysis.

We also examine whether there is a differential relationship between the impact of the ACPP and a teacher's prior productivity, where productivity is measured by the average test-score gain of students in the teacher's classroom in the baseline year. A growing body of literature suggests a substantial difference across teachers in their ability to produce student test-score gains.[8] One possible reason for such wide variation in teacher quality is that some teachers put forth more effort under the current system, even though the uniform pay schedule provides no direct incentive for them to do so. The idea of increasing marginal cost to effort, a fundamental assumption in economics, leads us to hypothesize that the ACPP will have its greatest motivational impact on those teachers who were trying the least under the past system.

To evaluate whether teachers of varying productivity had different responses to the ACPP, an interaction between the treatment status of a school and a measure of a teacher's pretreatment success at improving student test-score gains can be added to the model. Since treatment begins in the 2006–07 school year, and the first test-score observation comes from the 2004–05 school year in our sample, this analysis is limited to learning gains from the 2005–06 school year as the only measure of pretreatment productivity of a teacher.

This model takes the form

$$(3) \quad Y_{i,a,t} = \phi_0 + \phi_1 Y_{i,a,t} + \phi_2 \textbf{Student}_{i,t} + \phi_3 School_{i,t} + \phi_4 Year_t + \phi_5 Pre\text{-}Gain_{i,a}$$
$$+ \phi_6 Treat_{i,t} + \phi_7 \left(Pre\text{-}Gain_{i,a} * Treat_{i,t} \right) + \rho_{i,t},$$

where $Pre\text{-}Gain_{i,t}$ is the average test-score gain in 2005–06 school year for students in the class of student i's current teacher, and ρ is again a normally distributed mean-zero stochastic term. If the coefficient of the interaction of previous student gain and treatment is negative, that means lower-performing teachers in ACPP schools made the largest gains.

The first model examines whether students learn more when their teachers are eligible for performance awards as part of the ACPP relative to the achievement of those students before the program was introduced and relative to the performance of students in other schools; we control for observed demographic characteristics of students. The second model is the same as the first, but it also controls for the average effectiveness of teachers to produce gains in student learning. The third model is the same as the first, but it tries to identify whether performance pay had its largest effect on the best or worst teachers.

These analyses are able to estimate these equations in math, reading, and language in elementary schools. However, the grades included in the analyses of each subject differ owing to limitations of the testing scheduled in the Little Rock School District. Students were administered the math version of the Iowa Test of Basic Skills in all grades from kindergarten to fifth in each of the three school years from 2004–05 through 2006–07, so each of these grades is included in all analyses. However, the Iowa Test of Basic Skills language or reading tests were not administered to students in grades 3, 4, or 5 until the 2005–06 school year. Furthermore, the Iowa Test of Basic Skills reading test was not administered to students in kindergarten until the 2006–07 school year. These data limitations mean that only students in grades 2 and 3 for the reading analyses and students in grades 1, 2, or 3 in the language analyses can be included—the only grades for which there are both pretest and posttest scores for students in both the baseline and treatment eligible years.

The principal limitation of this study is that schools were not randomly assigned to be part of the ACPP. In particular, as discussed above, the program was targeted to traditionally low-performing schools with above-average proportions of disadvantaged students, and for this reason there may be unobserved differences between ACPP and non-ACPP schools that are beyond our control. We attempt to account for this bias by controlling for time-invariant characteristics of schools using a school fixed-effects estimator and, in one analysis, a teacher fixed-effects estimator in order to account for heterogeneity in school and teacher quality, respectively. These approaches assume the possibility that in the absence of treatment, ACPP schools were likely to have made smaller test-score improvements than non-ACPP schools, which would tend to bias the estimation of the treatment effect downward. At the same time, if the year-specific gains at the school are measured with error or influenced by random shocks that make them a noisy measure of the time-invariant component of school quality, then a school fixed-effects model may overestimate the impact of the ACPP on student outcomes. Thus even though we attempt to eliminate this confounding influence in our evaluation of ACPP, the nonrandom selection of schools participating in the ACPP may explain some or all of the estimated treatment effect reported in this study.

Findings

Marcus Winters and colleagues, in an interim evaluation report on the effect of the ACPP on student test-score gains, find that math scores for students in Wakefield Elementary improved by roughly 6 percentile points after the ACPP was implemented.[9] While these findings provide some cautious optimism for proponents of merit pay programs, they were limited by the small student sample and the fact that only math scores were available for analysis at that time. Here, we improve on the earlier analysis by employing additional subject area tests with a larger sample of students. Furthermore, we are able to consider the impact of the ACPP on the subgroup of teachers who were previously less productive. Finally, we augment these findings by providing insight on teacher attitudes toward the program.

Effect on Student Test-Score Gains

The results from the first model, which estimates the overall effect of the program on student achievement, are reported in table 12-4. Recall that these results are based on a more restricted group of grades in the reading and language analyses than in the math analysis, which accounts for the variation in the number of observations across subjects. In each subject there is a positive relationship between the teacher pay-for-performance treatment and student achievement. The effect is statistically significant at the 5 percent level in math and at the 10 percent level in reading. The analyses suggest that the ACPP led to an increase of about 3.5 normal curve equivalent points in math and 3.3 normal curve equivalent points in reading after only one year of participation in the program.

Table 12-5 reports on the estimation of the overall treatment effect, including a fixed effect for each individual teacher. The results are qualitatively similar to those reported in table 12-4, with the exception that the impact of the ACPP on reading is statistically significant at the 1 percent level. Somewhat surprisingly, the small gain in the R^2 value between the analyses reported in tables 12-4 and 12-5 suggests that the teacher fixed effect is explaining very little of the variance in student achievement. That is, there does not appear to be much of an improvement in the explanatory power of the model when we control for average teacher quality, despite the price that is paid for doing so.[10]

Table 12-4. *Regression Results: Overall Treatment Effect*[a]

Variable	Math		Reading		Language	
	Coefficient	t	Coefficient	t	Coefficient	t
Math t−1	0.70	69.42***				
Reading t−1			0.68	64.59***		
Language t−1					0.68	51.33***
Black	−4.60	−11.01***	−4.69	11.27***	−2.75	5.48***
Asian	3.65	4.46***	1.04	1.00	5.81	4.53***
Hispanic	−1.14	−1.72*	−1.62	2.38**	1.18	1.50
Indian	−1.80	−1.47	−3.78	−1.79*	−3.19	−1.01
Male	0.03	0.14	−0.41	−1.45	−2.87	−10.43***
Eligible for free or reduced-price lunch	−2.47	−10.17***	−2.88	6.06***	−3.19	−8.58***
Treat	3.52	2.32**	3.29	1.91*	4.56	1.57
Constant	23.11	20.24***	19.40	26.84***	20.04	27.49***
Teacher fixed effect	No		No		No	
N	13,389		5,948		8,933	
Adjusted R^2	0.6479		0.7118		0.6211	

a. Statistical significance at the 1 percent level is indicated by ***, at the 5 percent level by **, and at the 10 percent level by *.

Estimated using ordinary least squares. Models also control for school, grade, and year fixed effects. Standard errors clustered by school.

Nonetheless, the size of the effects reported in tables 12-4 and 12-5 are substantial. The summary statistics for baseline achievement in these subjects reported in table 12-3 can be used to put these results into terms of standard deviation units. If we divide the effect size by the standard deviation of the baseline test score in the subject, the results reported in table 12-4 suggest that the ACPP increased student proficiency by 0.16 standard deviations in math and 0.15 standard deviations in reading. These effect sizes are comparable to those reported on the impact of "highly-effective" comprehensive school reform models on student test-score gains.[11]

Effect on the Least Productive Teachers

Table 12-6 reports on the analysis exploring whether there is any differential impact of the ACPP on a teacher's previous productivity. In each of the three subjects, the coefficient on the treatment effect remains positive, although the effect is statistically significant only for math and language. However, in this model we must incorporate both the coefficient on the overall treatment effect and the

Table 12-5. *Overall Treatment Effect*[a]—*Includes Teacher Fixed Effect*[a]

Variable	Coefficient	t	Coefficient	t	Coefficient	t
Math $t-1$	0.71	71.94***				
Reading $t-1$			0.69	65.22***		
Language $t-1$					0.68	51.22***
Black	−4.41	−10.82***	−4.56	−11.04***	−2.70	4.69***
Asian	3.64	4.01***	1.33	1.23	5.92	5.37***
Hispanic	−0.86	−1.30	−1.27	−1.85*	1.68	2.10**
Indian	−1.34	−0.93	−2.89	−1.58	−3.11	−0.97
Male	0.06	0.29	−0.43	−1.32	−2.71	−10.30***
Eligible for free or reduced-price lunch	−2.24	8.33***	−2.82	5.55***	−2.90	6.96***
Treat	5.23	2.21**	3.05	2.76***	2.04	0.93
Constant	17.36	26.42***	22.60	6.87***	24.54	9.12***
Teacher fixed effect	Yes		Yes		Yes	
N	13,389		5,948		8,933	
Adjusted R^2	0.6780		0.7293		0.6541	

a. Statistical significance at the 1 percent level is indicated by ***, at the 5 percent level by **, and at the 10 percent level by *.

Estimated using ordinary least squares. Models also control for school, grade, and year fixed effects. Standard errors clustered by school.

impact of the interaction with prior teacher effectiveness in order to evaluate the overall treatment impact. Once we account for both coefficients, the analyses suggest that the ACPP led to an increase of about 5.97 normal curve equivalent points in math and 2.23 normal curve equivalent points in reading after only one year of participation in the program.

Intriguingly, in each of the three subjects, teacher performance pay has the greatest positive impact on the previously lowest-performing teachers. There is a negative relationship between the teacher's prior productivity (measured by the average test-score gain of students in the teacher's classroom in the baseline year) and the impact of the ACPP on teacher productivity. The inverse relationship between prior teacher productivity and the treatment effect is statistically significant in each of the three tested subjects.

Effect on Teacher Perceptions, Attitudes, and Behaviors

It is worthwhile here to place the student achievement and teacher productivity findings in the context of a broader two-year evaluation of the ACPP led by a team of researchers at the University of Arkansas's Department of Education Reform.[12]

Table 12-6. *Regression Results: Effect by Prior Teacher Productivity*[a]

Variable	Math Coefficient	t	Reading Coefficient	t	Language Coefficient	t
Math $t-1$	0.72	62.03***				
Reading $t-1$			0.66	50.93***		
Language $t-1$					0.65	38.16***
Black	−4.17	−9.10***	−4.57	−9.04***	−2.48	−4.03***
Asian	3.90	4.19***	−0.10	−0.07	6.48	5.54***
Hispanic	−0.79	−1.00	−1.80	−2.49**	0.89	0.94
Indian	0.87	0.62	−2.01	−0.93	−1.86	−0.43
Male	−0.05	−0.24	−0.56	−1.48	−2.90	−8.27***
Eligible for free or reduced-price lunch	−2.62	−10.02***	−3.07	−5.24***	−3.61	−8.14***
Average 2006 gain for teacher	0.62	17.42***	0.22	3.06***	0.37	6.59***
Treat	6.93	14.32***	3.63	1.65	4.24	3.93***
Treat* 2006 gain for teacher	−0.48	−13.72***	−0.35	−3.61***	−0.50	−9.76***
Constant	17.13	16.88***	17.66	17.77***	19.42	14.53***
N	10,305		4,560		6,695	
Adjusted R^2	0.6756		0.7015		0.6025	

a. Statistical significance at the 1 percent level is indicated by ***, at the 5 percent level by **, and at the 10 percent level by *.

Estimated using ordinary least squares. Models also control for school, grade, and year fixed effects. Standard errors clustered by school.

The comprehensive evaluation assessed the impact of the ACPP on teacher perceptions, attitudes, and behaviors, using data from a thirty-two-item survey administered to teachers at each ACPP school as well as at a set of comparison schools during the 2006–07 school year.[13] Comparison group schools were identified based on a series of demographic characteristics and student achievement results that were similar to those of the Geyer Springs, Mabelvale, and Romine schools, but their teachers were compensated on the traditional salary schedule and were not eligible to receive any bonus payouts.[14]

Table 12-7 shows teachers' responses to a set of eight questions drawn from the survey to illustrate beliefs about the single salary schedule, the role of merit pay in schools, and changes in behavior in the presence of a performance incentive system. Teachers in ACPP and comparison schools were similarly divided about the desirability of the current salary structure. For example, the majority of teachers

Table 12-7. *Teacher Beliefs about Merit Pay in ACPP and Comparison Schools,*
Spring 2007
Percent, except as indicated

Item		N	Strongly disagree	Disagree somewhat	Agree somewhat	Strongly agree
I am satisfied with the	ACPP	82	26	26	37	12
current salary system.	comparison	207	24	25	38	14
I think merit-pay	ACPP	84	19	42	38	1
programs increase	comparison	204	36	28	25	10
collaboration among						
teachers.						
Gains in student test	ACPP	85	25	36	35	4
scores are appropriate	comparison	198	28	39	30	3
measures of teacher						
effectiveness.						
I am paid well for the	ACPP	85	59	34	6	1
amount of effort that	comparison	202	41	31	24	4
I put into my work.						
Over the last school year,	ACPP	84	11	25	45	19
I researched more new	comparison	202	5	19	50	25
teaching strategies than						
in previous years.						
Over the last school year,	ACPP	83	2	11	52	35
I implemented new	comparison	198	1	10	47	42
"best practices"						
teaching strategies.						
Over the last school year,	ACPP	84	11	15	48	26
I spent more time	comparison	197	5	13	41	41
preparing for my job.						
Over the last school year,	ACPP	76	4	26	57	13
student performance	comparison	196	8	18	54	20
improved in my school.						

Source: Gary Ritter and others, "Year Two Evaluation of the Achievement Challenge Pilot Project in the Little Rock Public School District," University of Arkansas at Fayetteville, Department of Education Reform, January 22, 2008.

in both treatment schools (93 percent) and the comparison schools (62 percent) did not feel they were paid well for their work effort, whereas a significantly greater share of teachers in comparison schools were satisfied with their compensation (28 percent) relative to peers in pilot schools (7 percent). Even though these differences may be associated with the lower base pay of a less experienced body of teachers in schools participating in the ACPP, a practical interpretation of this survey finding in a different school context may be that the use of a performance incentive scheme will not necessarily improve the general level of teacher satisfaction with total compensation arrangements.

The table also presents data on the perceived impact of teacher pay-for-performance programs on the school environment. Survey results indicate that teachers in schools participating in the ACPP and those in comparison group schools tended to disagree about the impact of merit pay programs on teacher collaboration. However, practitioners and other education stakeholders may need to consider the structure of future programs to improve the likelihood of interaction among teachers, while also considering the consensus belief of teachers about the place of student achievement tests in evaluation: both groups appeared to generally agree that gains in student test scores were appropriate measures of teacher effectiveness.

Teachers in ACPP and non-ACPP schools reported comparable levels of activity in researching new instructional strategies, with similarly lower levels of implementation of best practices in classroom teaching, though treatment teachers indicated spending more time preparing for their jobs than the comparison group. It is also important to note that teachers did not associate the implementation of teacher pay for performance with having a more negative work environment, with increased counterproductive competition, or with the shunning of low-performing students. They did report that teacher pay for performance increases salary satisfaction and enhances their views of their own effectiveness.

Implications for Policy

There is much still to be learned about the effects of performance-pay programs on student achievement. The evaluation of Little Rock's ACPP reports evidence from only three elementary schools participating in a pay-for-performance program and can estimate the effects only after one year of participation in the ACPP. Furthermore, participating schools were not selected at random, a fact that potentially undermines confidence in these results because schools participating in the ACPP are systematically different from non-ACPP schools on characteristics that are statistically beyond our control.

Despite these study limitations, the evidence from Little Rock offers several noteworthy contributions to enhance the understanding of teacher compensation reform, especially given how little evidence is currently available. For starters, the program offered awards not only to teachers but also to principals, paraprofession-

als, and other staff. The bonus distribution scheme was transparent and not structured as a "fixed tournament." Furthermore, as the program matured, the district
and philanthropies supporting the initiative were willing to adjust design features
of the ACPP based on information gleaned from the educational research, practice, and policy communities.

The data provided by the Little Rock School District permitted analysis of the
ACPP that exploited longitudinally linked student data as well as data that enabled
students to be linked to their teachers over time. Study findings suggest that test-
score gains of students in schools participating in the ACPP increased by 0.16
standard deviations in math and 0.15 standard deviations in reading. These results
are robust to alternative specifications that control for time-invariant teacher or
school characteristics.

The most striking thing suggested by this analysis is that performance pay
may have the greatest effect on improving the teachers who were previously the
least effective at producing learning gains for students. This may be a result
of random shocks that make test scores a noisy measure of student ability.
Nonetheless, if this result holds across evaluations of other programs, performance
pay may be an effective strategy not just for improving overall achievement but
also for closing the achievement gap. Moreover, because of perverse sorting
effects of current teacher hiring, pay, and transfer policies, minority and low-
achieving students are more likely to be in schools with the least effective teachers. If it is those less effective teachers who improve more under performance
pay, minority and low-achieving students should experience the greatest gains.

The Little Rock School District will offer no further opportunities to evaluate the impact of teacher compensation reform on students and teachers in the
near term because the ACPP has been discontinued by the current school board.
While the program received considerable support from the educators at participating schools—a majority of teachers at those schools had to vote for the program to participate—the program failed to win the support of the local teacher
union affiliate. Political activity by that union and allied groups reversed the
narrow 4-3 school board majority that had supported the ACPP, leading to its
cancellation following the 2006–07 school year.

Fortunately, careful evaluations of educator performance-pay programs are
under way in other school systems across the United States. We are optimistic
these evaluation efforts will yield considerably more to our understanding of the
effects of teacher pay-for-performance programs. That broader set of knowledge
and empirical evidence is likely to have a strong influence on whether pay for

performance continues as another education reform fad or has the potential to be part of sound and lasting policy.

Notes

1. William Howell, Martin West, and Paul Peterson, "What Americans Think about Their Schools," *Education Next* 7, no. 4 (2007): 12-26.
2. David Figlio and Lawrence Kenny, "Individual Teacher Incentives and Student Performance," *Journal of Public Economics* 91 (2007): 901-14.
3. Thomas Dee and Benjamin Keys, "Does Merit Pay Reward Good Teachers? Evidence from a Randomized Experiment," *Journal of Policy Analysis and Management* 23, no. 3 (2005): 471-74.
4. See chapter 9 in this volume for additional examples of performance measures used to evaluate teachers in pay-for-performance programs.
5. For example, in March 2006 Little Rock teachers were asked to vote on a privately supported merit pay pilot project that would pay bonuses to fifty teachers across the district who volunteered for the program. The Little Rock Classroom Teachers Association actively opposed this plan, and the teachers rejected it with a vote of 256 to 42. Katherine Wright Knight, president of the teachers association, said at the time that "we hope this sends a clear message to the administration and to the Board that merit pay may never work in Little Rock." Cynthia Howell, "Teachers Reject Merit-Pay Plan; 256–42 Vote Scuttles LR Test Run," *Arkansas Democrat-Gazette*, March 25, 2006.
6. The press release announcing the first year of the rewards highlights the importance of the inclusion of all school staff in the program. Karen Carter, the principal of Meadowcliff school, stated, "As a school campus, we are very supportive of a project where all employees have an opportunity for a reward. We work as a team here, where everyone supports the effort and takes a special interest in our children's learning." Deeann Morgan, literacy coach at Meadowcliff, agreed: "This was really a very positive experience and one that we and our kids felt very lucky to be part of. . . . It truly takes a team to make it happen . . . [from] the cafeteria worker making sure everyone has a good breakfast, to the librarian making certain we have challenging books for every student."
7. Gary Ritter and others, "Year Two Evaluation of the Achievement Challenge Pilot Project in the Little Rock Public School District," University of Arkansas at Fayetteville, Department of Education Reform, January 22, 2008 (www.uark.edu/ua/der/research/merit_pay/year_two.html).
8. See, for example, Steven G. Rivkin, Eric A. Hanushek, and John F. Kain, "Teachers, Schools, and Academic Achievement," *Econometrica* 73, no. 2 (2005).
9. Marcus A. Winters, Gary W. Ritter, Joshua H. Barrett, and Jay P. Greene, "An Evaluation of Teacher Performance Pay in Arkansas," January 2007, University of Arkansas–Fayetteville, Department of Education Reform (www.uark.edu/ua/der/Research/performance_pay_ar.htm).
10. It is possible to test the explanatory power of the teacher fixed effect itself by estimating a regression of math test scores against only the teacher fixed effect. That is, the amount of variance explained by the teacher fixed effect can be computed by running the model with only that effect and no other variables. These analyses produced R^2 values between 0.20

and 0.25 for the three subjects. This indicates that there is variation in teacher effectiveness but that here it is correlated with other regressors included in the model. Analyses available from authors upon request.

11. See, for example, G. D. Borman and others, "Comprehensive School Reform and Achievement: A Meta-Analysis," *Review of Educational Research* 73, no. 2 (2003): 125-230.

12. Ritter and others, "Year Two Evaluation of the Achievement Challenge Pilot Project."

13. A copy of the survey instrument along with the construct scores and results for all individual survey items is provided in appendixes A, B, and C to Ritter and others, "Year Two Evaluation of the Achievement Challenge Pilot Project."

14. The two sets of schools were qualitatively similar with respect to racial composition, family income levels, and student performance. At the same time, the survey responses indicate that teachers in schools that volunteered to participate in the ACPP and provided age and experience data on their survey were younger and less experienced than their peers across the district. Fewer than half of all survey respondents in the treatment group provided their total years of experience (ibid., p. A-14).

13

Teacher Incentives in the Developing World

Paul Glewwe, Alaka Holla, and Michael Kremer

In many developing countries even children who attend school seem to learn remarkably little, as evidenced by their low scores on internationally comparable tests.[1] One, though certainly not the only, explanation for this may be that teacher incentives are extremely weak in many developing countries, with frequent teacher absences, despite salaries that are often far above market levels. Efforts to improve the quality of schooling in developing countries by changing teacher incentives have included policies that improve working conditions, so that teachers are more motivated to come to work; policies that provide direct payments to teachers, based on either their inputs (for example, their own attendance) or their outputs (for example, student performance on tests); and policies that change teacher incentives by modifying the management of the education system, such as local hiring of contract teachers and providing information on school and student performance to the local community. This paper focuses on student achievement and teacher effort in primary and secondary education, and on evidence from randomized evaluations since they allow one to isolate the causal impact of

We thank Rachel Glennerster and Matthew Springer for many useful comments on this chapter. We draw on Michael Kremer and Alaka Holla's World Bank working paper, "Increasing the Quantity and Quality of Human Capital Investment in the Developing World."

specific policies or programs from student or school characteristics that may be correlated with those policies.

In many societies, the enforcement of rules requiring teachers to attend school has broken down. Providing payments to teachers based on attendance does induce more teacher attendance and does not lead teachers to show up but then not teach. However, there may be a political challenge in implementing these. Evidence from developing countries on systems that link teacher pay to the student test scores is mixed; one study finds that such policies lead to teachers teaching to the test; another study (still in progress) finds more positive impacts. Regarding policies that modify the management of the education system, the limited evidence to date suggests that simply providing information to communities on teacher performance without actually changing authority over teachers has little impact. One promising and politically feasible policy is hiring additional contract teachers locally outside the civil service system. These teachers are much cheaper than civil service teachers, they attend school more often, and their students do better.

The following discussion reviews evidence that student performance is disturbingly low in much of the developing world and argues that teachers in many developing countries have very weak incentives. It continues with a review of the evidence on whether teacher effort increases in response to better working conditions and results from interventions that offer more direct incentives by differentiating teachers' pay based on their performance. The final section discusses more fundamental reforms of education systems, based on local empowerment and contract hiring.

Background: Student Achievement and Teacher Incentives in Developing Countries

This section provides basic information on education outcomes and teacher incentives in developing countries. It begins by presenting evidence that student performance in many developing countries is much lower than in developed countries. In addition, there are few pecuniary incentives in these countries for teachers to exert more than very minimal effort. This section describes both of these phenomena, drawing on recent evidence.

Low Student Achievement

Children currently attending school in developing countries often receive a poor quality education, leaving school with very low levels of achievement. In Bangladesh, for example, Vincent Greaney, Shahidur R. Khandker, and Mahmudul Alam find that 58 percent of rural children ages eleven and older could not identify seven of eight presented letters, and 59 percent correctly answered only five or fewer of eight questions requiring recognition of one- and two-digit numbers, writing one-digit numbers, and recognizing basic geometric shapes.[2] In Ghana, the mean score of grade 6 students on a very simple multiple-choice reading test was 25 percent, the score one would expect from random guessing.[3] In India, 36 percent of grade 6 students were unable to understand and correctly answer the following question: "The dog is black with a white spot on his back and one white leg. The color of the dog is mostly: (a) black, (b) brown, or (c) grey."[4]

Internationally comparable achievement data are rarely available for low-income countries, but the Trends in International Mathematics and Science Study (TIMSS) does include a few, and scores in these countries are particularly low.[5] The average eighth-grade test taker in South Africa, for example, answered only 18 percent of questions correctly on the math portion of the TIMSS in 2003, while test takers in the United States answered an average of 51 percent of questions correctly. The academic achievement gaps among all children of a given age are likely to be even larger than gaps among children who are currently in school, since developing countries have lower enrollment rates and low rates of progression to secondary school, so that the students in these countries who remain in school long enough to be tested in these evaluations are likely to be better than average students.

Eric A. Hanushek and Ludger Wössmann, using evidence from internationally comparable tests, show that, in many developing countries, students in a given grade or of a given age score much lower than comparable students in developed countries.[6] For example, the share of students who fail to achieve basic competence in math and science (defined as scores falling more than one standard deviation below the OECD mean) is quite small in almost all developed countries (usually less than 10 percent), while in many developing countries more than half of the students do not achieve this basic level of competence (examples include South Africa, Brazil, Morocco, Peru, and Saudi Arabia).

Weak Teacher Incentives

One possible cause of lower student performance in developing countries is weak incentives for teachers to work effectively, as evidenced by high rates of teacher absenteeism. In surveys of teacher and health care worker absence across countries and across states in India, Nazmul Chaudhury and others find that primary school teachers were absent from school 27 percent of the time in Uganda, 25 percent in India, 14 percent in Ecuador, and 11 percent in Peru.[7] Absence rates are typically higher in poorer countries, and within India poorer states have higher absence rates. Data from Kenya reveal a teacher absenteeism rate of 20 percent in rural primary schools; for comparison, the absence rate among staff at a nonprofit organization working in the same area was around 6 percent.[8]

These rates of teacher absence seem to be broadly distributed among the population of teachers rather than concentrated among a subset of teachers with very high absence rates. In India, for example, where the average absence rate among primary school teachers is 25 percent, if the same teachers were always absent, 75 percent of teachers would never have been absent during the three surprise visits made to schools, while 25 percent would have been absent at each visit. Instead, only 49 percent of teachers were absent zero times, while 33 percent were absent once, 14 percent twice, and only 5 percent three times. Chaudhury and colleagues find a similar pattern of widespread absence in Bangladesh, Indonesia, Peru, and Uganda (but not in Ecuador). Using data from two Kenyan districts, Paul Glewwe, Nauman Ilias, and Michael Kremer estimate the distribution of teacher absence in two districts of Kenya using a maximum likelihood approach (assuming that the underlying probability of absence follows a beta distribution).[9] They do this because a finite number of visits to each school causes the dispersion of absence rates in the true empirical distribution to exaggerate the underlying dispersion of probabilities of attendance among teachers. This calibration exercise shows that absences are not primarily due to a few teachers who have very high rates of absenteeism; instead, the majority of absences appear to be accounted for by teachers who attend between 50 percent and 80 percent of the time, with the median teacher being absent 14 to 19 percent of the time.

Even when teachers are in school, they are not necessarily teaching their students. In India, while 75 percent of teachers were present in the school, only about half of all teachers were actually teaching in the classroom when enumerators arrived.[10] Enumerators who visited classes in Kenya to observe pedagogy found that teachers were absent from class about 27 percent of the time, although they were absent from school only 20 percent of the time. Moreover, only a small percentage of Kenyan teachers were in the classroom at the time that the class officially started. Casual observation suggests that teachers are often drinking tea in the staff room with other teachers during class time. Public school teachers work under civil service protection in many developing countries.[11] For these teachers, effective sanctions are rarely imposed for behavior that would invite disciplinary action in developed countries. According to Chaudhury and others' survey of 3,000 headmasters of government schools in India, only one teacher in those 3,000 schools was reported to have been fired for repeated absence. Incentives seem to be somewhat stronger under other contractual or organizational forms, although absence rates are high under these as well.

The same survey also looks at absence among private school teachers in India and finds that, in general, their absence rates were only 2 percentage points lower than those of public school teachers. In villages with both public and private schools, however, teacher absence rates in private schools were about 8 percentage points lower, indicating that private schools are disproportionately located in villages with particularly high rates of teacher absence in public schools. One way to interpret this is that private schools tend to enter areas where public school performance is poor. Another interpretation, however, is that the entry of private schools triggers the exit of influential families from public schools and thus weakens pressure on public school teachers to attend.

Private school teachers in India are paid only about one fourth of what public school teachers are paid, and this higher attendance for lower pay may well reflect enforcement of sanctions for absence in private schools. Chaudhury and others find that 35 of 600 private schools in their survey reported a case of the head teacher dismissing a teacher for repeated absence or tardiness. Thus teacher dismissal for repeated absences was found to occur in about 6 percent of private schools, compared to only 0.03 percent of public schools.

Chaudhury and others find little evidence that high absence rates are due to low teacher salaries: in many developing countries teachers are paid up to five times per capita GDP. Teacher salaries across Indian states are relatively flat, so salaries for teachers in poor states are considerably higher relative to the cost of living and outside opportunities than are salaries in rich states. Absence rates are higher, however, in poor states. In many developing countries, salaries are highly correlated with the teacher's age, experience, educational background, and rank (such as head teacher status), but again there is little evidence that any of these factors is significantly associated with lower absence. In fact, across countries head teachers are significantly more likely to be absent, and point estimates suggest that better-educated and older teachers are, on average, more likely to be absent. This could be due to better outside opportunities for these teachers.

Working conditions, however, do appear to motivate teachers to come to school. Absence is negatively correlated with an index that measures school infrastructure (toilets, covered classrooms, nondirt floors, electricity, and a school library), with a one standard deviation improvement in school infrastructure associated with a 2.7 percentage point reduction in teacher absence on average across countries. If frequently absent teachers are sanctioned by being transferred to schools with poor facilities, then the direction of causality from this relationship would be unclear. However, when Chaudhury and others restrict the analysis to teachers on their first postings (determined by an algorithm unrelated to their performance), the relationship between absence and school infrastructure remains. Logically, if teachers' employment is not conditional on absence, pay is likely to have little effect on absence, but the attractiveness of the work environment might affect whether a teacher decides to come to work on a particular day.

Incentives from the School Environment

The discussion above suggests that school environment can influence teachers' propensity to come to work, since teachers are more likely to be present if their schools have good infrastructure. This section examines the impact on teacher attendance of changes in the school environment that make schools more attractive places for teachers to work but that do not attempt to reward some teachers more than others based on teacher behavior or on student outcomes. The evidence, which comes from two randomized interventions in Kenya, suggests that teacher effort is greater when students are better prepared and motivated to learn, although, as discussed below, it is not possible to rule out other hypotheses.

After primary school fees were abolished in Kenya in 2003, the associated influx of students increased both pupil-teacher ratios and the degree of heterogeneity in incoming students' academic preparation. In response, the International Child Support (ICS) Fund, a nongovernmental organization (NGO), launched the Extra Teacher Program (ETP), which provided school committees of randomly selected schools with funds to hire an extra teacher for first grade on a contractual basis, allowing the school to add another first-grade class. (Schools not randomly selected for the ETP serve as a comparison group.) First-grade children were split into two classes in two ways. In half of the schools that were randomly selected to receive an extra teacher, students were randomly assigned to either the contract teacher or the regular civil service teacher. In the other half, children were placed in classrooms based on their preintervention achievement scores, so that children above the median level would be taught in one classroom and those below the median level in another. These classrooms were then randomly assigned to either the contract teacher or the civil service teacher.

Civil service teachers in the tracked schools were around 5.4 percentage points more likely to be found in schools on a random day relative to their counterparts in the untracked schools.[12] This effect seems entirely due to greater presence of teachers assigned to the above-the-median class, which may reflect easier or more pleasant teaching conditions when students are better prepared and less heterogeneous, since teachers would not have to accommodate a wide range of achievement among the children.

Another randomized intervention offered merit-based scholarships to the top-scoring 15 percent of sixth-grade girls in Kenyan primary schools (the Girls Scholarship Program). These scholarships consisted of grants (to schools) that covered school fees, grants to parents for school supplies, and recognition in an awards ceremony. After the introduction of the program, average student test scores were 0.12 standard deviations higher in treatment schools, with spillover benefits for boys and for girls in the bottom of the achievement distribution (whose chances of winning the scholarships were small).[13] Teacher attendance in program schools increased by 4.8 percentage points from a baseline attendance rate of 84 percent, which implies a 30 percent decrease in absence. Teacher behavior in the classroom, however, did not change.

Teachers may have been more motivated to show up for school because their students were more motivated. However, other explanations are also possible. Anecdotal evidence shows that parental monitoring played a role: parents in treatment schools would visit schools more frequently to monitor teachers and pressure them to work hard so that their daughters could win scholarships.

Rewards for Performance

A potentially more powerful, but also more politically controversial, approach to provide incentives for teachers is to differentiate teacher compensation based on teachers' inputs or outputs. Input-based incentives reward improvements in what are thought to be behaviors that improve teaching—frequent attendance or improvements in pedagogy, for example. Outcome-based incentives tie rewards to output, most frequently student learning as measured by test scores. This section examines evidence on both types of such incentive schemes, focusing on experimental studies conducted in developing countries.

Input-Based Incentives

In many developing countries, headmasters are supposed to record teacher attendance, and school inspectors are supposed to visit periodically and (among other things) verify that teachers are present and that teacher attendance records are accurate. This is the standard mechanism for monitoring teacher attendance. While in theory this should work, in practice it often fails because it is not enforced. Three studies from India and Kenya suggest that input-based rewards can be effective if they are enforced, but it may be difficult for local monitors to enforce them.

Michael Kremer and Daniel Chen evaluate an inputs-based-incentive intervention in Kenyan preschools in which teachers were eligible for bonuses equivalent to as much as 85 percent of their salary, based on their attendance.[14] They find that the program affected neither teacher attendance nor most measures of teacher pedagogy. Moreover, it had no effect on either pupil test scores or pupil attendance. This input-based-incentive program assigned headmasters to monitor teacher absence and award bonuses based on a specified rule, in which bonuses were reduced for each day a teacher was absent without excuse. Any funds that were not paid to teachers went to the general school account, so headmasters had at least some financial incentive not to pay teachers bonuses if they were not present. Nonetheless, headmasters routinely paid the entire bonus to teachers even though independent monitoring showed that teacher absences did not significantly decline relative to the baseline rate of 29 percent.

Esther Duflo, Rema Hanna, and Stephan Ryan report on a randomized evaluation of an inputs-based program in remote nonformal education centers in India.[15] These nonformal schools typically teach basic numeracy and literacy skills with the aim of eventually mainstreaming children into the regular school system. The teachers at these schools do not have civil service protection, are typically paid very low wages, and have less education than regular teachers. The fact that these teachers are not part of the civil service system and were hired by an NGO rather than the government made it easier to implement the incentive program.

The program was implemented in a poor, sparsely populated rural area, where the NGO administering the nonformal schools found it difficult to monitor the education centers. Perhaps as a consequence of this difficulty, teacher absenteeism was high (around 44 percent) before the intervention, despite an official policy of dismissal for absent teachers in these nonformal schools.

The incentive program provided teachers with cameras with tamper-proof time and date functions. A child was to photograph the teacher and the other children at the beginning and the end of each school day. Teachers' salaries were then a function of the number of "valid school days," days in which the morning and afternoon pictures were separated by a minimum of five hours, with at least eight children appearing in each picture. Teachers received a base salary for working at least twenty days a month and a bonus for each day in excess of twenty; they were fined for each day they fell short of the minimum requirement of twenty days. The program had a large effect on teacher absence over its thirty-month duration: it decreased teacher absence in treatment schools by 19 percentage points, which is roughly equivalent to halving the absence rate.

One key question with input-incentive-based programs such as this one, which reward teachers for being at school but not for what they do there, is whether teachers find ways to increase the measured input without actually producing the desired educational output. For example, teachers might come to school but then not bother to teach. Reassuringly, however, Duflo, Hanna, and Ryan find that the teachers in treatment schools were no less likely to be teaching on the days they were at school than were the teachers in comparison schools.

Further evidence that the camera program did not lead to an ineffective increase in inputs is that students scored higher on tests at the end of the program. After one year, the program increased language scores by 0.21 standard deviations, math scores by 0.16 standard deviations, and overall test scores by 0.17 standard deviations. In addition, the graduation rate to mainstream government schools increased by 10 percentage points (from a baseline of 16 percent). This improvement may simply reflect increased student time in school. While students' attendance rates (measured by unannounced spot checks) on the days their schools were open did not increase, the total amount of time children spent in school did increase, since schools were open more days: children in treatment schools obtained, on average, 2.7 more days of schooling per month.

Duflo, Hanna, and Ryan also show that the camera program was relatively cost effective. The average salary was the same in treatment and comparison schools. All other costs of the program amounted to roughly $6 a child per year (assuming twenty children per teacher), which implies a cost of $60 for an additional school year. In terms of raising test scores, the per child cost of increasing test scores by 0.10 standard deviations was only $3.58.

Since teacher unions often have substantial political influence and may oppose efforts to link payments to either inputs or outputs, it is worth asking whether such programs could be sustained politically in government schools. Some discouraging evidence is provided by examining an intervention among government health care workers in rural areas of Udaipur district, India.[16] In these areas, subcenters are facilities that provide the most basic health care services (such as first-aid and pre-natal care) and should be staffed by at least one assistant nurse midwife (ANM). They are supposed to be open six hours a day, six days a week. A 2003 survey, however, shows that subcenters were closed 56 percent of the time and that in only 12 percent of the cases was the ANM on duty somewhere around the center.[17]

The NGO that had administered the camera program collaborated with state and local health administrations to provide ANMs with incentives to show up to their assigned health centers on certain days on which they knew they would be monitored, by using time and day stamp machines and a specific schedule of fines and other punishments to determine an ANM's wages. During each month, if an ANM was absent for more than 50 percent of the time on the monitored days, then her pay would be reduced by the recorded number of absences for that month. If she were absent more than 50 percent of the monitored days for a second straight month, she was to be suspended from government service. Some absences, such as government-mandated meetings, survey work, or other health-related work were excused and not counted as absences. If a stamp machine broke, an ANM could not be monitored until it was fixed.

Abhijit Banerjee, Esther Duflo, and Rachel Glennerster find that in the first six months, the stamp machine program doubled ANM presence, as observed in random unannounced visits to the subcenters. On the days when they were supposed to be monitored, ANMs in the treatment group were present 60 percent of the time, while the comparison group of ANMs was present less than 30 percent of the time. The ANMs in the treatment group were present in the subcenter less than 40 percent of the time on the days when they were not expecting to be monitored.

In the next nine-month period, however, ANM presence in treatment sub-centers fell dramatically, to 25 percent on monitored days, while the comparison ANMs were present 35 percent of the time, so that by the end of the period, the treatment ANMs had higher absence rates than the ANMs in the comparison group. On the nonmonitored days, the presence of treatment and comparison ANMs converged by the end of the period to a rate of less than 20 percent.

The administrative data, however, did not reflect this decrease in presence. The number of days marked as exempt, as well as days with machine problems, did increase over the life of the program. Program monitors, in fact, reported that a number of machines had been deliberately broken and that ANMs were not present to meet the monitors when they came to subcenters to replace the malfunctioning machines, thus extending the period in which they could not be monitored under program rules.

Although one should be cautious about drawing broad generalizations from only three studies, these studies suggest that the effectiveness of input-based incentives depends on their design and implementation, in particular on the system for monitoring the inputs on which payments are based. The use of an external observation technology that produces frequent, clear-cut yes-or-no measurements of absence and so cannot be vulnerable to shadings of excuse (such as the cameras in India, with payments determined by distant NGO workers) appears to be more effective than using local observers, such as headmasters, who might be very close to teachers and therefore unlikely to sanction them. A simple yes-no technology with an infrequent inspection system is less likely to be effective because then a teacher who is usually absent a small fraction of the time, but who by chance is absent on the days the inspector happens to visit, would be subject to disciplinary action. Finally, the Udaipur stamp machine example suggests that, at least in some settings, it is politically difficult to sustain efforts to increase service provider attendance through more frequent monitoring, perhaps due to the political power of providers and their unions.

Output-Based Incentives

Linking teacher pay to student performance could potentially lead teachers not only to increase school attendance but also to provide other inputs, such as better pedagogy, more homework, or more time spent teaching conditional on their presence in school. In developed countries, opponents of teacher incentives based on students' test scores argue that, since teachers' tasks are multidimensional and only some aspects are measured by test scores, linking compensation to test scores could cause teachers to sacrifice the promotion of curiosity and creative thinking in order to teach the skills tested on standardized exams.[18]

The extremely weak teacher incentives and teacher supervision systems in many developing countries raise the potential for both these benefits and these costs if output-based incentives are implemented. On the one hand, it can be argued that teachers in many developing countries are already teaching to the test and that the main problem is to get teachers to come to school, and thus teacher incentives are particularly appropriate for developing countries. On the other hand, developing countries with weak teacher accountability systems may be more prone to attempts by teachers to game any incentive system.

It is not a priori clear whether teacher incentives will improve long-run learning. Suppose teachers can exert two types of effort: genuine teaching effort to promote long-run learning and "signaling effort," which improves scores in the short run but has little effect on long-run learning. Observable test scores depend both on underlying learning (produced by current and past teaching effort) and contemporaneous signaling effort. Test-score-based incentives could either increase or decrease teaching effort, since teaching effort and signaling effort could be either substitutes or complements. For example, they can be substitutes if there is a fixed amount of time in the day that must be allocated between them. On the other hand, they can be complements if there is a fixed cost to teachers of attending school at all.

Although it would be expensive and very difficult to monitor both kinds of effort on an ongoing basis, there may be ways to distinguish teaching and signaling efforts empirically at the aggregate level for incentive programs that pay rewards based on test scores. First, direct observation of teacher behavior can provide some clues. Teacher attendance or homework assignments would most likely contribute to students' long-run learning, while other activities are likely to have a higher signaling component. In many countries, for example, some schools conduct extra test preparation or coaching sessions outside of normal class time, often during school vacations. While these sessions may include some genuine learning, relative to normal classes they contain a higher proportion of effort aimed at raising test scores, such as reviewing old exams or teaching students not to leave blanks on multiple-choice exams.

Second, improved learning should have a longer lasting effect on test scores than would signaling effort. Thus a finding that test score gains do not persist beyond the end of an incentive program suggests that the program led to an increase in signaling effort but not to an increase in effort aimed at promoting long-run learning.

A third way to distinguish efforts to increase long-run learning from test preparation activities is to examine in more detail the pattern of any test score increases. If test scores increased only on exams linked to incentives, were concentrated in subjects prone to memorization, or increased primarily on exams with formats that are more amenable to coaching, such as multiple-choice exams, one can infer that test preparation activities were more common than efforts to increase long-run learning.

A program in Kenya that linked teacher bonuses to student performance led teachers to modify their behavior in ways that raised scores on the tests that were used to allocate the bonuses but that did not improve teacher attendance. Although students had higher test scores on the tests tied to the incentives while the program was in effect, similar increases were not present on tests not linked to the incentives, and a year after the program ended the gains in student achievement on the tests linked to the incentives had completely dissipated.[19]

This output-based program, which was implemented in randomly selected schools in western Kenya, provided prizes to all teachers in grades 4 to 8 based on the school's average performance on the government (district) exams administered in those grades each year. These prizes, which were awarded at the end of each year to top-scoring and most-improved schools, ranged in value from 21 to 43 percent of the typical teacher's monthly salary. The program created incentives not only to raise test scores but also to reduce dropout rates, since all students enrolled at the beginning of the program were included in the computation of scores and, for purposes of awarding prizes, students who did not take the government exams were assigned a score less than what they could have obtained by random guessing. The school's score was calculated using only initially enrolled students in order to discourage schools from recruiting strong students to take the exams.

More students in treatment schools took the government exam than in comparison schools during the two years that the Kenyan output-based program operated (6.0 percentage points higher in the first year and 10.8 percentage points higher in the second year, from a base of 70 percent). The program did not affect dropout or repetition rates, nor did it change eighth-grade graduation rates. Teachers apparently induced more students to take the exams, which improved their scores on the formula used to reward teachers, but they do not appear to have induced them to stay in school.

The program did generate gains in test scores, but these gains were short-lived, which is consistent with teachers' being focused on raising test scores in the short run rather than on raising long-run learning. Students in the treatment schools scored an average of 0.14 standard deviations higher on the government exams in the second year of the program relative to students in comparison schools, when the sample is restricted to students who took the exam in both the pre-intervention and intervention years. Yet one year after the intervention ended there were no significant achievement differences between the treatment and comparison schools on the government exams.

It is possible that achievement gains did not persist because of a natural process of depreciation (or forgetting) in what has been learned over time, as noted by Tahir Andrabi and colleagues.[20] Several other patterns in the data, however, suggest that teachers did not modify their behavior to improve long-term learning but rather focused on short-run signaling.

First, teacher absence rates did not decline; teachers continued to be absent from school 20 percent of school days. Second, students did not report an increase in homework assignments, nor did observers notice any change in pedagogy (such as increases in the use of blackboards or teaching aids or in teachers' levels of energy or caring). Instead, schools increased their number of exam preparation sessions, especially during vacation periods. In the second year of the intervention, for example, treatment schools were 7.4 percentage points more likely to conduct exam preparation sessions than were comparison schools.

Third, the achievement gains during the intervention appear to be the strongest in the subjects—geography, history, and Christian religion—that arguably require the most memorization. In the second year of the program, students in treatment schools scored 0.34 standard deviations higher on the government exams for these subjects. Fourth, the NGO administering the program also tested students; this exam differed from the government exams in content and format and was designed to detect performance differences among a wider range of students. Whereas the program's incentives were set in terms of performance on the government exam, no incentives existed with respect to performance on the NGO exam. Strikingly, in neither of the intervention years did students in the treatment schools display any statistically significant gains on the NGO exam relative to their counterparts in the comparison schools.

Finally, there is evidence that the Kenyan output-based program improved students' test-taking techniques. Standard test-taking advice includes not leaving blanks on multiple-choice questions and managing time so as to reach the end of exams. Examination of specific questions on the NGO tests suggests that students in treatment schools were less likely to leave blanks, more likely to answer multiple-choice questions, and less likely to leave answers blank at the end of the test. Together, these results suggest that the extra preparation sessions in program schools increased students' test-taking skills. This may help explain the absence of a significant effect on the NGO exams (which were not the sort of test that prep classes were designed to teach to), particularly on questions with a format different from that of the government tests.

A program in India that linked teacher pay to student test scores had effects that were in many ways similar to the effects of the Kenyan program, except that students also performed better on exams not linked to incentives, which suggests that the program may have improved long-run learning. Karthik Muralidharan and Venkatesh Sundararaman examine a teacher-incentive program in India that was part of the Andhra Pradesh Randomized Evaluation Study (APRESt).[21] There were two variants of the program: a group-based teacher incentive and an individual teacher incentive. In the individual-incentive intervention, each teacher was paid 500 rupees (more than $10) for every percentage point improvement in his or her students' test scores beyond a minimum improvement of 5 percentage points. An improvement in scores of 10 percentage points would yield a bonus equivalent to about 30 percent of an average teacher's monthly salary. In the group-incentive intervention, the same bonus was paid to all teachers based on the average performance of all students in the school. In both interventions, there were provisions to prevent gaming, (such as exclusion of weaker students from taking the exams).

The APRESt teacher-incentive program led to gains in scores on tests linked to incentives. In the first year, the gains of 0.12 to 0.19 standard deviations were similar for the teacher-based and the school-based incentive groups. In the second year of the program, however, teacher-based incentive schools displayed achievement gains of 0.27 standard deviations, which were significantly higher (at the 10 percent level) than the 0.16 standard deviation gains in the school-based incentive group.

As in the Kenyan output-based program, the APRESt teacher-incentive program did not change teacher absence rates, nor did it change various indicators of classroom processes that were measured by direct observation. There is also evidence that teachers in treatment schools conducted more extra classes after school hours and gave more practice tests. Although teachers in treatment schools were more likely to self-report that after the program they assigned more homework and in-class work relative to their counterparts in the comparison schools, these self-reports should be taken with a grain of salt, since incentive school teachers in Kenya also reported assigning more homework, but interviews with students suggest that they increased only the prep sessions and did not actually assign more homework. Indeed, classroom observation data from India show no statistically significant differences between treatment and comparison schools in assigning homework, providing homework guidance or feedback, giving tests, encouraging participation, or providing help to groups or individuals. Teachers in program schools were 18 percentage points more likely to report conducting extra classes after school hours (from a base of 4 percent) and 11 percentage points more likely to report giving practice tests (from a base of 10 percent). Thus these results appear quite similar to those from the Kenyan program: improvements in test scores coupled with increases in test preparation. Test score improvements were identical on questions with an unfamiliar format that were designed to be conceptual and on questions with a more familiar format. Since the program is ongoing at the time of this writing, it is not possible to know whether these improvements in achievement will be sustained after the incentives have been removed.

These results suggest that, unlike the Kenya program, the APRESt teacher-incentive program increased long-run learning rather than simply improving students' test-taking techniques, although it is difficult to rule out the possibility that test-taking techniques, which helped on the mechanical questions, also helped on the conceptual ones. It is also worth noting that pupils in incentive schools scored 0.11 and 0.18 standard deviations higher in science and social studies, respectively, subjects for which there were no incentives. This is consistent either with positive spillover effects or with an improvement in test-taking skills that could transfer across subjects. Definitive evidence on the impact of the program in India will have to await tests administered after the program is over, at which point teachers will no longer have any incentive to produce high scores. If the participants show higher test scores after the incentives end, that will provide strong evidence that the program led to actual increases in long-run learning.

Summary

The evidence on input-based systems suggests that if teachers can be given effective incentives to come to school more regularly, they will do so. In societies in which existing input-based incentive systems have broken down, and teacher absence is high, one approach to strengthening teacher incentives is to use technologies that allow monitoring by people who are not closely connected to the teachers and that provide frequent and unambiguous signals of whether teachers are present. However, the political obstacles to implementing such programs may be quite formidable.

Regarding output-based incentives, the experimental evidence from developing countries is mixed. Table 13-1 summarizes the results from Kenya and India. The study from Kenya suggests that linking teacher pay to a formula based on test scores led to unintended outcomes and produced little or no long-term gains in learning. The study in India finds some evidence of impacts on long-term learning, but the program has not been in place long enough to see how long these impacts will last. It is not clear whether the differences reflect differences in the context or differences in the design of the two programs.

Table 13-1. *Test-Score-Based Teacher Incentives*

Item	Glewwe, Ilias, and Kremer[a]	Muralidharan and Sundararaman[b]
Context	Kenyan primary schools	Indian primary schools
Basis of prize	School average scores	School average scores, individual teacher scores
Teacher attendance	No	No
Pedagogy (direct observation)	No	No
Test scores	0.14 increase in standard deviation	0.19 SD (math) and 0.12 SD (language)
Homework (direct observations)	No	No
Exam prep sessions	Increase	Increase
Effects on tests not related to incentives	No	Yes
Evidence that test gains reflect improvements in test-taking techniques	Yes	Not discussed
Gains retained after end of program	No	Results not yet available

a. Paul Glewwe, Nauman Ilias, and Michael Kremer, "Teacher Incentives," mimeo (2008).
b. Karthik Muralidharan and Venkatesh Sundararaman, "Teaching Incentives in Developing Countries: Experimental Evidence from India," mimeo (2008).
"No" indicates no statistically significant effect.

System Reforms

An alternative approach to improving teacher incentives is not simply more appealing working conditions or input- or output-based merit pay within the context of a civil service system but rather a change in the lines of authority so that teachers are subject to community monitoring, local control over hiring, or a system in which schools must compete for students. Such policies have been advocated in response to the perceived failures of centralized school systems and are increasingly being adopted, but at this point rigorous empirical evidence on their impact is still limited. This section reviews evidence from two sources: interventions that provide communities with information on schools in an attempt to empower parents and programs that transfer real control over hiring and firing decisions to parents.

Information and Parental Involvement

If lack of information or awareness about how schools should be functioning prevents people from demanding a certain standard of quality and holding schools accountable, one approach to improving social service delivery would be to provide communities with information about the quality of their schools and to make them aware of their rights, under national and state laws, to keep service providers accountable. A project in rural Uttar Pradesh (UP) in India sheds light on this hypothesis.

To understand the project, some background information is useful. In 2000 the UP government set up Village Education Committees (VECs) in each village. These committees were to consist of the elected head of the village government, the head teacher of the village's government school, and three parents whose children are enrolled in the village's government school. The committees' functions include monitoring the performance of the government school, reporting problems to higher authorities, requesting additional resources, deciding whether the contracts of community-based teachers should be renewed, recruiting new hires, and allocating any additional resources for school improvement that the school receives from a national education program.

Surveys undertaken before the interventions, however, show that the simple creation of local agencies does not ensure that people are informed about the state of social services or even are aware that such agencies exist.[22] For example, 92 percent of households surveyed did not know that a VEC existed, and among those that were aware of the committee, only 2 percent could name its members. Among the nonheadmaster members of the committees, 23 percent did not even know that they were members. Only 3.6 percent of committee members mentioned that requesting government funds to hire a contract teacher from the community is one of the functions of the VEC. These surveys, combined with assessment tests given to children in their homes, also show that parents considerably overestimate their children's reading and math abilities and are not fully aware of how poorly their schools are functioning.

The project in UP included three distinct interventions. In the first intervention, a team of NGO workers visited areas for two days and organized a village meeting to inform people about the status of education in their village, the quality of village schools, state-mandated provisions for schools (pupil-teacher ratios, infrastructure, midday meals, and scholarships), local funds available for education, and the responsibilities of the VEC. The second intervention did all of this and also gave villagers a specific monitoring tool by actively encouraging and equipping communities to participate in testing of their children's reading and arithmetic skills. The third intervention contained all of the components of the first two and also added an option for villagers to deal with poor learning outcomes without engaging in local political institutions or the school system. It did so by adding a training component in which community volunteers with an education of tenth or twelfth grade were trained for four days to teach children how to read.

An average village of about 360 households sent about 100 people to the meetings, but none of the three interventions had much impact on the awareness or activism of either the VECs or the parents.[23] VECs in all three of the treatment groups, for example, were no more likely to perform any of their functions (such as filing complaints or hiring a contract teacher from the community) than the VECs in the comparison group. In none of the treatment groups were parents more involved with their children's school (through volunteering or filing a complaint, for example) than their comparison counterparts, nor were they more likely to know about the state of education in their village or consider it a major issue. All three interventions also failed to improve teacher and student absence, which remained high, at 25 percent and 50 percent, respectively.

The third intervention, however, dramatically improved community participation in teaching children to read and significantly improved reading achievement. In fifty-five of the sixty-five villages that received the third intervention, volunteers from the community started more than 400 reading camps, with 7,500 children enrolled (roughly 8 percent of all children). When the third intervention is used to predict reading camp attendance (to avoid endogeneity bias), children who attended reading camps were 22.3 percentage points more likely to be able to read at least several letters, 23.2 percentage points more likely to be able to read at least a word or paragraph, and 22.4 percentage points more likely to be able to read a story, although this last result is not significant at the 10 percent level. Of course, these results apply only to the 8 percent of children attending the reading camps, who tended to be the weakest readers initially (13.1 percent of children who could not read even letters at baseline attended the camps, whereas only 3 percent of children who could already read a story attended them).

The results of the first two interventions suggest that giving villagers information about the state of public goods in the village, without facilitating the use of that information, may not be useful (the first intervention). Even when a tool for monitoring student performance was given, if community members do not act upon the additional information from the monitoring and engage with the political institutions designed to address complaints or put pressure directly on schools, then the tool might not be an effective means of improving the quality of publicly provided social services (the second intervention). There is an obvious public good–free rider problem in motivating political action to address these problems. The results under the third program suggest that moving beyond the civil service system may have favorable results.

Two evaluations in Kenya shed light on programs that moved further in providing parents with influence, albeit limited, over teachers.[24] As in India, it is useful to know the context. In Kenya, teachers in public primary schools are hired centrally through the teacher service commission and are assigned to schools. Their promotion is determined by the Ministry of Education, not by parents. However, Kenya also has a long-standing tradition of local school committees, most of whose members are students' parents. These school committees have historically been concerned primarily with raising funds, for classroom repairs or textbook purchases, for example. But they also potentially provide a vehicle for communication between parents and the ministry. Moreover, school committees sometimes use some of the funds they have raised to hire contract teachers locally, whom they pay much lower wages, to supplement regular teachers provided by the Ministry of Education.

A recent program in Kenya aimed to strengthen ties between school committees and local educational authorities through training and joint meetings and to improve teacher incentives through prizes awarded by school committee members. Preliminary results show that average teacher attendance did not change.[25] In treatment schools, committee members met more often with teachers, but teacher behavior in school was rarely discussed and teacher absence was never discussed. Local education officials did not increase the total number of visits to treatment schools. There is also little systematic and significant evidence that pedagogy within the classroom changed or that student achievement improved.

Under the overall ETP program—which, as described above, provided funds to school committees to hire these extra contract teachers—half of the school committees in untracked schools with extra contract teachers and half in the tracked schools were also randomly selected for training to help them monitor these contract teachers (soliciting inputs from parents, checking teacher attendance, and so forth), and a formal review meeting was arranged for the committees to review the contract teachers' performance and decide whether their contracts should be renewed. An evaluation shows that the monitoring program had no impact on attendance rates of contract teachers or on the test scores of these teachers' students, since these outcomes were statistically indistinguishable for contract teachers in the ETP schools without extra school committee monitoring and the contract teachers in the ETP schools with extra school committee monitoring.[26] This might have occurred because the contract teachers already had very high attendance rates, as discussed below.

However, the program may have had some impact on the attendance rates of the regular civil service teachers and on the test scores of their students. Training in monitoring increased the attendance rates of civil service teachers in the ETP schools by 7.3 percentage points relative to civil service teachers in ETP schools, whose school committees did not receive the monitoring training, although this result is not quite significant at the 10 percent level.

The monitoring program also increased the attendance rates of students assigned to the civil service teachers by 2.8 percentage points relative to pupil attendance trends experienced by comparable civil service teachers in ETP schools without the monitoring program. Students assigned to civil service teachers in ETP schools with trained committees also experienced test score gains of 0.18 standard deviations in math relative to students assigned to civil service teachers in ETP schools without the training program. Overall it seems that the program had a modest effect on teacher incentives. A number of questions remain open, however, including whether the effect persists or is only a short-run effect and whether it generalizes beyond the particular context here, to one in which all schools had contract teachers.

Local Hiring of Contract Teachers

A number of countries have moved toward local hiring of contract teachers to supplement civil service teachers. These contract teachers are usually paid a fraction of what civil service teachers are paid, often only a quarter as much. They are often hired locally rather than through the central government. Often they have lower formal educational qualifications than are required of regular teachers. The move toward hiring contract teachers is motivated partly by concern about the weak incentives faced by civil service teachers and partly by fiscal concerns, since these teachers are much less expensive than regular teachers. In the cross-country study of absence discussed earlier, Nazmul Chaudhury and others find that teachers from the local area are less likely to be absent in all six countries and that this association is statistically significant for India and Indonesia.[27] Limited experimental evidence exists on the effectiveness of these teachers.[28]

Evidence from India suggests that hiring outside of the civil service system can be an effective way to improve the quality of teaching. The Balsakhi program implemented in India paid young women from the community, who had completed only secondary school (tenth grade), roughly one-tenth of a regular teacher's salary to teach basic literacy and numeracy skills to children who had reached third or fourth grade but had not yet mastered basic skills.[29] These children left the regular classroom each day for two hours of tutoring. Abhijit Banerjee and colleagues find that the Balsakhi program increased average test scores in treatment schools by 0.14 standard deviations in the first year and by 0.28 standard deviations after two years, with most of this increase due to large gains experienced by children at the bottom of the initial test-score distribution and by the children who received the remedial instruction.[30] One year after the program ended, the average student in program schools had a 0.1 standard deviation advantage over the average student in comparison schools, suggesting that at least some of the effect of the program persisted.

The Kenyan ETP intervention provided funds to a randomly selected set of school committees for hiring a local contract teacher. In this project, the contract teachers had the same academic qualifications as regular teachers.[31] Unlike their civil service counterparts, local contract teachers could be fired by school committees and were paid only a fraction of the civil service pay. The probability that contract teachers were in class and teaching was roughly 16 percentage points higher than that for civil service teachers in comparison schools, who attended 58.6 percent of the time, and 29.1 percentage points higher than that for civil service teachers in the ETP schools.

In the absence of the monitoring program and of tracking of students by initial achievement, the presence of these contract teachers increased absence among the civil service teachers in ETP schools. The probability that a civil service teacher was in class and teaching in the ETP schools fell by 12.9 percentage points relative to civil service teachers in the comparison schools. Their classes would sometimes be combined with a class whose teacher was present, but at other times students would simply sit unsupervised in their classrooms. However, training school committees in monitoring and tracking students by initial achievement prevented a statistically significant decline in attendance by civil service teachers after the hiring of local contract teachers.

Overall the ETP program raised student test scores by 0.22 standard deviations. Students assigned to contract teachers scored 0.23 standard deviations higher and attended school 1.7 percentage points more often (from a baseline attendance rate of 86.1 percent) than students who had been randomly assigned to civil service teachers.

In a program conducted in India alongside the APRESt teacher incentives program, one set of schools also randomly received a contract teacher for two years. Unlike Kenya's ETP program, the APRESt contract teacher program did not assign the contract teachers to particular classrooms and did not employ contract teachers with similar academic qualifications to their civil service counterparts. For example, 72 percent of contract teachers were female, and their average age was twenty-seven, while only 34 percent of their civil service teacher counterparts were female, and their average age was forty. Only 44 percent of contract teachers had at least a college degree; only 8 percent had received a formal teacher training degree or certificate, while 85 percent of civil service teachers had a college degree, and 99 percent had received a formal teacher training degree or certificate. These contract teachers were also more likely to be local: 85 percent lived in their assigned school's village, compared to only 11 percent of civil service teachers.

For the first year of the APRESt contract teacher program, Muralidharan and Sundararaman find that contract teachers were 11 percentage points less likely to be absent than their civil service counterparts in the same school, who were absent 24 percent of the time; in the second year, contract teachers were 17 percentage points less likely to be absent than civil service teachers, who were absent 29 percent of the time.[32] In both years of the program, contract teachers were also significantly more likely than civil service teachers to be teaching during random spot checks at the schools. Like the ETP program in Kenya, the contract teacher program in India induced 2.4 percentage points greater absence of civil service teachers and decreased their teaching activity by 3.2 percentage points.

Contract teachers with lower absence rates and higher rates of teaching activity in the first year of the APRESt contract teacher program were more likely to have had their contracts renewed in the second year. Since good performance seems to translate into contract renewal in this context, this potential for renewal could have been an important incentive for the contract teachers. Muralidharan and Sundararaman also find that the APRESt contract teacher program improved test scores. After two years, students in schools assigned a contract teacher scored

0.11 standard deviations higher than their counterparts in the same grade in schools without contract teachers.

It is not clear which characteristics of contract teachers were responsible for the success in Kenya and India. That contract teachers were more likely to come from the local area than regular civil service teachers were could have increased their accountability to their schools' parents since they could have faced effective sanctions outside of the school environment. Contract teachers in Kenya and India were also chosen by school committees rather than by a central bureaucracy, so they might have been better matched to the schools than civil service teachers. Finally, the observed differences between contract and civil service teachers could also have resulted from differences in the nature of their contracts: namely, that contract teachers were not guaranteed employment security and could be fired.

Conclusion

Many students in developing countries score very low on standardized tests, and one potential explanation is the weak incentives faced by teachers, as evidenced by their very high absence rates. In many developing countries, systems for monitoring and enforcing teacher presence have broken down. Higher pay alone is therefore unlikely to induce acceptable attendance, although teacher attendance does appear to be responsive to working conditions. This chapter discusses a number of policies that attempt to increase student performance in developing countries by increasing teacher incentives (see table 13-2).

While more research is needed before generalizations can be drawn with confidence, several themes seem to emerge from these studies. There is evidence that if teachers do face strong, well-designed incentives to reduce their high absence rates, they will be absent less often and students will learn more. Using technologies that provide frequent and unambiguous signals of teacher presence to monitors who are more distant from the teachers may be a promising policy. However, there could be political obstacles to putting such systems in place. There is mixed evidence on the impact of more ambitious programs, which differentiate teacher pay through formulas based on student test scores. More experimentation with these approaches is warranted, but such experimentation should be accompanied by careful evaluation so that programs that are successful can be scaled up, while unsuccessful programs can be modified or terminated.

More fundamental changes to the incentive system also seem promising. While simply providing information to communities about the performance of students and the absence rates of teachers may have a limited impact, empowering local

Table 13-2. *Summary of Programs' Effects on Teacher Incentives*

Policy	Country	Results	Source
Incentives from the school environment			
Tracking by initial test scores	Kenya	Attendance of civil service teachers 9.2 percentage points higher in tracked classes relative to civil service teachers in untracked classes Effect concentrated in classrooms with "above the median" students	Esther Duflo, Pascaline Dupas, and Michael Kremer, "Peer Effects, Pupil-Teacher Ratios, and Teacher Incentives," mimeo (2007)
Merit scholarships for students	Kenya	Increased teacher attendance rates by 4.8 percentage points from baseline of 84 percent	Michael Kremer, Edward Miguel, and Rebecca Thornton, "Incentives to Learn," *Review of Economics and Statistics* (forthcoming)
Input-based incentives			
Cameras used to verify teacher attendance and teachers paid for higher attendance in nonformal schools	India	Teacher absence drops by 19 percentage points from baseline of 42 percent No effect on pedagogy in the classroom Students' test scores increase by 0.17 standard deviations Graduation rate to mainstream government schools increased by 10 percentage points from a baseline of 16 percent	Esther Duflo, Rema Hanna, and Stephan Ryan, "Monitoring Works: Getting Teachers to Come to School," Working Paper 11880 (Cambridge, Mass.: National Bureau of Economic Research, 2007)
School headmasters monitor teacher attendance and teachers paid bonuses for higher attendance	Kenya	No increase in teacher attendance Headmasters paid bonuses regardless of attendance	Michael Kremer and Daniel Chen, "Interim Report on a Teacher Incentive Program in Kenya," mimeo (2001)

Table 13-2. *Summary of Programs' Effects on Teacher Incentives (continued)*

Policy	Country	Results	Source
		Output-based incentives	
Teachers received prizes for higher (school average) student test scores	Kenya	Test scores increased by 0.14 standard deviations on tests linked to the incentives Gains highest in subjects requiring the most memorization Gains not sustained one year after program No gains on tests not linked to the incentives Improvement in students' test-taking techniques Increase in exam preparation sessions held by teachers but no other changes in pedagogy No decrease in teacher absence	Paul Glewwe, Nauman Ilias, and Michael Kremer, "Teacher Incentives," mimeo (2008)
Teachers received prizes for higher (school average and teacher specific) student test scores	India	Test scores increased by 0.12–0.19 standard deviations in first year and by 0.22 standard deviations in second year Test scores also increased on non-incentivized subjects Test score gains also made on questions with unfamiliar format No change in pedagogy as measured by direct observation Too early to tell if gains sustained because programs are ongoing	Karthik Muralidharan and Venkatesh Sundararaman, "Teaching Incentives in Developing Countries: Experimental Evidence from India," mimeo (2008)

(continued)

Table 13-2. *Summary of Programs' Effects on Teacher Incentives (continued)*

Policy	Country	Results	Source
Information provision and parental involvement			
Three interventions: (1) Villagers informed about local school quality and responsibilities of local leaders (2) Same as (1) + parents taught how to test children (3) Same as (2) + training of community volunteers to teach children to read at reading camps	India	No effect of pure information intervention No effect of training parents to test children at home 8 percent of all children attended reading camps; these children were 22.3 percentage points more likely to be able to read at least letters, 23.2 percentage points more likely to be able to read at least a word or paragraph, and 22.4 percentage points more likely to be able to read at least a story	Abhijit Banerjee, Esther Duflo, and Rachel Glennerster, "Putting a Band-Aid on a Corpse: Incentives for Nurses in the Indian Public Health Care System," mimeo (2008)
Training parent school committees to monitor contract teacher	Kenya	Increased attendance of civil service teachers by 7.3 percentage points relative to civil service teachers in non-monitored schools Increased attendance of students assigned to the civil service teacher by 2.8 percentage points relative to pupil attendance gains in nonmonitored schools Increased math test scores of students of civil service teachers by 0.18 standard deviations No effect on contract teachers or their students	Esther Duflo, Pascaline Dupas, and Michael Kremer, "Peer Effects, Pupil-Teacher Ratios, and Teacher Incentives," mimeo (2007)

Table 13-2. *Summary of Programs' Effects on Teacher Incentives (continued)*

Policy	Country	Results	Source
		Local hiring of contract teachers	
Young women from community paid to give remedial education to some students for 2 hours a day	India	Increased average test scores by 0.14 standard deviations in first year and by 0.28 standard deviations in second year Largest gains by children at bottom of initial test score distribution and by children receiving remedial education Average gain of 0.1 standard deviations persists one year after program ended	Abhijit Banerjee and others, "Remedying Education: Evidence from Two Randomized Experiments in India," *Quarterly Journal of Economics* 122 (2007): 1235–64.
Hiring of local contract teachers to split first-grade classes	Kenya	Probability of being in class and teaching drops by 12.9 percentage points for civil service teachers from baseline of 58.6 percent Contract teachers roughly 16 percentage points more likely to be in class and teaching relative to civil service teachers in comparison schools, and 29 percentage points more likely relative to civil service teachers in program schools	Esther Duflo, Pascaline Dupas, and Michael Kremer, "Peer Effects, Pupil-Teacher Ratios, and Teacher Incentives," mimeo (2007)

(continued)

Table 13-2. *Summary of Programs' Effects on Teacher Incentives (continued)*

Policy	Country	Results	Source
Hiring of local contract teachers	India	After one year, absence rates of contract teachers 10.6 percentage points less than absence rates of civil service teachers in schools without contract teachers, and 24.1 percentage points less than civil service teachers in the same school After second year, absence rates of contract teachers 17 percentage points less than absence rates of civil service teachers in schools without contract teachers, and 29.4 percentage points less than civil services teachers in the same school No significant increase in absence for civil service teachers Decreased rate of multigrade teaching Decreased class size	Karthik Muralidharan and Venkatesh Sundararaman, "Teaching Incentives in Developing Countries: Experimental Evidence from India," mimeo (2008)

communities to hire teachers on a contract basis can have a significant impact. It is worth noting, however, that many of these teachers are subsequently given jobs in the formal system, and that may be an important part of their motivation to work hard, so one should not assume that moving to a system in which there are only contract teachers and no civil service positions would have the desired incentive effects. That, however, is not achievable politically in many countries, and the relevant question is whether it would be better to have a system in which teachers worked on a contract basis for several years before being given civil service positions. The evidence presented here suggests that that would be a clear improvement. Aside from the potential incentive benefits documented here, there may also be selection benefits to the extent that only those who perform well as contract teachers are given civil service positions.

Recent research in the United States shows that there are large differences in students' test-score gains associated with different teachers within schools, but indicators such as teacher certification, years of experience, and master's degrees have little predictive power for these achievement gains.[33] Yet Robert Gordon, Thomas Kane, and Douglas Staiger present evidence that suggests that school districts can predict which teachers are effective in generating test score gains, and which are not, with only two years of student outcome data.[34] Given these two empirical findings, they recommend reducing the barriers to entering the teaching profession for teachers without traditional teacher certification and requiring a two-year trial period once teachers are hired, after which they can receive tenure based on their performance in the classroom. In order to work, however, these policies would require a reliable data infrastructure to measure teacher performance.

A policy of first hiring teachers on a contract basis and then awarding civil service status to those who are successful could be politically viable because it offers the opportunity, at modest cost, to expand the ranks of teachers in response to rising enrollment without threatening existing civil service teachers or the long-run viability of teachers' unions. In contrast, programs that differentiate pay among civil service teachers based on either attendance or students' test scores are likely to run into opposition from teachers unions.

A few final comments concern a policy direction that this chapter has not examined but that would perhaps generate the most fundamental change in teacher incentives: expansion of school choice under a system in which schools compete for students. Experimental results from Colombia's PACES program, which distributed private school vouchers to students from poor neighborhoods, demonstrate substantial gains in both student attendance and achievement.[35] Yet nonexperimental studies from Chile's national voucher program yield mixed results, with Francisco Gallego arguing that there are student achievement benefits in both public and private schools and Chang-Tai Hsieh and Miguel Urquiola arguing that student achievement does not improve and that increased school choice leads to increased sorting by parental income and education background.[36]

The PACES studies, however, do not examine whether these gains resulted from changes in teacher behavior, and there is some evidence that the program induced greater effort from students, since students who won a voucher through the program's lottery worked fewer labor hours in subsequent years than did students who did not win a voucher. Better matching of students to schools might also account for the observed achievement gains. More experiments in expanding school choice, with special efforts to collect data on teacher attendance and other indicators of effort, will be necessary to determine whether such policies can improve teacher incentives.

Notes

1. Eric A. Hanushek and Ludger Wössmann, "The Role of Education Quality in Economic Growth," Policy Research Working Paper 4122 (Washington: World Bank, 2007).
2. Vincent Greaney, Shahidur R. Khandker, and Mahmudul Alam, *Bangladesh: Assessing Basic Learning Skills* (Dhaka, Bangladesh: University Press, 1999).
3. Paul Glewwe, *The Economics of School Quality Investments in Developing Countries: An Empirical Study of Ghana* (New York: St. Martin's Press, 1999).
4. Marlaine Lockheed and Adriaan Verspoor, *Improving Primary Education in Developing Countries* (Oxford University Press, 1991).
5. Patrick Gonzales and others, "Highlights from the Trends in International Mathematics and Science Study (TIMSS) 2003 (NCES 2005–005)," U.S. Department of Education, National Center for Education Statistics (Washington: U.S. Government Printing Office, 2004).
6. Hanushek and Wössmann, "The Role of Education Quality in Economic Growth."
7. Nazmul Chaudhury and others, "Missing in Action: Teacher and Health Worker Absence in Developing Countries," *Journal of Economic Perspectives* 20, no. 1 (2006): 91–116.
8. Paul Glewwe, Nauman Ilias, and Michael Kremer, "Teacher Incentives," Working Paper (Cambridge, Mass.: Harvard University, 2008); also "Teacher Incentives," Working Paper 9671 (Cambridge, Mass.: National Bureau of Economic Research, April 2003).
9. Ibid.
10. Chaudhury and others, "Missing in Action."
11. Civil service protection refers to job security provisions that are associated with being a government employee, which are often supported by membership in a labor union. Such protections include job security, relatively high wages, the right to strike, and pensions.
12. Esther Duflo, Pascaline Dupas, and Michael Kremer, "Peer Effects, Pupil-Teacher Ratios, and Teacher Incentives: Evidence from a Randomized Evaluation in Kenya," Working Paper (Cambridge, Mass.: Harvard University, 2008).
13. Michael Kremer, Edward Miguel and Rebecca Thornton, "Incentives to Learn," *Review of Economics and Statistics,* forthcoming.
14. Michael Kremer and Daniel Chen, "Interim Report on a Teacher Incentive Program in Kenya," Harvard University (www.people.fas.harvard.edu/~dlchen/papers/Preschool.pdf).
15. Esther Duflo, Rema Hanna, and Stephan Ryan, "Monitoring Works: Getting Teachers to Come to School," Working Paper 11880 (Cambridge, Mass.: National Bureau of Economic Research, 2007).
16. Abhijit Banerjee, Esther Duflo, and Rachel Glennerster, "Putting a Band-Aid on a Corpse: Incentives for Nurses in the Indian Public Health Care System," *Journal of European Economic Association* 6, nos. 2–3 (2007): 487–500.
17. Abhijit Banerjee, Angus Deaton, and Esther Duflo, "Health Care Delivery in Rural Rajasthan," *Economic and Political Weekly* (February 2004): 944–49.
18. Bengt Holmstrom and Paul Milgrom, "Multi-Task Principal-Agent Analysis: Incentive Contracts, Asset Ownership, and Job Design," special issue, *Journal of Law, Economics, and Organization* 7 (1991): 24–52; Jane Hannaway, "Higher Order Thinking, Job Design, and Incentives: An Analysis and Proposal," *American Education Research Journal* 29, no. 1 (1992): 3–21.
19. Glewwe, Ilias, and Kremer, "Teacher Incentives."

20. Tahir Andrabi and others, "Here Today, Gone Tomorrow? Examining the Extent and Implications of Low Persistence in Child Learning," Working Paper, Kennedy School, Harvard University, 2008.

21. Karthik Muralidharan and Venkatesh Sundararaman, "Teacher Performance Pay: Experimental Evidence from India," Working Paper, University of California–San Diego.

22. Abhijit Banerjee and others, "Can Informational Campaigns Spark Local Participation and Improve Outcomes?: A Study of Primary Education in Uttar Pradesh, India," Policy Working Paper 3967 (Washington: World Bank, 2006).

23. Abhijit Banerjee and others, "Pitfalls of Participatory Programs: Evidence from a Randomized Evaluation in Education in India," Working Paper 14311 (Cambridge, Mass.: National Bureau of Economic Research).

24. Joost de Laat, Michael Kremer, and Christel Vermeersch, "Local Participation and Teacher Incentives: Evidence from a Randomized Experiment," Working Paper, Harvard University, 2008; Duflo, Dupas, and Kremer, "Peer Effects, Pupil-Teacher Ratios, and Teacher Incentives."

25. de Laat, Kremer, and Vermeersch, "Teacher Incentives and Local Participation."

26. Duflo, Dupas, and Kremer, "Peer Effects, Pupil-Teacher Ratios, and Teacher Incentives."

27. Chaudhury and others, "Missing in Action."

28. For nonexperimental results, see Emiliana Vegas and Joost de Laat, "Do Differences in Teacher Contracts Affect Student Performance?" *World Development Report 2004* (Washington: World Bank, 2005); Emiliana Vegas, "Teacher Labor Markets in Developing Countries," *Future of Children* 17, no. 1 (2007): 219–32; Ilana Umansky and Emiliana Vegas, "Inside Decentralization: How Three Central American School-Based Management Reforms Affect Student Learning through Teacher Incentives," *World Bank Research Observer* 22, no. 2 (2007): 197–215; Emmanual Jimenez and Yasuyuki Sawada, "Do Community-Managed Schools Work? An Evaluation of El Salvador's EDUCO Program," *World Bank Economic Review* 13, no. 3 (1999): 415–41.

29. *Balsakhi* means "child's friend."

30. Abhijit Banerjee and others, "Remedying Education: Evidence from Two Randomized Experiments in India," *Quarterly Journal of Economics* 122, no. 3 (2007): 1235–64.

31. Duflo, Dupas, and Kremer, "Peer Effects, Pupil-Teacher Ratios, and Teacher Incentives."

32. Karthik Muralidharan and Venkatesh Sundararaman, "Contract Teachers: Experimental Evidence from India," Working Paper, University of California–San Diego.

33. Eric A. Hanushek and Steven G. Rivkin, "How to Improve the Supply of High Quality Teachers," in *Brookings Papers on Education Policy: 2004,* edited by Diane Ravitch, pp. 7–25 (Brookings, 2004).

34. Robert Gordon, Thomas J. Kane, and Douglas O. Staiger, "Identifying Effective Teachers Using Performance on the Job," Discussion Paper 2006-01 (Hamilton Project, Brookings, 2006).

35. Joshua Angrist and others, "Vouchers for Private Schooling in Colombia: Evidence from a Randomized Natural Experiment," *American Economic Review* 92 (2002): 1535–58.

36. Francisco Gallego, "Voucher-School Competition, Incentives, and Outcomes: Evidence from Chile," Working Paper (Catholic University of Chile: 2006); Chang-Tai Hsieh and Miguel Urquiola, "The Effects of Generalized School Choice on Achievement and Stratification: Evidence from Chile's School Voucher Program," *Journal of Public Economics* 90 (2006): 1477–503.

Contributors

MATTHEW M. CHINGOS
Harvard University

MARK EHLERT
University of Missouri–Columbia

PAUL GLEWWE
University of Minnesota

DAN GOLDHABER
University of Washington and Urban Institute

JAY P. GREENE
University of Arkansas

BING HAN
RAND Corporation

ALAKA HOLLA
Innovations for Poverty Action

MICHAEL KREMER
Harvard University

WARREN E. LANGEVIN
Peabody College of Vanderbilt University

J. R. LOCKWOOD
RAND Corporation

RYAN MARSH
University of Arkansas

DANIEL F. MCCAFFREY
RAND Corporation

DEREK NEAL
*University of Chicago and
National Bureau of
Economic Research*

MICHAEL PODGURSKY
University of Missouri–Columbia

GARY W. RITTER
University of Arkansas

RICHARD ROTHSTEIN
Economic Policy Institute

JAMES E. RYAN
University of Virginia

WILLIAM L. SANDERS
SAS Institute

MATTHEW G. SPRINGER
*Vanderbilt University and National
Center on Performance Incentives*

LORI L. TAYLOR
Texas A&M University

JACOB L. VIGDOR
*Duke University and National Bureau
of Economic Research*

MARTIN R. WEST
Brown University

MARCUS A. WINTERS
Manhattan Institute for Policy Research

S. PAUL WRIGHT
SAS Institute

Index